International law in Europe, 700–1200

MANCHESTER
1824

Manchester University Press

artes liberales

Series Editors

Carrie E. Beneš, T. J. H. McCarthy,
Stephen Mossman, and Jochen Schenk

Artes Liberales aims to promote the study of the Middle Ages –
broadly defined in geography and chronology – from a perspective
that transcends modern disciplinary divisions. It seeks to publish
scholarship of the highest quality that is interdisciplinary in topic
or approach, integrating elements such as history, art history,
musicology, literature, religion, political thought, philosophy, and
science. The series particularly seeks to support research based
on the study of original manuscripts and archival sources, and to
provide a recognised venue for increased exposure for scholars at
all career stages around the world.

Previously published
Writing the Welsh borderlands in Anglo-Saxon England
Lindy Brady

Justice and mercy: Moral theology and the exercise of law in
twelfth-century England
Philippa Byrne

Rethinking Norman Italy: Studies in honour of Graham A. Loud
Joanna H. Drell and Paul Oldfield (eds)

Emotional monasticism: Affective piety in the eleventh-century
monastery of John of Fécamp
Lauren Mancia

International law in Europe, 700–1200

Jenny Benham

MANCHESTER UNIVERSITY PRESS

Published by Manchester University Press
Oxford Road, Manchester M13 9PL

www.manchesteruniversitypress.co.uk

British Library Cataloguing-in-Publication Data
A catalogue record for this book is available from the British
Library

ISBN 978 1 5261 4228 3 hardback

First published 2022

Typeset by Newgen Publishing UK

Till min mor,
Ewa Johansson

Contents

Acknowledgements

This book has been long in the making. It was while I was working on the Early English Laws project with Jane Winters and Bruce O'Brien at the Institute of Historical Research that I first started to seriously consider what international law in the medieval period might have entailed. Partly, it was a reaction to the categorisation of a number of pre-1066 English treaties as laws, while those originating in the twelfth century were suddenly termed treaties despite there being no obvious explanation for this, and despite those treaties containing similar legal clauses to the earlier ones. An opportunity to explore this more closely came in 2011 for the project's final conference in Copenhagen. I was subsequently encouraged to publish that paper as 'Law or Treaty? Defining the Edge of Legal Studies in the Early and High Medieval Periods', in *Historical Research* in 2013, and through that a commitment to write a book on international law was born.

Writing this book, I have racked up a mass of professional and personal debts, most of which I can never satisfy by mere brief mentions here. The greatest professional debt should be paid to Matthew McHaffie, without whose comments and suggestions on several chapters, and many conversations about all things medieval legal history, this would have been a very different book. The following were also kind enough to read and comment on various chapters or aspects of chapters: Hermann Kamp, Jón Viðar Sigurðsson, Rachel Herrmann, Jamie Smith, Ben Morris, and Stephanie Ward. Many kindly provided materials or made suggestions of readings, including Adam Kosto, Bjørn Poulsen, Björn Weiler, Charles West, Dominik Waßenhoven, Fredrik Rosén,

Geoffrey Koziol, Gerd Althoff, Hans Jacob Orning, Harald Siems, Helen Nicholson, James Ryan, Kenneth Duggan, Levi Roach, Matt Raven, Paul Webster, Randall Lesaffer, Scott Chaussée, and Yvonne Friedmann. The support, encouragement, knowledge, and scholarly generosity of my colleagues within the Voices of Law international network – Carole Hough, Paul Russell, John Hines, Sara Pons-Sanz, Helle Vogt, and Han Nijdam – has been invaluable too. A special thank you goes to Bill Aird, for the invitation to Edinburgh to discuss the chapter on legal redress; and to Jens Meierhenrich and Campbell Craig for the invitations to attend and contribute to the workshops on transitional justice, and history and political theory. I would also like to thank Isabella Lazzarini for the opportunity to come to Toronto to discuss treaties, law, and diplomacy with the rest of her diplomacy network: John Watkins, Diego Pirillo, Luciano Piffanelli, Timothy Hampton, Randall Lesaffer, Brian Sandberg, Mohamed Ouerfelli, and Bram de Ridder. I learnt a lot!

In addition, I want to acknowledge my considerable debt to my former students Naomi Maher and Eleanor Collingwood, who helped to gather materials for my database on treaties and 'unemendable' crimes. So many other students have provided me with opportunities to discuss medieval treaties; Jamie Smith, Ben Morris, Thomas Tollefsen, and Eleanor Stinson in particular, but any student who has taken my Year 2 module 'War, Peace and Diplomacy' at Cardiff since 2013 has contributed to the thought process of many aspects of this book. More generally, my colleagues in the History department should be thanked for their continued collegiality and support. Finally, I want to thank the anonymous readers for their incisive comments and suggestions, the copy editor Victoria Chow, Rebecca Wilford of Newgen Publishing, and the team at Manchester University Press – Alun Richards, Jen Mellor, and especially the ever-patient Meredith Carroll.

I gratefully acknowledge the generous financial support I have received from the Leverhulme Trust (for the international network 'Voices of Law: Language, Text and Practice'); the Centre of Advanced Studies (facilitating my stay in Oslo during 2017–18); and the College of Arts, Humanities and Social Sciences at Cardiff University.

Among my personal debts, those who have frequently provided tea, cake, friendship, and football chat: Ann Shopland, Emily Archer, Lesley Farthing, Tracey Loughran, Federica Ferlanti, Mary Heimann, and Danny Pucknell. For providing my home away from home with so much care: Alan Lane and Gill Boden. To Ellinor and Malene, for continuous sisterly support and indulging my love of 'piles of stones'. Last, to Keiran and especially to Mel, for always showing that a life of laughter, crazy antics, and good food is 'where it's at'!

This book is dedicated to my mother who sadly passed away in the early stages of researching this book. She was the master of boardgames, always up for some foraging adventure in the northern wilderness – I still recall like it was yesterday climbing that 3m fence to reach the mire with cloudberries and the bear lurking in the background – and yet, she always encouraged my thirst for knowledge and books. She instilled in me to never give up, to take risks, to dare to challenge, and to problem-solve at a practical level. In writing this book, I like to think I have used all of these, and so it is right that the dedication of it belongs to her.

Norwich, October 2020

Abbreviations

II Cn	'Cnut's Winchester code' in *Die Gesetze der Angelsachsen*, 3 vols., ed. Felix Liebermann (Halle, 1903–1916), i, 278–370.
II Edw	'Edward the Elder's second code', in *Die Gesetze*, i, 140–4.
II-III Eg	'Edgar's Andover code', in *Die Gesetze*, i, 194–206.
III As	'Æthelstan's Faversham code', in *Die Gesetze*, i, 170.
IV As Latin	'Æthelstan's Thunderfield code', in *Die Gesetze*, i, 171–2.
V As	'Æthelstan's Exeter code', in *Die Gesetze*, i, 166–8.
V Atr	'Law-making council at Enham, 1008', in *Die Gesetze*, i, 236–47.
VI Atr	'VI Æthelred', in *Die Gesetze*, i, 246–56.
AB	*Annales Bertiniani*, ed. G. Waitz, *MGH SRG*, 5 (Hanover, 1883). Available in English as *The Annals of St-Bertin*, ed. Janet L. Nelson (Manchester, 1991). References to the translation are given within brackets.
Abt	'Æthelberht's code', in *Die Gesetze*, i, 3–8.
Abulafia, *Two Italies*	David Abulafia, *The Two Italies. Economic Relations between the Norman Kingdom of Sicily and the Northern Communes* (Cambridge, 1977).
ACM	*Gli atti del commune di Milano*, ed. C. Manaresi (Milan, 1919).

AF	*Annales Fuldenses*, ed. F. Kurze, *MGH SRG*, 7 (Hanover; Hahn, 1891). Available in English as *The Annals of Fulda*, ed. Timothy Reuter (Manchester, 1992). References to the translation are given within brackets.
Af	'Alfred's *domboc*', in *Die Gesetze*, i, 16–20, 26–89.
AGu	*Treaty between Alfred and Guthrum*, in *Die Gesetze*, I, 126–8. Translation in *EHD*, I, 380–1.
AHR	*American Historical Review.*
AJIL	*American Journal of International Law.*
AJLH	*American Journal of Legal History.*
The Alexiad	*The Alexiad of Anna Comnena*, tr. E. R. A. Sewter (London, 1969).
Althoff, *SP*	Gerd Althoff, *Spielregeln der Politik im Mittelalter: Kommunikation in Frieden und Fehde* (Darmstadt, 1997).
Annali Genovesi	*Annali Genovesi di Caffaro e de' suoi continuatori*, 4 vols., ed. L. T. Belgrano and Cesare Imperiale di Sant'Angelo (Rome, 1890–1929).
ANS	*Anglo-Norman Studies* (the first four volumes were published as *Proceedings of the Battle Conference*), eds. R. Allen Brown (1979–89), Marjorie Chibnall (1990–4), Christopher Harper-Bill (1995–9), John Gillingham (2000–4), C.P. Lewis (2005–11), David Bates (2012–14), Elisabeth van Houts (2015–19).
ARF	*Annales Regni Francorum*, ed. F. Kurze, *MGH SRG*, 6 (Hanover, 1895). Available in English as *Royal Frankish Annals*, in *Carolingian Chronicles*, tr. B.W. Scholz (Ann Arbor, 1972).
ASE	*Anglo-Saxon England.*
Assize of Clarendon	William Stubbs, ed., *Select Charters and Other Illustrations of English Constitutional History*, 9th edn, rev. by H. W. C. Davis (Oxford, 1921), 170–3.

Benham, 'The Earliest Arbitration Treaty?'	Jenny Benham, 'The Earliest Arbitration Treaty? A Re-assessment of the Anglo-Norman Treaty of 991', *Historical Research*, 93 (2020).
Benham, *PMA*	Jenny Benham, *Peacemaking in the Middle Ages: Principles and Practice* (Manchester, 2011; repr. 2017).
BJRL	*Bulletin of the John Rylands Library.*
'Capitulary of Herstal, 779'	'Capitulare Haristallense', in *MGH Capit. I*, ed. A. Boretius (Hanover: Hahn, 1883), no. 20, 46–51. Translation in *Charlemagne: Translated Sources*, ed. P. D. King (Kendal, 1987), 203–5.
'Capitulary of Mantua, 781'	'Capitulare Mantuanum 781', in *MGH Capit. I*, no. 90, 190–1.
'Capitulary concerning the Saxons, 797'	'Capitulare Saxonicum, 797', in *MGH Capit. I*, no. 27, 71–2. Translation in *The Reign of Charlemagne: Documents on Carolingian Government and Administration*, eds. H. R. Loyn and John Percival (London, 1975), 230–2.
'Capitulary of Aachen, 802–3'	'Capitulare Aquisgranense, 801–13', *MGH Capit. I*, no. 77, 170–2. Translation in *Charlemagne: Translated Sources*, 244–5.
'Capitulary of Quierzy, 857'	*Capitulare Carisiacense 857*, in *MGH Capit. II*, eds. A. Boretius and V. Krause (Hanover, 1897), 286–9.
'Capitulary of Quierzy, 873'	*Capitulare Carisiacense 873*, in *MGH Capit. II*, 343–7.
CDRG	*Codice diplomatico della repubblica di Genova*, 4 vols., ed. C. Imperiale di Santangelo (Genoa, 1936–42).
CFB	*The Crusade of Frederick Barbarossa. The History of the Expedition of the Emperor Frederick and Related Texts*, tr. G. A. Loud (Farnham, 2010).
Chaplais, *EDP*	Pierre Chaplais, *English Diplomatic Practice in the Middle Ages* (London, 2003).

The Chronicle of Regino of Prüm	*History and Politics in Late Carolingian and Ottonian Europe. The Chronicle of Regino of Prüm and Adalbert of Magdeburg*, tr. Simon MacLean (Manchester, 2009).
Cicero, *On Duties*	Cicero, *On Duties*, tr. Walter Miller (Cambridge, MA, 1913).
Cn 1027	'Cnut's Letter of 1027' in *Die Gesetze*, i, 276–7. Translation in *EHD, I*, no. 53.
'Constitutio de Hispanis, 815'	*Constitutio de Hispanis in Francorum regnum profugus prima* (815), in *MGH Capit, I*, no. 132, 261–3.
Crawford, *State Responsibility*	James Crawford, *State Responsibility. The General Part* (Cambridge, 2013).
DA	*Deutsches Archiv für Erforschung des Mittelalters*
DD FI	i: *Die Urkunden Friedrichs I, 1152–1158*, ed. H. Appelt (Hanover, 1975); ii: *Die Urkunden Friedrichs I, 1158–1167*, ed. H. Appelt (Hanover, 1979); iii: *Die Urkunden Friedrichs I, 1168–1180*, ed. H. Appelt (Hanover, 1985); iv: *Die Urkunden Friedrichs I, 1181–1190*, ed. H. Appelt (Hanover, 1990).
The Decree of King Childebert	In *Capitula legi Salicae addita – Capitulare VI*, ed. K.A. Eckhardt, *MGH Leges nationum germanicarum*, vol. 4, pt. 1 (Hanover, 1962), 267–9. Translation in *The Laws of the Salian Franks*, tr. Katherine Fischer Drew (Philadelphia, 1991), 156–9.
Decretum	*Decretum Magistri Gratiani*, ed. Emil Friedberg, *Corpus Iuris Canonici*, I (Leipzig, 1879).
Diceto	*The Historical Works of Master Ralph de Diceto*, 2 vols., ed. W. Stubbs, Rolls Series, 68 (London, 1876).
Digest	*The Digest of Justinian*, 4 vols., ed. T. Mommsen, tr. Alan Watson (Philadelphia, 1985).
Dip. Dan	*Diplomatarium Danicum*, vol. 1, parts i–vii, ed. C.A. Christensen (Copenhagen, 1975–93).

Dip. Docs	*Diplomatic Documents Preserved in the Public Record Office, 1101–1279*, ed. P. Chaplais (London, 1964).
Dixon, *Textbook on IL*	Martin Dixon, *Textbook on International Law*, 7th edn. (Oxford, 2013).
EHD	i: *English Historical Documents. Volume 1 c.500–1042*, ed. D. Whitelock, 2nd edn. (London, 1979; repr. 1996); ii: *English Historical Documents. Volume II 1042–1189*, eds. D. C. Douglas and G. W. Greenaway, 2nd edn. (London, 1981; repr. 1996); iii: *English Historical Documents, Volume 3: 1189–1327*, ed. Harry Rothwell (London, 1996).
EHR	*English Historical Review.*
EJIL	*European Journal of International Law.*
EMDP	*English Medieval Diplomatic Practice Part I*, 2 vols., ed. Pierre Chaplais (London, 1982).
EME	*Early Medieval Europe.*
Epstein, *Genoa and the Genoese*	Steven A. Epstein, *Genoa and the Genoese 958–1528* (Chapel Hill, NC, 1996).
ESjL	*Eriks Sjællandske Lov*, ed. E. Kroman, in *Danmarks gamle landskabslove*, vol. 8 (Copenhagen, 1941). Translation in *The Danish Medieval Laws*, eds. Ditlev Tamm and Helle Vogt (London, 2016), 156–232.
Formulae Andecavenses	*Formulae Merowingici et Karolini aevi*, ed. K. Zeumer (Hanover, 1886), 1–25. Translation in *The Formularies of Angers and Marculf: Two Merovingian Legal Handbooks*, tr. Alice Rio (Liverpool, 2008).
Ganshof, *MA*	François L. Ganshof, *The Middle Ages. A History of International Relations*, 4th edn., tr. Rémy Inglis Hall (London, 1968).
'General Capitulary of Thionville, 806'	'Capitulare Missorum in Theodonis villa datum secundum, generale', in *MGH Capit, I*, nos. 43–4, 121–6. Translation in *Charlemagne: Translated Sources*. Quoted by

chapter number with page number to King's
edition in brackets.

Gerald of Wales, Expugnatio Hibernica	Gerald of Wales, *Expugnatio Hibernica: The Conquest of Ireland*, eds. A.B. Scott and F.X. Martin (Dublin, 1978).
Gesta Friderici	*Ottonis et Rahewini Gesta Friderici I imperatoris*, 3rd edn., ed. G. Waitz, revised by B. de Simson, *MGH SRG*, 46 (Hanover, 1912).
GL	*Gulathingslov* in *Norges gamle love indtil 1387*, vol. 1, eds. R. Keyser and P. A. Munch (Christiania, 1846). Translation in *The Earliest Norwegian Laws, being the Gulathing Law and the Frostathing Law*, ed. L. M. Larson (New York, 1935).
Glanvill	*The Treatise on the Laws and Customs of the Realm of England Commonly Called Glanvill*, ed. G. D. G. Hall (Oxford, 1993).
González, El reino de Castilla	*El reino de Castilla el la epoca de Alfonso VIII, vol. II: Documentos 1145 a 1190*, ed. Julio Gonzalez (Madrid, 1960).
Hall, Caffaro	*Caffaro, Genoa and the Twelfth-Century Crusades*, tr. Martin Hall and Jonathan Phillips (Farnham, 2013).
Historia de Expeditione	*Historia de Expeditione Friderici Imperatoris*, in *Quellen zur Geschichte des Kreuzzuges Kaiser Friedrichs I*, ed. A. Chroust, *MGH SRG* n.s., 5 (Berlin, 1928).
Howden, Chronica	*Chronica Magistri Rogeri de Hovedene*, 4 vols., ed. W. Stubbs, Rolls Series, 51 (London, 1868–71).
Howden, Gesta	*Gesta Regis Henrici Secundi Benedicti Abbatis*, 2 vols., ed. W. Stubbs, Rolls Series, 49 (London, 1867).
ILC Articles 2001	International Law Commission, Draft Articles on Responsibility of States for Internationally Wrongful Acts, 2001: http://legal.un.org/ilc/texts/instruments/english/draft_articles/9_6_2001.pdf

Ine	'Ine's code', in Felix Liebermann, ed., *Die Gesetze der Angelsachsen*, 3 vols (Halle, 1903–16), vol. 1, 20–7, 89–123.
Isidore, *Etymologiae*	*Isidori Hispalensis episcopi Etymologiarum sive Originum libri XX*, ed. W. M. Lindsay, 2 vols. (Oxford, 1911). Translation in *The Etymologies of Isidore of Seville*, trans. Stephen A. Barney et al. (Cambridge, 2006). References to the translation are given in brackets.
JHIL	*Journal of the History of International Law.*
JL	*Jyske lov*, ed. P. Skautrup, in *Danmarks gamle landskabslove*, vol. 2 (Copenhagen, 1933). Translation in *The Danish Medieval Laws*, 242–93.
JMH	*Journal of Medieval History.*
Kamp, *Friedensstifter und Vermittler*	Hermann Kamp, *Friedensstifter und Vermittler im Mittelalter* (Darmstadt, 2001).
The Law of Gundobad	*Liber Legum Gundebati*, ed. F. Bluhme, in MGH LL, iii, ed. G. H. Pertz (Hanover, 1863), 526–74. Translation in *The Burgundian Code*, tr. Katherine Fischer Drew (Philadelphia, 1972), 17–87.
The Laws of King Aistulf	*Ahistulfi Leges*, ed. F. Bluhme, in MGH LL, iv, ed. G. H. Pertz (Hanover, 1868), 194–205. Translation in *The Lombard Laws*, 227–38.
The Laws of King Liutprand	*Liutprandi Leges*, ed. F. Bluhme, in MGH LL, iv, 96–182. Translation in *The Lombard Laws*, 137–214.
The Laws of King Ratchis	*Ratchis Leges*, ed. F. Bluhme, in MGH LL, iv, 183–93. Translation in *The Lombard Laws*, 215–25.
LIRG	*I libri iurium della repubblica di Genova*, 11 vols., eds. Dino Puncuh, Antonella Rovere, et al. (Rome, 1992–2011).
The Lombard Laws	*The Lombard Laws*, tr. Katherine Fischer Drew (Philadelphia, 1973; repr. 1989).

LP	*Le Liber Pontificalis: texte, introduction et commentaire*, 3 vols., ed. L. Duchesne (Paris, 1886).
Marculfi Formularum Liber I	*Formulae Merowingici et Karolini aevi*, ed. K. Zeumer (Hanover, 1886), 32–112. Translation in *The Formularies of Angers and Marculf*.
Martin, *Guerre*	Jean-Marie Martin, *Guerre, accords et frontières en Italie méridionale pendant le haut Moyen Âge* (Rome, 2005).
Mas Latrie, *Traités de paix*	M. L. de Mas Latrie, *Traités de paix et de commerce et documents divers concernant les relations des chrétiens avec les Arabes de l'Afrique septentrionale au moyen âge, part II: documents* (Paris, 1865).
MGH Capit.	*MGH Capitularia Regum Francorum.*
MGH Const.	*MGH Constitutiones et acta publica imperatorum et regum.*
MGH Epp.	*MGH Epistolae.*
MGH Epp. sel.	*MGH Epistolae selectae.*
MGH LL	*MGH Leges (in folio).*
MGH SRG	*MGH Scriptores rerum Germanicarum in usum scholarum separatim editi.*
MGH SRG n.s.	*MGH Scriptores rerum Germanicarum, Nova series.*
Moeglin, Diplomatie	Jean-Marie Moeglin and Stéphane Péquignot, *Diplomatie et 'relations internationals' au Moyen Âge (IXe–XVe siècle)* (Paris, 2017).
Nithard, *Histoire*	*Nithard: Histoire des fils de Louis le Pieux*, ed. and tr. P. Lauer (Paris, 1926); Translation in *Nithard's Histories* in *Carolingian Chronicles*, tr. B. W. Scholz (Ann Arbor, 1972). References to the translation are given in brackets.
OHHIL	*Oxford Handbook of the History of International Law*, eds. Bardo Fassbender and Anne Peters (Oxford, 2012).
P&P	*Past & Present.*

Paddeu, *Justification*	Federica Paddeu, *Justification and Excuse in International Law. Concept and Theory of General Defences* (Cambridge, 2018).
Pryce, *The Acts of Welsh Rulers*	*The Acts of Welsh Rulers 1120–1283*, ed. Huw Pryce (Cardiff, 2005).
Rec. des actes de Philippe Auguste	*Recueil des actes de Philippe Auguste*, 4 vols., ed. H. F. Delaborde (Paris, 1916–79).
Ripuarian Laws	*Lex Ribuaria*, eds. Franz Beyerle and Rudolf Buchner, in *MGH Leges nationum germanicarum*, vol. 3, pt. 2 (Hanover, 1954), 73–194; Translation in *Laws of the Salian and Ripuarian Franks*, tr. T. J. Rivers (New York, 1986).
RIS	*Review of International Studies*.
Rothair's Edict	*Edictus Rothari*, ed. F. Bluhme, in *MGH LL*, iv, 13–90. Translation in *The Lombard Laws*, 39–130.
RPC	*The Russian Primary Chronicle. The Laurentian Text*, eds. S. H. Cross and O. P. Sherbowitz-Wetzor (Cambridge, MA, 1953).
Saxo, *GD*	Saxo Grammaticus, *Gesta Danorum: the History of the Danes*, 2 vols., eds. Peter Fisher and Karsten Friis-Jensen (Oxford, 2015).
SL	*Skånske Lov*, ed. Johannes Brøndum-Nielsen and Poul Johannes Jørgensen, in *Danmarks gamle landskabslove*, vol. 1 (Copenhagen, 1933). Translation in *The Danish Medieval Laws*, 56–96.
Steiger, *Die Ordnung der Welt*	Heinhard Steiger, *Die Ordnung der Welt. Eine Völkerrechtsgeschichte des karolingischen Zeitalters (741 bis 840)* (Cologne, 2010).
TRHS	*Transactions of the Royal Historical Society*.
UHSRV	*Urkunden zur älteren Handels- und Staatsgeschichte der Republik Venedig*, eds. G. Tafel and G. Thomas, 3 vols. (Vienna, 1857).

VSL	*Valdemars Sjællandske Lov*, ed. Johannes Brøndum-Nielsen, in *Danmarks gamle landskabslove*, vol. 8 (Copenhagen, 1941). Translation in *The Danish Medieval Laws*, 111–52.
Widukind, *Deeds*	Widukind of Corvey, *Deeds of the Saxons*, tr. Bernard S. Bachrach and David S. Bachrach (Washington, DC, 2014).
Widukind, *RGS*	*Widukindi monachi Corbeiensis Rerum gestarum Saxonicarum libri tres*, ed. H. E. Lohmann and Paul Hirsch, *MGH SRG*, 60 (Hanover, 1935).
WM, *GRA*	William of Malmesbury, *Gesta Regum Anglorum*, 2 vols., ed. and tr. by R. A. B. Mynors, R. M. Thomson, and M. Winterbottom (Oxford, 1998–9).

Maps of medieval Europe

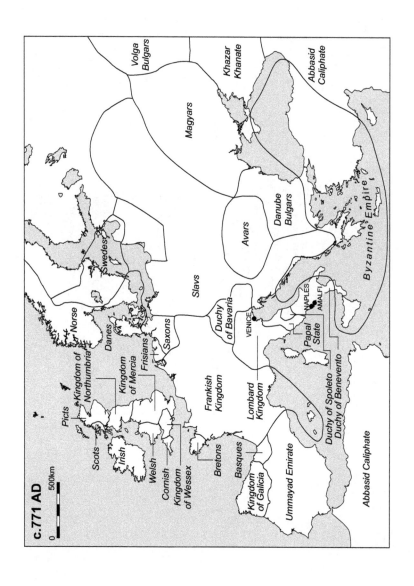

c.771 AD

0   500km

Picts
Scots
Irish
Welsh
Cornish
Kingdom of Wessex
Bretons
Basques
Kingdom of Galicia
Ummayad Emirate
Abbasid Caliphate

Norse
Danes
Frisians
Saxons
Kingdom of Northumbria
Kingdom of Mercia
Swedes
Slavs
Frankish Kingdom
Lombard Kingdom
Duchy of Bavaria
VENICE
NAPLES
AMALFI
Papal State
Duchy of Spoleto
Duchy of Benevento

Volga Bulgars
Magyars
Avars
Danube Bulgars
Khazar Khanate
Byzantine Empire
Abbasid Caliphate

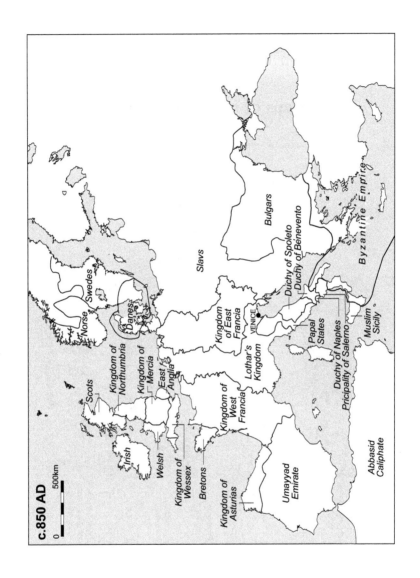

c.850 AD

0 — 500km

Scots

Irish

Welsh

Norse

Swedes

Danes

Kingdom of Northumbria

Kingdom of Mercia

East Anglia

Kingdom of Wessex

Bretons

Kingdom of West Francia

Kingdom of Asturias

Umayyad Emirate

Kingdom of East Francia

Lothar's Kingdom

Slavs

Bulgars

Duchy of Spoleto

Duchy of Beinevento

VENICE

Papal States

Duchy of Naples

Pricipality of Salerno

Muslim Sicily

Byzantine Empire

Abbasid Caliphate

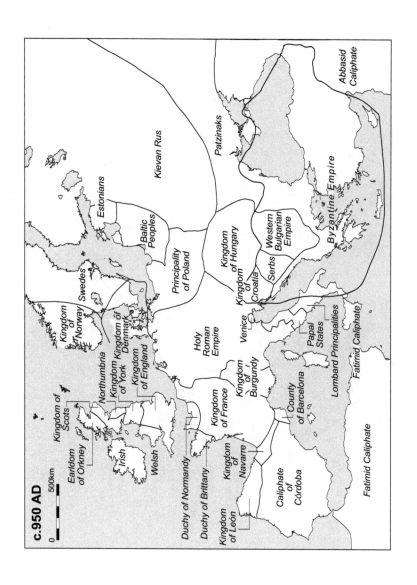

c.950 AD

0 500km

Earldom of Orkney

Kingdom of Scots

Irish

Welsh

Northumbria

Kingdom of York

Kingdom of Denmark

Kingdom of England

Kingdom of Norway

Swedes

Estonians

Baltic Peoples

Kievan Rus

Principality of Poland

Kingdom of Hungary

Kingdom of Croatia

Serbs

Western Bulgarian Empire

Patzinaks

Byzantine Empire

Abbasid Caliphate

Holy Roman Empire

Venice

Papal States

Lombard Principalities

Fatimid Caliphate

Duchy of Normandy

Duchy of Brittany

Kingdom of France

Kingdom of Burgundy

County of Barcelona

Kingdom of Navarre

Kingdom of León

Caliphate of Córdoba

Fatimid Caliphate

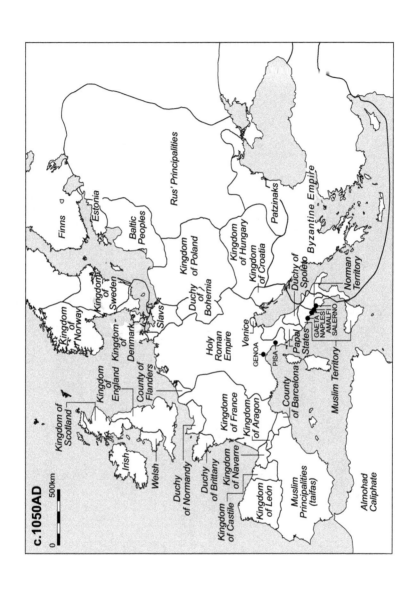

c.1050AD

0   500km

Kingdom of Scotland

Irish

Welsh

Kingdom of England

County of Flanders

Duchy of Normandy

Duchy of Brittany

Kingdom of Navarre

Kingdom of Castile

Kingdom of León

Muslim Principalities (taifas)

Kingdom of France

Kingdom of Aragon

County of Barcelona

Almohad Caliphate

Finns

Estonia

Baltic Peoples

Kingdom of Norway

Kingdom of Sweden

Kingdom of Denmark

Slavs

Rus' Principalities

Kingdom of Poland

Duchy of Bohemia

Holy Roman Empire

Venice

GENOA

PISA

Kingdom of Hungary

Kingdom of Croatia

Patzinaks

Duchy of Spoleto

Papal States

GAETA
NAPLES
AMALFI
SALERNO

Norman Territory

Muslim Territory

Byzantine Empire

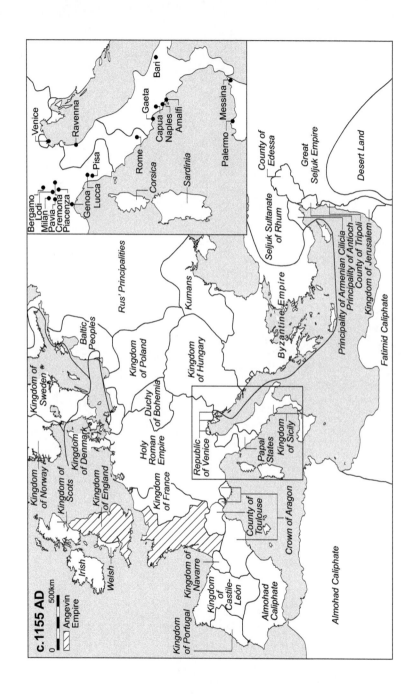

c.1155 AD

0 — 500km

Angevin Empire

Inset (top):

Bergamo
Lodi
Milan
Pavia
Cremona
Piacenza
Genoa
Lucca
Pisa
Venice
Ravenna
Gaeta
Rome
Corsica
Capua
Naples
Amalfi
Sardinia
Bari
Messina
Palermo

Main map:

Kingdom of Norway
Kingdom of Sweden
Kingdom of Scots
Kingdom of Denmark
Irish
Welsh
Kingdom of England
Baltic Peoples
Rus' Principalities
Kingdom of France
Holy Roman Empire
Duchy of Bohemia
Kingdom of Poland
Kingdom of Hungary
Kumans
Republic of Venice
County of Toulouse
Papal States
Kingdom of Sicily
Byzantine Empire
Kingdom of Portugal
Kingdom of Navarre
Kingdom of Castile-León
Almohad Caliphate
Crown of Aragon
Almohad Caliphate
Seljuk Sultanate of Rhum
County of Edessa
Great Seljuk Empire
Principality of Armenian Cilicia
Principality of Antioch
County of Tripoli
Kingdom of Jerusalem
Fatimid Caliphate
Desert Land

Introduction

It is the contention of this book that there was a notion of international law in the period c. 700–1200. While it is true that there was nothing that contemporaries referred to as 'international law' in this period nor were there any physical international institutions along the lines of the United Nations or the International Criminal Court, I argue, nonetheless, that there were laws, customs, and institutions that guided interactions between different communities and political entities, protected the rights and status of people and their goods in foreign lands, and acted as deterrents to future conflict. As there were no nation states in medieval Europe but there were still diplomacy and interactions between different communities, it is important that traditional views of state-centred international law and institutions give way to a different paradigm, which recognises the plurality of law and that the locus of political and legal power in the Middle Ages was multi-layered.[1] Recognising this legal plurality allows us to understand how conflict resolution operated within different contexts – cultural, economic, legal, political, and social – and how this translated into what we might think of as international law.

This move would mirror where the field of modern international law is going in the twenty-first century following the increasing challenges of globalisation and terrorism over the past thirty years and the move away from a Euro-centric view of international law.[2] Indeed, how people resolved conflict at a time when wars and violence may have been more pervasive both between and within polities than today and in a period before fully-fledged nation states, international institutions, and law, has acquired timely relevance in an age of asymmetrical warfare, tensions over natural resources, unilateralism, and '*ad hocery*'; an age in which the world is multipolar but at the same becoming more polarised; and an age of international protection of individual rights but also protection of the global environment in which those individuals live.[3] These trends have resulted in lessening the importance of the nation state as a dominant factor in war and in securing peace, and in the proliferation of non-state actors involved in both conflict and conflict resolution. Conflicts now are frequently not between states but rather expand across states thereby blurring the lines between wars and civil wars. Violence has become harder to categorise into that carried out during war or peace, or between that which is political or criminal.[4] In short, there are many analogies in the contexts of war and conflict resolution between the medieval and modern periods, and this has also resulted in a resurgent interest in the history of international law.[5]

In this context then, it is important that scholars cease thinking of international law in the very narrow way of it being a law between nations or nation states as it was perceived in the nineteenth or twentieth centuries. As argued by Hathaway and Shapiro, 'Modern State Conception is both an excessively narrow and historically incomplete account of law. Legal systems can and have existed despite lacking the capacities of a modern state.'[6] According to Jörg Fisch, 'International law is, and always has been, law between States and thus between political entities, not law between nations, peoples, or other groups of human beings'.[7] This is despite the fact that 'in European languages, the terms for international law used today do not refer to the State but to concepts with different backgrounds: to nations, from which "international law", *droit international,* etc. comes, or to peoples (*gentes*), from which *droit des gens, derecho de gentes, diritto delle genti, Völkerrecht,* etc. are derived'.[8] Evidently, the crucial issue in all of this is what a 'state' is – an issue hotly debated among scholars of many historical periods and disciplines. This study follows a similar approach as that proposed by Randall Lesaffer, that international law 'as a historical concept should be defined as the law regulating relations between political entities that do not recognise a higher authority', or what Heinhard Steiger has referred to as 'the law between political powers'.[9]

Despite the renewed interest in medieval international law, the debate on the history of international law in the Middle Ages has rarely moved beyond the contribution of canon law and even the best treatments of the topic tend to leave a gap from the end of the western Roman empire to the revival of Roman and natural law in the twelfth and thirteenth centuries – nearly 800 years. A few examples will suffice to demonstrate.[10] Without dedicating a sentence to developments in the earlier Middle Ages, Stephen Neff declared in his 2014 monograph 'What medieval Europe did *not* have was a conception of international law in our modern sense, as a law applying *specifically* to relations between independent sovereign states'. Medieval people, he argues 'envisaged a world in which the rule of law made no concessions to even the mightiest of monarchs – and in which those monarchs were accorded no privileged position in drafting the laws. Emperors and kings could no more alter the strictures of natural law than the fabled King Canute could command the tide to recede.'[11] The revised version of Wilhelm G. Grewe's *The Epochs of International Law* did better; covering the period c. 500–1200 across nearly seven pages, but using these mainly to describe the order of political and spiritual authority (emperor and pope), and the conflict between them.[12] More successfully, the *Oxford Handbook of the History of International Law*, published in 2012, and Randall Lesaffer's edited collection, *Peace Treaties and International Law in European History* (2004), are characterised by a range of strong chapters on different aspects of historical developments, yet most of these seem to start in the later Middle Ages or leave a gap for the period c. 500–1200.[13] Bruno Paradisi's collections of essays on the history of international law in the Middle Ages likewise have done much to examine the doctrine and legal institutions of the Middle Ages, even though, again, much of it is focused either on the later period or in tracing the transformation from antiquity to the early medieval.[14] The point about the gap in the scholarly literature is borne out well in Rasilla Del Moral's overview of international law for the Oxford bibliographies series, which for the period 400 to 1000 lists only a single scholarly work; that of Heinhard Steiger covering the Carolingian period.[15] This gap does not necessarily mean that there was no equivalent of international law in the early Middle Ages, but rather that there seems to have been no systematic reflection on it. While Augustine's *The City of God* is the classic work on the idea of the international community, and Isidore's *Etymologiae* contains a definition of the *ius gentium* based on natural law, no early medieval writer in Europe attempted to systemise relations between rulers or how they were regulated.[16] This is in contrast to the Islamic world, where Muhammad al-Shaybānī produced a compilation and systemisation of the rules of Islamic international law under a specialised subject area of Islamic law termed *al-Siyar*, which covers the laws of war and peace according to the *Shari'ah*.[17] In other words, scholars interested in the history of international law in medieval Europe have found few sources with which to investigate it, prior to the renewed interest in natural and Roman law in the twelfth and thirteenth centuries.[18]

International law is more than doctrine, however, and scholars frequently accept that it has developed in practice over a long time.[19] Yet, works examining international legal practice across any historical period are significantly fewer than those exploring doctrine. The most obvious explanation for this discrepancy, Lesaffer explains as being that the abundance of source material for legal practice makes such studies huge undertakings.[20] Heinhard Steiger's 2010 monograph *Die Ordnung der Welt* (The Order of the World), with the subtitle *Eine Völkerrechtsgeschichte des karolingischen Zeitalters* (A History of International Law in the Carolingian Period), is the most successful work to investigate some of these customary practices and their legal context for the earlier medieval period. To avoid anachronistic terminology, he examines specific terms, some of which have a direct link to Roman international law, including *ius* (law), *regnum* (realm), *territorium* (territory), *foedus* (treaty), *pax* (peace), *societas* (community), and *deditio* (surrender), using these to demonstrate the hierarchical or reciprocal relationships between different powers ('Zwischen-Mächte-Verbindungen').[21] The study's overarching aim is to investigate the link between legal order and political order, and much of the evidence on specific diplomatic encounters and agreements is analysed with the main purpose of understanding how the two sides conceptualised their relationship with one another into an ordered world. Steiger traces the continuities and discontinuities with international law as it was perceived in the late Roman empire and through the writings of Augustine, and further compares and contrasts this to modern international law. This analytical framework explains his choice of dates for the study: 741–840. That is, the period which he characterises as showing the rapid expansion of the Frankish kingdom into a Carolingian empire through the coronation of Charlemagne in 800, and which ends with the death of Emperor Louis the Pious, Charlemagne's son, since it was followed by a period of divisions and the eventual demise of the empire created.[22] Steiger emphasises the importance of religion for the unity of this empire, which created a common Christian normativity – and a common language in Latin – within which the various 'powers' thought and acted.[23] From this, he concludes that during this time of Carolingian dominance, people were generally convinced that there was a common legal-normative order into which they were integrated and that regulated their relationships with one another. He recognises the difficulty of identifying common standards and instead refers to parallel norms of individual legal systems, e.g., for the protection of ambassadors or the taking of oaths, which Steiger highlights corresponds to the concept of *ius gentium*, the norms that apply to all peoples.[24]

Steiger's immense study, covering some 800 pages, is detailed and important; his conclusions have been developed over a lifetime of research as a scholar of the history of international law. While the overall argument about the presence of recognised rules that we can think of as international law is well-made, nevertheless, some of its details are less convincing. For instance, the argument that relations with non-Christian powers were fundamentally different from those with Christian powers cannot be sustained based on the evidence of diplomatic practices. Similarly, the point that the year 751 – the change from the Merovingian to the Carolingian dynasty – was a watershed in the practice of foreign relations is made without much supporting evidence or consideration of the historiography.[25] Many of the problems with Steiger's argument arise from his self-imposed limitations of focusing on the Carolingian realm(s) 741–840. His methodology of examining specific terms and phrases could, as an example, have been significantly enhanced if he had extended the chronology to include the whole of the ninth century. It would also have avoided conclusions such as that it is not possible to determine if contemporaries perceived of methods for the peaceful settlement of disputes arising from treaties, when the flurry of treaties from subsequent decades demonstrates this amply, and not in a way to suggest this was a new practice. Moreover, Steiger's notion of the Carolingian whole, for all its claim to plurality, and the focus on specific terminology, have led to a lack of sensitivity to nuances between theory and practice in the sources. Furthermore, in focusing on the idea of the Christian empire as the basis of international law – based on Augustine's *City of God* – Steiger followed a long tradition of the connection between legal and political theory, so that, ultimately, his study is still closer to the idea of international law than to the practice.[26] This present study aims to take Steiger's work on international law in early medieval Europe one step further by expanding its chronological and geographical focus, but also by diverging from the scholarly focus on doctrine to explore a different type of evidence: treaties. Indeed, treaties and customs (or legal practice) – two of the most important sources of international law – have never received a full scholarly treatment for the period c. 500–c. 1500. Hence, many assertions about international law in the medieval period are currently not based on an examination of the available evidence.

That the treaty is older than the idea of international law seems certain. Indeed, Allott has argued that the 'practice of treaty-making has continued from the days of the earliest recorded human history to the present day, more or less in isolation from the troubled development of international law in general'.[27] In the Middle Ages, as now, the treaty was a central, even fundamental, means of regulating and shaping relations between different political entities.[28] A treaty between two or more parties could create obligations and responsibilities; outline new or old rights; establish, amend, or suspend customary practice; and devise shared solutions for a range of problems and disputes that faced medieval princes and the societies over which they ruled. It was, in short, the main way in which international law could be consciously created. This study takes as its focus c. 200 written treaties from the period 700 to 1200. The time period has been deliberately chosen to begin before the accession of the Carolingians to the Frankish kingdom in the mid-eighth century – Steiger's starting point but also the first century from which written treaties have survived from more than a single entity – and to end roughly mid-point between the compilation of Gratian's *Decretum* (1130s) and Thomas Aquinas's *Summa Theologiae* (1260s) – the most influential works carrying the Roman and natural law traditions, and hence commonly viewed as the starting point for the history of international law in the medieval period. As a corpus of evidence, the number of treaties has certain limitations that should be acknowledged from the outset. As a start, it should be noted that the survival of written treaties is not distributed evenly across every century nor every geographical area in Europe.[29] In the ninth and tenth centuries, the majority of treaties originate in the Frankish kingdoms (modern-day France, Germany, and the Benelux countries), the Lombard and later Italian kingdoms, and the Anglo-Saxon kingdoms (modern-day England) (Map 2, 3). Treaties, furthermore, survive in greater numbers from the whole of Europe after 1100, but the real explosion of both treaties and other written evidence comes in the second half of that century. From that period after 1150, we can be very specific about where and from whom the majority of treaties have survived: those involving the English kings Henry II, Richard I, and John; those involving the Emperor Frederick I; and those involving one of the Italian cities (often called city-states) (Map 5). The latter, in fact, are so abundant that it has been necessary to set further limitations.[30] Genoa has been chosen as the focus because in its archives survive a large number of treaties with different entities; those of the Latin west and east, as well as Byzantium, and various Muslim powers. The advantage of focusing on Genoa in the twelfth century is hence that its diplomatic relations radiated outwards in all directions, and this sets it apart from other Italian cities, such as Venice, whose relations mainly went eastwards. Moreover, treaties involving the Italian cities are often quite similar, and those from Genoa provide a good representative sample of issues and practices. It is worth noting that even with these particular restrictions, if only a single treaty survives from a certain city, it has more often than not been included, e.g., the 1126 *Treaty of Pisa* is the sole surviving written treaty of that period involving the city of Amalfi.

A few further comments can be made about the geographical and chronological distribution of surviving treaties. There are no written treaties from most areas inhabited by peoples such as Slavs, e.g., areas known today as Poland and the Baltic States, and only two involving a ruler or other entity from Scandinavia. Similarly, there is only a single written treaty surviving for the whole period involving an Irish ruler, and the first treaty with a Welsh ruler that has come down to us in written form dates to 1201, i.e., outside the chronological scope of this study, but has been included as it is a sole treaty. Moreover, it should be noted that both the eighth century and the eleventh century have a relatively small number of written treaties surviving from the whole of Europe (Map 1, 4). In particular, it is noteworthy that for the reigns of rulers seen by previous scholars as the heyday of the empire doctrine of international law in the period before 1100 – that is, the reigns of Charlemagne (760 011), the three Ottos (936–1002) and Henry III (1039–56) – only five written treaties have survived.[31] An attempt has been made to draw in, as far as possible, other evidence of international legal practice from those geographical areas or particular centuries. In addition, while this is perceived as a study of international law in Europe, based on the evidence from written treaties, there are some significant exceptions. The first concerns treaties written in Greek or Arabic, which have been excluded due to linguistic limitations. In the small number of cases where a Latin version exists, or where there is a translation in a modern language, a treaty may have been included for comparative purposes. It should be acknowledged, however, that this is not always a satisfactory substitute. The second exception concerns treaties from the Iberian peninsula. Although Latin is known as the lingua franca of medieval Europe, it remains the case that treaties frequently contain terminology specific to a geographical area or to particular political or cultural circumstances. Unfamiliarity with these historical contexts and linguistic limitations in accessing the modern secondary literature, vital for the analysis of both the treaties and the history of the region, has prompted this exclusion. Nevertheless, certain treaties from this geographical region have been included for purposes of comparison and contrast. The figure of c. 200 treaties then, evidently, does not represent the total number of treaties in this period, but has been arrived at through the particular limitations described. How to identify treaties, and the problems and possibilities of using such documents as evidence for international law c. 700–1200 have formed the basis of Chapter 1.

The methodology of this book is by definition and practice comparative. The objective is not to outline for each treaty its historical context, purpose(s), or the relationship between the individuals or communities involved. Some of the treaties covered by this study already have a large literature on these aspects, and examples have been noted in each chapter where relevant. Such studies are important in providing a contemporary context, but because they typically deal with a single treaty or a small number of treaties between two specific entities, they tend to disguise wider trends and practices across both time and space, and/or speak mainly to a particular historiographical tradition. Examples of this include

François Ganshof's work on Merovingian and Carolingian treaties, the work by Pierre Chaplais and others on the treaties concluded by West Saxon and English rulers, and the studies by Thomas Madden and others on the eleventh-century Byzantine treaties with Venice.[32] Instead, to explore how we can build up a picture of what international law might have been, and how it was understood and practised in a period when no outline of this exists, this study employs a simple framework; namely, that 'the most cogent argument for the existence of international law is that members of the international community recognise that there exists a body of rules binding upon them as law'.[33] Evidence of this belief can be cited in four ways. First, that it is practised on a daily basis. Second, that there is a reliance upon justification of action. Third, that the majority of international legal rules are consistently obeyed. And finally, that 'it is a function of all legal systems to resolve disputed questions of fact and law'.[34] These four categories have provided the basis for the main part of the book. Chapter 2 begins by arguing that one of the best ways to see that international law was practised on a daily basis in the medieval period is to look to displacement of people and, in particular, to expulsion – exile, banishment, outlawry, or whatever we want to call it. The expulsion of individuals who had committed reprehensible acts was one of the ways in which medieval rulers and whole communities dealt with law and order. As an alternative to punishment such as mutilation or death, expulsion from a political entity – whether we view this as a city, region, or kingdom – was reserved for the most serious offences; those which could not be atoned for with compensation. However, while expulsion was intended to ensure law and order on a domestic level, it could result in becoming a threat to peace and security on an 'international' level. Primarily this was because, once expelled, such individuals, shorn of their social and economic status, often committed further reprehensible acts and/or engaged in conflict against the entity from whence they had come. As a consequence, one of the foremost purposes of concluding treaties between rulers was to ensure that those who had been expelled from one political entity did not find shelter in another, and almost every treaty concluded in the period contains a clause about not harbouring each other's enemies. Chapter 2 examines the evidence available in treaties, putting it into a wide legal context of expulsion at both a domestic and international level. It further explores the strategies for dealing with expulsion and the extent to which there was enforcement of the clauses found in treaties by using a range of complementary evidence available in laws, letters, and chronicles.

The extent to which the international legal rules may have been consistently obeyed is the focus of Chapter 3. It is the most difficult part of international law to assess, both in the medieval period and in the modern world, yet the extent to which rules were obeyed is a notion that goes right to the heart of the question about effectiveness or enforcement. Medieval writers were often more interested in law-breaking because obedience was not newsworthy. Moreover, in the ecclesiastical thought-world inhabited by chroniclers, writing providential history was the order of the day and the breaking of oaths is frequently commented upon because it was followed by divine retribution. The problem with our evidence aside, this chapter considers carefully how useful the notion of effectiveness or enforcement is with regards to international law, because even in the modern period it is not the only facilitator or controller of state conduct, nor is it designed to be. Indeed, the practice of international law is fundamentally linked to diplomacy, politics, and the conduct of foreign relations. The chapter argues that scholarly ideas about effectiveness and enforcement are often fundamentally flawed, because they insist that legal rules only affect behaviour when they are enforced, and they furthermore adopt an excessively narrow conception of law enforcement as something done violently, i.e., through the threat and exercise of physical force. In other words, the chapter argues that if the only enforcement one is willing to recognise is that characterised by violence by state institutions, then international law will always look pretty ineffective. By contrast, if we perceive of enforcement through a medieval perspective of shared cultural values, one can point to certain enforcement procedures, such as loss of legal rights and privileges. This can be best seen through an exploration of the use of redress for injuries and loss of property, amnesty, and mechanisms of transitional justice (e.g., international shaming) in treaties, their link to domestic laws and institutions, and how they functioned in different situations.

In the modern period, no states claim to be above the law or that international law does not bind them. Chapter 4 argues likewise that, in the medieval period, rulers and political entities justified their actions in legal terms when they departed from a legal norm. In the later medieval period, the issue of justification has been explored mainly through the development of the 'just war' doctrine and canon law. This chapter builds on that historiography by examining how in the period before 1200, treaties, diplomatic documents, and narratives often give evidence of such justifications, thereby providing strong indications that rulers followed the rules of international law as a matter of obligation and not only as a matter of choice or on moral grounds. To explore this fully, the chapter returns to familiar questions about violence and peace, e.g., how and in what circumstances violent action was justified, and who had the authority to carry out such violence. It further identifies what constituted breaches of international law and how parties dealt with such breaches, thereby revealing medieval conceptions of responsibility and liability. Examining justifications hence demonstrates something of how deterrence worked in the medieval period and the effectiveness of this.

Finally, Chapter 5 investigates how medieval entities and rulers resolved disputed questions of fact and law through one particular method: arbitration. It was, and continues to be, one of the most common ways to resolve conflict, secure peace, and deter future violence. Its frequent and sustained use as a method to settle disputes at lower levels of society during the whole of the medieval period and across most geographical areas has often been acknowledged by scholars, but, in an international context, it has been seen primarily as a late-medieval phenomenon, involving the papacy or merchant towns, e.g., those of the Hanseatic League. This chapter argues that in the period before 1200, arbitration was a relatively rare method for determining disputes between rulers, yet it was one that had a clear process with specific terminology, procedure, and expectations. More commonly, the evidence show that parties used arbitration panels, drawing an equal number of men from each side, to discuss, determine, and decide disputes over individual stipulations in treaties. Chapter 5 demonstrates the involvement of both individuals and communities in conflict resolution, their authority and ability to make decisions on matters in dispute, and how they encouraged, coerced, or reinforced obligations and responsibilities agreed in treaties. In short, there were well-developed strategies for resolving international disputes, employing judicial institutions that were widely used and known to all parties.

Comparing widely across time and space is a difficult endeavour. For instance, I am conscious that comparing examples separated by hundreds of years has drawbacks; in particular, in divorcing the evidence from the many real differences among medieval societies, cultures, and historical contexts. It is not possible to give due attention to all and every example of a particular practice, nor is it possible to be an expert on every geographical region, time period, topic, or discipline, and their wider literatures.[35] As far as possible, I have tried to highlight important differences in the evidence, and certainly nuances, between geographical areas or different time periods. There has also been an attempt to give a sense of the wider literature for particular topics/disciplines or historical contexts, although not only the sheer scope of the task but also working out the terminology used in different modern languages for particular topics, e.g., 'reprisals', 'self-defence', or 'amnesty', have proved interesting challenges. Despite these issues, comparison is essential for this study and there are advantages to such a methodology. The nature of the medieval sources, often sporadic and chance survivals, means that analyses of a single treaty from a particular time period, or a small group of treaties from a particular region, can lead to conclusions that look less convincing in the context of other available treaties. More generally, the medieval world was interconnected in lots of different and sometimes surprising ways, and comparing the evidence for treaties and legal practice across time and space highlights the connections between international and domestic law and institutions particularly well. This further enables the historian to identify and answer broader questions, e.g., about the nature of authority and jurisdiction, or about war and peace.

It is possible to perceive of international law in Europe c. 700–1200. This study is intended to provide the starting point for a new discourse of how to investigate the laws, customs, and institutions that guided interactions between different rulers, communities, and political entities, protected the rights and status of people and their goods, and acted as deterrents to future conflict. This book then is an exploration of the place of medieval Europe in the history of international law, and a search for points of similarity and contrast with other historical periods and geographical regions.

Notes

1 Martin Kintzinger, 'From the Late Middle Ages to the Peace of Westphalia', in *OHHIL*, 616, 626–7; Antonio Padoa-Schioppa, 'Profili del diritto internazionale nell'alto medioevo', in *Le relazioni internazionali nell'alto medioevo: Spoleto, 8–12 aprile 2010, Settimane di studio della Fondazione Centro italiano di studi sull'alto Medioevo*, 58 (Spoleto, 2011), 3.

2 On the changing nature of international law, see Carl Landauer, 'The Ever-Ending Geography of International Law: the Changing Nature of the International System and the Challenge to International Law: A Reply to Daniel Bethlehem', *EJIL*, 25 (2014), 31–4; Yasuaki Onuma, 'When was the Law of International Society born? An Inquiry of the History of International Law from an Intercivilizational Perspective', *JHIL*, 2 (2000), 1–66; Mary Ellen O'Connell and Lenore VanderZee, 'The History of International Adjudication', in *The Oxford Handbook of International Adjudication*, eds. Cesare P. R. Romano, Karen J. Alter, and Yuval Shany (Oxford, 2013), 40–62; Martti Koskenniemi, 'Histories of International Law: Dealing with Eurocentrism', *Rechtsgeschichte*, 19 (2011), 152–76; Armin Steinbach, 'The Trend towards Non-Consensualism in Public International Law: A (Behavioural) Law and Economics Perspective', *EJIL*, 27 (2016), 643–68.

3 María Fernanda Espinosa Garcés, President of the 73rd Session of the UN General Assembly, 'Current Challenges to International Law: The Role of Societies of International Law', as delivered on 3 September 2019, available at www.un.org/pga/73/2019/09/03/current-challenges-to-international-law-the-role-of-societies-of-international-law/ (accessed 16 July 2021); Robert Falkner, 'Rethinking Europe's External Relations in an Age of Global Turmoil: An Introduction', *International Politics*, 54 (2017), 389–404. On the medieval period providing a paradigm for both regionalism and globalism in contemporary IR, see Jan Zielonka, 'The International System in Europe: Westphalian Anarchy or Medieval Chaos?', *Journal of European Integration*, 35 (2013), 1–18.

4 There is a large literature on this. For some of the more useful for this study, see Cristofer Berglund, 'What is (Not) Asymmetric Conflict? From Conceptual Stretching to Conceptual Structuring', *Dynamics of*

Asymmetric Conflict, 13 (2020), 87–98; Mary Kaldor, 'In Defence of New Wars', *Stability*, 2 (2013), 1–16; Mats Berdal, 'The "New Wars" Thesis Revisited', in *The Changing Character of War*, eds. H. Strachan and S. Scheipers (Oxford, 2011), 109–28; Edward Newman, 'The "New Wars" Debate: A Historical Perspective is Needed', *Security Dialogue*, 35 (2004), 173–89.

5 Randall Lesaffer, 'International Law and its History: The Story of an Unrequited Love', in *Time, History and International Law*, eds. M. Craven et al. (Leiden, 2006), 28–9. See also Patrick Quinton-Brown, 'The South, the West, and the Meanings of Humanitarian Intervention in History', *RIS*, 46 (2020), 514–33; C. F. Amerasinghe, 'The Historical Development of International Law – Universal Aspects', *Archiv des Völkerrechts*, 39 (2001), 367–93; James A. Caporaso, 'Changes in the Westphalian Order: Territory, Public Authority, and Sovereignty', *International Studies Review*, 2 (2000), 1–28; D. Blaney and N. Inayatullah, 'The Westphalian Deferral', *International Studies Review*, 2 (2000), 29–64; H. Duchhardt, ' "Westphalian System". Zur Problematik einer Denkfigur', *Historische Zeitschrift*, 269 (1999), 305–15.

6 Oona Hathaway and Scott Shapiro, 'Outcasting: Enforcement in Domestic and International Law', *Yale Law Journal*, 121 (2011), 258. See also Stanley Anderson, 'Human Rights and the Structure of International Law', *New-York Law School Journal of International and Comparative Law*, 12 (1991), 2–3, 5–8.

7 Jörg Fisch, 'Peoples and Nations', in *OHHIL*, 27.

8 Ibid.

9 Lesaffer, 'International Law and its History', 32; Heinhard Steiger, 'From the International Law of Christianity to the International Law of the World Citizen. Reflections on the Formation of the Epochs of the History of International Law', *JHIL*, 3 (2001), 181. See also Steiger, *Die Ordnung der Welt*, 17. For what this meant in the period c. 700–1200 and how it emerges in the medieval evidence, see Chapter 1, pp. 18–23.

10 For a few examples of the wider literature, see William E. Butler, ed., *On the History of International Law and International Organization. Collected Papers of Sir Paul Vinogradoff* (Clark, NJ, 2009); A. S. Hershey, 'The History of International Relations during Antiquity and the Middle Ages', *AJIL*, 5 (1911), 901–33; Steiger, 'From the International Law of Christianity', 180–93.

11 Stephen C. Neff, *Justice among Nations: A History of International Law* (Cambridge, MA, 2014), 51–2.

12 Wilhelm G. Grewe, *The Epochs of International Law*, tr. Michael Byers (Berlin, 2000), 39–45. Karl-Heinz Ziegler, *Völkerrechtsgeschichte*

(Munich, 1994) has a similar structure, and likewise deals with the earlier period in the same manner. That this structure has a long tradition is evident from Ernest Nys, *Les origines du droit international* (Paris, 1894), 7–26.

13 For specific examples, see the chapters by Martin Kintzinger on historical developments in Europe, Mary Ellen O'Connor on peace and war, and Randall Lesaffer on peace treaties, in *OHHIL*. See also chapters by Ziegler and Vollrath in *Peace Treaties and International Law in European History*, ed. R. Lesaffer (Cambridge, 2004).

14 Bruno Paradisi, *Storia del diritto internazionale nel medio evo: L'età de transizione* (Naples, 1956); Bruno Paradisi, Civitas Maxima, 2 vols. (Florence, 1974).

15 Ignacio De La Rasilla Del Moral, 'Medieval International Law', *Oxford Bibliographies. International Law* (Oxford, 2014). On Steiger's work, see below.

16 Isidore, *Etymologiae*, V:6.1 (118). On the intellectual developments in this period, see Joseph Canning, *History of Medieval Political Thought, 300–1450* (London, 2005), and the recent discussion in Geoffrey Koziol, *The Peace of God* (Leeds, 2018), esp. 5–7.

17 *The Islamic Law of Nations. Shaybānī's Siyar*, tr. Majid Khadduri (Baltimore, 1966). For a brief introduction to al-Shaybānī and his contribution to the history of international law, see Mashood A. Baderin, 'Muhammad Al-Shaybānī (749/50–805)', in *OHHIL*, 1081–5.

18 The earliest medieval treatise on peace originates with Rufinus of Sorrento's *De Bono Pacis*, tr. Roman Deutinger (Hanover, 1997), written against the backdrop of the conflict between the cities of the Lombard League and the Emperor Frederick I. The inclusion of the *Peace of Constance* (1183), which concluded this conflict, in one version of Justinian's *Digest*, was the subject of extensive commentary in the fourteenth century, for which see G. Dolezalek, 'I commentari di Odofredo e Baldo alla pace di Constanza', in *La pace di Costanza 1183* (Bologna, 1984), 59–75.

19 Phillip Allott, 'The Concept of International Law', *EJIL*, 10 (1999), 38; Anderson, 'Human Rights and the Structure of International Law', 5. On the 'structural hostility' between the theory and practice of law, see Pierre Bourdieu, 'The Force of Law: Toward a Sociology of the Juridical Field', *Hastings Law Journal*, 38 (1987), 821.

20 Lesaffer, 'International Law and its History', 32.

21 Steiger, *Die Ordnung der Welt*, 107–293, 373–457

22 Ibid., 523, 700.

23 Ibid., 701–5.

24 Ibid., 705–6.

25 The notion is similarly asserted by Padoa-Schioppa, 'Profili del diritto internazionale', 9

26 On this, see also Padoa-Schioppa, 'Profili del diritto internazionale', 4; Grewe, *The Epochs of International Law*, 39–45; Ziegler, *Völkerrechtsgeschichte*; Nys, *Les origines du droit international*, 7–26.

27 Allott, 'The Concept', 42 (key point 31). See also Padoa-Schioppa, 'Profili del diritto internazionale', 40.

28 Steiger, *Die Ordnung der Welt*, 712.

29 A detailed description of the treaties used in this study is available in Chapter 1, pp. 24–8.

30 David Abulafia's *The Two Italies*, published in 1977, is still an excellent discussion of the context and importance of many of these treaties.

31 These are: *Treaty between Charlemagne and Offa of Mercia* (796), *Division of the Realms* (806); *Treaty of Rome* (962, 967); and *Treaty of Verona* (983). One further document could be considered: the submission of Tassilo and his renouncement of Bavaria as recorded in the announcement in the Capitulary of Frankfurt of 794, for which see 'Synodus Franconofurtensis', in *MGH Capit.* i, no. 28, c. 3 (p. 74).

32 For some examples, see F. L. Ganshof, 'The Treaties of the Carolingians', *Medieval and Renaissance Studies*, 3 (1967), 23–50; F. L. Ganshof, 'Les traités des rois mérovingiens', *Tijdschrift voor Rechsgeschiedenis*, 32 (1964), 163–192; Chaplais, *EDP*, 36–45; R. H. C. Davies, 'Alfred and Guthrum's Frontier', *EHR*, 97 (1982), 803–10; Paul J. E. Kershaw, 'The Alfred-Guthrum Treaty: Scripting Accommodation and Interaction in Viking Age England', in *Cultures in Contact: Scandinavian Settlement in England in the Ninth and Tenth Centuries*, eds. Dawn Hadley and Julian D. Richards (Turnhout, 2000), 43–64; Thomas F. Madden, 'The Chrysobull of Alexius I Comnenus to the Venetians: the Date and the Debate', *JMH*, 28 (2002), 23–41; Peter Frankopan, 'Byzantine Trade Privileges to Venice in the Eleventh Century: The Chrysobull of 1092', *JMH*, 30 (2004), 135–60; John Mark Nicovich, 'The Poverty of the Patriarchate of Grado and the Byzantine-Venetian Treaty of 1082', *Mediterranean Historical Review*, 24 (2009), 1–16.

33 Dixon, *Textbook on IL*, 4. For some other examples of the various approaches to the study of international law, see Andrei Marmor, 'The Nature of Law', *Stanford Encyclopedia of Philosophy*, ed. Edward N. Zalta (2011), available at http://plato.stanford.edu/archives/win2011/entries/lawphil-nature/ (accessed 16 July 2021); A. Javier Treviño, *The Sociology of Law. Classical and Contemporary*

Perspectives (New Brunswick, NJ, 2001), 5–6; Oren Perez, 'Fuzzy Law: A Theory of Quasi-Legal Systems', *Canadian Journal of Law and Jurisprudence*, 28 (2015), 343–70; Patrick Capps, *Human Dignity and the Foundations of International Law* (Oxford, 2009), esp. 6–7, 11–21.

34 Dixon, *Textbook on IL*, 4–6.

35 For an excellent discussion of the problems and possibilities of doing comparative history, see Chris Wickham, 'Problems in Doing Comparative History', in *Challenging the Boundaries of Medieval History. The Legacy of Timothy Reuter*, ed. Patricia Skinner (Turnhout, 2009), 5–28, esp. 6–14.

1

The sources of international law: treaties

The starting point for any discussion of the sources of international law is usually Art. 38(1) of the Statute of the International Court of Justice, which describes the three types of material that should be considered international law. Treaties are the first listed, followed by international custom (or legal practice) and general principles of law (e.g., canon or Roman law through its use of natural law).[1] While the statement seems easy enough to interpret – if we're looking for international law, we need first to look to treaties – establishing exactly what a treaty was in the period before 1200 is more difficult. David J. Bederman, in his study of international law in the ancient world, saw treaties as 'the chief means of regulating peaceful relations between States'.[2] Yet, his deliberate use of the word 'state' and the choice to explore the topic on the selection of three specific time periods when there was 'an undisputed, and authentic, system of States in place', would be untenable for the period 700 to 1200.[3] Indeed, J. L. Holzgrefe commented that 'the political structure of Medieval Europe, was so different from that of a system of sovereign territorial states that it is difficult to see in it what came to be called "international" relations'. Particularly problematic for Holzgrefe, and a host of other scholars, was the division of power among a multitude of different actors.[4] The problem has been clearly explained by Randall Lesaffer:

> During the Middle Ages, sovereignty – *superiorem non recognoscens* or the non-recognition of a superior – was a relative concept and extended to a variety of rulers and groups including kings, feudal lords, and vassals, clerical institutions, towns, and even rural communities. The right to use force and make peace was not restricted to supreme princes such as the pope, emperor, or kings. Consequently, there was no strict distinction between public and private peacemaking.[5]

While these assertions are not necessarily untrue, it should be noted that despite the emergence of the nation state, physical international institutions, and a body of international law, they contain a kernel of truth also for more recent historical periods and even the contemporary world. Indeed, the debate over so-called new wars since 1989 has highlighted that how to draw a distinction between law and politics, between war and peace, between the domestic and the international, between the individual and the 'state', is always likely to be subject to great discussion.[6]

Recognising the difficulty and that the locus of political and legal power in the Middle Ages was multi-layered does not mean that it is impossible to point to international matters or to treaties as international agreements.[7] As a start, as highlighted in 2013, when most dictionaries and scholars use definitions of 'treaty' that involve the words 'state' or 'international', both of which are tricky to use in a period before nation states, it is important to qualify the usage by noting that a 'state' between 700 and 1200 usually equates to a ruler or a ruling council (whose authority and jurisdiction, was different to that of, say, local lords or bishops), and 'international' should be taken to mean 'inter-ruler'.[8] Some treaties are even explicit about this by including a so-called amnesty clause, which cancels all expectations and obligations for redress at the expense of the rights of individuals, showing that rulers, and only rulers, had the authority (over all of their subjects) and jurisdiction (over all their territory) to conclude treaties with other foreign entities.[9] Documents from those entities governed by ruling councils corroborate this, showing a clear concept of the authority that should be invested in those dealing with matters of war and peace. For instance, in the 1140s, a certain Filippo di Lamberto was excluded from office in Genoa, after the failure of a mission of his own accord, showing that the 'commune' as a whole – represented by the consuls – and alone, negotiated and concluded treaties with foreign entities.[10] This is not to say that only rulers, or ruling councils, concluded treaties, but rather to point out that such treaties are rarer and usually strictly limited in terms of both authority and jurisdiction. For instance, the *Treaty of Artlenburg*, by which Duke Henry the Lion of Saxony (a subject of the Emperor Frederick I) concluded peace with the Gotlanders (the men of a semi-independent island nominally under the Swedish king) in the 1160s, is clear that not only was this agreement a renewal of laws and privileges previously granted by the Emperor Lothar III but its terms applied only to areas under Henry's authority and jurisdiction.[11] A different example is the *Treaty of Pavia*, concluded in 840 under the supervision of the Emperor Lothar I, and hence often known as the 'Pactum Lotharii'. Despite the involvement of Lothar, who in theory ruled over a vast empire, there can be no doubt that the terms of this treaty applied only to the Venetians (an independent lagoon community headed by a *doge* and their neighbouring communities on the Italian mainland ('vicinos eorum'), the inhabitants of which are named in the prologue of the treaty.[12] It was in essence a treaty regulating the relations between two border communities, not two rulers and their kingdoms. Similarly, the *Ordinance of Dunsæte* sets out the rules for interactions between an English and a Welsh community separated by an unnamed river, most likely the Wye. The prologue states that the treaty had been established by the English *witan* (the royal council) and the counsellors of the Welsh people but without referring to any specific ruler.[13]

What is evident from these examples is that while local communities or lords might conclude treaties with foreign entities, these were limited in scope and they all recognise this fact. Such treaties tend to imply a ruler's consent or involvement in some way, and it is clear from other treaties that rulers had the right to extend, limit or exclude such treaties from any treaty he, himself, concluded.[14] In many ways, this is simply a reflection of the fact that medieval political entities were polycentric and it also hints at the origins of the terminology of international law (*ius gentium*), where, as argued by Jörg Fisch, 'the emphasis is on a (real or invented) group or community and not on an organization; it is not law between states but instead between groups of human beings'.[15] For many reasons, but if for no others at least for reasons of economics, logistics, and communication, on the periphery of an entity, there needed to be individuals who could take up arms as well as lay them down, deal with foreign commerce, and resolve cross-border disputes and interactions relating to property, inheritance, and redress, without a ruler's direct involvement.[16] In addition, the Church acted as a supranational institution with an authority and jurisdiction that, at different times, could both complement and contrast that of secular powers.[17] This polycentrism and legal pluralism is highlighted clearly in how treaties were concluded and implemented. Treaties frequently involved the swearing of oaths not only by the contracting parties, usually rulers, but also their supporters – ecclesiastical and lay – to achieve maximum effect and engage different sections of society in keeping the terms. This created a complicated web of obligations that was not only individual but also communal.[18] Scholars hence need to take a pragmatic approach to finding treaties and the 'international' in the period 700 to 1200. Treaties, as international agreements, were in the vast majority of cases concluded between rulers (or ruling councils), or between two different border communities or lords.[19] Of course this is not unambiguous, but it is important that we continue to grapple with the complex relation of medieval treaties to an outdated state-centred understanding of international law, rather than denying that such agreements ever filled functions that contributed to how rulers, communities, and political entities conducted diplomacy and regulated their interactions with each other.[20] Indeed, as will be shown in this and subsequent chapters, ambiguities are often key to understanding international law in the medieval period rather than the impediments.

A treaty was a formal recognition that both parties had the required authority and jurisdiction.[21] Indeed, treaties of friendship or non-aggression pacts were common throughout the whole Middle Ages and one of their main purposes was simply to recognise that each party had the capacity and authority to enter into such agreements. That external recognition was an important tool in establishing legitimacy and authority, as well as a jurisdiction that might be deemed territorial, can be seen from the *Treaty of Melfi* (1059). This treaty, detailing the oath of Robert Guiscard to Pope Nicholas II, recognised Robert – who was from Normandy but had no claims to rule it – as 'Duke of Apulia and Calabria' in southern Italy.[22] Other examples include the treaty by which Alfred and the viking leader Guthrum recognised each other as kings, and the *Treaty of Bonn* (921), which formally recognised the East and West Frankish kings and kingdoms, following the repeated divisions and disputes over the middle kingdom (often termed Lotharingia) at the end of the ninth and beginning of the tenth centuries.[23] However, that early medieval rulers, unlike modern states, primarily ruled over people not territory and that it was possible to be recognised as having international personality and legal authority without any territorial jurisdiction is clear from the treaty concluded between the English king, Æthelred II, and an army ('here') with which were three leaders, Olaf, Josteinn, and Guthmund.[24] More generally, the importance of recognition can be highlighted through the diplomatic efforts of those rulers and entities whose status was contested, or through the fact that the beginning of a ruler's reign often resulted in a flurry of negotiations, peace conferences, and treaties.[25] The former can be seen clearly in the 1198 alliance between the French king, Philip II, and Philip of Swabia, whose candidacy to be king and emperor was contested with Otto of Brunswick, count of Poitou. The final clause of the treaty specifically noted that if, God willing, Philip was crowned emperor, they would renew the treaty between them. The French king's recognition of Philip's possible change in status was hence important enough to enshrine as one of the legal obligations in the treaty already before the event.[26] Other examples are the *Treaty of Genoa* (1164, 1168), in which the Genoese recognised and treated with Barisone II as king of Sardinia, a status that was reduced to king of Arborea (one of four jurisdictions in Sardinia), and recognised as such in the subsequent treaties of 1168 and 1172.[27] An inversion of this recognition, and of the ability to act independently, can be seen in 794 through the final submission of Duke Tassilo III and the renouncement of his claim to rule Bavaria. According to the announcement of this, the renouncement, like many treaties, was drawn up in three copies; one kept in the palace, one kept by Tassilo, and the third kept in the chapel of the palace.[28] Determining whether or not parties had the required authority and jurisdiction is obviously tricky for the medieval period. Yet, as I argued in 2011, in many instances terminology and context, showing a capacity to act independently can be used for this. Moreover, the customary principle of recognition by or between rulers or peoples – often focused on more political acts of meeting and other principles of conducting diplomacy or contracting treaties – is one of the clearest indicators of the 'international' in the Middle Ages.[29] Such recognition was thus expressed in treaties, moving it from the political and symbolic spheres to the legal.

A treaty, then, is a deliberately entered into agreement, which may cover any aspect of international relations, between 'legal equals', typically princes or entities recognised as having the ability to act independently in an international context.[30] That is, the ruler had to be perceived to be an 'international legal person', capable of making claims, contracts, shouldering responsibilities and obligations, and enjoying some immunity from the jurisdiction of domestic courts of other rulers or political entities.[31] The term 'legal equals' simply means that parties have an equal right to redress or justice.[32] It is not the same as having equality in power – e.g., military or economic – and treaties between distinctly unequal parties, such as submission treaties, still recognise that the parties are 'legal equals' and bind both to carry out the stipulated terms. It is noteworthy that a treaty might also create obligations or rights for one party only.[33] Clear examples of this include the *Treaty of Canterbury* (1189), by which Richard I released William, king of Scots, from the obligations in the *Treaty of Falaise* exacted by Henry II, Richard's father, and the numerous treaties by which the Genoese and Venetians were granted trading privileges by various rulers.[34] It should be noted, however, that even seemingly one-sided grants of trade privileges tended to include commitments and obligations on behalf of the recipients, demonstrating the importance of parties being 'legal equals' and of binding them to carry out the terms.[35] This is based on the fundamental principle of *pacta sunt servanda* ('agreements must be kept'), that good faith and an oath properly demanded and properly taken was binding, in whatever form the sworn agreement had been prepared and published.[36] It is difficult to trace the exact origins of the principle of *pacta sunt servanda* other than to say that it followed a long legal tradition of how to conclude treaties, which can be seen at least as far back as 3,000 BCE, and that prior to the seventeenth century its focus was indisputably on the oath as a cross-cultural and cross-religious concept.[37] By the Middle Ages, the notion that good faith was pledged through oaths and that this was the case even against enemies was firmly embedded in religious writings and wider scholarship.[38] This explains why oaths between parties of different religions or cultures were frequently universally accepted.[39] It also explains why the majority of treaties from the period 700 to 1200 are preserved as oaths or as texts containing oaths.[40] In short, *pacta sunt servanda* can be seen as, on the one hand, a general principle of law found across many cultures and legal systems, and, on the other, as a customary rule, the consistent practice of which is evident in how treaties were concluded over several thousand years.[41]

The fact that the basic premise of any treaty is the principle of *pacta sunt servanda* presents some very practical problems when dealing with medieval treaties as evidence. In order to say something about treaties as possible sources of international law, it should be made clear that this is a study based on those treaties for which a written text has survived. Here, c. 200 such texts have formed the basis of the study, but it is important not to place too much interpretative weight on this figure. Aside from the chronological and geographical scope of this study highlighted in the introduction, which limits the figure, a number of other factors should be noted. The first is that although 200 or so treaties may seem like a surprisingly large number, it is worth emphasising that the majority of treaties from the earlier medieval period have no surviving text at all.[42] Between 700 and 1200 there are more than 1,040 mentions of treaties in narrative sources and other documents. Where possible, some mentions of treaties, giving glimpses of the terms agreed, have been included in each chapter as a separate comparator, to show that stipulations and practices found in actual treaty documents are reflected more broadly also across the narrative evidence. That more written treaties once existed cannot be doubted, and we should be careful to assume, as has so often been done, that the majority of early treaties were only oral.[43] Nevertheless, those treaties for which a written text, in some form, have survived into modern times are but a fraction of the total number of treaties once made.

Other factors affecting the number of written treaties are closely related and concern how the texts have been drawn up and preserved. For instance, some treaties were renewals and many such texts have been copied almost verbatim from one treaty to the next, with only occasional modifications or additions to the terms. One of the longest running sequences of such treaties is that between the Venetians and their neighbours on the mainland, contracted under the supervision of a king or emperor. The first surviving text is the *Treaty of Pavia*, concluded in 840, but it is evident that it had been preceded by earlier ones.[44] The treaty was renewed several times over the next three centuries, although not all texts have survived, and only one, the *Treaty of Verona*, concluded in 983 between the Emperor Otto II and the Venetians, has come down to us in a contemporary copy.[45] While each renewal obviously contributes towards the total figure of treaties, for the purpose of this study, only the *Treaty of Pavia* as the text in which the wording was formalised, will be discussed in any detail. A similar approach has been adopted for other renewals of treaties, including the Anglo-Flemish alliances, known as the treaties of Dover, for which the first surviving text – preserved in the original – dates from 1101.[46] While some treaties were renewals and produced several similar texts, other treaties were proposals and produced texts that never came into effect. Some of these show the negotiating process and the tweaking of the terms over an extended period of time. One example is the *Treaty of Anagni*, drawn up in November 1176 by the representatives of Pope Alexander III and the Emperor Frederick I as the proposed terms for ending the decades-long strife between them, with the peace being amended and finalised in the *Treaty of Venice* of July 1177.[47] Proposed terms of treaties have been counted individually as part of the total, but it is worth noting that in the small number of cases where both a finalised treaty text and the ratified version has survived, these have been counted as a single treaty.

More problematic, for the purpose of putting a number to the available written treaties from the period 700 to 1200, are those which have several surviving constituent parts. One example of this is the *Treaty of Koblenz*, concluded in 860 between Charles the Bald, king of West Frankia, Louis the German, king of East Frankia, and Lothar II, king of the middle Frankish kingdom later known as Lotharingia. This particular treaty appears to have had at least five parts – the oath of Louis the German, a short *adnuntiatio* (announcement or speech) of the peace by Charles the Bald, a longer announcement by Louis the German, a witness list, and the terms of the agreement. These parts likely had different purposes and/or different audiences. This can be seen with the announcement by each king, which was made in the vernacular, likely for their followers, just as was intended with the oaths of Strasbourg in 842.[48] The originals of these various parts do not survive but there are early, pre-twelfth century, copies, for instance in the large tenth- or eleventh-century collection of legal materials MS Lat. 9654 preserved at the Bibliothèque nationale de France in Paris.[49] Only very late manuscripts, such as the Vatican Library's MS Vat. Lat. 4982, preserve all five parts of the treaty, with earlier ones often only preserving one or two.[50] For instance, MS Lat. 9654 records only the twelve clauses of the agreement, the witness list, and the oath of Louis the German, while manuscripts containing the treaty as recorded in the *Annals of Fulda* preserve only the oath of Louis the German.[51] A number of other ninth-century treaties also had several parts, including the *Treaty of Meersen* (851), which has the terms of the agreement as well as the announcements of all three parties; the *Treaty of Liège* (854), which has the announcements of both parties and their mutual oath; and likely also the *Pactum Sicardi* (836), for which only the terms of the agreement has come down to us but with the headings indicating that oaths once accompanied them. By the time we get into the twelfth century, we usually only see combination of documents in Italy.[52] Elsewhere, the various parts are often, but not always, compacted into a single document. Having treaties with lots of parts across several documents is obviously problematic in terms of putting a figure to the available evidence. For the purpose of this study, all documents pertaining to a particular occasion at which a treaty was concluded has been counted as one, but where relevant for the legal implications, differences between the texts have been noted. More importantly, the fact that there can be several parts, and/or several documents, to a treaty raises lots of questions, the most pertinent of which is what a treaty document might have been in the period 700–1200.

Some forty years ago Wilhelm G. Grewe noted that for a long time, treaty documents followed a traditional scheme developed in the Middle Ages. They open up with a general preamble

> setting out the motives and goals of the contracting parties, they attribute guilt or stipulate amnesty and forgiveness, and they promise peace and friendship for the future. The central part of the text consists of a general peace clause (terminating the state of war and restoring friendly relations) and more detailed territorial and political clauses; they are followed by provisions dealing with financial, economic and juridical questions. Sometimes special arrangements are provided for safeguarding and guaranteeing the execution of the treaty and for settling disputes arising out of the interpretation and application of the treaty. Final clauses generally deal with ratification, the date of effectiveness and the authentic language(s).[53]

More recently, Moeglin and Péquignot have similarly highlighted that the preparation, form, ratification, and public announcement of a treaty were subject to particularly standardised forms.[54] However, with some treaties in the period 700 to 1200 surviving as several parts, or even as several documents, it is evident that much of the format and the practices of writing down treaties anticipated by these scholars apply mainly to treaties from the period after 1200.[55] One of the reasons for this is that very few pre-1100 treaties survive in what can be shown to have been their original forms.[56] From the twelfth century, a number of treaties survive in the original, including the alliance of 1101 between Henry I of England and Count Robert of Flanders, known as the *Treaty of Dover*, and the surrender of the city of Piacenza in 1162 to the Emperor Frederick I, known as the *Treaty of San Salvatore*. More commonly for the whole period, treaties survive in contemporary or near-contemporary copies, such as the *Treaty of Verona* (983) mentioned above, or in later, often thirteenth-century, copies, e.g., the *Treaty of Grosseto* – a papal arbitration of 1133 between the cities of Pisa and Genoa. Pisan treaties can be particularly interesting because those among the city's own records have frequently been preserved as texts within texts of later documents. Such examples include the 1113 treaty with Count Ramon Berenguer III of Barcelona, which has been inserted into a 1233 charter by James I of Aragon to Pisa, and the treaty of 1111 with the Byzantine emperor, Alexios I Komnenos, which survives inserted with the text of the 1192 treaty with the Byzantine emperor, Isaac II Angelos.[57] Others yet again, have come down to us in various chronicles and narrative sources, and as I discussed in 2011, some such authors have preserved the texts in full, while others have done so in abridged versions.[58] Texts of treaties in such narratives are particularly susceptible to manipulations resulting from the author's wish to shape his writing for various purposes, and often it is impossible to know the extent of any alterations.[59] Consequently, such texts must be approached with great care and throughout this study obvious attempts to shape texts of treaties are noted where possible and pertinent.

Another reason why much of the format anticipated in later treaties is tricky to apply to those from before 1200 is because it seems to have pertained specifically to peace treaties. By contrast, the majority of treaties surviving from before 1200, or even any historical period, are not peace treaties, if we think of these as being treaties concluded after a period of armed conflict. Most treaties were intended to prevent conflict rather than end it and therefore had the more general aims of peace and friendship, which could be expressed in lots of different ways both orally and in writing. As discussed in 2011, this further explains why the terminology for treaties (e.g., *pax, pactum, amicitia, concordia, repromissio, conventus, confederatio, feodus, treugae*) is wide-ranging yet not the sole indicator that a treaty has been concluded.[60] What is obvious from this very short summary of some of the challenges to using the available evidence is that it would be impossible to speak of a specific treaty document for the earlier Middle Ages.[61] In thinking about what a treaty was in the period 700 to 1200, it is important to note, however, that there is no such thing as a specific treaty document under modern international law either. In the modern world, 'the instrument will be a treaty so long as it is intended to be legally binding in the sense of creating rights and duties enforceable under international law, and this is to be judged objectively according to the nature and content of the agreement and the circumstances in which it was concluded'.[62] The problem for the medieval period thus lies in the fact that there was no Vienna Convention on the Law of Treaties 1969, setting out the scope of treaties and treaty-making, and no physical international institutions, that could objectively judge the nature and content of any agreements nor the circumstances in which they were concluded. Without this, the historian of the medieval period has to take a different approach to deciding which documents were, and which were not, treaties. As a start, and with such a wide variety of types and provenances of treaties, it should be made clear that the treaties in this study 'share a legal-looking structure, with preambles, sections, articles, and annexes', even though not all have every one of these features. They also share 'legal-type language, speaking of parties, signatories, and binding obligations', and, most importantly, 'the structure and language… suggest that the parties viewed them as legal documents'.[63] Most importantly, it is by combining and balancing the various issues discussed above – international; state; recognition; format, terminology, and provenance of texts; and *pacta sunt servanda* – that it is possible to arrive at a corpus of treaties which can be used as sources of international law c. 700–1200.[64]

Having examined the problems of defining a treaty and offering some solutions, the second part of this chapter will explore the extent to which they, like their modern counterparts, were intended to be legally binding in the sense of creating rights and duties that were enforceable. This is important to do, because it allows the historian to think more clearly also about when an international obligation has been violated, its consequences, and permissible means of reaction – issues explored further in Chapter 4.[65] Treaties are typically discussed by scholars in terms of whether they are 'contract treaties' or 'law-making treaties'.[66] Treaties that are contracts create obligations on the parties that agree to enter into them.[67] In the period 700 to 1200, some of the obligations and duties created were very general. The best examples of this are often alliances or treaties of friendship. For instance, with the *Oath of Strasbourg* of February 842, Louis the German, king of the East Franks, swore to 'protect this brother of mine, Charles, with aid or anything else, as a man should rightfully protect his brother'.[68] Charles the Bald, king of the West Franks, in turn then swore to protect his brother, Louis, in the same manner.[69] Some eighty years later, in 921, King Charles the Simple of the West Franks, similarly swore to 'be a friend to this friend of mine, Henry, king of the East [Franks], as a friend should rightfully be to his friend'. Although Henry's copy of this treaty has not survived, it seems certain that he swore a similar oath, as the preserved text notes that Charles had sworn his oath 'on condition that he [Henry] himself swears the same oath to me'.[70] Rules such as these, which do not stipulate concrete rights or obligations for the legal persons to whom they are addressed, are frequently referred to as 'soft law'. They are normative in that they are rules of law, but 'their content is inherently flexible or vague.'[71] Dixon has commented that such rules 'lessen the chances of conflict between competing ideologies' but that 'the disadvantage is that such law may be so vague or imprecise as to have no practical legal content at all' – the latter of which is a sentiment shared by many scholars commenting on treaties and international law across historical periods.[72] However, the *Oaths of Strasbourg* show that it is certainly possible to hazard a guess as to what might have been involved in promising to protect the other party as a friend/brother should or against all (*contra omnes*). Louis' oath specifically stipulates that he would not make any agreement ('nul plaid nunquam prindrai') with Lothar – the brother of Charles and Louis against whom the treaty was directed – which might with Louis' consent harm Charles. Likewise, Charles promised not to enter into any dealings with Lothar ('mit Ludheren in nohheiniu thing ne gegango') that might harm Louis.[73] In other words, the minimum requirement to be an ally (whether as a brother, a friend, or against all men) was to not conclude a similar agreement with the enemy. As this would not have prevented either party from concluding a different type of agreement with the enemy, this particular obligation seems to have become increasingly defined as we get into the eleventh and twelfth century. By the time King Alfonso of Aragon concluded the *Treaty of Najac-de-Rouergue* with Richard, count of Poitou (son of Henry II of England) in the mid-1180s, neither party was allowed to make any 'truces, peace, concord or agreement whatsoever (treugas, pacem, concordiam, sive aliquam composicionem)' with their enemy Count Raymond V of Toulouse, without the other's consent.[74]

With the increase in the survival of written treaties from the twelfth century, it is possible to see that phrases promising to aid the other party as a friend/brother should or against all often became embedded among other stipulations in treaties, showing that the obligations, rights, and duties created became more varied.[75] For instance, the aid became specified as a certain number of men (e.g., *Treaty of Dover*, 1101, 1110, 1163; *Pact between Milan and Piacenza*, 1156; *Treaty of Najac-de-Rouergue*, 1185) and extended to advice, not revealing secrets, and to dissuading enemies (e.g., *Treaty of Melfi*, 1059; *Treaty of Ceprano*, 1080; *Treaty of Dover*, 1101). The aid frequently also specified who it was directed at and the involvement of any third parties (e.g., *Treaty of Dover*, 1101; *Treaty between Roger of Sicily and Savona*, 1127; *Treaty of Sahagún*, 1158; *Pact of Philip of Swabia and Philip II of France*, 1198), it could be defined geographically (e.g., *Treaty between Baldwin of Jerusalem and Genoa*, 1104; *Treaty of Toul*, 1171; *Treaty of Ivry*, 1177), and there could be some form of payment or supplies involved (e.g., *II Æthelred*, 994; *Treaty of Devol*, 1108). One treaty, between Raymond of Toulouse, Sancho of Provence, William of Forcalquier, and Genoa of 1184, even specifically stated that restoring or rebuilding Marseille and its port, after the allies had destroyed them, would exceed the traditional obligation of counsel and aid.[76] While this looks as if obligations became more defined over time, so as to have precise legal implications, we must not underestimate the fact that it might be the greater survival of documents that makes it appear this way. A different interpretation could be that princes always had a range of different relationships, and therefore treaties, with each other; from ones with vague promises to those creating more defined legal obligations. A ruler might conclude one treaty – perhaps typically with his greatest rival or ally – that had vague or broad obligations, while other treaties concluded by that same ruler would hence need to be more defined, so as not to encroach on that broader treaty, which further explains why many such treaties name the individuals against whom the terms applied as well as where and when.[77] That such an interpretation has some merits can be seen by looking at the Anglo-Flemish alliances across the whole of the twelfth century. For most of that century, the obligations between the English king and the Flemish count were clearly defined in terms of what aid would be provided, where, and against whom, as well as the payment for this. The alliance was perhaps important but certainly eclipsed by any relationship that both the Flemish count and the English king had with the French king.[78] In 1197, however, in the midst of significant warfare between the English and French kings, Count Baldwin IX and King Richard I concluded an alliance, known as the *Treaty of Andeli*, which was very different to the many obligations and terms set out in earlier alliances in the treaties of Dover. The *Treaty of Andeli*, like the *Oaths of Strasbourg*, simply promised mutual aid ('mutuum subsidium et auxilium') and not to conclude any agreement ('pacem aut treugam') with the French king without the other's consent but made little attempt to define these obligations further.[79] Indeed, the one specific stipulation shows the broad conception of this alliance between Richard and Baldwin: it would be in force not only during the war but in perpetuity.[80]

That less defined obligations in friendship treaties were often preserved for the ruler's most important external relationship can be seen, moreover, from the way some treaties anticipate that breaches would be dealt with. The announcement accompanying the *Oaths of Strasbourg* stipulates that if either Charles the Bald or Louis the German reneged on their promises, their followers would be released from the obedience and oath they had sworn to their king.[81] Effectively, this would deprive the offending party of his supporters, and thereby undermine his ability to rule as an independent prince. Similarly, the *Treaty of Andeli* anticipated that in case of breaches, those of the supporters who had sworn to the treaty would hand themselves over into the captivity of the other ruler without being summoned to do so.[82] Like the *Oaths of Strasbourg*, this would effectively deprive the offender of his supporters and seriously impede his ability to rule. Such clauses show that the margin between war and peace was very small, because any breach immediately anticipated an action that would terminate the relationship between the contracting parties.[83] By contrast, treaties of friendship or alliance with lots of defined obligations often recognised that there were several ways of dealing with breaches. For instance, the sureties given as guarantors of the *Treaty of Dover* (1101) show that, in case of violation, they could be expected to work in three different ways: by persuading the violator to make amends; by each surety paying his share of a specified fine; and, if the first two failed, by each surety presenting himself for imprisonment at a specified location. In addition, half of the sureties undertook to fulfil the count of Flanders's military obligations to the English king in case the count defaulted on account of a lawful excuse (e.g., illness), and the sureties themselves could be replaced if they failed to fulfil their duties for some reason.[84] The renewal of the alliance in 1110 set out yet another way of resolving breaches, namely by appointing an arbiter, Count Eustace of Boulogne, who would decide what obligation had been breached and the remedy.[85]

These various strategies highlight that these treaties were contracts that the parties were expected to negotiate their way around and out of rather than enforce. In other words, resolving breaches of the terms or terminating the relationship between the two contracting parties required several steps of negotiation because the different legal obligations and their effect could be resolved in many ways. Seemingly, it would have been difficult to get to the stage that required the men of either party to hand themselves over to the other side. One of the most notable things about this is that it is difficult to envisage exactly how having monopoly on force – often seen as a necessary characteristic for a 'state' and hence for international law – would have aided the ability of the parties to negotiate their way around any breaches of the terms in this treaty.[86] Often scholars view effectiveness or enforcement of international law and deterrence to violence and war through this narrow lens of monopoly on force without noting that such measures are possibly better suited to dealing with crimes rather than contracts, which is what many treaties are.[87] Indeed, as has been noted by modern commentators, so-called 'soft law' measures – whether expressed in a lack of defined treaty obligations or in a lack of defined enforcement methods – facilitate compromise and mutually beneficial cooperation, reflect particular problems actors are trying to resolve, and are 'frequently dynamic' in that they can initiate 'a process and a discourse that may involve learning and other changes over time'.[88]

More generally, treaties that were contracts were often intended to terminate either when the particular object for which they were entered into had been achieved or if other unforeseen circumstances intervened.[89] For instance, the *Treaty of Seligenstadt* was a contract setting out the terms of the betrothal of 1188 between the Emperor Frederick I's son, Conrad, and Berenguela, the daughter of King Alfonso VIII of Castile. The terms focus on Berenguela's right to succeed her father if he should die without a male heir and Conrad's rights as her husband, as well as the marriage gift ('donationem... nuptias') which among Alfonso's Romance-speaking subjects was known as 'doaire' and among the Spanish-speaking subjects as 'arras'.[90] However, just a year or so later, King Alfonso produced a male heir and the parties ceased to be interested in the fulfilment of the terms of this treaty, which was later annulled by the archbishop of Toledo and a papal legate.[91] Similarly, the *Treaty of Montferrand*, by which Henry II of England contracted a marriage for his youngest son, John, with the daughter, Alice, of Count Humbert III of Maurienne in 1173, did clearly not remain in force once Alice passed away in 1174.[92] A different example, the *Treaty of Genoa*, concluded in 1190 with the French king, Philip II, for the purpose of transporting him and his fleet to the Holy Land, seems to anticipate that the obligations would end once this had been completed. For instance, the treaty stipulated that the Genoese only had to carry enough food supplies for men and horses for eight months, starting from the day that the king's journey would begin, and the full payment for the service of the Genoese would be made in June of 1190, shortly before the anticipated starting date.[93] In recognition of the partial fulfilment of the terms – presumably the preparations for the transportation – Philip then, on his way to the Holy Land, re-confirmed the promises regarding Genoese rights in areas that would be conquered.[94] There can thus be no doubt that treaties such as these ended when they had achieved their purpose or in the case of unforeseen circumstances, even if this is not always explicitly set out in the treaty.

Other treaties were law-making, intended to endure and lay down rules of conduct for the, usually, indefinite future.[95] This is easiest seen through treaties concluded between rulers or communities for the purposes of frequent interactions. Often such treaties share features and format with domestic laws of the same period and regulate a similar range of interactions or procedures for dealing with disputes, including movement of people (e.g., merchants, captives, pilgrims), commerce, violent offences, land ownership, and inheritance. Three out of the four treaties surviving from the Anglo-Saxon period carry terms that indicate that they were law-making treaties rather than contracts, and show great similarity both in content and procedure to domestic laws from the same period. For instance, the short ninth-century treaty between the West Saxon king, Alfred, and Guthrum, as king of the people in East Anglia, only has five clauses (in its longest version), four of which deal with regulating future interactions between the kings' subjects.[96] Many law-making treaties were, furthermore, looking to firmly establish long-practised customs or to implement reforms. Some of the best such examples can be found in treaties concluded with the papacy.[97] For instance, the *Treaty of Benevento*, ending the dispute between the Roman Church and William I, king of Sicily, in 1156, sets out the terms for dealing with ecclesiastical affairs, and, in accordance with papal reforms, confirming to the papacy the rights, in Apulia and Calabria, to celebrate councils in whatever city it chooses, to freely send legations, and to hold appeals in disputes.[98] Sicily, by contrast, was to remain a special case, in accordance with Pope Urban II's grant of powers to Count Roger I in 1098, and on the island the king could 'retain... whatever it [the majesty] considers necessary to retain for promoting Christianity and for upholding the crown'.[99] The next clause, however, shows that even long-held ecclesiastical customs could be amended to suit circumstances. Clause 11 of the treaty stipulated that ecclesiastical elections – which the Church usually insisted should be free – needed the assent of the king, who would only grant it once it had been established that the nominated and designated person was 'not among the traitors or enemies of us or our heirs'.[100] The clause is a clear reference to the troubles that had plagued the kingdom in the lead-up to the treaty, showing that even treaties that enshrined many long-established customs and practices could set out new rules for the future. Most importantly, this treaty, as also that between Alfred and Guthrum, is clear that the terms as set out would remain in force in perpetuity, showing the intention to be law-making.[101]

Intra-community treaties often anticipate that disputes over the terms were to be resolved through arbitration panels, made up of an equal number of men drawn from each side. For instance, in the *Ordinance of the Dunsæte*, dating to the tenth or early eleventh century, such a panel of 'lahmen' (lit. lawmen) was to decide whether or not measures for dealing with disputes over cattle were just.[102] The *Treaty of Grosseto*, itself an arbitration by the pope dating to 1133, stipulated that disputes arising over the customs and rights of the cities of Genoa and Pisa would be decided by a panel of four men from either side, who had to investigate and make a judgment within two months.[103] The *Treaty of Montebello*, concluded between the Emperor Frederick Barbarossa and the cities of the Lombard League in 1175, likewise set out that six arbiters from each side would investigate and decide on various issues in dispute.[104] An interesting example, also linking arbitration to powerful ecclesiastics, can be found in the *Treaty of Jarnègues* of 1190. According to one of the stipulations, if it should happen that a complaint or dispute arose between the two parties – the king of Aragon and the count of Toulouse – over the terms of the treaty, the matter would be decided by two archbishops (Berenguer de Vilademuls of Tarragona and Bernat Gaucelin of Narbonne) – one acting on behalf of each ruler – if the issue arose in the parts beyond (i.e., to the west of) the river Hérault.[105] For matters arising in the parts between the river Hérault and Montgenèvre (i.e., to the east) two men from each side acted as arbiters, all of whom seem to have been secular lords and one of whom was Barral, viscount of Marseille. A different strategy, but one that also drew on known judicial institutions, was anticipated in the *Treaty of Messina* (1190). Here, it was the enforcement methods that Richard I of England sought to put on a firm legal footing by approaching Pope Clement III and giving him power to 'coerce' either Richard himself or his lands if he breached the terms of the treaty or if he failed to return the money paid for the contracted marriage between Richard's nephew and Tancred's daughter, in the event that it did not take place.[106] The intention was to authorise the pope to excommunicate Richard or put his lands under interdict, even though the text as outlined in the letter sent to the pope seems to acknowledge that this was a last resort, as it refers also to the 'mediation of the Church'.[107] In other words, this particular third-party involvement reinforced compliance. All of these examples show then that many law-making treaties included measures whereby the circumstances, nature and terms could be, if not 'objectively' judged as stipulated in the Vienna Convention on the Law of Treaties 1969, at least interpreted by judicial institutions that were widely used and known to all parties. This is powerful evidence that medieval rulers and communities considered treaties as law-making in an international sense.[108]

Often the best examples of how, in practice, treaties were agreed and interpreted by judicial bodies can be found with partition treaties. For instance, the Treaty of Verdun, agreed in August 843, divided the Frankish Empire into three kingdoms among the surviving sons of the Emperor Louis the Pious – Charles the Bald, Louis the German, and Lothar I. The issues at stake centred not only on the division of the realm but also on the reparation of damages suffered during the war. Contemporaries report that a commission of the leading men from each side were chosen to investigate the parts that each brother should have in the division with the intention to make it as fair as possible.[109] Although no text of the Treaty of Verdun has survived into modern times, the exact provisions of the treaty are usually reconstructed with the help of a series of subsequent partitions and treaties; in particular, that agreed at Meerssen in 870. The division at Meerssen is recorded in the *Annals of St. Bertin* by Hincmar, archbishop of Rheims, who was an eyewitness, and in it he lists each share in terms of ecclesiastical provinces and then counties, before finally outlining some additional cities and settlements as well as an area, defined by rivers and roads, which was put to arbitration.[110] This tallies with the evidence explored by Ganshof, showing that, in 843, the commission of leading men had made inventories (*descriptiones*) of the realm, after which the division at Verdun was made on several principles including proximity to the lands already held by each king, equivalents between portions, and resources to distribute to followers.[111] This process was then replicated for subsequent partitions, including that at Meerssen in 870.

While it is useful for our understanding of the legal scope to distinguish between treaties that were contracts and those which were law-making, it is evident that many were both. There are lots of ways of showing this for the period 700 to 1200. For instance, the *Treaty of Logroño*, concluded between King Alfonso VIII of Castile and King Sancho VI of Navarre in 1176, specifically sets out that it had been agreed for the purpose of submitting their points of dispute to the arbitration of King Henry II of England.[112] Once Henry had given his judgment on their dispute in the *Treaty of London* of 1177, some of the terms in the *Treaty of Logroño* – relating specifically to whom the parties would send to the English king, when they would travel and the nature of the envoys' authority – would have ceased to be in force. However, the parties had also agreed to a truce of seven years while the arbitration was going ahead – allowing the free movement of people and goods, and redress for injuries – which was still in force even after Henry's judgment, enabling the parties to continue to negotiate and eventually conclude a firm peace in the second *Treaty of Logroño* of 1179.[113] Similarly, the series of treaties between Genoa, King Alfonso VII of Léon-Castile and Count Ramon Berenguer IV of Barcelona, agreed in 1146 for the purpose of conquering the cities of Almería and Tortosa, created some obligations and duties that were not only specific in time but also had a particular purpose. The *Treaty of Genoa* stipulated that Alfonso VII would assemble his army in May of 1147, immediately pay the Genoese envoy 10,000 *marabotini* for the cost of siege engines, and pay a further 10,000 *marabotini* by Easter 1147.[114] At the same time, the treaty gave rights that were intended to be long-lasting. For instance, upon capture of Almería or any other settlement, the Genoese would receive one third of the city and this would include a church 'with sufficient real estate and dwellings to support five presbyters with their attendant priests', as well as a trading post, an oven, a bath, and a garden. Furthermore, Alfonso allowed Genoese men and their goods free and secure movement across all his lands without paying tolls and other dues.[115] The Genoese treaty with the count of Barcelona mirrors these terms but applied to the expedition to Tortosa and its capture.[116] In short, some of the obligations in these treaties had a very particular, often time-limited purpose, but they also set out rules of conduct for the indefinite future.

Conversely, some treaties were clearly perceived to be law-making but were limited in time. The *Treaty of Pavia* of 840 is an obvious example of this. As noted above, this treaty essentially regulated the daily interactions between two border communities and its terms bear all the hallmarks of, and similarities to, domestic laws, yet, it was concluded for five years at a time. Similarly, the so-called *Pactum Sicardi* of 836, concluded between the prince of Benevento, Sicard, and the cities of Naples, Sorrento, and Amalfi for the fixed term of five years, sets out a range of terms intended to regulate interactions between these regions. For instance, neither party was to buy Lombard subjects or sell them overseas, and doing so could incur hefty fines.[117] Anyone committing homicide would be handed over to the other party for justice to be done, and anyone who presumed to bind or strike another would pay for the injury with 100 *solidos*.[118] Merchants and other men were allowed to cross rivers freely at recognised fords, and ships and goods would remain unharmed in the territory of the other party.[119] In short, this treaty not only looks similar to that of Pavia in terms of the range of interactions covered, but it also shares features and phrases with the Lombard laws more generally.[120] It would thus be difficult to think of this treaty as being anything other than law-making, even though it was concluded only for five years. Such treaties further raise the issue of how long a period might be required to make customs, another source of international law. One can certainly imagine that since the *Treaty of Pavia* (840) was renewed several times, at some point, the rights, practices, and procedures it set out had become customary and remained in force even if the treaty was not renewed exactly every five years. In fact, the terms of the *Treaty of Pavia* (840), or rather its first written predecessor, might simply have set down in writing practices and procedures that were customary. Either way, there can be little doubt that the community of Venice and the communities on the mainland under its ruler regarded the treaty's terms as binding and as regulating the relations between them. What all of these examples show is the futility of trying to separate clearly between those treaties that were contracts and those which were law-making. Indeed, the legal effect of treaties was the same regardless of whether we view them as law creating or as obligation creating: the parties were bound to act in accordance with the terms of the treaty to which they were a party. In short, 'the distinction between the various types of treaty is not one of legal effect but one of purpose and aim'.[121]

In the period 700 to 1200, there was no equivalent to the Vienna Convention on the Law of Treaties 1969 that set out the parameters for, and governed, written treaties. Nevertheless, there manifestly were customary rules that governed who could conclude treaties and how this should be done. Furthermore, such documents were perceived as creating legally binding obligations and rights that could be determined and interpreted by recognised legal institutions in an international context, and that could be terminated in a number of ways not just enforced. That treaties then were the main source of international law in the period 700 to 1200, as in historical periods both before and beyond, seems certain.

Notes

1 *Statute of the International Court of Justice*, available at www.icj-cij.org/en/statute#CHAPTER_II (accessed 16 July 2021), Art. 38(1).

2 David J. Bederman, *International Law in Antiquity* (Cambridge, 2004), 2, 205–6.

3 There has been significant debate over the medieval 'state'. For one of the most useful summaries, highlighting the shift in ideas in the twenty-first century, see Steffen Patzold, 'Human security, fragile Staatlichkeit und Governance im Frühmittelalter. Zur Fragwürdigkeit der Scheidung von Vormoderne und Moderne', *Geschichte und Gesellschaft*, 38 (2012), 406–22. See also Stefan Esders and Gunnar Folke Schuppert, *Mittelalterliches Regieren in der Moderne oder modernes Regieren im Mittelalter?* (Baden-Baden, 2015); R. R. Davies, 'The Medieval State: The Tyranny of a Concept?', *Journal of Historical Sociology*, 16 (2003), 280–300; Susan Reynolds, 'There Were States in Medieval Europe. A Response to Rees Davies', *Journal of Historical Sociology*, 16 (2003), 550–5; Hans-Werner Goetz, '*Regnum*. Zum politischen Denken der Karolingerzeit', *Zeitschrift der Savigny-Stiftung für Rechtsgeschichte, Germanische Abteilung*, 104 (1987), 110–89; Hans-Werner Goetz, 'Die Wahrnehmung von "Staat" und "Herrschaft" im frühen Mittelalter', in *Staat im frühen Mittelalter* (Vienna, 2006), 39–58; Johannes Fried, 'Der karolingische Herrschaftsverband im 9. Jahrhundert zwischen "Kirche" und "Königshaus"', *Historische*

Zeitschrift, 235 (1982), 1–43; Otto Brunner, *Land und Herrschaft* (Darmstadt, 1956), esp. 132–93.

4 J. L. Holzgrefe, 'The Origins of Modern International Relations Theory', *RIS*, 15 (1989), 11–14. See also Moeglin, *Diplomatie*, 598–602; Jeffrey L. Dunoff, Steven R. Ratner, and David Wippman, *International Law: Norms, Actors, Process* (Aspen, 2006), 441; Amerasinghe, 'The Historical Development of International Law', 374; John G. Ruggie, 'Continuity and Transformation in the World Polity: Toward a Neorealist Synthesis', *World Politics*, 35 (1983), 273–4.

5 Randall Lesaffer, 'Peace Treaties and the Formation of International Law', in *OHHIL*, 75. There is significant critique of viewing international law through this lens of sovereignty. For two of the most relevant examples, see Allott, 'The Concept', 31–50; Geoffrey A. Hoffman, 'Critique, Culture and Commitment: The Dangerous and Counterproductive Paths of International Legal Discourse', *Dalhousie Law Journal*, 27 (2004), 439–502, esp. 439–72.

6 For the most relevant for this study, see Newman, 'The "New Wars" Debate', 173–89; Christine Bell, *On the Law of Peace: Peace Agreements and the Lex Pacificatoria* (Oxford, 2008), esp. 17; Christopher Clapham, 'Rwanda: The Perils of Peacemaking', *Journal of Peace Research*, 35 (1998), 193–210, esp. 193–4; Mary Kaldor, 'How Peace Agreements Undermine the Rule of Law in New War Settings', *Global Policy*, 7 (2016), 146–55; Blaney and Inayatullah, 'The Westphalian Deferral', 29–64; Jakub Grygiel, 'The Primacy of Premodern History', *Security Studies*, 22 (2013), 1–32; Yasuaki Onuma, *A Transcivilizational Perspective of International Law* (Leiden, 2010).

7 On legal pluralism, see Margaret Davies, 'Legal Pluralism', in *The Oxford Handbook of Empirical Legal Research*, eds. Peter Cane and Herbert M. Kritzer (Oxford, 2010), 805–27; James G. Stewart and Asad Kiyani, 'The Ahistoricism of Legal Pluralism in International Criminal Law', *American Journal of Comparative Law*, 65 (2017), 393–450; Paul S. Berman, *Global Legal Pluralism. A Jurisprudence of Law Beyond Borders* (Cambridge, 2012), esp. 3–58. An interesting example of medieval legal pluralism can be found in Claudia Storti's discussion juxtaposing the 'natio', the kingdom and the community: 'Ascertainment of Customs and Personal Laws in Medieval Italy from the Lombard Kingdom to the Communes', *Rechtsgeschichte-Legal History*, 24 (2016), 257–65. See also Caroline Humfress, 'Thinking through the Lens of Legal Pluralism: "Forum Shopping" in the Later Roman Empire', in *Law and Empire: Ideas, Practices, Actors*,

eds., J. Duindam et al. (Leiden, 2013), 225–50; Brigitte Pohl-Resl, 'Legal Practice and Ethnic Identity in Lombard Italy', in *Strategies of Distinction: The Construction of Ethnic Communities 300–800*, eds. Walter Pohl and Helmut Reimitz (Leiden, 1998), 205–19, esp. 205–6.

8 Jenny Benham, 'Law or Treaty? Defining the Edge of Legal Studies in the Early and High Medieval Periods', *Historical Research*, 86 (2013), 488; Moeglin, *Diplomatie*, 521–2. Steiger similarly categorised inter-powers relations (*Zwischen-Mächte-Beziehungen*), inter-powers law (*Zwischen-Mächte-Recht*), inter-powers associations (*Zwischen-Mächte-Verbindungen*). Steiger, *Die Ordnung der Welt*, 107–293, 373–457. Compare Ganshof, who argued that a treaty was 'an agreement between states, peoples, tribes or rulers', but without qualifying this further. Ganshof, 'The Treaties of the Carolingians', 23.

9 On amnesty clauses and legal redress in treaties, see Chapter 3, pp. 99–103. There is a large literature on sovereignty and the challenges of amnesty and human rights in later historical periods. For examples, see Kieran McEvoy and Louise Mallinder, 'Amnesties in Transition: Punishment, Restoration, and the Governance of Mercy', *Journal of Law and Society*, 39 (2012), 410–40, esp. 413–15; Ulrich Haltern, *Was bedeutet Souveränität?* (Tübingen, 2007), esp. 75–97; Lisa Ford, *Settler Sovereignty: Jurisdiction and Indigenous People in America and Australia, 1788–1836* (Cambridge, MA, 2010). See also summary of development of 'sovereignty' and the just war in Rory Cox, 'The Ethics of War up to Thomas Aquinas', in *The Oxford Handbook of Ethics of War*, eds. S. Lazar and H. Frowe (Oxford, 2018), 110–12.

10 *CDRG*, I, no. 178. Philip was later re-instated, as shown by nos. 180, 182.

11 *Treaty of Artlenburg*, prol: 'Per universe potestatis nostre ditionem Gutenses pacem firmam habeant, ita ut, quicquid dispendii rerum suarum seu iniurie infra terminos nostri regiminis pertulerint, plenam ex iudicaria potestate nostram iusticiam et correctionem consequantur...' Cf. *Treaty of Mallorca* (1188), c. 1, setting out the places along the coast and the islands where the peace between the King of Mallorca and the Genoese applied.

12 *Treaty of Pavia* (840), prol. This treaty was renewed several times and the precise communities to which it applied altered but are always specified. For a good discussion of the context of this treaty, see G. V. B. West, 'Communities and *Pacta* in Early Medieval Italy: Jurisdiction, Regulatory Authority and Dispute Avoidance', *EME*, 18 (2010), 367–93, esp. 367–75. On the nature of Venice, see Stefano Gasparri,

'Venezia fra l'Italia bizantina e il regno italico: la civitas e l'assemblea', in *Venezia. Itinerari per la storia della città*, eds. S. Gasparri, G. Levi, and P. Moro (Bologna, 1997), 61 110; Stefano Gasparri, 'The First Dukes and the Origins of Venice', in *Venice and its Neighbors from the 8th to the 11th Century. Through Renovation and Continuity*, eds. Sauro Gelichi and Stefano Gasparri (Leiden, 2017), 5–26.

13 *Dunsæte*, prol: 'Ðis is seo gerædnes ðe Angelcynnes witan 7 Wealhðeode rædboran betweox Dunsetan gesetton.' As noted by Molyneux, the wording of the text is slightly ambiguous, making it unclear if the Dunsæte covered both the English and Welsh communities or pertained only to the Welsh side. George Molyneux, 'The *Ordinance Concerning the Dunsæte* and the Anglo-Welsh Frontier in the Late Tenth and Eleventh Centuries', *ASE*, 40 (2012), 249–50. On this treaty, see also Lindy Brady, *Writing the Welsh Borderlands in Anglo-Saxon England* (Manchester, 2017), 1–22.

14 E.g., *II Æthelred*, c. 1; *Treaty between Bertrand of Saint-Gilles and Genoa* (1109); *Treaty of Gisors* (1160), c. 13; *Treaty of Ivry*, c. 3; *Treaty of Toul*, c. 2. For discussion of this, see Chapter 3, pp. 64, 107–11. See also Walter Pohl, 'The Empire and the Lombards: Treaties and Negotiations in the Sixth Century', in *Kingdoms of the Empire. The Integration of Barbarians in Late Antiquity*, ed. Walter Pohl (Leiden, 1997), 106–7, 111; R. R. Davies, 'Frontier Arrangements in Fragmented Societies: Ireland and Wales', in *Medieval Frontier Societies*, eds. R. Bartlett and Angus MacKay (Oxford, 1989), 85–7. That a similar concept and approach to those who could conclude treaties existed in Muslim law is evident, e.g., in the writings of Muhammad al-Shaybani (d. 805). *The Islamic Law of Nations*, 152–70. On this, see also Viorel Panaite, *Ottoman Law of War and Peace* (Leiden, 2019), 166.

15 Fisch, 'Peoples and Nations', 28. On polycentrism as a legal concept, see Gunther Teubner, 'The King's Many Bodies: The Self-Deconstruction of Law's Hierarchy', *Law & Society Review*, 31 (1997), 763–88, esp. 780–4; Brian Druzin, 'Towards a Theory of Spontaneous Legal Standardization', *Journal of International Dispute Settlement*, 8 (2017), 403–31.

16 Other historians working on similar problems have also noted this. For three good examples, see Patzold, 'Human security', 421; Janet L. Nelson, 'Kingdom and Empire in the Carolingian World', in *Carolingian Culture: Emulation and Innovation*, ed. Rosamond McKitterick (Cambridge, 1993), 52; Esther Pascua, 'South of the Pyrenees: Kings, Magnates and Political Bargaining in Twelfth-century Spain', *JMH*, 27 (2001), 103–4.

17 A good sketch of this in the ninth century is Mayke de Jong's 'The Two Republics. *Ecclesia* and the Public Domain in the Carolingian World', in *Italy and Early Medieval Europe. Papers for Chris Wickham*, eds. Ross Balzaretti, Julia Barrow, and Patricia Skinner (Oxford, 2018), 486–500.

18 Jenny Benham, 'Peace, Security and Deterrence', in *A Cultural History of Peace in the Medieval Age 800–1450*, ed. Walter P. Simons (London, 2020), 125–6.

19 Ferdinand Feldbrugge has advocated a similar approach in dealing with treaties from medieval Russia, which often involved the prince dealing with groups of foreign merchants rather than other rulers. F. Feldbrugge, *Law in Medieval Russia* (Leiden, 2009), 182.

20 Christine Bell's excellent study of peace agreements and the *lex pacificatoria* in the contemporary world deals with many similar issues and provides a strong context for my own study. See, for instance, her comments on the term 'peace agreements', highlighting that the involvement of both state and non-state actors, as well as domestic parties, means that 'the act of comparing agreements is immediately open to the challenge that the term "peace agreement" in fact has no core meaning'. Bell, *On the Law of Peace*, 47.

21 On recognition in international law generally, see Allott, 'The Concept', 37 (key point 21); Anne Schuit, 'Recognition of Governments in International Law and the Recent Conflict in Libya', *International Community Law Review*, 14 (2012), 381–402, esp. 381–3; Dixon, *Textbook on IL*, 123–4; James Crawford, *The Creation of States in International Law*, 2nd edn. (Oxford, 2006); José María Ruda, 'Recognition of States and Governments', in *International Law: Achievements and Prospects*, ed. M. Bedjaoui (Dordrecht, 1991), 449–65; Anthony Murphy and Vlad Stancescu, 'State Formation and Recognition in International Law', *Juridical Tribune*, 7 (2017), 6–14.

22 *Treaty of Melfi*: 'Ego Robertus Dei gratia et sancti Petri dux Apulie et Calabrie et utroque subveniente futurus Sicilie…' Cf. the renewal of this treaty in 1080, which clearly recognised Robert's status as duke also of Sicily. *Treaty of Ceprano*: 'Ego Robertus Dei gratia et sancti Petri Apulie, Calabrie et Sicilie dux…'

23 *AGu*, prol: 'Ðis is ðæt frið, ðæt Ælfred cyninc 7 Gyðrum cyning…'; *Treaty of Bonn*, c. 2: 'Ego Karolus… rex Francorum occidentalium amodo ero huic amico meo regi orientali Heinrico amicus…' The historiography on the *Treaty of Bonn* has often focused on the issue of recognition and the means by which this achieved, for which see Grewe, *The Epochs of International Law*, 77; Bernd Schneidmüller, 'Die Begegnung der Könige und die erste Nationalisierung Europas

(9.-11. Jahrhundert)', in *Le relazioni internazionali nell'alto medioevo* (Spoleto, 2011), 568–73; Susanne Kaeding, Kerstin Seidel and Britta Kümmerlen, 'Heinrich I. – ein Freundschaftskönig?', *Concilium medii aevi*, 3 (2000), 269–81; Gerd Althoff, *Amicitiae und Pacta. Bündnis, Einigung, Politik und Gebetsgedenken im beginnenden 10. Jahrhundert* (Hanover, 1992), 23–26.

24 *II Æthelred*, prol. On this problem in the modern world, see the contrasting arguments of Shaw and Bell: 'Without territory a legal person cannot be a state. It is undoubtedly the basic characteristic of a state and the one most widely accepted and understood... Most nations indeed developed through a close relationship with the land they inhabited.' Malcolm N. Shaw, *International Law*, 6th edn. (Cambridge, 2008), 487–8. 'The dislocation of power in contemporary times, separates the nation from the territorial state, giving competing nationalisms a stake in the state and in peace agreements.' Bell, *On the Law of Peace*, conclusion of part I.

25 This fits with Björn Weiler's argument that royal successions were 'moments of crisis', for which see his 'Describing Rituals of Succession and the Legitimation of Kingship in the West, ca.1000–ca.1150', in *Court Ceremonies and Rituals of Power in Byzantium and the Medieval Mediterranean: Comparative Perspectives*, eds. Alexander D. Beihammer, Stavroula Constantinou, and Maria G. Parani (Leiden, 2013), 115. On this phenomenon in an earlier period and the issuing of charters by new kings, see also Geoffrey Koziol, *The Politics of Memory and Identity in Carolingian Royal Diplomas. The West Frankish Kingdom (840–987)* (Turnhout, 2012), 63–5.

26 *Pact of Philip of Swabia and Philip II of France*, c. 6.

27 For a discussion of the conflicts and events surrounding these treaties, see Johannes Bernwieser, *Honor civitatis. Kommunikation, Interaktion und Konfliktbeilegung im hochmittelalterlichen Oberitalien* (Munich, 2012), 68–127, 150–240. For summaries in English, see Charles D. Stanton, *Medieval Maritime Warfare* (Barnsley, 2015), 123–4; Marco Tangheroni, 'Sardinia and Corsica from the Mid-Twelfth to the Early Fourteenth Century', in *The New Cambridge Medieval History, volume V, c. 1198–c.1300*, ed. D. Abulafia (Cambridge, 1999), 448–9; Henrike Haug, 'The Struggle for Sardinia in the Twelfth Century: Textual and Architectural Evidence from Genoa and Pisa', in *A Companion to Sardinian History 500–1500*, ed. M. Hobart (Leiden, 2017), 215–18.

28 'Capitulary of Frankfurt, 794' in *MGH Capit.* I, no. 28, c. 3 (p. 74). In this context it is also worth noting that Tassilo appealed for the pope's intervention in his conflict with Charlemagne (*ARF*, s.a. 787), as if he

was an independent prince, and the second clause of the *Division of the Realms* (806) awarded Bavaria to Charlemagne's son Pippin 'just as Tassilo held it.' On Tassilo's relationship with Charlemagne, see the excellent discussion in Stuart Airlie, 'Narratives of Triumph and Rituals of Submission: Charlemagne's Mastering of Bavaria', *TRHS*, 9 (1999), 93–120, esp. 97–106. See also Peter Classen, 'Bayern und die politischen Mächte im Zeitalter Karls des Grossen und Tassilos III', in *Ausgewählte Aufsätze*, ed. J. Fleckenstein (Sigmaringen, 1983), 231–48, esp. 245–6; Philippe Depreux, 'Tassilon III et le roi des Francs: examen d'une vassalité controversée', *Revue Historique*, 293 (1995), 23–73.

29 On terminology and context, see Benham, *PMA*, 7–11, esp. 8, 190–5. On the customary principle of recognition through meetings, see ibid., 21–62, esp. 21–3, 44; Ingrid Voss, *Herrschertreffen im frühen und hohen Mittelalter* (Cologne, 1987), 49; Esther Pascua, 'Peace among Equals: War and Treaties in Twelfth-century Europe', in *War and Peace in Ancient and Medieval History*, eds. Philip de Souza and John France (Cambridge, 2008), 193–4; Pascua, 'South of the Pyrenees', 113.

30 On treaties as agreements between 'equals', see also Reinhard Schneider, *Brüdergemeine und Schwurfreundschaft der Auflösungsprozess des Karlingerreiches im Spiegel der Caritas-Terminologie in den Verträgen der karlingischen Teilkönige des 9. Jahrhunderts* (Lübeck, 1964); Gerd Althoff, *Verwandte, Freunde und Getreue. Zum politischen Stellenwert der Gruppenbindungen im frühen Mittelalter* (Darmstadt, 1990); Rodolphe Dreillard, ' "A jure foederis recedente": respect et irrespect des traités dans le monde franc au VIII siècle', in *L'autorité du passé dans les sociétés médiévales*, ed. Jean-Maries Sansterre (Rome, 2004), 57–77.

31 Dixon, *Textbook on IL*, 115–17. On medieval rulers grappling with immunity from courts of other rulers, see *Treaty of Orvieto*, cc. 3–4; *Radulphi de Coggeshall Chronicon Anglicanum*, ed. Joseph Stevenson, Rolls Series, 66 (London, 1875), 135–6. For discussion, see Benham, *PMA*, 21–37.

32 On legal redress in medieval treaties, see Chapter 3, pp. 92–126.

33 Dixon, *Textbook on IL*, 57.

34 *Treaty of Canterbury* (1189). For but a few examples of treaties granting trade privileges, see *LIRG*, vol. 1/2, nos. 353, 359; *Treaty of Constantinople* (991).

35 For three examples, see *Treaty of Antioch* (1098, 1101, 1169).

36 K.-H. Ziegler, 'The Influence of Medieval Roman Law on Peace Treaties', in *Peace Treaties and International Law*, ed. R. Lesaffer (Cambridge, 2000), 148.

37 K.-H. Ziegler, 'Conclusion and Publication of International Treaties in Antiquity', *Israel Law Review*, 29 (1995), 233–49.

38 Cf. the similarity of such statements in Cicero's *De Officiis* (3.31), the writings of Augustine and the Qur'an. Hans Wehberg, '*Pacta Sunt Servanda*', *AJIL*, 53 (1959), 775–6.

39 For examples of cross-religious/cultural oaths in treaties, see *Treaty between Sancho IV of Navarre and al-Muktadir of Zaragoza* (1073), c. 11 ('per omnes iuras quas omnes gentes in Deo iurant'); *Treaty of Mallorca* (1181); *Treaty of Constantinople* (911); *Treaty between Mu-Tsung of China and Tritsuk Detsen of Tibet* (821–2). This is also reflected in narrative sources across the whole medieval period, e.g., *The Fourth Book of the Chronicle of Fredegar with its Continuations*, tr. J. M. Wallace-Hadrill (London, 1960), 63; *Heinrici Chronicon Lyvonie*, ed. W. Arndt, in *MGH SS*, 23 (Hanover, 1874; repr. Stuttgart, 1986), 281.

40 Examples of treaties preserved as oaths include the *Oaths of Strasbourg* (842), *Treaty of Melfi* (1059) and *Treaty between Coloman of Hungary and Venice* (1098x1101). Those containing oaths within the treaty itself include the *Treaty of Bonn* (921), or as an additional but separate record to it, e.g., *Treaty of Portovenere* (1149), *Treaty of Messina* (1190).

41 On this principle more generally, see J. H. Gebhardt, '*Pacta Sunt Servanda*', *Modern Law Review*, 10 (1947), 159–70; Wehberg, '*Pacta Sunt Servanda*', 775–86, esp. 782–6; Md Anowar Zahid and Rohimi Shapiee, '*Pacta Sunt Servanda*: Islamic Perception', *Journal of East Asia and International Law*, 3 (2010), 375–86; Panaite, *Ottoman Law of War and Peace*, 205–29. For challenges to this principle, see D. Davison-Vecchione, 'Beyond the Forms of Faith: *Pacta Sunt Servanda* and Loyalty', *German Law Journal*, 16 (2015), 1163–90; Christina Binder, 'Stability and Change in Times of Fragmentation: The Limits of *Pacta Sunt Servanda* Revisited', *Leiden Journal of International Law*, 25 (2012), 909–34.

42 Antonio Padoa-Schioppa also makes this point, for which see his 'Profili del diritto internazionale', 41–2.

43 Discussions of the problems and possibilities with the survival of treaties can be found in Paul J. E. Kershaw, *Peaceful Kings. Peace, Power and the Early Medieval Political Imagination* (Oxford, 2011), 26–8; Benham, *PMA*, 10–11, 181–5; Mohamed Ouerfelli, 'Diplomatic Exchanges between the City of Pisa and the States of the Maghrib (from the 12th to the 14th Century)', *Mediterranean World*, 22 (2015), 98–101. On oral and oral-written treaties, see Steiger, *Die Ordnung der Welt*, 379–406; Christopher Holdsworth, 'Peacemaking

in the Twelfth Century', *ANS*, 19 (1998), 3. Written treaties based on prior negotiated oral promises or agreements often acknowledge this with the word 'prolocutione' or variations thereof. For examples see *II Æthelred* (994; Latin version), *Treaty of Acre* (1124), Treaty of Gerberoy (1182).

44 A treaty was concluded with Venice in 713 and another with Comacchio in 715, a town whose rights were later intermingled and subsumed by those of Venice. For these agreements, see L. M. Hartmann, *Zur Wirtschaftsgeschichte Italiens im frühen Mittelalter* (Gotha, 1904); Massimo Montanari, 'Il capitolare di Liutprando: note di storia dell'economia e dell'alimentazione', in *La Civiltà Comacchiese e Pomposiana dalle origini preistoriche al tardo medioevo* (Bologna, 1986), 461–5.

45 A good summary of the documents until the eleventh century can be found in West, 'Communities and *Pacta*', 367–70. On the Treaty of Verona, see A. Fanta, 'Die Verträge der Kaiser mit Venedig bis zum Jahre 983', *Mitteilungen des Instituts für Österreichische Geschichtsforschung, Ergänzungsband*, 1 (1885), 51–128; G. Rösch, *Venezia e l'Impero, 962–1250. I rapporti politici, commerciali e di traffico nel periodo imperiale germanico* (Rome, 1985). For the treaties of the high Middle Ages, see G. Rösch, *Venedig und das Reich. Handels- und verkehrspolitische Beziehungen in der deutschen Kaiserzeit* (Tübingen, 1982). See also List of Treaties, pp. 257–77.

46 On the treaties of Dover, see F. L. Ganshof, 'Note sur le premier traité anglo-flamand de Douvres', *Revue du Nord*, 40 (1958), 245–57. Similar series of treaties include also those between the kings of Sicily/dukes of Apulia/Capua and the papacy, and those between the Frankish and Ottonian rulers and the papacy. There is a large literature on the latter series, for examples, see T. H. Sickel, *Das Privilegium Otto I. für die römische Kirche vom Jahre 962* (Innsbruck, 1883); Walter Ullmann, 'The Origins of the *Ottonianum*', *The Cambridge Historical Journal*, 11 (1953), 114–28; Adalheid Hahn, 'Das *Hludowicianum*. Die Urkunde Ludwig den Fromme für die römische Kirche von 817', *Archiv für Diplomatik*, 21 (1975), 15–135; O. Bertolini, 'Osservazioni sulla Constitutio Romana e sull Sacramentum Cleri et Populi Romani dell'anno 824', in his *Scritti scelti di storia medioevale*, 2 vols., ed. O. Banti (Livorno, 1968), II, 705–38.

47 On the *Treaty of Anagni* and the negotiations surrounding it, see Johannes Laudage, *Alexander III. und Friedrich Barbarossa* (Cologne, 1997), 202–14; Knut Görich, *Die Ehre Friedrich Barbarossas: Kommunikation, Konflikt und politisches Handeln im 12. Jahrhundert* (Darmstadt, 2001), 162–6; Helmut Plechl, 'Studien

zur Tegernseer Briefsammlung des 12. Jahrhunderts II: Briefe zur Reichspolitik aus der Zeit der Verhandlungen in Anagni und der Vorbereitungen des Venetianer Friedenskongresses (Oktober 1176– Januar 1177)', *DA*, 12 (1956), 73–113.

48 On this phenomenon, see Patrick J. Geary, 'Oathtaking and Conflict Management in the Ninth Century', in *Rechtsverständnis und Handlungsstrategien im mittelalterlichen Konfliktaustrag: Festschrift für Hanna Vollrath*, eds. Stefan Esders and Christine Reinle (Munich, 2007), 247–8; Rosamond McKitterick, 'Latin and Romance: An Historian's Perspective', in *The Frankish Kings and Culture in the Early Middle Ages*, ed. Rosamond McKitterick (Aldershot, 1995), 130–45.

49 A description of the content of this collection is available at http:// capitularia.uni-koeln.de/en/mss/paris-bn-lat-9654/ (accessed 16 July 2021). A detailed discussion of the various versions of this treaty can be found in Geary, 'Oathtaking and Conflict Management', 243–9.

50 All parts of the treaty in MS Vat. Lat. 4982 are available at https://digi. vatlib.it/view/MSS_Vat.lat.4982 (accessed 16 July 2021), 122r–125r. A full study of the manuscripts and provenance of the treaties I have used is sorely needed but is outside the scope of this current study.

51 *AF*, 54–5. For a brief overview of the manuscripts, see *The Annals of Fulda*, 2–4.

52 E.g., *Treaty of Genoa I* (1146); *Treaty of Palermo* (1156); *Treaty of Genoa* (1190); *Treaty of Naples* (1191).

53 Wilhelm G. Grewe, 'Peace Treaties', in *Encyclopedia of Public International Law: Use of Force. War and Neutrality. Peace Treaties, vol. 4*, ed. Rudolf Bernhardt (Amsterdam, 1982), 106.

54 Moeglin, *Diplomatie*, 498–519.

55 Kershaw made a similar observation based on those treaties surviving mainly from ninth-century Frankia. Kershaw, *Peaceful Kings*, 27.

56 For two eleventh-century exceptions from the Iberian peninsula, see J. M. Lacarra, 'Dos Tratados de paz y alianza entre Sancho el de Peñalén y Moctádir de Zaragoza (1069 y 1073)', in *Homenaje a Johannes Vincke*, 2 vols. (Madrid, 1962–3), i, 121–34.

57 On the 1113 *Treaty of Sant Feliu de Guíxols*, see *Liber maiolichinus de gestis pisanorum illustribus*, ed. C. Calisse (Rome, 1904), appendix 1, 137–40. For a discussion of the historical context, see Giuseppe Scalia, 'Contributi pisani alla lotta anti-islamica nel Mediterraneo centro-occidentale durante il secolo XI e nei prime deceni del XII', *Anuario de estudios medievales*, 10 (1980), 135–44. On the 1111 treaty, see *Documenti sulle relazioni delle citta Toscane coll'oriente Cristiano e coi Turchi*, ed. Giuseppe Müller (Florence, 1879), 40–58. On the

context, see the PhD thesis by Daphne Penna, 'The Byzantine imperial acts to Venice, Pisa and Genoa, 10th–12th centuries: A Comparative Legal Study', unpublished PhD thesis (Groningen, 2012), 13, 101–18. The treaty of 1082x1092 by which the Byzantine emperor awarded trade privileges to the Venetians similarly survives in two Latin translations of the original Greek folded inside later treaties. Madden, 'The Chrysobull of Alexius I Comnenus to the Venetians', 38.

58   Benham, *PMA*, 181–2.

59   For a discussion of the effects of one chronicler's shaping of a treaty text, see Jenny Benham, 'Writing Peace, Writing War: Roger of Howden and Saxo Grammaticus Compared', in *History and Intellectual Culture in the Long Twelfth Century: The Scandinavian Connection*, eds. Sigbjørn Sønnesyn, Mia Münster-Swendsen, and Thomas Heebøll-Holm (Durham, 2016), 278–83. James H. Merrell has highlighted similar problems with reference to treaties between colonial settlers and native Americans in the Early Modern period, for which see his ' "I Desire All That I Have Said ... May Be Taken down Aright": Revisiting Teedyuscung's 1756 Treaty Council Speeches', *The William and Mary Quarterly*, 63 (2006), 777–826.

60   Benham, *PMA*, 188–95. See also Moeglin, *Diplomatie*, 496; Pascua, 'Peace among Equals', 194–5; Schneider, *Brüdergemeine und Schwurfreundschaft*.

61   For an opposing opinion, see M. Wielers, 'Zwischenstaatliche Beziehungsformen im frühen Mittelalter (*Pax, Foedus, Amicitias, Fraternitas*)', unpublished PhD thesis (Münster, 1959).

62   Dixon, *Textbook on IL*, 57. One modern example of a treaty that contains several different texts, supplements, and clarifying notes is the Molotov-Ribbentrop Non-Aggression Pact, 1939, for which see *Nazi-Soviet Relations: Documents from the German Foreign Office*, eds. Raymond James Sontag and James Stuart Beddie (Washington, DC, 1948), 76–8; 'Secret Supplementary Protocols of the Molotov-Ribbentrop Non-Aggression Pact, 1939', *History and Public Policy Program Digital Archive. Nazi-Soviet Relations, 1939–1941: Documents from the Archives of the German Foreign Office* available at https://digitalarchive.wilsoncenter.org/document/110994 (accessed 16 July 2021).

63   Bell made this observation about the peace agreements she was examining, and although she concluded that her agreements were not treaties, because they dealt with conflicts that were 'neither clearly interstate nor clearly internal' and often had non-state signatories – therefore not fitting the criteria of the Vienna Convention on the Law of Treaties 1969 – the description neatly captures what all medieval

treaties have in common. Christine Bell, 'Peace Agreements: Their Nature and Legal Status', *AJIL*, 100 (2006), 378.

64 Moeglin and Péquignot have made a similar point, for which see Moeglin, *Diplomatie*, 497.

65 See Chapter 4, pp. 145–80. In modern international law, these obligations are also important in establishing the nature of the law of state responsibility, for which see Dixon, *Textbook on IL*, 252–85; Philip Allot, 'State Responsibility and the Unmaking of International Law', *Harvard International Law Journal*, 29 (1988), 1–26; Robert Rosenstock, 'The ILC and State Responsibility', *AJIL*, 96 (2002), 792–97.

66 Some scholars also use the terms 'contracts' and 'covenants'. For some examples of this debate over types of treaties, see Kenneth W. Abbott and Duncan Snidal, 'Hard and Soft Law in International Governance', *International Organization*, 54 (2000), 424–5.

67 This is primarily under the customary *pacta sunt servanda* rule, as discussed above. On the scope of legal obligation, see also Dixon, *Textbook on IL*, 68–80.

68 *Oaths of Strasbourg* in *Nithard Histoire*, 104: '...si saluarai eo cist meon fradre Karlo, et in aiudha et in cadhuna cosa si cum om per dreit son fradra saluar dift...' Note that Louis swore in Romance, the language of his brother's supporters. Charles, likewise, swore in Old High German, the language of Louis' supporters. On these oaths, see Jonathan Beck, ' "Pro... salvament" in the Strasbourg Oaths: "Safety" or "Salvation"?', *Romance Philology*, 30 (1976), 144–51; McKitterick, 'Latin and Romance', 130–45. On vernacular oaths generally, see Patrick J. Geary, 'Land, Language and Memory in Europe, 700–1100', *TRHS*, 9 (1999), 169–84.

69 *Nithard Histoire*, 106: '...so haldih thesan minan bruodher, soso man mit rehtu sinan bruher scal...'

70 *Treaty of Bonn*, c. 2: '...amodo ero huic amico meo regi orientali Heinrico amicus, sicut amicus per rectum debet esse suo amico... ea vero ratione, si ipse mihi iuraverit ipsum eundemque sacramentum...' Such 'friendship' phrasing also occurs in the 898 promise of Berengar I, king of Italy, to Angiltrude, the widow of his rival Guy III (Wido) of Spoleto, and in the treaty of 1073 between Sancho IV and al-Muktadir. For these, see *MGH Capit.* II, no. 231; *Treaty between Sancho IV of Navarre and al-Muktadir of Zaragoza* (1073), c. 2. A later treaty between the Emperor Frederick I and the north Italian city of Lucca uses similar phrasing, replacing 'friend' for 'emperor', but without stipulating exactly what this meant. *Treaty of Burgo San Genesio* in *DD FI*, ii, 239.

71 Dixon, *Textbook on IL*, 52.
72 Ibid., 52. See also Abbott and Snidal, 'Hard and Soft Law', 421–56, esp. 422–3.
73 Nithard, *Histoire*, 104–6 (162).
74 *Treaty of Najac-de-Rouergue*, c. 2. Other treaties with a similar clause include *Treaty of Devol* (1108), c. 9; *Treaty of the Basilica of Cosmas and Damian* (1120); *Treaty of Andeli* (1197), c. 1; *Treaty of Constance* (1153), c. 1. For a modern example encompassing these same obligations, see Molotov-Ribbentrop Non-Aggression Pact, 1939, Art. 1–4.
75 That treaties of friendship and their obligations have much in common with the fealty Fulbert of Chartres, in the eleventh century, anticipated a man should swear to his lord is evident and well known. For his famous letter to Duke William V of Aquitaine setting out the obligations between man and lord, see *The Letters and Poems of Fulbert of Chartres*, ed. F. Behrends (Oxford, 1976), no. 51, 90–3. For discussion of some of the historiography, see Stephen D. White, 'A Crisis of Fidelity in c.1000', in *Building Legitimacy: Political Discourses and Forms of Legitimacy in Medieval Societies*, eds. I. Alfonso, H. Kennedy, and J. Escalona (Leiden, 2004), 27–49, esp. 36–9). More generally, see K. Pennington, 'The Formation of the Jurisprudence of the Feudal Oath of Fealty', *Rivista internazionale di diritto comune*, xv (2004), 57–76; K. Pennington, 'Feudal Oath of Fidelity and Homage', in *Law as Profession and Practice in Medieval Europe: Essays in Honor of James A. Brundage*, eds. K. Pennington and M. Harris Eichbauer (Farnham, 2011), 93–115; cf. M. Ryan, 'The Oath of Fealty and the Lawyers', in *Political Thought and the Realities of Power in the Middle Ages*, eds. J. P. Canning and O. G. Oexle (Göttingen, 1998), 211–28.
76 *Treaty between Genoa and Raymond of Toulouse, Sancho of Provence, William of Forcalquier*, c. 4.
77 Examples of treaties specifying the enemy, as well as where and when aid against this enemy might be given include *Treaty of Dover* (1101), cc. 1, 5, 9, 11, 14; *Treaty of Devol*; *Treaty of Constance*, cc. 1, 3–4; *Treaty of Messina* (1190) in Howden, *Gesta*, ii, 134; *Pact between Philip of Swabia and Philip II of France*, cc. 1, 4. More rarely, different parties specifically set out that there were no competing obligations in agreements concluded with a third party. For instance, the *Treaty of Sardinia* (c. 8) decreed that the terms sworn by Peter, the *iudex* of Cagliari, to Barisone II, the *iudex* of Arborea, had been agreed without prejudice to agreements he had made with the Genoese and

that those obligations would not be diminished by the observance of this new treaty

78 Abulafia made a similar point about the *Treaty of Messina* (1177), in which the Savonese obligations to Roger II of Sicily would be performed 'salva amicitiam januensium', that is, saving always their relationship with Genoa. Abulafia, *Two Italies*, 66–7. On the Anglo-Flemish alliance and its context, see Eljas Oksanen, *Flanders and the Anglo-Norman World, 1066–1216* (Cambridge, 2012), 54–81; Ganshof, 'Note sur le premier traité', 245–57; Renée Nip, 'The Political Relations between England and Flanders (1066–1128)', *ANS*, 21 (1998), 145–68.

79 *Treaty of Andeli*, cc. 1–2.

80 *Treaty of Andeli*, c. 3: 'Et sciendum est quod hoc fedus et hec conventio non solummodo duratura tempore guerre, set imperpetuum...' On obligations in time, see below pp. 37–9.

81 *Nithard Histoire*, 104: 'a subditione mea necnon et a juramento quod mihi jurastis unumquemque vestrum absolvo'.

82 *Treaty of Andeli*, c. 3.

83 This tallies with Abbott and Snidal's observation that 'softer legalization is often easier to achieve than hard legalization. This is especially true when the actors are states that are jealous of their autonomy and when the issues at hand challenge state sovereignty.' Abbott and Snidal, 'Hard and Soft Law', 423.

84 *Treaty of Dover* (1101), c. 17. The count's lawful excuses are listed under clause 13. On the role and function of sureties in treaties, see Adam J. Kosto, *Hostages in the Middle Ages* (Oxford, 2012), 130–56, esp. 148–56; Benham, *PMA*, 165–71; Benham, 'Peace, Security and Deterrence', 127–9.

85 *Dip. Docs*, i, 7. On arbitration more generally, see Chapter 5, pp. 196–221.

86 Grygiel, 'The Primacy of Premodern History', 15.

87 Harold Hongju Koh, 'Why Do Nations Obey International Law?', *Yale Law Journal*, 106 (1997), 2603.

88 Abbott and Snidal, 'Hard and Soft Law', 423. See also Bell, 'Peace Agreements', 384.

89 Dixon, *Textbook on IL*, 31. On *force majeure*, see Chapter 4, pp. 171–9.

90 *DD FI*, iv, 248–51. For the historical context, see Peter Wanner, 'Der staufisch-kastilische Ehepakt des Jahres 1188. Erkenntnisse aus Anlass einiger "Kleiner" Stadtteilsund Gemeindejubiläen 2013', *Quellen und Forschungen zur Geschichte der Stadt Heilbronn*, 22 (2016), 453–60.

91 Wanner, 'Der staufisch-kastilische Ehepakt', 457. On the context, see also Miriam Shadis, *Berenguela of Castile (1180–1246) and Political Women in the High Middle Ages* (New York, 2009), 52–7; Evelyn S. Procter, *Curia and Cortes in Leon and Castile 1072–1295* (Cambridge, 1980), 74–6.

92 Howden, *Gesta*, I, 36–41. On the format of this treaty, see Chaplais, *EDP*, 52. Whether or not the treaty would have gone ahead even if she had not died is uncertain, as the conclusion of it sparked the great rebellion of 1173–4. For the historical context, see Stephen Church, *King John, England and the Making of a Tyrant* (London, 2015), 7–8; John Gillingham, *Richard I* (New Haven, 1999), 41–3.

93 *LIRG*, vol. 1/6, 12–13; Hall, *Caffaro*, 219. Note that the French paid 2,000 marks at the conclusion of the treaty in February 1190, with the remaining 3,850 marks due in June of the same year.

94 *LIRG*, vol. 1/2, no. 353 (pp. 189–92); Hall, *Caffaro*, 221–2.

95 Dixon, *Textbook on IL*, 31; Abbott and Snidal, 'Hard and Soft Law', 424.

96 *AGu*, cc. 2–5. These clauses can be compared to those dealing with similar matters in West Saxon domestic laws, e.g., *Af*, cc. 2, 4 (on harbouring fugitives or outlaws), 26–8 (on killing), 4.1–4.2, 33 (on clearing oneself from an accusation), 34 (on trading), 37 (on seeking the service of another); *Ine*, cc. 14–15, 19 (on clearing oneself from an accusation), 23, 34 (on killing), 25 (on trading), 39 (on seeking the service of another).

97 The *Peace of Constance*, 1183, is another example of this. For good discussions of both the historical and legal contexts, see Gianluca Raccagni, *The Lombard League, 1167–1225* (Oxford, 2010), 1–146; Gianluca Raccagni, 'When the Emperor Submitted to his Rebellious Subjects: A Neglected and Innovative Legal Account of the Peace of Constance, 1183', *EHR*, 131 (2016), 520–39.

98 *Treaty of Benevento* (1156), cc. 4–8. This reflects papal aims as set out in *Dictatus Papae*, cc. 3–4, 20–21. Cf. the *Pact of Louis the Pious* (817), cc. 8–9, and the *Treaty of Rome* (824), c. 3, which outlined the election process of the pope. On the latter treaty and papal elections, see West, 'Communities and *Pacta*', 379–83.

99 *Treaty of Benevento* (1156), c. 9. On this grant, see Geoffrey Malaterra, *De rebus gestis Rogeri Calabriae et Siciliae comitis et Roberti Gusicardi ducis fratris eius*, ed. Ernesto Pontieri, RIS, 2nd edn., V, pt. I (Bologna, 1925–8), Bk, IV, c. 29.

100 The exception granted here bears similarities to that outlined by Pope Calixtus II to the Emperor Henry V in the *Concordat of Worms* (1122), Callixtus' promise, c. 1. On elections to ecclesiastical office

being free of lay investiture and of simony, see *Bibliotheca rerum germanicarum, tomus secundus: Monumenta gregoriana*, ed. P. Jaffé (Berlin, 1865), 332; 'The Canons of the First Lateran Council, 1123', in *Decrees of the Ecumenical Councils, vol. 1*, ed. Norman P. Tanner (Washington, DC, 1990), c. 1; 'The Canons of the Second Lateran Council, 1139', in ibid., cc. 2, 16.

101 *Treaty of Benevento* (1156), c. 15; *AGu*, prol. For a discussion of rulers concluding treaties in perpetuity, see also Moeglin, *Diplomatie*, 538–40.

102 *Dunsæte*, cc. 3.2–3.3.

103 *Treaty of Grosseto*, cc. 4–5.

104 *DD FI*, iii, 136–8. On this treaty, see W. Heinemeyer, 'Der Friede von Montebello (1175)', *DA*, 11 (1954), 101–39.

105 *Treaty of Jarnègues*, c. 5: 'Quod si forte inter eos de supradictis conventionibus et pactis questio vel discordia aliqua oriatur, arbitrio Berengarii archiepiscopi Tarraconensis, qui constitutus arbiter pro parte domini regis est, et arbitrio Bernardi Narbonensis archiepiscopi, qui constitutus arbiter pro parte domini comitis est, in partibus illis que ultra flumen Erarium sunt, terminetur.' Cf. *Treaty of Constantinople* (992), c. 2, which stipulated that disputes would be settled by the logothete, a Byzantine official, rather than any other judges.

106 Howden, *Gesta*, ii, 135: '...si forte... ex parte nostra pacis integritas frangeretur, potestatem habeat ecclesia Romana nos et terram nostram districtius coercere. Similiter, et ad matrimonium contrahendum, potestatem habeat nos et partem nepotis nostri constringere; vel si propter causas praedictas non fieret matrimonium, ad restituendam pecuniam nos et heredes nostros, aut terram nostram cogere habeat potestatem.'

107 Howden, *Gesta*, ii, 137. Cf. *Treaty of Acre* (1124), c. 11, which shows reliance on papal instructions for interpretation of the obligations and rights.

108 Cf. Abbott and Snidal's observation that 'hard legal commitments... are interpreted and applied by arbitral or judicial institutions'. Abbott and Snidal, 'Hard and Soft Law', 427. See also Bell, 'Peace Agreements', 403–4.

109 Nithard, *Histoire*, 116–43 (165–73); *AB*, 29 (54); *AF*, 33 (21). For a summary of the context, content, and legacy of Verdun, see Jenny Benham, 'The Treaty of Verdun, 843', in *Encyclopedia of Diplomacy*, ed. Gordon Martel (London, 2018).

110 *Treaty of Meerssen* (870); *The Annals of St-Bertin*, 168–9.

111 F. L. Ganshof, 'The Genesis and Significance of the Treaty of Verdun (843)', in *The Carolingians and the Frankish Monarchy*, tr. J. Sondheimer (London, 1971), 289–302.

112 Howden, *Gesta*, i, 140: '...de querelis videlicet quas inter se habebant, ut judicio regis Anglie sibi satisfacerent.' On this arbitration, see Chapter 5, pp. 197–8, 205–9.

113 Howden, *Gesta*, i, 140–3.

114 *LIRG*, vol. 1/6, 3–4.

115 Ibid., 4; Hall, *Caffaro*, 179.

116 *LIRG*, vol. 1/6, 8–9. The *Treaty of San Salvatore II* (1162), with the Emperor Frederick I, and the *Treaty of Genoa I* (1190), concluded with Philip II of France for the Third Crusade, also mirror these terms, for which see *LIRG*, vol. 1/6, 12–14; *DD FI*, ii, 222. English translations in Hall, *Caffaro*, 198, 219.

117 *Pactum Sicardi*, c. 3.

118 Ibid., cc. 7–9.

119 Ibid., c. 13.

120 E.g. the phrase 'manum ad prendendum' meaning 'to offer one's hands to be bound', i.e., to be arrested, is found also in *Rothair's Edict*, cc. 32–3, 253.

121 Dixon, *Textbook on IL*, 31. See also Abbott and Snidal, 'Hard and Soft Law', 424–6.

2

That which is practised on a daily basis: displacement of people

One of the most consistent threats to peace and security across the whole of the medieval period, or at least the one rulers and other political entities were most worried about in an international context, was displacement of people. It is a useful issue for thinking about how to achieve peace, security, and deterrence, primarily because the main conflict drivers of the medieval period – land, jurisdiction, and resources – converge and are reflected in displacement. It was also an issue that operated at several levels – local, regional, and international – and as such required several, overlapping, solutions that could be executed and implemented at each of the different levels. Some of these measures were intended to deter, while others dealt with the effects of the measures taken or were intended to restore peace and order. Others, yet again, became part of the problem for which they had been devised. Exploring this issue is consequently one of the best ways to see that international law was practised on a daily basis in the medieval period. Displacement of people could of course come in many forms but for the purposes of this chapter, the focus will be on just a single aspect; namely, the expulsion of those deemed to have committed some form of reprehensible act.

Expulsion – exile, banishment, outlawry, or whatever we want to call it – has been defined by William Walters as a practice 'used against the individual who is understood to be a member of the political community or nation. It is used as a form of punishment, but also security.'[1] Scholars are generally agreed that it was an ancient practice.[2] Yet, while scholars have readily acknowledged this ancient practice, historical analysis of it for the early medieval period has been curiously absent.[3] In the medieval period, the expulsion of individuals who had committed reprehensible acts was one of the ways in which rulers and communities dealt with law and order. As an alternative to punishment such as mutilation or death, expulsion from a political entity – whether we view this as a city, region, or kingdom – was reserved for the most serious offences; those which could not be atoned for with compensation and fines.[4] Across the medieval West, these 'unemendable crimes' tended to include arson; counterfeiting (coins or documents); thefts (recurring or above a certain amount), plundering, or robbery; indiscriminate homicide (e.g., poisoning), murder, or killing in certain spaces (e.g., at the assembly or the king's residence); flight from accusations of an 'unemendable crime'; and treacherous or disloyal behaviour (e.g., plotting against a king's life, fleeing the army, or bringing a foreign army into a political entity).[5] In the earlier period, there is not always an exact distinction between the different types of offences and by the time we get into the twelfth century, they are frequently lumped together under what one might think of as umbrella terms, such as dishonourable/serious/unemendable deeds or *lese/crimine maiestatis*.[6] The latter term shows that by the twelfth century, and with the revival of Roman law, some of these offences were falling under what would eventually develop into treason. An interesting statement in John of Salisbury's *Policraticus*, made in the midst of the twelfth-century renaissance with its revival of Roman law and based on Justinian's *Digest* of the sixth century, shows that the term was suitably vague:

> The acts are many which constitute the crime of lèse majesté ['crimen maiestas'], as for example if one conceives the death of the prince or magistrates, or has borne arms against his country, or, forsaking his prince, has deserted in a public war, or has incited or solicited the people to rebel against the commonwealth; or if by the act or criminal intent of any, the enemies of the people and commonwealth are aided with supplies, armor, weapons, money, or any thing else whatsoever, or if, from being friends, they are turned into enemies of the commonwealth; or if by the criminal intent or act of any, it comes to pass that pledges or money are given against the commonwealth, or the people of a foreign country are perverted from their obedience to the commonwealth; likewise he commits the crime who effects the escape of one who after confessing his guilt in court has on this account been thrown into chains; and many other acts of this nature, which it would be too long or impossible to enumerate.[7]

In the contemporary world, treason is often considered the archetyp-ical domestic crime, which should never fall under the jurisdiction of international criminal law.[8] In the later Middle Ages, however, through the development of the just war theory, treason – in par-ticular taking up arms against a ruler – was a breach of the faith that held Christian society together. Rebels hence 'placed them-selves beyond the pale of peaceful Christian society and were now no more than mere brigands and thieves'.[9] Ziv Bohrer has recently argued that this shows that 'treason was considered an international crime, and traitors/rebels were considered international outlaws'.[10] Furthermore, other serious crimes such as murder, theft, robbery, or arson could be condemned as crimes against humanity, and therefore considered international, if they did not have the sanction of just war or royal authorisation.[11]

In the earlier period, this theory on the just war was much less developed, yet we must not for this reason think that serious crime pertained to domestic law and justice only or, even, specifically to Christian communities.[12] Expulsion provides an opportunity for investigating this issue for the period before 1200 since, while expulsion was intended to ensure law and order on a domestic level, it could result in becoming a threat to peace and security on an 'international' level. Primarily this was because, once expelled, such individuals, shorn of their social and economic status, often committed further reprehensible acts and/or engaged in conflict against the entity from whence they had come. This phenomenon, similar to the modern crime-conflict nexus, is described well in the Norwegian didactic text known as *The King's Mirror*:

> the wicked take refuge in the service of some other master; and, though they have been driven from home because of their misdeeds, they pretend to have come in innocence to escape the cruel wrath of their lord... But those who had to flee because of their evil conduct and lawbreaking soon begin to show hostility toward the lord whose subjects they formerly were and to rouse as much enmity as they can between him and the one to whom they have come. They take revenge for their exile by carrying murder, rapine and plundering into the kingdom...[13]

The King's Mirror was composed in the middle of the thirteenth century but it is clear that the author commented on what was a common problem throughout the medieval period and it is hardly surprising to find that one of the foremost purposes of concluding treaties between rulers was to ensure that those who had been expelled from one political entity did not find shelter in another. There are numerous examples from treaties about participants of treaties not harbouring the enemies of the other, in fact, as outlined in an article in 2013, almost every treaty concluded in the period 700 to 1200 contains such a clause.[14] Frequently, such clauses are specific in stating that they apply to those who had committed crimes or who had fled. For instance, the *Treaty of Pavia*, concluded between Emperor Lothar I and the Venetians in 840, has a number of clauses dedicated to those that should not be harboured by the other party, which included fugitives, spies ('scamera'), as well as any other enemies ('hostis').[15] The so-called *Pactum Sicardi* of 836, concluded between the prince of Benevento, Sicard, and the cities of Naples, Sorrento, and Amalfi, additionally promised to return murderers, thieves, and not to shelter other known criminals, as did also the 849 *Partition of Benevento* between Radelchis and Sicard's successor, Sikenolf.[16] In the treaty of 911 between the Rus' and the Byzantine emperor, both sides agreed that any escaped criminal would be arrested and returned – 'regardless of his protests' – upon the other side making a complaint, and similar provisions were also in place for escaped slaves.[17] Some thirty years later, this treaty was renewed and the clause about criminals was replaced by one that implicitly required them to be returned.[18] In addition, a clause concerning slaves who had committed theft was added to the stipulations covering those who should not be sheltered but returned.[19] The treaty concluded in 994 between the English king, Æthelred, and the three Scandinavian leaders, Olaf, Guthmund, and Josteinn, stipulated that neither party would receive any escaped 'slave, or thief, or person concerned in a feud', and both the *Division of the Realms* (806) and the *Treaty of Meersen* (851) recorded that the royal brothers involved were not to receive or retain a man of the others who was seeking to evade justice for offences committed.[20] Though not explicitly stated, it seems reasonable to assume that both the 'person concerned in a feud' and the one trying to evade justice in these treaties indicated someone who had committed serious wrongs. In the *Treaty of Meersen* (851) this seems to be further corroborated by the next clause in the treaty, which advocates that no man excommunicated for 'any capital or public crime' by a bishop in one realm should be harboured in another realm.[21] The *Treaty of Fouron*, 878, simi-larly referred to those trying to evade justice who should not be received, commenting that they were rootless men who behaved like tyrants.[22] That the issue of not harbouring those convicted of an offence or who had fled from an accusation of wrongdoing was a shared concern across the domestic and international spheres is evident from a law of the early tenth century in which the West Saxon King, Edward the Elder, decreed that the compensation for harbouring a fugitive should be in accordance with the *domboc* – a reference to the laws of King Alfred – if the offence was committed in his own kingdom, and in accordance with 'written treaties' ('friðgewritu') if the offence was committed in the 'east' or in the 'north', that is, the areas not ruled by the West Saxon king.[23]

Narrative descriptions of treaties and negotiations further support the evidence from treaties. For instance, a letter of the early eighth century from the bishop of London to the archbishop of Canterbury, commenting on the negotiations between the East Saxon and the West Saxon kings, states that the parties had concluded a treaty aimed at driving out each other's exiles ('...in utrorumque partium conventibus pacem verbis firmabant fædusque ingerunt ut exules eliminarentur...').[24] In another example, the *Historia Regum* of Symeon of Durham records for the year 801 how Eardwulf, king of the Northumbrians, led an army against Coenwulf, king of the Mercians, because he had harboured his enemies.[25] Similarly, in c. 863 Archbishop Hincmar of Rheims wrote to Rorik (who, himself, had been expelled from the Danish kingdom and put in charge of parts of Frisia by successive Frankish kings to defend against raiders), urging him not to shelter Baldwin of Flanders. According to Hincmar, Baldwin had stolen the daughter of King Charles the Bald ('in uxorem furatus fuerat'), had fled, and been excommunicated as a result.[26] This particular incident is interesting in that it also highlights that excommunication and secular expul-sion often operated in tandem, as is also evident from the *Treaty of Meerssen* (851) and the later legislations of Frederick Barbarossa.[27]

As records become more frequent from the mid-twelfth century onwards, there is evidence of stipulations specifically relating to not harbouring those who had committed crimes from across the whole of medieval Europe. We find it, for instance, in the treaties of Falaise and Montlouis, both of which were concluded in the aftermath of the great rebellion of 1173–4 against the English king, Henry II.[28] Similarly, the *Treaty of Logroño* (1176), which was concluded between Sancho VI of Navarre and Alfonso VIII of Castile and which outlined their intention to submit one of their disputes to the arbitration of Henry II of England, granted secure passage to all men between the kingdoms 'except known murderers'.[29] Furthermore, Anna Komnena gives a text in *The Alexiad*, which purports to be the *Treaty of Devol* of 1108, concluded between the Byzantine Emperor Alexios Komnenos and Bohemond of Antioch, in which she detailed that Bohemond agreed not to receive any fugitives from the empire but would 'compel them to retrace their steps and return'. Other clauses of that treaty reveal that such fugitives included those who had plotted against the emperor.[30] The *Treaty of Montlouis* is particularly interesting because, in detailing pardons, it shows both that anyone who had committed murder, treason, or maiming of any limb would have to answer for his wrongs in accordance with the English king's laws, and that those who took flight for any cause before the rebellion broke out in 1173 and who subsequently joined the service of his rebellious sons against him, would be allowed to return in peace only if they resumed their trials at whatever stage they were at.[31] Similar notions can be discerned in the *Treaty of San Salvatore I*, whereby Frederick I received the submission of the citizens of Piacenza in 1162. According to the terms, if a citizen and his accomplices did not appear in court to answer for a murder, he would be placed under the ban and the citizens were expected to expel him from the city.[32] In both of these cases, we can clearly see those worries expressed by the author of *The King's Mirror* being acted upon in treaties with the expectancy that domestic institutions would carry out and dispense justice according to these stipulations.

While treaties that are specific about who should not be harboured nearly always refer to those who had committed wrongdoings of some sort, it is evident that many treaties were less specific in their stipulations. For instance, Æthelred's agreement with the Norman duke, Richard I, of 991 simply stated that neither side would harbour the enemy of the other.[33] A number of treaties, including the late ninth-century agreement between King Alfred and the viking king, Guthrum, and the pact between the imperial candidate, Philip of Swabia, and Philip II of France struck in 1198, further stipulate that men were not allowed to enter the territory of the other party nor join the other party's army contrary to their ruler's wishes, the latter of which could, of course, be viewed as the crime of betraying one's lord.[34] There is, furthermore, corresponding evidence of this in domestic laws. For instance, the laws of the English king Athelstan set out that 'no one shall receive a man who has been in the service of another, without the permission of him he has been serving, whether within our borders or beyond them'.[35] Athelstan's next law went even further and stipulated that this specifically applied to a man who had been dismissed for wrongdoing, linking very clearly to the criminal aspect found in many treaties.[36] In addition, there are also lots of phrases in treaties that practically must have referred to not harbouring each other's enemies even if it is not specified, for instance 'being a friend to the other's friend and an enemy to his enemies', found in the *Treaty of Bonn* of 921 and the *Treaty between Genoa and Fos* of 1138, or 'aiding and defending against all men', which we find in the *Oaths of Strasbourg* of 842, Robert Guiscard's oath to the pope of 1059 (otherwise known as the *Treaty of Melfi*), the Anglo-Flemish alliances of 1101, 1110, and 1163 (known as the treaties of Dover), the *Treaty of Sahagún* of 1158 between the kings of Castile and Leon, and the 1162 *Treaty of San Salvatore I*.[37]

It has been argued that some of the statements about not harbouring the other party's enemies are generic and likely covered any enemies. To some extent this is true and certainly practical, because distinguishing between those who were murderers, arsonists, robbers, exiles, hostages, fugitives, spies, captives, slaves, and a whole host of other terms found in treaties and narratives is not an exact science. In particular, scholars have pointed to the difficulty of distinguishing between 'criminal' exiles and 'political' exiles.[38] For instance, Elisabeth van Houts' article on exile in England and Normandy makes a distinction between domestic exile in England – outlawry – and international exile, which she seems to have deemed to always be political, even though she acknowledges that the legal process may have been very similar for both types.[39] Yet, it is not entirely clear that such a distinction is necessary, primarily because treachery, which encompasses a myriad of different acts, and fleeing or evading justice, of whatever nature, were regarded as the most serious crimes and 'political' exiles often fall into one of those two categories. Furthermore, there could be lots of reasons why a person's status might change in the course of a sojourn abroad. For instance, a number of writers recording Frederick Barbarossa's expedition to the Holy Land in 1189–90 refer to the Turkish prisoner turned guide, who was likely seen as a traitor by his compatriots for leading the crusaders, and at this latter point then, he may have been more of an exile than a captive.[40] This blurring of an individual's status is further borne out in treaties where three groups of people consistently appear within the context of displacement: criminals, slaves, and captives.[41] Nevertheless, we should not underestimate that enemies are frequently defined in treaties and, overwhelmingly, this evidence shows that when they are, they nearly always refer to those of a 'criminal' kind. A convenience maybe, but in terms of international law, an important point to make, because it shows the need to provide justification for action – one of the principles used to test whether or not there is a system of international law.[42] This can be seen even more clearly in some treaties from the twelfth century, which, rather than referring only to those who had been expelled for crimes or enemies more generally, name specific enemies. For instance, in 1186, King Alfonso VIII of Castile and King Alfonso II of Aragon concluded the *Treaty of Agreda*, which was specifically aimed at the Azagra family, who held the important border lordship of Albarracín. The text states that neither king was to 'receive Pedro Rodríguez, nor his brothers or relatives who live at his expense, nor his followers except Gonzalo Rodríguez who is the vassal of lord Alfonso'.[43] In another example, while the *Treaty of Dover* (1101) anticipated that the summons of military aid to the count of Flanders would be valid against all men or people, it also specified those whom the English king, Henry I, clearly thought were likely to do him harm: the French king Philip I and any English baron or magnate ('aliquis comes Anglie vel alii homines illius terre regi').[44] As argued in 2013, this stipulation was specific because Henry had recently faced rebellion from his brother Robert Curthose, duke of Normandy, and some prominent English noblemen, and the French king had in the past been keen to help such rebellious elements against his English rival.[45] It is furthermore clear that the majority of evidence relating to specifically named individuals comes from agreements involving the English king and his lands on the Continent, and also treaties concluded by the various Iberian kings. This likely reflects the circumstances of the overlapping lordships in these regions, which gave their subjects immediate sources of alternative lordship to whom they could apply for redress in any matter.[46] The treaties hence frequently reflect this aspect by naming individuals who should be included in, or excluded from, the terms of the treaty, or against whom certain terms were directed. It is important to point out that in these cases of individuals being named as enemies or potential enemies, those individuals are always portrayed as having committed a wrongful or evil act or as potentially committing one in the future.[47] This shows again that couching justification for action, of whatever nature, in a legal context was important.

Scholars have often argued that the clauses in treaties about not harbouring enemies were aimed at curbing the exploits of displaced groups of people, perhaps particularly the vikings. Much of this discussion has focused on the reign of Æthelred II 'the Unready', king of the English, and the *Treaty of Rouen* (991).[48] For instance, van Houts believed that in tenth-century Normandy, the use of expulsion was an intensification of the Frankish practice specifically targeted at troublesome Danish immigrants and cited the *Treaty of Rouen* (991) as evidence.[49] However, such arguments are not entirely convincing in context of the overwhelming evidence showing that 'enemies' most frequently referred to domestic, 'criminal' ones. In the period covered by this study, there are only two examples of specific groups of people named in treaties. The first is the *Partition of Benevento* of 849, which stipulated that all 'Saracens', except those who had converted to Christianity in the days of Sico and Sicard (i.e., c. 817–39), were to be expelled and that neither party was to seek them out for aid or alliance.[50] This particular clause was directed at limiting the large number of Muslim mercenaries present in southern Italy at the time, and which were being used by all sides in the conflict(s) to assert authority in the area. The second example is the *Treaty of Toul*, concluded between the French king, Louis VII, and the Emperor Frederick Barbarossa in 1171, in which the two kings promised to expel all 'wicked men, called Brabançons and Coterelli', between the Rhine, the Alps and the city of Paris and not to keep them for the purpose of war.[51] The most recent editor of this treaty, Heinrich Appelt, commented that these measures were likely part of efforts to limit violence, which were promoted by churchmen under the auspices of the Peace and Truce of God movements. Indeed, it is clear that the treaty stipulations mirrored church legislation such as the canons of the Third Lateran Council of 1179, which decreed that those who hired, kept, or supported 'Brabanters, Aragonese, Navarrese, Basques, Coterelli and Triaverdini' would be denounced publicly, denied mass and Christian burial, just as if they were heretics.[52]

The treaties of 849 and 1171 remind the historian that there is another aspect of displacement of people for which there is plentiful evidence in a context of international relations; namely, employing those expelled. We know for instance that some of the men that emerge raiding Europe in the eighth to the twelfth centuries had been expelled, even though the wider Scandinavian, Slav, and Muslim expansions cannot be explained through this factor alone.[53] Our primary sources from this period are replete with references to the chaos caused by these expansions, in the form of raiding of, but also settlements in, existing political entities, though we should be wary of wholly believing these ecclesiastical authors, who often described events as apocalyptic by applying Christian moral and providential frameworks to their narratives. One of the most common ways medieval rulers dealt with the threat of raids or invasions was to use military force. A large number of agreements from the medieval period details the employment of foreign raiders and their military men, who were provisioned or paid in return for defending the ruler, his people and territory 'against all enemies', including other raiders.[54] The majority of such agreements are known to us in brief mentions in chronicle evidence with only a single treaty giving us the semblance of a full text: *II Æthelred*, concluded between the English king, Æthelred II, and the leaders of an army ('here').[55] *II Æthelred* names the leaders of the army as 'Anlaf, Josteinn and Guthmund Steitason', the first of whom scholars have reasonably concluded to be Olaf Tryggvason, who later became king of Norway.[56] Olaf's own biography is interesting in terms of the issues discussed here, because having supposedly started out as a refugee – fleeing twice as a small child with his mother – Olaf ends up being captured and sold as a slave on his way to 'Gardariki', before taking revenge on the man who killed his foster-father and subsequently having to seek refuge in the household of King Vladimir. However, Olaf's descent and penchant for killing eventually worried Vladimir to the extent that he expelled the Norwegian from 'Gardariki', and hence begins Olaf's career as a 'viking' proper, harrying and raiding in many regions in north-western Europe, including, of course, England.[57] Now, we shouldn't wholly believe the thirteenth-century saga's version of Olaf's rise to fame, but it is certainly clear that Olaf's shifting status and his subsequent employment as a mercenary bear all the hallmarks of similar exile literature from the period and puts a context to the surviving treaty.[58]

While the agreement of 994 is seemingly the only treaty where at least one contracting party had a clear connection to expulsion, there are other treaties where one party was displaced but perhaps not expelled. For instance, the *Treaty of Melfi*, of 1059, by which the Norman Robert Guiscard promised to be the ally of Pope Nicholas II and the holy Roman Church against all men.[59] Unlike Olaf, Robert's arrival in Italy does not seem to have been the result of expulsion. William of Apulia, writing his poem about the Norman leader in the last years of the eleventh century, recorded merely that he had followed his brothers.[60] A few years later, Geoffrey Malaterra expanded on this by recalling that Robert and his brothers, having realised that there was not enough land in Normandy for all of them, decided to seek their fortune through arms in southern Italy.[61] Elsewhere in the text, Geoffrey explains that at least one brother ended up in exile in Brittany after fleeing from charges of having sought revenge and killed a man who had wronged him, but there is no notion that such a legal context surrounded Robert.[62] Certainly, it would appear that those writing about the Normans in this period had an expectancy of them being adventurers and seeking wealth outside the duchy, and Dudo, in describing their Scandinavian origins, implies that this followed a long tradition: 'For they are exiled by fathers, boldly to batter kings. They are sent away without wealth from their own people, that they may enrich themselves out of the plenty of foreigners... They are expelled as exiles, that they may be rewarded as warriors.'[63] The similarity to the description in the *King's Mirror*, referred to at the beginning of this chapter, is obvious, although missing – perhaps deliberately – the clear link to serious offences found in that narrative. In both cases, however, there is that essential ingredient of displacement; namely, that it was forced.[64] Whether or not Robert Guiscard's relocation to Italy was forced, for economic or other reasons, is perhaps debatable. What is evident is that by the time Robert contracted the agreement with the pope, he had a new territorial connection, and the payment for his military services seems to have been the recognition and his investiture as Duke of Apulia and Calabria, as well as Sicily if he managed to secure it.[65] It would thus seem that with the *Treaty of Melfi*, unlike the treaty of 994, the requirement to defend and supply fighting men against all enemies formed part of a more formal military alliance between two contracting parties who were trying to consolidate territory they already held or expand on that territory. This is a feature also with the *Treaty of Dover* (1101), and subsequent renewals throughout the twelfth century. These treaties, each concluded between a count of Flanders and an English king, effectively employed fighting men against enemies of the English king but with the main intention to serve in Normandy. In the case of the treaty of 1101 at least, this was away from the heartland of both contracting parties.[66] Furthermore, by contrast to *II Æthelred* and the *Treaty of Melfi*, which anticipated that the leaders and their armies would repel and look out for enemies on a continuous basis, the treaties of Dover would only come into force if the English king specifically requested it. As Eljas Oksanen has argued, there is no clear evidence that the military obligations in the treaties of Dover were ever 'activated exactly in the manner outlined in the clauses'.[67] Indeed, as noted in 2011, when the count of Flanders did engage in conflict together with the English king in 1197–9, the two parties concluded an agreement that said nothing about the supply of fighting men but merely stated that neither Richard I nor Baldwin IX would make any peace or truce without the other's consent.[68] The twelfth century saw a large number of agreements that are similar to the treaties of Melfi and Dover. For instance, the treaty between the Genoese and Alfonso VII of Castile in 1146 effectively hired out the Genoese fleet for an expedition to Almeria, which could be viewed in a context of the preparations for the Second Crusade.[69]

From the evidence it would appear then, that while treaties for mercenaries became more widely used the further into the medieval period we proceed, they also lost some of their connection to displacement and in particular to expulsion. Despite this, the

careers of men such as the mercenary captain Mercadier show that
agreements made with individual leaders (who had been expelled
or displaced in some way or another) and their followers continued
into the twelfth century, but the texts of most of these have not
been preserved.[70] Even though it might be possible to argue that
the greater availability of mercenary treaties between rulers in the
twelfth century perhaps reflects a diversification in the nature of
these types of agreements, rather than a decrease in importance of
the link to expulsion and displacement more generally, it is evident
that most of the twelfth-century treaties we have were concluded
between rulers who had some form of permanent territorial base
and who had not themselves been expelled for wrongdoing. This
clearly differs from the treaties of the ninth and tenth century. One
of the most interesting things about this development is that it raises
questions about the ability of leaders, such as Olaf, Josteinn, and
Guthmund, to contract treaties, such as *II Æthelred*, as instruments
of international law. As is well known, 'legal personality' is a pre-
requisite for entering into any international agreement. However,
even in modern times the nature of personality is relative, and the
subjects of international law are, likewise, many and varied. There
is no reason to believe that this would have been different in the
earlier Middle Ages, in particular, because personality 'denotes the
capacity to act in some measure under international law' and this
concept can 'mean different things in different circumstances'.[71]
The exact legal personality enjoyed is dependent on several factors.
In 994, we can point to two important factors that show that
Olaf, at the very least, enjoyed legal personality: first, the treaty
was part of a peacemaking whole, the particulars of which are
similar to other occasions of peacemaking between rulers and
should be regarded as customary practice – itself a source of international law;[72] and second, and most importantly, the recognition
by King Æthelred that Olaf could enter into a treaty – a general
peace ('worold friŏ'[73]) – on behalf of the group of men – the army
('here') – that he was leading. The latter is significant at a time when
princes ruled over people not territory.[74] In short, Olaf was seen as
having the capacity to act independently in some measure and to
fulfil the obligations and the responsibilities set out in the treaty.
Other leaders in the ninth and tenth century held a similar status,
including Rorik, who, as noted by Coupland in 1998, was referred

to as *rex* by some contemporaries even though he theoretically held Frisia from the Frankish kings.[75] It might be possible to conclude from this that while agreements with men who had suffered expulsion continued into the eleventh and twelfth centuries, these individuals did not have the capacity to act independently in the way those of the earlier period had, and so these later agreements contracted cannot be considered treaties or international law. However, where there is a continued connection to international law is in the activities of these fighting men. For instance, they often resorted to plunder when not employed, which in turn could lead to expulsion.[76] There evidently was a somewhat ambiguous attitude to the use of such military men, with the Church providing on the one hand sanction and on the other condemnation. As a consequence, expulsion and the use of paid fighting men became inextricably linked to the development of the just war theory and to international criminal law according to which plundering, raiding, and fighting unjust wars formed part of those criminal acts which rendered a perpetrator *hostis humani generis* ('an enemy of all mankind').[77]

Treaties, narrative accounts, and domestic laws give evidence of the connection between wrongdoing and expulsion at a local, regional, and international level across both time and space in the period 700 to 1200. However, to further consider the extent to which this significant concern to contain the movements of certain people was practised on a regular basis, we need to also consider how rulers ensured that enemies were not harboured. This, first of all, involves thinking about how such malefactors could be identified; and second, what action could be, or was, subsequently taken. Several treaties set out that neither side was to receive the men of the other without some form of identification that they came on legitimate business. In the late tenth-century *Treaty of Rouen* between Æthelred II and the Norman duke, Richard I, this item was seemingly a seal and likely referred to seals being carried loose.[78] This seems to have imitated practice elsewhere. For instance, the *Russian Primary Chronicle*, refers to an occasion in 944–5 when Prince Igor I of Kiev and the Byzantine emperor, Constantine VII, concluded a treaty which stated that until then the prince's agents going to Greece had carried gold seals and his merchants silver ones.[79] The link between this occasion and the statement in the treaty is strengthened by the recent find of a copper-alloy seal matrix, dating to Æthelred's reign, with remnants of gilding, which would have made it appear to have been made of gold.[80] Pierre Chaplais argued in 2003 that finger rings and loose impressions of seal matrices may provide further evidence of this diplomatic practice from Anglo-Saxon England, and one could speculate that the seventh-century gold signet ring of Queen Balthild, wife of the Merovingian King Clovis II, which was found a few kilometres east of Norwich, England, in 1998, is a Frankish example.[81] Most of the evidence relating to identification of foreigners concern merchants and pilgrims, and this can be seen in both treaties and domestic laws. For instance, a number of agreements mention that men should turn up and immediately announce themselves to certain appointed persons or officials or that they would have to provide a hostage to guarantee their behaviour – essentially a safe conduct.[82] This evidence tallies with what can be found in laws from the same period, for instance, those of Alfred, Cnut, or some of the capitularies of the Frankish kings.

Perhaps the most discussed feature of identification has been that found among the additions of King Ratchis to the Lombard laws, which details that foreign men would have to be in possession of a document carrying the seal of the king ('signo aut epistola regis'). The stipulation makes it clear that this functioned in such a way that specific border stations were guarded so that 'neither our enemies nor our people can send spies through them or allow fugitives to go out and in'. A judge should enquire from where they had come and if deemed to be without evil intent, the judge or the gate warden could issue a document ('syngraphus') that the traveller would show on his onward journey to Rome. On the way back, this document had to be validated with the seal of the king's ring.[83] This clause of course related to the Alpine passes where large number of people passed through and one might think that such bureaucracy likely did not appear elsewhere until the late twelfth century. In fact, as Walter Pohl points out, many scholars have rightly been cautious in their analysis of the clause, deeming it pertinent to the conditions at the time of issue in 746 rather than to any longstanding practices.[84] Drawing on this contemporary context of the contest for domination between the Lombard and Carolingian rulers and the papacy in northern Italy, Tangl argued that it was aimed at controlling the movements of papal and Frankish messengers.[85] Pohl has further argued that the legislation of both Ratchis and his successor Aistulf formed a whole 'in trying to introduce firmer checks and balances against undesired movements within and across the boundaries of the [Lombard] kingdom'.[86] In essence then, both Tangl and Pohl attribute such legislation to paranoid rulers concerned with their own survival in the face of the Carolingian expansion of the eighth century. However, while this interpretation is both sensible and convincing, there is a point to putting such clauses into a wider chronological and geographical context. As the evidence in treaties and legislation from across Europe relating to expulsion shows, containing the movements of specific people was essential. Not just because of the threat to individual rulers at specific times but because those who had committed serious wrongs – whether this be murder, robbery, plunder, treachery, or evading justice of any kind – were threats to communities in general. It will thus come as no surprise that some semblance of Ratchis' clause can be seen across the period 700 to 1200, and not just relating to the Alpine passes.[87] For instance, Cnut's letter to the English of 1027, issued on his way home from a sojourn in Rome, shows that some such procedure was still in place almost 300 years later:

> I therefore spoke with the Emperor and the lord pope and the princes who were present,[88] concerning the needs of all the people of my whole kingdom, whether English or Danes, that they might be granted more equitable law and *greater security on their way to Rome, and that they should not be hindered by so many barriers on the way* and so oppressed by unjust tolls; and the emperor consented to my demands; and *King Rudolf [of Burgundy], who chiefly had dominion over those barriers, and all the princes confirmed by edicts that my men, whether merchants or others travelling for the sake of prayer, should go and return from Rome in safety with firm peace and just law, free from hindrances of barriers* and toll-gatherers.[89]

The letter clearly shows that King Rudolf of Burgundy was in charge of some of the Alpine passes at this time but, furthermore, that similar provisions could be found in other political entities, as Cnut concluded treaties with several rulers to ease the journey of those from England who had legitimate business to be travelling through an area.[90] Furthermore, among the Merovingian and Carolingian formularies edited by Zeumann, there are templates for documents that could be adapted for those travelling as merchants or pilgrims.[91] Hence, it would seem that the common expectancy across Europe was that those with legitimate business to travel should be able to identify themselves in some way.[92] That this was not without its problems is evident from a letter of Charlemagne to Offa, king of the Mercians, usually dated to 796, which shows that at times subjects tried to circumvent more formal agreements and customary practices. Charlemagne writes: 'But we have discovered that certain persons fraudulently mingle with them [the pilgrims] for the sake of commerce, seeking gain, not serving religion. If such are found among them, they are to pay the established toll at the proper places; the others may go in peace.'[93]

The idea that there was an expectancy that foreigners could identify themselves, proving that they were not of ill repute or criminals and had legitimate business to travel, can be strengthened by exploring a range of other evidence. It is clear from treaties, laws, and from descriptions in chronicles and letters that lists of 'undesirable' individuals were kept, and we know that, in certain contexts, such lists were also exchanged. For instance, at the end of the account of the agreement to partition Denmark between the three rivals Cnut, Sven, and Valdemar in 1157, Saxo Grammaticus notes that 'it was also agreed that they should mutually deliver up informers (*delatores mutuo prodi debere*), to ensure that their sincerity might not be injured by dark lies and the soundness of their alliance shaken'.[94] Many scholars have speculated that Saxo may have had access to an actual document recording the terms of the treaty but, if nothing else, he must have been well aware of the wording of such agreements and of actual practices because other chroniclers similarly describe this. To take one similar example, Roger of Howden, writing about the conclusion of peace between King Henry II of England and Philip II of France and Henry's son, Richard, in 1189, stated that, having agreed to the treaty, Henry requested that a list of all traitors, in writing, be given to him.[95] We can find similar notions on the Iberian peninsula, for instance, in the *Treaty of Zaragoza* of 1170, in which the kings of Castile and Aragon promised to inform each other, either by letter or by envoy, about men who had lost their king's mercy.[96] In the twelfth century, England provides the most complete evidence of how fugitives or those expelled were identified, sought and returned. According to the *Assize of Clarendon*, officials – termed *vicecomes* (sheriffs) in the text – were responsible for keeping a register of all fugitives and outlaws so that they could be sought throughout all of England.[97] These officials likely acted together with the 'ballivos' (bailiffs) mentioned in the *Treaty of Falaise*, who were expected to capture and return fugitives 'on account of felony (pro felonia)'.[98] Safe conducts and peace conferences then provided the opportunity for the actual, physical, return of any such individuals apprehended. For instance, the 1194 letter of King Richard I outlining the safe conduct of the Scottish king, records that sheriffs, bishops, and barons should meet and conduct the latter king through their particular counties until the party arrived at the English king's court. During this safe conduct, the Scottish king had the right to bring with him any fugitives who wished to clear themselves of felony.[99] Although this evidence is late and may arguably have pertained to Anglo-Scottish relations only, fragmentary documentary evidence across space and time seem to indicate that not only were lists of fugitives or exiles kept but some men assumed responsibility for bringing them to justice. For instance, both the ninth-century treaty between Emperor Lothar and the Venetians and the Rus-Byzantine treaty of 944 has the feature that men would be returned if the other party enquired or made a claim for specific individuals.[100] Similarly, the *Treaty of Ivry* of 1177, concluded between the English and French kings, state that neither of the kings 'will harbour any enemy of the other in his dominions, from the time that delivery of him shall have been demanded'.[101] It is difficult to imagine how such requests could be satisfied unless rulers tried to keep an eye on those who might potentially be asked about at a later date. We should also put such practices into the wider context of conflict and displacement, because we know that rulers also kept lists of hostages and more valuable captives.[102] Bishops similarly seem to have had lists of those who had been excommunicated and Richard Allen has argued that the majority of those which have survived 'concern the excommunication of national or international figures'.[103] Furthermore, keeping lists of those who had been expelled was ancient practice, as is evident, for instance, from the writings of Isidore of Seville.[104]

The *Division of the Realms* of 806 states that those sent into exile ('in exilium missi vel mittendi sunt'), like hostages, would only be returned with the permission of the brother from whose kingdom they had come and further that, in the future, the reception of such men should be rendered mutually upon 'a reasonable request'.[105] The statement in the *Division of the Realms* further make it appear that those expelled occasionally went to designated places, and that this could be negotiated between the parties.[106] One could compare this to what can be found in domestic laws too. One of the laws of the tenth-century English king Athelstan stipulates that disturbers of the peace 'are to be ready, themselves, their wives and their cattle and all things, to go whither I wish – unless they are willing to desist after this – on condition that they never come back into their native district'.[107] This particular stipulation is almost word for word the same as that found in Charlemagne's capitulary concerning the Saxons of 797, in which it is stated that criminals were to be removed with their wives and goods and be settled elsewhere in the kingdom or in the march or wherever the king wished.[108] It is unclear whether the *wherever the king wishes* in either law was always aimed at sending such men elsewhere within a kingdom or outside it, but it shows, in any case, consistent provision of controlled expulsion across both the domestic and international spheres. Other evidence seems to corroborate this or at least indicate that rulers tried to keep tabs on those expelled after conflict and/or negotiated how and where the displacement would take place. As an example, an entry in *Domesday Book* records how a certain Eadric, the helmsman of King Edward the Confessor's ship, had been outlawed to Denmark for opposing William after he came to England in 1066.[109] Similarly, in the late 930s, after the count of Flanders had captured Montreuil, he expelled ('trans mare... mittit'/'deportat') the wife and children of the rebel Count Herluin of Ponthieu, who had been captured, to the court of the English king Athelstan.[110] At other times, expulsion to specific areas had clear purposes. Although he never referred to exile or expulsion, it seems likely that Widukind of Corvey's famous account of the legion of thieves should be seen in such a legal context. According to Widukind, this legion was recruited from thieves as King Henry I [of East Frankia] was 'severe with foreigners but showed mercy to his countrymen in all cases. When he saw that a thief or highway man was strong and suited to war, Henry spared the man from the punishment that was due, and settled him in a suburb of Merseburg.' There, these men were to spare their countrymen but 'exercise their thievery against the barbarians as much as they dared'.[111] The employment of such individuals – both countrymen and foreigners – and the fact that high-status men actively sought shelter at foreign courts indicate that many who had been expelled were hiding in clear view.

Keeping lists or designating the place of exile were not the only ways to keep track of those expelled. As noted by Claire Judde de Larivière in 2007, in smaller communities, identification was based on knowledge.[112] This knowledge, oral in nature, is well documented in a domestic legal context with medieval writers often reporting on those who were 'notorious' wrongdoers, and there is a significant scholarly literature on the role of 'gossip' in medieval legal culture.[113] It seems logical that this would have applied more widely too, as decisions and judgments relating to expulsions were announced publicly across the period. However, the case is perhaps best strengthened by the fact that the onus of determining whether someone was in foreign parts for legitimate business or not, fell on officials (individuals) but also on whole communities, and that failure to uphold such duties and obligations, including providing swift justice in case of complaints about damage to people or goods or for harbouring or aiding fugitives, can be seen in treaties but also in domestic laws. To take one example, the *Formulary of Marculf*, dating from the late seventh century but popular as a textbook in the Carolingian period, contains a template which is headed: 'If anyone acted against the will of the king, [this is a] security for the man whom he has ordered to pursue him.'[114] The document was intended to provide immunity from prosecution for those obeying royal commands. In this case, the commands were for pursuing a man, who had rebelled ('faciente revello') or committed other wrongs against the king ('alias causas contra regi') and who had subsequently fled ('de regno nostro se transtulit'), and for confiscating his property and that of his followers.[115] Obviously, it is tricky to know the extent to which such commands were carried out and hence the extent of need for this type of immunity, but it clearly indicates that there were men who were expected to deal with expulsion and its results at a local level.[116] The Lombard laws similarly contain a number of provisions, including how much a judge or other resident who apprehended a freeman or slave trying to flee outside the country ('foris provincia') would be paid for this – presumably a good incentive to do so – and how much a ferryman would be fined for transporting a fugitive or a thief across a river.[117]

That officials and whole communities, ecclesiastical as well as secular, were involved in dealing with the issue of expulsion is further apparent if we examine how enquiries were dealt with by different parties. Indeed, that enquiries about those who had been expelled were frequently made is not in doubt nor that this could take different forms. For instance, one of the versions of *Baglarsaga* has a story about how King Sverre of Norway, at some point in the 1190s, found out that there was a man in exile in Denmark who was calling himself Erling, son of Sverre's former rival King Magnus. Upon hearing this, Sverre sent men to Denmark to look for him but Erling fled to the province of Göta in the kingdom of Sweden.[118] Sverre then sent a letter to the Swedish king, Cnut, who was related to him by marriage, and told him that there was a man in his realm, who was calling himself a son of King Magnus, and who likely wanted to cause 'ofrið' (lit. non-peace) in Norway. As soon as King Cnut heard this, he sent men to look for Erling and put him in the stone tower on the island of Vising in Lake Vättern, where he remained for a while.[119] One thing that is particularly interesting about this example is that it shows two different ways in which an expelled person might be sought: by sending royal agents to a foreign entity or by engaging a neighbouring ruler to use domestic enforcement. Elsewhere, one of the clauses from the laws of the Lombard king, Ratchis, makes it clear that only the king's agent ('missum'), or someone with the king's permission, could be sent into another political entity, suggesting perhaps that such agents, even in an earlier period, could have a similar purpose as those sent to apprehend the exile Erling.[120] Certainly, the *Treaty of Meersen* (851) anticipated that 'all should join together to pursue him [a man fleeing justice], into the realm of whomsoever he may come, until either he be brought to reason or wiped out from the realm', and a similar statement can also be found in the 878 *Treaty of Fouron*.[121] In any case, it seems likely that the method chosen for dealing with such matters, depended on the relationship between the parties and whether or not there already was a treaty of some sort in place. Ultimately, of course, the threat of military force could accompany such enquiries if the other side refused to comply, as seems to have been the case with Eardwulf's invasion of Mercia in 801.[122]

Other examples show that recipients of exiles could also intervene and it won't come as any big surprise that the Church and churchmen played a vital role in such negotiations, just as they did in diplomatic matters more broadly.[123] One instance, which offers one of the best examples of how the whole issue of expulsion discussed here may have played out, can be glimpsed from a letter of Charlemagne to Archbishop Æthelheard of Canterbury and Bishop Ceolwulf of Lindsey. The letter, dated 793–6, records how Charlemagne had sent a group of exiles to the archbishop and bishop, hoping that they 'may deign to intercede for them with... King Offa [of Mercia], that they may be allowed to return to their native land in peace and without unjust oppression of any kind, and to serve anyone whatever'.[124] These particular exiles were the loyal followers of a lord named Hringstan, who had seemingly died in exile.[125] The letter hints that Hringstan's crime centred on an accusation of treachery to his lord: '...he would have been faithful to his lord (fidelis suo fuisset domino), if he had been allowed to remain in his own country....[he] was ever ready to purge himself with oath from all disloyalty (semper paratus se ab omni purgare infidelitate)'.[126] It would seem then that the followers were guilty by association and that with Hringstan's death, Charlemagne was optimistic enough that they would receive a favourable welcome that he sent them back across the channel. Interestingly, Charlemagne further asked that if the bishops were unable to obtain peace for the exiles, they were to send them back to the Frankish king uninjured ('inlesos'), and he hints that they would under such circumstances be better off to 'serve in a foreign land (in aliena servire)' – perhaps referring to service in arms.[127] It is furthermore clear that some sort of treaty, although we do not have the text, must have existed between Charlemagne and Offa because throughout the letter, the language (e.g., the use of 'brother') indicates a formal relationship between the two. Additionally, it would appear that such a treaty specified that exiles were not to be harboured, since Charlemagne is careful to point out that he kept Hringstan with him 'for the sake of reconciliation, not out of enmity', thereby justifying his action and indicating it was not a breach of their agreement.[128] Here then, is an almost complete cycle of how expulsion worked and its move from a domestic to an international sphere and back again. It shows that it operated at several levels and involved strategies to both prevent and to deal with its consequences, which, out of necessity, were hence both complementing and conflicting.[129] Indeed, what one ruler solved through expulsion became another ruler's problem.

We can compare the provisions and strategies examined in this chapter with how expulsion, international criminal law, and international law more generally work in the modern period. In the contemporary world, the Rome Statute of the International Criminal Court (ICC) sets out the provisions for the arrest and surrender of those evading or fleeing justice following an accusation of a crime.[130] However, not all countries have signed up to this statute and others have done so only partially. Furthermore, the jurisdiction of the ICC is limited to only 'the most serious crimes of concern to the international community as a whole': genocide, crimes against humanity (e.g., murder, enslavement, torture, apartheid, forced displacement of people), war crimes (e.g., hostage taking, unlawful confinement, intentionally attacking civilians, conscripting children, plundering), and the crime of aggression (e.g., annexation by force of another state's territory).[131] By contrast, the arrest and surrender of domestic criminals trying to evade justice by fleeing abroad are subject to individual or collective extradition treaties and schemes, such as the European Arrest Warrant, under which some crimes are again more serious than others (the dual criminality principle or those that carry a sentence of more than three years), including arson, murder, counterfeiting or forgery, trafficking of certain goods or people, terrorism, and money laundering.[132] Requests for an arrest, surrender, or extradition can be made through diplomatic channels or by engaging a relevant international, regional, or domestic institution (e.g., Interpol) and often time limits apply.[133] Additionally, there might be provisions for costs or compensation; for cooperation in gathering evidence, witness statements, and other assistance; and for dispute resolution.[134] These provisions can then be put into context through cases such as that of the former president of Liberia, Charles Taylor, who, in 2012 (upheld on appeal in 2013), was found guilty of eleven counts of war crimes and crimes against humanity committed during the civil war in Sierra Leone, including aiding and abetting and planning murder; rape, sexual slavery, and enslavement; pillage; and conscription of children. In March 2003, an arrest warrant was issued for Taylor by the Special Court for Sierra Leone and, having stepped down as president in August of the same year, he went into exile in Nigeria where he was arrested in 2006.[135] Following his conviction, Taylor was sent to serve his fifty-year sentence in the UK, in accordance with the International Tribunals (Sierra Leone) Act 2007.[136] It is apparent from this, that just as in the early medieval period, provision centres around certain serious crimes; it is not universal but based on a range of legal instruments and practices; and, as a consequence, it is grounded in cooperation rather than enforcement at local, national, regional, and international levels.[137]

The period 700 to 1200 did not produce the equivalent records that would allow the historian to follow a case similar to that of Charles Taylor, nor does it need to. Effectively, what we have is evidence of a system of European arrest warrants: the treaties set out the agreement that apprehending or not harbouring enemies was a desirable outcome or aim of the relationship between two rulers or groups of people, while supplementary evidence, both laws and descriptions of customs or legal practice, show how this agreement was implemented by engaging and using domestic institutions and actors. The evidence in treaties further show that while containing the movement of those expelled was a prime motivator for concluding treaties, employing such individuals was another solution for dealing with them as well as a source of further conflict.[138] Ambiguity, plurality, conflicting as well as complementing strategies were the order of the day, and just as in the modern period, we should not think of treaties and customs as imposing universal legal obligations or creating a universal international law that could be practised regularly. Instead, what we have is enough evidence across time and space – although more abundant in certain locations at specific times – to show great consistency in legislation (laws and treaties) and in practice over this particular issue. This shows that international law was practised, if not on a daily basis, at least regularly, in the early medieval period.

Notes

1 William Walters, 'Deportation, Expulsion, and the International Police of Aliens', *Citizenship Studies*, 6 (2002), 268. For a short

summary of the literature on the topic and the terminology, see Elisabeth van Houts, 'The Vocabulary of Exile and Outlawry in the North Sea Area around the First Millenium', in *Exile in the Middle Ages*, eds. Laura Napran and Elisabeth van Houts (Turnhout, 2004), 13–28. On the terminology more generally across historical periods, see also Ziv Bohrer, 'International Criminal Law's Millennium of Forgotten History', *Law and History Review*, 34 (2016), 395, 422–3; Markus Dubber and Tatjana Hörnle, *Criminal Law: A Comparative Approach* (Oxford, 2014), 153–4.

2 Walters, 'Deportation, Expulsion', 268; Bohrer, 'International Criminal Law's Millennium of Forgotten History', 424–6; C. Forstein, 'Challenging Extradition: The Doctrine of Specialty in Customary International Law', *Columbia Journal of International Law*, 53 (2015), 364; Julius Goebel, *Felony and Misdemeanor: a Study in the History of English Criminal Procedure* (New York, 1937; repr., 1976), 51–9, esp. fn. 133.

3 Walters, 'Deportation, Expulsion', 268–9; Laura Napran, 'Introduction', in *Exile in the Middle Ages*, 3–4; Elisabeth van Houts, 'L'exil dans l'espace Anglo-Normand', in *La Normandie et l'Angleterre au Moyen Âge*, eds. Pierre Bouet and Véronique Gazeau (Caen, 2003), 117–27. The best introduction to the legal context in England, and the similarities to Frankish procedures, is still Goebel, *Felony and Misdemeanor*, esp. 51–9, 110–22. Another excellent study of the legal context, but dealing with the period just beyond this book, is William Chester Jordan, *From England to France: Felony and Exile in the High Middle Ages* (Princeton, NJ, 2015). On the practice in the Italian city states, see Giuliano Milani, *L'esclusione dal comune: conflitti e bandi politici a Bologna e in altre città italiane tra XII e XIV secolo* (Rome, 2003). For a summary of practices across early medieval period and link to modern practice and international law, see Michael E. Moore, 'Wolves, Outlaws and Enemy Combatants', in *Cultural Studies of the Modern Middle Ages*, eds. E. Joy et al. (New York, 2007), 217–34, esp. 218–23. Bohrer's study is similarly interesting from a perspective of international law, but deftly skips the earlier medieval period. Bohrer, 'International Criminal Law's Millennium of Forgotten History', 393–485.

4 Hathaway and Shapiro refer to 'outcasting', i.e., expulsion, as 'denying the disobedient the benefits of social cooperation and membership'. Hathaway and Shapiro, 'Outcasting', 258.

5 For but a few examples across space and time, see *Af* 4; *V As* prologue 5; *II-III Eg* 7.3; *V Atr* 30; *VI Atr* 35, 37; *II Cn* 57; *Glanvill*, 171; 'Capitulary of Herstal, March 770', c. 23; 'Capitulary concerning the

Saxons, 797', c. 10; 'Capitulary of Aachen, 802–3', c. 12; 'Capitulary of Boulogne October 811', c. 4; 'Constitutio de Hispanis, 815', c. 2; 'Capitulary of Quierzy, 873', c. 1; *Rothair's Edict*, cc. 1, 3–7; *DD FI*, i, no. 25, cc. 6–7; 'Frederick I's Edict against Incendiaries', in *MGH Const.*, I, no. 318; *GL*, cc. 159, 170, 178, 253, 302, 312; *ESjL*, Bk. II, c. 27.

6 *Leges Henrici Primi*, ed. L. J. Downer (Oxford: 1972), c. 12.1a; *Glanvill*, 175–77; *GL*, c. 178; *VSL*, cc. 53–4.

7 John of Salisbury, *Policraticus*, Bk. VI, cap. 25; *Digest*, 48: 4.1–4.

8 George P. Fletcher, 'Parochial Versus Universal Criminal Law', *Journal of International Criminal Justice*, 3 (2005), 22–6.

9 F. H. Russell, *The Just War in the Middle Ages* (Cambridge, 1975; repr. 1979), 141–2.

10 Bohrer, 'International Criminal Law's Millennium of Forgotten History', 433.

11 Bohrer, 'International Criminal Law's Millennium of Forgotten History', 437; Neil Jamieson, ' "Sons of Iniquity": The Problem of Unlawfulness and Criminality amongst Professional Soldiers in the Middle-Ages', in *Outlaws in Medieval and Early Modern England*, eds. John C. Appleby and Paul Dalton (Burlington, VT, 2009), 91; Maurice Keen, *Laws of War in the Late Middle Ages* (London, 1965), 96–100.

12 On this, see Koziol, *The Peace of God*, 15–24.

13 *Konungs Skuggsià*, ed. L. Holm-Olsen (Oslo, 1983), 53. Translation in *The King's Mirror*, tr. L. M. Larson (New York, 1917), 199. For the crime-conflict nexus, see Christina Steenkamp, 'The Crime-Conflict Nexus and the Civil War in Syria', *Stability: International Journal of Security and Development*, 6 (2017), 1–18; J. Goodhand, 'Corrupting or Consolidating the Peace? The Drugs Economy and Post-Conflict Peacebuilding in Afghanistan', *International Peacekeeping*, 15 (2008), 405–423; J. Bergeron, 'Transnational Organised Crime and International Security: A Primer', *The RUSI Journal*, 158 (2013), 6–9.

14 Benham, 'Law or Treaty?', 491–2; Ganshof, 'The Treaties of the Carolingians', 37.

15 *Treaty of Pavia* (840), cc. 3–6. The treaty concluded in 713 between Abd al-Aziz, governor of North Africa, and Theodemir (Tudmir), the Visigothic leader of Murcia, has a clause phrased in a similar way: 'He [Theodemir] will not give shelter to fugitives, nor to our enemies, nor encourage any protected person to fear us, nor conceal news of our enemies.' 'Treaty of Tudmir', in *Reading the Middle Ages: Sources from Europe, Byzantium, and the Islamic World*, 3rd edn., ed. Barbara H. Rosenwein (Toronto, 2018), 79.

16 *Pactum Sicardi*, c. 11; *Partition of Benevento*, cc. 19–20. The latter here divulges that the crimes committed were acts of reprisal not sanctioned by the ruler.

17 *RPC*, 68.

18 *RPC*, 76: 'If any crime is committed by a Greek subject to our Empire, the Russes shall not have the right to punish him, but according to the legislation of our Empire, he shall suffer in proportion to his misdeed.'

19 *RPC*, 75.

20 *II Æthelred*, c. 6.2; *Division of the Realms*, c. 7; *Treaty of Meersen* (851), c. 4. Note that the twelfth-century Latin translation of *II Æthelred* in *Quadripartitus* merely says 'slave or enemy' ('servum vel inimicum').

21 *Treaty of Meersen* (851), c. 5.

22 *Treaty of Fouron*, c. 8: 'Et quia per vagos et in tyrannica consuetudine inreverentes homines pax et quies regni perturbari solet, volumus, ut, ad quemcumque nostrum talis venerit... rationem et iustitiam subterfugere possit, nemo ex nobis illum ad aliud recipiat vel retineat...'

23 *II Edw 5.2.*

24 London, British Library Cotton Augustus II, 18; P. H. Sawyer, *Anglo-Saxon Charters: An Annotated List and Bibliography* (London, 1968), in its revised form available online as the 'Electronic Sawyer', at http://esawyer.org.uk/charter/1428b.html (accessed 16 July 2021), S1428b. Translated as 'Letter of Wealdhere, Bishop of London, to Brihtwold, Archbishop of Canterbury (704–705)', in *EHD*, I, no. 164. On the authenticity and context of this letter, see Pierre Chaplais, 'The Letter from Bishop Wealdhere of London to Archbishop Brihtwold of Canterbury; the Earliest Original "Letter Close" Extant in the West', in *Medieval Scribes, Manuscripts and Libraries: Essays presented to N.R. Ker*, eds. M. B. Parkes and A. G. Watson (London, 1978), 3–23.

25 *Symeonis monachis Opera Omnia*, 2 vols., ed. T. Arnold (London, 1885), ii, 65; *The Historical Works of Simeon of Durham*, tr. J. Stevenson (London, 1855), 463.

26 Flodoard, Historia Remensis ecclesiae, eds. J. Heller and G. Waitz, *MGH SS*, 13 (Hanover: Hahn, 1881), 541. On the career of Rorik, see Simon Coupland, 'From Poachers to Gamekeepers: Scandinavian Warlords and Carolingian Kings', *EME*, 7 (1998), 95–101. On Baldwin's crime and the legal context, see *MGH Capit.* II, no. 245, c. 5; *AB*, 56–7 (97–8).

27 See above pp. 60–1, n. 21; 'Frederick I's Edict against Incendiaries', cc. 1, 7, 10. For offences that could result in excommunication in the eleventh and twelfth centuries, see Brian A. Pavlac, 'Excommunication

and Territorial Politics in High Medieval Trier', *Church History*, 60 (1991), 23; *Councils and Synods, with Other Documents Relating to the English Church. I, A.D. 871–1204*, 2 vols., eds. D. Whitelock, M. Brett, and C. N. L. Brooke (Oxford, 1981), ii, 606. The role of the Church is perhaps best seen in the practice of sanctuary, for which see Karl Shoemaker, *Sanctuary and Crime in the Middle Ages* (New York, 2011).

28 *Treaty of Falaise*, 4–7; Howden, *Gesta*, i, 79.

29 Howden, *Chronica*, ii, 124.

30 *Treaty of Devol*, cc. 6, 12.

31 Howden, *Chronica*, ii, 69.

32 *Treaty of San Salvatore I*, c. 9. 'Si Amizo Sacco Amizonem Bataliam vel aliquos alios appellaverit de morte filiorum suorum et illi ad curiam venire noluerint facturi et recepturi iusticiam, erunt in banno domini imperatoris et Placentini eos eicient extra civitatem et episcopatum eorum et persequentur eos tamquam hostes et omnia bona eorum mobilia et inmobilia fisco applicabuntur.'

33 *Treaty of Rouen* (991).

34 Examples include *AGu*, c. 5; *Division of the Realms* (806), c. 8; *Pact of Philip of Swabia and Philip II of France*, c. 3.

35 *III As* 4.

36 *IV As Latin* c. 3.

37 *Dip. Docs*, 1; *Treaty of Bonn*, c. 2; *Treaty between Genoa and Fos*, c. 2; *Treaty of Melfi*; *Oaths of Strasbourg*; *Treaty of Sahagún*, c. 1; *Treaty of San Salvatore I*, c. 4. For the Iberian treaty and who these 'all men' might have been, see Pascua, 'South of the Pyrenees', 113.

38 On the issue of definition, see Ewan Johnson, 'The Process of Norman Exile into Southern Italy', in *Exile in the Middle Ages*, 30–4.

39 Van Houts, 'L'exil dans l'espace Anglo-Normand', 118–19. See also the discussions by Elisabeth van Houts and Ewan Johnson in *Exile in the Middle Ages*, or the introduction to the detailed study of thirteenth-century conditions in Jordan, *From England to France*.

40 *Historia de Expeditione*, 78 (*The History of the Expedition of Emperor Frederick*, in *CFB*, 102); *Magni Presbiteri Chronicon*, ed. Wilhelm Wattenbach, *MGH SS*, 17 (Hanover, 1861), 513 (*The Chronicle of Magnus of Reichersberg*, in *CFB*, 157–8).

41 In that order of frequency. For four examples of treaties containing this trifecta of stipulations, see *Treaty of Pavia* (840); *Treaty of Constantinople* (911, 945); *II Æthelred* (994). Captives are furthermore interlinked with hostages and exiles, for which see Kosto, *Hostages*, 8–9, 69–70.

42 On this, see Chapter 4, pp. 145–80.

43 *Treaty of Agreda*, prol.: 'ut nullus reciperet Petrum Roderici, nec eum nec fratres suos, nec parentes suos qui ad suum proficium ibi essent... nec aliquibus hominibus qui ad proficium Petri Roderici forent, preter Gonzaluum Roderici, qui tunc temporis erat uassallus domini Aldefonsi.'

44 *Dip. Docs*, 2.

45 Jenny Benham, 'A Changing Perception of War: The Role of Treaties from the Tenth to the Early Thirteenth Centuries', in *Battle and Bloodshed: The Medieval World at War*, eds. Lorna Bleach and Keira Borrill (Newcastle, 2013), 219.

46 The *Pact of Philip of Swabia and Philip II of France*, c. 4, also names specific enemies. However, this clause related to the count of Flanders who held lands from both the French king and the German emperor, and in addition was frequently allied to the king of England.

47 One example of this is the French copy of the *Treaty of Le Goulet* which stipulates that any 'liege man', naming specifically only the count of Flanders, would be an enemy if he attempted to do the French king any harm. Howden, *Chronica*, iv, 151.

48 A useful summary of the literature is discussed in Bauduin, 'La papauté, les Vikings et les relations Anglo-Normandes: autour du traité de 991', in *Échanges, communications et réseaux dans le haut Moyen Âge*, eds. Alban Gautier and Céline Martin (Turnhout, 2011), 202–6. See also Levi Roach, *Æthelred the Unready* (London, 2016), 117; Eric John, 'War and Society in the Tenth Century: The Maldon Campaign', *TRHS*, 5th ser., 27 (1977), 189; Philippe Grierson, 'The Relations between England and Flanders before the Norman Conquest', *TRHS*, 4th ser., 23 (1941), 89, 93 fn. 2. For a different view, see Benham, 'The Earliest Arbitration Treaty?', 189–204.

49 Van Houts, 'The Vocabulary of Exile', 20–1.

50 *Partition of Benevento*, c. 24. For the context, see Barbara M. Kreutz, *Before the Normans* (Philadelphia, 1996), 20–33; Graham A. Loud, *The Age of Robert Guiscard: Southern Italy and the Norman Conquest* (Harlow, 2000), 17–18; Gustavo Adolfo Nobile Mattei, 'Il problema della qualificazione giuridica della "Divisio Ducatus"', *Historia et Ius*, 4 (2013), 1–3.

51 *DD FI*, iii, no. 575. On the context, see H. Géraud, 'Les routiers au douzième siècle', *Bibliothèque de l'école des chartes*, 3 (1842), 125–47.

52 'Canons of the Third Lateran Council 1179', at www.papalencyclicals. net/Councils/ecum11.htm (accessed 16 July 2021), c. 27.

53 There is a large literature on this topic. For examples, see Guy Halsall, *Warfare and Society in the Barbarian West, 450–900* (London, 2003),

111–16; Jesse Byock, *Viking Age Iceland* (London, 2001), 5–24; John Godfrey, 'The Defeated Anglo-Saxons Take Service with the Eastern Emperor', *ANS*, 1 (1978), 63–74.

54 Coupland, 'From Poachers to Gamekeepers', 89–101; Benham, 'Law or Treaty?', 491; Charles Bowlus, 'The Early Hungarians as Mercenaries 860–955', in *Mercenaries and Paid Men. The Mercenary Identity in the Middle Ages*, ed. John France (Leiden, 2008), 194–5.

55 II *Æthelred*, prologue.

56 There is a large literature on this treaty and its context. For some examples, see Benham, 'Law or Treaty?', 490–1; Simon Keynes, 'Historical Context', in *The Battle of Maldon AD 991*, ed. Donald Scragg (Oxford, 1991), 103–7; Roach, *Æthelred the Unready*, 175–7; T. M. Anderson, 'The Viking Policy of Ethelred the Unready', *Scandinavian Studies*, 53 (1987), 284–95.

57 *Olafs saga Tryggvasonar*, ed. Olafur Halldorsson (Reykjavik, 2006), cc. 1, 6, 8, 21, 25, 29–30.

58 For some examples, see Maurice Keen, *The Outlaws of Medieval Legend* (London, 2000; repr. 2007), 9–63.

59 *Treaty of Melfi*.

60 Guillaume de Pouille, *La geste de Robert Guiscard*, ed. M. Mathieu (Palermo, 1963), 139.

61 Geoffrey Malaterra, *De rebus gestis Rogeri Calabriae*, Bk, I, c. 5.

62 Ibid., Bk. I, cc. 38–9.

63 'Exsulant quippe a patribus ut arietent viriliter cum regibus. Dimittuntur a suis inopes, ut mercentur ex extraneis dapes... Pelluntur extorres, ut fenerentur praeliantes.' *De moribus et actis primorum Normannorum Ducum auctore Dudone Sancti Quintini decano*, ed. J. Lair (Caen, 1865), 130. Translation from Dudo of St Quentin, *History of the Normans*, tr. Eric Christiansen (Woodbridge, 1998), 16.

64 For the UN definition of displacement, see www.unesco.org/new/en/ social-and-human-sciences/themes/international-migration/glossary/ displaced-person-displacement/ (accessed 16 July 2021).

65 *Treaty of Melfi*.

66 For a good analysis of these treaties with references to the historiography, see Oksanen, *Flanders and the Anglo-Norman World*, 54–81.

67 Eljas Oksanen, 'The Anglo-Flemish Treaties and Flemish Soldiers in England 1101–1163', in *Mercenaries and Paid Men*, 261.

68 Benham, *PMA*, 104–5; *Treaty of Andeli*, cc.1–2.

69 *Treaty of Genoa I*. For a brief summary of the context with references to relevant primary sources, see Epstein, *Genoa and the Genoese*, 49–52.

70 Matthew Strickland, 'Mercadier', *ODNB*, http://doi.org/10.1093/ref. odnb/50123 (accessed 16 July 2021).

71 Dixon, *Textbook on IL*, 115–17, 130–1. On legal personality in medieval treaties, see also Chapter 1, p. 23.

72 On the peacemaking process in 994, see *Two of the Saxon Chronicles Parallel*, i, 132–3. For commentary, see Benham, 'Law or Treaty?', 490–1; Keynes, 'Historical Context', 103–7; Roach, *Æthelred the Unready*, 175–7; Anderson, 'The Viking Policy of Ethelred the Unready', 284–95. On the principles and customary nature of peacemaking, see Benham, *PMA*, esp. chs. 3–7.

73 Tom Lambert has recently noted how the word *frið* tended to have been used to 'justify legislative initiatives and to exhort people to assist in their implementation' and that this was furthermore a communal matter, the peace of the kingdom as a whole. Tom Lambert, *Law and Order in Anglo-Saxon England* (Oxford, 2017), 208.

74 Compare this to Grewe's comments on the *Treaty of Bonn* (921), which he argued should be regarded as a 'legal act corresponding to international legal recognition'. *The Epochs of International Law*, 77.

75 Coupland, 'From Poachers to Gamekeepers', 100.

76 'Canons of the Third Lateran Council 1179', at www.papalencyclicals. net/Councils/ecum11.htm (accessed 16 July 2021), c. 27. Chroniclers further show that these men were used frequently in conflicts in the twelfth century, e.g., 1173–4 rebellion. There is a large historiography on this, for some examples see articles by John D. Hosler, Eljas Oksanen, and David Crouch in *Mercenaries and Paid Men*.

77 Russell, *The Just War*, 240–3; Dixon, *Textbook on IL*, 128; Bohrer, 'International Criminal Law's Millennium of Forgotten History', 395–404, 409–10, 419–64. The phrase is derived from Cicero's 'communis hostis omnium' in his *De Officiis* III: 29 and in *Contra Verres* II, iv, 21.

78 *Treaty of Rouen* (991), 38.

79 *RPC*, 74.

80 J. Kershaw and R. Naismith, 'A New Late Anglo-Saxon Seal Matrix', *ASE*, 42 (2013), 291–8.

81 Chaplais, *EDP*, 30; Portable Antiquities Scheme, Unique ID: PAS-8709C3 https://finds.org.uk/database/artefacts/record/id/509468 (accessed 16 July 2012).

82 E.g., *Dunsæte*, c. 6; *AGu*, c. 5.

83 *The Laws of King Ratchis*, c. 13. For a good discussion of this provision and the literature, see Walter Pohl, 'Frontiers in Lombard Italy: the Laws of Ratchis and Aistulf', in *The Transformation of Frontiers. From Late Antiquity to the Carolingians*, eds. Walter Pohl, Ian Wood, and Helmut Reimitz (Leiden, 2001), 117–42.

84 Pohl, 'Frontiers in Lombard Italy', 119. For a summary of the historical background to the relations between the Lombard rulers, the Frankish kings, and the papacy, see Chris Wickham, *Early Medieval Italy. Central Power and Local Society 400–1000* (London, 1981), 44–6.

85 Georgine Tangl, 'Die Paßvorschrift des Königs Ratchis und ihre Beziehung zu dem Verhaltnis zwischen Franken und Langobarden vom 6.-8. Jahrhundert', *Quellen und Forschungen aus italienischen Archiven und Bibliotheken*, 38 (1958), 52. Note, however, that the clause itself is not specific on this issue but is merely aimed at spies or fugitives.

86 Pohl, 'Frontiers in Lombard Italy', 121–5.

87 Most scholars discussing identification have specifically focused on the Alpine passes. For some examples, see Neil Middleton, 'Early Medieval Port Customs, Tolls and Controls on Foreign Trade', *EME*, 13 (2005), 319–20; David Pelteret, 'Not All Roads Lead to Rome', in *England and Rome in the Early Middle Ages: Pilgrimage, Art and Politics*, ed. Francesca Tinti (Turnhout, 2014), 26–9.

88 Earlier in the letter these are referred to as 'all the princes of the nations from Mount Garganus [southern Italy] to the sea nearest to us', likely the North Sea. *Cn 1027*, c. 5.

89 *Cn 1027*, c. 6. Emphasis added.

90 A letter of Gregory VII to Philip I of France shows that the French king collected payments in cash from traders and pilgrims, giving further evidence of such provisions and the economic incentive behind them. Gregory VII, *Registrum II*, 5 and 18, ed. E. Caspar, *MGH Epp. sel. 2,1*, 130–1, 150–1. Translation from *The Register of Pope Gregory VII, 1073–85: An English Translation*, tr. H. E. J. Cowdrey (Oxford, 2002), 97, 112.

91 *Formulae Merowingici et Karolini aevi*, ed. K. Zeumer (Hanover, 1886), 314–15 (merchants) and 439–40 (pilgrims).

92 Claire Judde de Larivière has argued that diplomatic contacts were localised and limited in this period and hence so was the issue of identification, which the evidence from treaties seems to contradict. Claire Judde de Larivière, 'Du sceau au passeport: genèse des pratiques médiévales de l'identification', in *L'identification. Genèse d'un travail d'État*, ed. Gérard Noiriel (Paris, 2007), 59.

93 'Sed probavimus quosdam fraudolenter negociandi causa se intermiscere, lucra sectantes, non religioni servientes. Si tales inter eos inveniantur, locis oportunis statuta solvent telonea. Ceteri absoluti vadant in pace.' *Epistolae Karolini Aevi, vol. II*, ed. E. Dümmler, *MGH Epp.*, 4 (Berlin, 1895), no. 100, p. 145. Available in English as 'Charles the Great to Offa, king of Mercia, 796', in *EHD, I*, no. 197.

94 Saxo, *GD*, ii, 1088–9.

95 Howden, *Chronica*, ii, 366. For a short discussion of the treaty and context of this list of traitors, see Benham, 'Writing Peace, Writing War', 280–2.

96 *Treaty of Zaragoza*, c. 2: 'et si aliquis nostrum disfidiaverit aliquem hominem, significet alteri per litteras suas vel per notos nuncios, et ex tunc, similiter disficet disfidatum et adiuuet disfidantem, et faciat ei omnem malum quodcumque facere poterit.'

97 *Assize of Clarendon*, c. 18.

98 *Treaty of Falaise*, 2–3.

99 '...fugitivis qui de felonia se defendere voluerint...' *Anglo-Scottish Relations 1174–1328: Some Selected Documents*, ed. E. L. G. Stones (London, 1965), 10.

100 *Treaty of Pavia* (840), cc. 2, 6; *RPC*, 74.

101 Howden, *Gesta*, i, 191; Howden, *Chronica*, ii, 144; *Treaty of Ivry* (1180), c. 2.

102 For a few examples with date in square brackets, see *Indiculus obsidum Saxonum Moguntiam deducendorum*, in *MGH Capit.*, I, 233–4 [805x6]; Ferdinand Güterbock, 'Alla vigilia della Lega Lombarda', *Archivio storico italiano*, 95 (1937), 181–5 [1162]; *Les registres de Philippe Auguste, 1: Texte*, ed. John Baldwin (Paris, 1992), 558–66 [1213]. On lists of hostages in the later Middle Ages, see also Kosto, *Hostages*, 95–9, 179–80, 185–7.

103 Richard Allen, 'The Earliest Known List of Excommunicates from Ducal Normandy', *JMH*, 39 (2013), 394–415, esp. 398–9 fn. 24.

104 Isidore, *Etymologiae*, V:27.30.

105 *Division of the Realms*, c. 13.

106 This seems to have Roman precedents in *deportatio*, which was a forcible removal to a specified place for life and was the most extreme case of banishment. Isidore, *Etymologiae*, V:27.30; *Digest*, 48:19.2, 4.

107 *V As*, Prol. 1. Cf. *IV As Latin*, c. 3, which indicates more clearly that the intention was to move them to another part within Athelstan's kingdom.

108 'Capitulary concerning the Saxons, 797', c. 10. Charlemagne's stipulations seem to have been harsher than those of Athelstan as he was said to have possession of these men 'as though dead', perhaps indicating that this was a form of enforced slavery. Domestically, specified exile could be an act of mercy, as can be seen in the case of Count Bera of Barcelona (*ARF*, s.a. 820) and that of Duke Eberhard of Franconia (Widukind, *RGS*, Bk. II, cap. 13 (p. 78); Widukind, *Deeds*, 75).

109 'postquam rex W. venit in Angliam fuit iste Edricus ex lex in Daciam.' *DB*, ii, 200a. There seems to have been a few men whose resistance

to William resulted in this same fate, for which see F. M. Stenton, 'St Benet of Holme and the Norman Conquest', *EHR*, 37 (1922), 233.

110 *Les annales de Flodoard*, tr. Philippe Lauer (Paris, 1905), 72 (translation in *The Annals of Flodoard of Rheims 919–966*, eds. Steven Fanning and Bernard S. Bachrach (North York ON, 2011), 31); *Richer von Saint-Remi Historiae*, ed. Hartmut Hoffmann, *MGH SS*, 38 (Hanover, 2000), 107. On this, see also Grierson, 'The Relations between England and Flanders', 89.

111 Widukind, *RGS*, Bk. II, cap. 3 (p. 69); Widukind, *Deeds*, 66. On this legion see also Karl Leyser, 'Henry I and the Beginnings of the Saxon Empire', *EHR*, 83 (1968), 12.

112 Judde de Larivière, 'Du sceau au passeport', 59.

113 Chris Wickham, 'Gossip and Resistance among the Medieval Peasantry', *P&P*, 160 (1998), 3–24; Thelma S. Fenster and Daniel Lord Smail, eds., *Fama: The Politics of Talk and Reputation in Medieval Europe* (Ithaca, NY, 2003). For examples, with dates in brackets, of being 'notorious', see Burchard of Worms, *Lex Familiae Wormatiensis ecclesiae* [1023x1025], in *MGH Const.* I, no. 438, c. 31; *Assize of Clarendon* [1166], cc. 12, 14; 'Frederick I's Edict against Incendiaries' [1186x1188], cc. 7, 13; *Glanvill* [1180s], 171.

114 *Marculfi Formularum Liber I*, in *Formulae Merowingici et Karolini aevi*, 62 (no. 32). Translation from *The Formularies of Angers and Marculf: Two Merovingian Legal Handbooks*, tr. Alice Rio (Liverpool, 2008), 165.

115 *Marculfi Formularum Liber I*, 62–3; *The Formularies of Angers and Marculf*, 165–6.

116 On the link between *formulae* and legal practice, see Alice Rio, 'Formulae, Legal Practice and the Settlement of Disputes', in *Law before Gratian. Law in Western Europe c. 500–1100*, eds. Per Andersen, Mia Münster-Swendsen, and Helle Vogt (Copenhagen, 2007), 21–34, esp. 22–4.

117 *Rothair's Edict*, cc. 264–8; *Laws of King Liutprand*, c. 11.V. Such provisions can also be found in the much earlier Burgundian laws and in certain treaties, for which see *The Law of Gundobad*, VI:1, 5; *Treaty of Pavia* (840), c. 10.

118 There were two such provinces in the Swedish kingdom: West Göta and East Göta. It is not clear from the narrative which one of these provinces is meant but subsequent events and geography perhaps indicate that the western province is the more likely.

119 *Bǫglunga Sǫgur*, 2 vols., ed. Hallvard Magerøy (Oslo, 1988), ii, 11–12; *Saga om baglarar og birkebeinar*, in *Noregs kongesoger*, vol. 3, eds., Finn Hødnebø and Hallvard Magerøy (Oslo, 1979), 281.

120 *The Laws of King Ratchis*, c. 9.V.

121 *Treaty of Meersen* (851), c. 4; *Treaty of Fouron*, c. 8.

122 *Symeonis monachis Opera Omnia*, ii, 65; *The Historical Works of Simeon of Durham*, 463.

123 That such diplomatic contacts had a long history can be seen in the narrative of Priscus of Panius who records a Roman embassy intended to negotiate the return of Hunnic fugitives, after a written request by Attila to return deserters. *Prisci Panitae Historia Byzantina*, in *Fragmenta Historicorum Graecorum, volume 4*, ed. C. Müller (Paris, 1851), 78–9.

124 *MGH Epp.*, IV, no. 85. Available in English as 'Charles the Great to Æthelheard, archbishop of Canterbury, and Ceolwulf, bishop of Lindsey, 793–6', in *EHD, I*, no. 196.

125 On Hringstan, these negotiations, and on exiles at Charlemagne's court more generally, see Joanna Story, *Carolingian Connections: Anglo-Saxon England and Carolingian Francia c. 750–870* (Aldershot, 2003), 135–51.

126 *MGH Epp.*, IV, no. 85.

127 *MGH Epp.*, IV, no. 85.

128 *MGH Epp.*, IV, no. 85. For more on this letter and the case of the exiles, see Chapter 5, pp. 200–1. On justifications and breaches of treaties, see Chapter 4, pp. 145–80.

129 That this process of expulsion and how to deal with those expelled is reflected elsewhere in medieval society is clear from a letter of Bernard of Clairvaux to the abbot of St Nicholas detailing how Bernard dealt with a fugitive monk, for which see *Some Letters of Saint Bernard, Abbott of Clairvaux*, ed. F. A. Gasquet and tr. Samuel J. Eales (London, 1904), no. XXIII (p. 58).

130 *Rome Statute of the International Criminal Court*, available at www. icc-cpi.int/NR/rdonlyres/ADD16852-AEE9-4757-ABE7-9CDC7CF02886/283503/RomeStatutEng1.pdf (accessed 16 July 2021).

131 *Rome Statute*, art. 5–8.

132 *2002/584/JHA: Council Framework Decision of 13 June 2002 on the European arrest warrant and the surrender procedures between Member States*, available at http://eur-lex.europa.eu/legal-content/EN/ALL/?uri=CELEX:32002F0584 (accessed 16 July 2021), art. 2.2.

133 *Rome Statute*, art. 87–9, 91; *2002/584/JHA*, art. 8–10, 12, 17, 23, 25. Practical guidance and statistics on the number of EAWs issued and executed can also be found at https://e-justice.europa.eu/content_european_arrest_warrant-90-en.do (accessed 16 July 2021).

134 For some examples, see *Rome Statute*, art. 93, 96, 99–100, 109, 113–17, 119; *2002/584/JHA*, art. 6–7, 29–31.

135 Prosecutor v. Taylor, Case No. SCSL-03–01-A, Appeals Judgment (Spec. Ct. Sierra Leone Sept. 26, 2013) at www.rscsl.org/Documents/Decisions/Taylor/Appeal/1389/SCSL-03-01-A-1389.pdf (accessed 16 July 2021), 10775–8.
136 International Tribunals (Sierra Leone) Act 2007 at www.legislation.gov.uk/ukpga/2007/7/introduction (accessed 16 July 2021).
137 There is a huge literature on this topic. For examples, see Stewart and Kiyani, 'The Ahistoricism of Legal Pluralism', 393–450; Nadia Banteka, 'Mind the Gap: A Systematic Approach to the International Criminal Court's Arrest Warrants Enforcement Problem', *Cornell International Law Journal*, 49 (2016), 523–8; Göran Sluiter, 'The Surrender of War Criminals to the International Criminal Court', *Loyola of Los Angeles International and Comparative Law Review*, 25 (2003), 607–16; Sunil Kumar Gupta, 'Sanctum for the War Criminal: Extradition Law and the International Criminal Court', *Berkeley Journal of Criminal Law*, 3 (2000), 1–35; Forstein, 'Challenging Extradition', 363–95.
138 For examples of how this played out across the medieval period, see Benham, 'Peace, Security and Deterrence', 120–2.

3

The rules consistently obeyed: redress, amnesty, and transitional justice

Acknowledgement and redress of wrongs is one of the most enduring legal principles across time and space. It can be found in the many codes of justice of the ancient worlds as well as in the monetary restitutions and fixed penalties prescribed for a range of offences and actions in modern law. In the period 700–1200, this legal principle was one of the pillars of medieval society with its emphasis on collective responsibility, both in how redress was demanded – from the perpetrator, as far as s/he could pay, to his/her kin – and in how redress was distributed to the victim and his/her family.[1] In a context of relations between rulers, redress of wrongful acts goes to the heart of whether or not there was international law because it shows the extent to which there was an expectation that redress could be sought, whether or not there was an obligation to provide redress and if so, how and by what means redress was provided. The causes, effects, and provisions of redress could be physically felt beyond the highest, international or inter-ruler, level of society, but they also, for this reason, pitted the aims, rights, authority, and jurisdiction of different individuals, communities or sections of society against each other at different times in the peace process. Exploring the issue of redress hence not only tells us about the extent to which international rules were consistently obeyed but also about the nature of enforcement and the perception of peace.

Redress of legal wrongs in international law – compensation, reparation, restitution, indemnity, or whatever we want to call it – entails obligations, the exact nature of which are not entirely clear even in the modern period since 'there is no such thing as a uniform code of international law, reflecting the obligations of all States'.[2] Yet, in the late eleventh century, Lampert of Hersfeld records how the young Henry IV was abducted from the care of Empress Agnes, who governed the German kingdom during her son's minority, into the hands of another court faction led by Archbishop Anno of Cologne, and that afterwards she resolved 'neither to follow her son nor complain of the injuries inflicted on her with an appeal to the law of nations (Imperatrix nec filium sequi nec iniurias suas iure gentium expostulare voluit)', but retired from public life.[3] There has been some debate over the rhetoric of Lampert's statement and scholars have pointed to his significant use of the Roman writer Livy in his chronicle to explain his reference to the *ius gentium*.[4] Nevertheless, that Lampert may not have been completely out of touch with the reality of conflict resolution of his day, or with his appeal to a specific international rule is clear.[5] In fact, nearly every treaty in the period 700 to 1200 sets out some sort of framework whereby redress would be made for damages, injuries, and losses incurred during or as a result of violence or conflict, either that which had already taken place or that which might occur in the future. Some are quite general stipulations stating that any wrongs committed against each other should be atoned for, but without giving specific details as to how much would be paid or for what. For instance, the *Treaty of Rouen*, concluded in 991, simply hinted that if the men of both King Æthelred II and Richard I, leader of the Normans, were to commit any wrong against the other, it should be atoned for with fitting compensation ('digna emendatione purgetur').[6] Likewise, the *Treaty of Túy*, concluded in 1137 between the kings of Castile and Portugal, merely set out that any man who breached the terms of the treaty should make amends ('emmendet'), without further elaborating what forms this might take.[7] Similar statements can often be found also in narrative evidence describing treaties and negotiations. For instance, the eighth-century letter of Bishop Wealdhere, detailing the attempts to establish peace between the East and West Saxon rulers, refers to a conference where the parties decided that if anyone could be shown to have committed wrongs, he would 'make amends with rightful compensation (recta emendatione satisfaciat)'.[8] Just as in the two treaties, exactly what 'rightful compensation' might have entailed is never divulged in this letter.

Other treaties have very detailed stipulations, which roughly fall into three categories: redress for injuries to, or killing of, freemen;

redress for damages to, or loss of, goods; and redress for slaves and their actions.⁹ One example of the first category is the treaty concluded between the West Saxon king, Alfred, and Guthrum, the Scandinavian king of the people in East Anglia towards the end of the ninth century. The second clause of this treaty sets out that free men killed were valued at the same amount, eight half-marks of refined gold. The killing of an English *ceorl*, who occupied rented land, and a freed man in East Anglia, was also valued the same, at 200 shillings.[10] The next clause continued by outlining how a man accused of manslaughter ('manslihtes') could clear himself with an oath taken together with twelve of his peers, and, in addition, a king's thegn if he was of lower status. If he was unable to do so, he would pay three-fold compensation ('gylde hit ðrygylde').[11] This treaty then first sets out the wergilds – that is, the value placed on a particular individual – before establishing the procedure of cases of manslaughter as well as the level of redress that could be sought. A line in the third clause adds that the procedure would be the same in any case brought that was worth more than four mancuses, and would be compensated according to its value.[12] A late example can be found with the alliance between the cities of Genoa and Pavia of 1140. This treaty stipulated that homicide would be compensated with seven and a half pounds of 'brune' money ('emendabitur libras septem dimidiam brune monetam') and if, in addition to the homicide, a person was injured, amends should be made according to the practice of the land ('emendabitur secundum usum terre').[13] The last part of this clause hints at the link to domestic laws and customs, yet the exact level of redress in domestic laws does not always correspond to what can be seen in treaties.[14] Perhaps the closest link between stipulations in treaties and domestic laws can be found with those involving the Lombards. For instance, the *Partition of Benevento* stipulates that those of Prince Radelchis' men who had committed homicide in the part belonging to Prince Sikenolf would pay ('componam') the latter three thousand gold byzants for 'nobilibus' and for 'rusticis' they would 'pay according to the law (fiat compositio secundum legem)'.[15] Exactly which one of the Lombard law stipulations for homicide is meant is unclear, but as an example, if 'rustici' is an umbrella term for various agricultural workers, then clauses 129 to 137 of *Rothair's Edict* list the compositions for killing such men, valued according to their precise duties.[16] More general, but retaining the clear link to domestic laws, is the renewal of the treaty between the princes of Naples and Benevento in 936, which sets out that all cases should be decided according to Roman or Lombard law – an acknowledgement of the juridical dualism of the region.[17] Clause six of this treaty, further-more, contains a reference to the 'launegilt' (a return or counter gift), which is well attested in the Lombard laws.[18] We find similar links also in northern Italy, where some of the clauses of the *Treaty of Pavia* of 840 are taken directly from the Lombard laws, other treaties, or Justinian's *Institutes*.[19] Interestingly, the close link between domestic law and treaties seemingly went both ways, with the tenth-century *Treaty of Rialto* indicating that anyone who committed an offence against the law – which law is not clear – should make amends according to the terms of the treaty.[20]

Detailed stipulations for redress – regardless of whether this concerned injuries to men or goods – occur most frequently in treaties where at least one party had significant involvement in commerce or in treaties between communities with longstanding and recurrent contacts with each other. One early example is the ninth-century *Treaty of Pavia*. Among its many stipulations, it records that if anyone led a raid into the territory of the Venetians, they would be handed over and all that had been taken would be compensated twofold ('in duplum restituantur'). If the emperor and the mainlanders failed to do so within the prescribed sixty-day limit, they would pay ('componamus') 500 *solidos* of gold for each person who had committed a wrong ('malitiam').[21] Another example can be found with the tenth- or early eleventh-century *Ordinance of the Dunsæte*, concluded between two communities living on opposite sides of a river, often thought to be the Wye. The treaty focuses mainly on the issue of cattle theft, setting out that if anyone followed the track of stolen cattle from one river bank to the other, the owner of that land would be responsible for finding the cattle within nine days or within that time pay com-pensation, or deposit a pledge worth half as much again, which, in turn, had to be redeemed within another nine days.[22] Finally, clause 2.2 states that 'from one bank to the other one may take a pledge, unless he can get justice in another way' while the *Treaty of Pavia* likewise recorded that if two appeals to return stolen cattle had gone unheeded, the injured party could seize something in pledge from the other until he received satisfaction.[23] Dante Fedele has argued that clauses such as these show that reprisals were frequent and accepted as a 'de facto in most European territories'.[24] While this is one way of interpreting the clauses in treaties like those of Pavia and *Dunsæte*, such an argument also perpetuates a view of the Middle Ages as a period of irrational violence for its own sake. A different way of looking at this evidence might be to think of reprisals as a last resort once all other alternatives to seek redress had been exhausted. Likely the truth lies somewhere between these two points. It is worth bearing in mind that the most detailed clauses of redress occur in treaties concluded between communities with frequent and recurrent contacts with each other. In such a context, reprisals, violent raids, and counterraids may have been carried out at specific times or over specific disputes but we should be careful to assume they were the default mode of achieving redress.[25] Rather, these clauses show that non-violent redress for legal wrongs was the default but that reprisals could form part of the many different procedures of how to achieve redress. It could be argued that setting this out explicitly in treaties may have been an attempt at deterrence, inducing parties to agree redress for any wrongs before such escalation. This is further confirmed by the fact that these types of treaties usually also stipulate the use of arbitration panels for deciding issues of redress and other disputes that might occur locally.[26]

Though laws, customs, or even reprisals may underpin some treaties in terms of the nature and form of redress, it is evident that many treaties assume that the parties involved knew what redress could be sought. Unsurprisingly, this is particularly common with regards to the provision for the peaceful and secure passage of merchants. For instance, the 1180 renewal of the *Treaty of Ivry* sets out that merchants and their goods of both the French King, Philip II, and the English king, Henry II, would enjoy peace and security throughout their lands ('mercatores… cum omnibus rebus suis securi sint et pacem habeant per omnes terras meas').[27] This is a frequently occurring clause in treaties but one that rarely outlines what redress could be sought if this was not adhered to.[28] One interesting insight to such clauses can be gleaned from the *Treaty of Artlenburg*, concluded in 1161 between Duke Henry the Lion of Saxony and the men of the island of Gotland in the Baltic Sea. The prologue of this treaty sets out that Henry granted the Gotlanders a firm peace so that whatever was the loss of their property or injuries done within the boundaries of his authority, they could demand full justice and redress.[29] Peace, in other words, was a state that entitled the parties to redress for legal wrongs relating to commercial activities as a default, and this seems to be confirmed by the fact that the detailed clauses of this treaty deal only with killing and wounding. None of this tells us exactly what redress could be sought for wrongs relating to commercial activities, but some treaties seem to have anticipated the single simple rule of returning that which had been taken or replacing it with the same. After detailing the circumstances and areas where a man and his goods would enjoy peace, the late tenth-century treaty between Æthelred II and the viking leaders sets out that 'if a man is robbed of his goods, and he knows by which ship [referring to those of the viking leaders], the steersman is to give back the goods' or deny it with an oath of five men, being himself the fifth.[30] In a similar manner the *Treaty of Pavia* decreed that if any horse or cattle or other four-legged animal 'have been taken or wandered away by themselves, we [referring to the Emperor Lothar and the mainlanders] will in every way restore them to you [the Venetians]'.[31] In 1167, King Alfonso II of Aragon, in his treaty with the Genoese, likewise stipulated that if any of his subjects took anything from them, he would return the property or give them full satisfaction.[32] Evidently, every effort was made to recover the exact item lost or stolen, or to replace like for like. This is further confirmed by the fact that several treaties stipulate that redress would be recovered from the perpetrator's own possessions, but not in the sense of reprisals, i.e., forceable seizure. One example is the treaty of 944–5 between the Rus' Prince Igor I of Kiev and the Byzantine emperor, Constantine VII, which states:

> If a Russ assault a Greek, or a Greek a Russ, with sword, spear, or any other weapon, he who has committed this crime shall pay five pounds of silver according to the Russian law, but if he is poor, all his available property shall be sold, even to the garments he walks in, and these too shall be taken from him. Finally, he shall swear upon his faith that he has no possessions, and then he shall be released.[33]

A later example can be found in the *Treaty of San Salvatore II* by which the Emperor Frederick Barbarossa granted the Genoese the right to an accused's portable assets 'whether in gold, silver, coin, or lengths of silk cloth'.[34] Such stipulations show the clear connection between redress and materiality, hinting that even international law was something that could be physically felt, handled, and manipulated at a local level.[35]

Stipulations for redress of legal wrongs in treaties were usually set out on the basis of reciprocity, but not necessarily equality. For instance, the treaty between the English king Æthelred II and three viking leaders and their army ('here'), employing them against other such raiders, made clear that going forward peace between the English and those in the army would be maintained by a similar system of compensation as that which regulated interactions between all of the king's subjects. However, the treaty deviated from provision of equality in redress in how it dealt with multiple killings. If the English killed more than eight men, this would be considered a breach of the agreed peace ('friðbrec') and a return to hostilities, but a similar offence on the other side resulted in the perpetrators alone being outlawed ('utlage').[36] These stipulations make it seem as if there was an acceptance on the English side that those in the viking army were unlikely to leave their 'savage' past fully behind them and so killing more than eight men did not result in the breakdown of the treaty, while the 'peaceful' English were expected not to kill large numbers of men and doing so was a declaration of war. Such stipulations perhaps fed into Christian ideas of war and peace against a perceived 'other', some of whom were non-Christians, thereby immediately justifying the actions of the English while avowing those of the viking army. Theory aside, it is important to remember that practical considerations usually underpinned strategies for restoring and maintaining peace. Hence, the stipulations likely simply reflected that the English king was prepared to make significant compromises to achieve peace and to retain a useful ally against other, similar, threats. Another possibility is that only Æthelred had jurisdiction that one might consider territorial, from which a man could be physically outlawed. The leaders of the army were just that and could not have outlawed any offender from anything but the army. Hence, the different authority and jurisdiction of the parties is evident, and it seems implied that viewing these offences as 'breaches of the peace' rendered the leaders responsible for them at which point they either could be ousted from the English kingdom or allowed to renew the agreement after suitable atonement. Such an interpretation would render the level of redress on a par with that set for the English, but highlights also that this clause may have acted as a surety against the 'army' splitting up, enabling different leaders to be in or outside the peace. Such practical considerations with regards to redress can be seen in other treaties too. For instance, the *Partition of Benevento* has a number of clauses relating to redress, most of which, unsurprisingly, concern people – whether churchmen, nobles, free men of lower status, or slaves – finding themselves on the 'wrong' side after the division of the principality. The redress in most of these clauses did not centre around equality but rather on returning these people to the part where they belonged or to do justice in some other way if this was not possible.[37] By the time we get into the twelfth century, some treaties have very complex ways of calculating redress; occasionally based on equity if not equality. For instance, the *Treaty of San Salvatore II* between Frederick I and Genoa anticipates that injuries to persons or goods caused by King William I of Sicily would be recovered from Sicilian goods seized by either party. The Genoese would receive one twentieth of all the goods seized, if their loss was that much. If it was less, however, redress would be made in accordance to how much had been lost, determined by an oath of the victims.[38] Most treaties do not have such complex stipulations relating to redress and likely those that have were created for a very particular context. Nevertheless, it highlights that reciprocity in redress does not mean equality or equity, merely that the parties were 'legal equals': that is, parties had an equal right to redress or justice, regardless of any inequality in nature or distribution.[39]

The evidence so far is unequivocal that asking for redress for wrongful acts was an international rule in the medieval period. However, that there was an expectation that redress for wrongs could be sought in the early medieval period, and that this was a rule consistently obeyed, is perhaps most evident from those times that treaties set out that redress should not be expected. For instance, Æthelred II's treaty with three viking leaders and their army recorded that 'all the slaughter and all the harrying and all the injuries which were committed before the peace was established, all of them are to be dismissed, and no one is to avenge it or ask for compensation'.[40] Clauses that wiped the slate clean, as it were – stipulating that all violence, damage, and injury done by one party to another during conflict would be forgotten – are known as amnesty clauses. They have become a hotly debated topic in the contemporary world because they can pit different sources of international law against each other. For instance, amnesty clauses in treaties suspending legal proceedings against individuals, such as military or political leaders, for crimes which might otherwise be sought under the Rome Statute of the International Criminal Court.[41] Randall Lesaffer has argued that amnesty clauses appear with some regularity in treaties from the twelfth century onwards, though this comment is more of a reflection that the issue has not been explored for the earlier medieval period than the appearance of new legal ideas.[42] Nevertheless, one of the most interesting things about amnesty clauses is that by cancelling opportunities for redress, rulers disposed of the rights of individuals, usually without offering any compensation, and this shows a clear concept of princes having the authority and jurisdiction to conclude treaties with other foreign entities: in other words, they were the 'state'. Examining amnesty clauses is thus one of the best ways to understand the rules consistently obeyed because by their very nature they imply that the right to seek redress for injuries and losses suffered during hostility was a general principle of law across Europe in the period 700 to 1200, and that this principle had to be explicitly cancelled for it not to apply.

The treaty between Æthelred and the viking leaders has one of the clearest amnesty clauses from the period before 1200, stating specifically that no one could ask for redress for any offence, injury or loss. Less specific with regards to redress but evidently cancelling all violent and criminal acts committed in conflict is the second *Treaty of Meerssen*, concluded in 851 between the three royal brothers Lothar I, Louis ('the German'), and Charles ('the Bald'). The first clause of this treaty sets out: 'That between us we blot out the evildoing that existed before, and all perpetrators of discords and of rebellions and evil plottings and injurious acts against each other.'[43] Nearly ten years later, this clause was repeated in the *Treaty of Koblenz*, and may also have formed part of the agreement between Louis and Charles concluded at Tusey in 865.[44] Although no eleventh-century treaty seems to have had an amnesty clause, narrative evidence confirms that they continued to be used. The anonymous author of the eleventh-century epic poem *The Ruodlieb* wrote about a treaty concluded between 'the greater' and 'lesser king' (likely referring to the emperor and the king of the Franks), noting that they should 'forget whatever stupidity our people on both sides have committed... Let no one recall what adversity he suffered; let him forget revenge and not think about it.'[45] By the twelfth century, amnesty clauses were seemingly used in treaties across the whole of Europe. For instance, when Alfonso VII of Léon and Castile and Ramon Berenguer IV, count of Barcelona, concluded the *Treaty of Tudején* in 1151, the first clause set out that 'all the complaints and all the claims and all the wrongs' between them would be forgiven ('perdonant').[46] A slightly later example can be found in the *Treaty of Adrianople*, concluded between the two emperors Frederick I and Isaac II Angelos in February 1190 during Frederick's crusade to the Holy Land. It stipulated that 'the Emperor of Constantinople willingly remitted (voluntarie pureque remisit) in full all claims for damages (damnum) with regard to the theft of property, the destruction of towns, the deaths of men and every [other] injury (iniuriam) unexpectedly inflicted upon him'.[47] The 1201 treaty between Llywelyn, prince of Gwynedd (north Wales), and the representatives of King John likewise set out that the king would pardon ('condonabit') all offences ('forisfacta') committed before the peace was concluded.[48] Although the latter two examples seemingly show one-sided dismissal of the principle of redress, as if these were a granting of mercy by a superior power to an inferior, it should be noted that these examples may reflect specific formats and survival of treaties in the twelfth century. The text of the *Treaty of Adrianople* can be deduced from the history of Frederick Barbarossa's crusade, but it has not been copied into the chronicle as a whole and faithful copy of it; lacking a prologue, any dating clause or witness list.[49] Nevertheless, the text seemingly indicates that what the chronicler had seen or heard was the copy drawn up by the emperor of Constantinople as only his obligations are outlined. In England, we know that treaties were frequently issued jointly in the name of the contracting parties and sealed interchangeably until the 1190s, after which they were drawn up in the form of individual letters and subsequently exchanged.[50] From the reign of John (1199–1216), many such outgoing letters were, furthermore, enrolled, and, indeed, the treaty with Llywelyn has survived in this form.[51] Consequently, in both of these cases, we don't know whether or not the other party also dismissed the violence and the opportunity to seek redress, making it very difficult to know exactly how widespread amnesty clauses were. Just as an indication, similar examples of seemingly one-sided amnesty clauses occur also in the *Peace of Constance* of 1183, which formally ended the long conflict between the Emperor Frederick Barbarossa and the cities of the Lombard League, as well as a number of Iberian treaties.[52] By contrast, the treaty between Genoa and Narbonne of 1132 is an example of a treaty with a definite one-sided amnesty clause. This text details not only how all offences ('omnia forisfacta') the Genoese had committed against Viscount Aimery, the archbishop, and the people of Narbonne were forgiven ('perdonarunt'), but also that Aimery made amends ('pro emendandis') for the injuries ('offensis') to the Genoese.[53]

Amnesty clauses appear most frequently in treaties concluded during or following conflicts which we might think of as civil wars or those which had no clear winner.[54] Dealing with redress in such a context could be a particularly tricky issue. In ninth-century Frankia, tradition dictated that fathers distribute lands equally among legitimate sons, and while the Emperor Louis the Pious had been his father Charlemagne's only such surviving heir, Louis himself was survived by three legitimate sons – Lothar, the eldest; Louis the German; and Charles the Bald. This led to prolonged conflicts over the Frankish (or Carolingian) empire between the brothers and their successors throughout the second half of the ninth century. Agreements recording repeated divisions of the kingdoms show, however, that often it was the kings' supporters who were hardest hit by these years of conflict interspersed with attempts at reconciliation. For instance, in 860, Charles the Bald and Louis the German met at the fortress of Koblenz and made a treaty whereby they promised to restore the family lands of those supporters who had defected to the other during the hostilities, on condition that they would be loyal in the future. Charles further undertook to consider restoring any grants of land and *honores* (grants of offices, which often carried lands with them), which he had made to them before they defected.[55] In other words, upon reconciliation, those who had hedged their bets in the conflict – likely tempted by offers and counter-offers of lands and privileges – were in the end left with only their family lands, which according to custom were inalienable. All other grants effectively reverted to the respective kings.[56] Similarly, in the *Treaty of Logroño* (1176), the kings of Castile and Navarre, after a prolonged conflict with no clear winner, agreed that all subjects of the two kings who had 'lost their inherited property (hæreditates) since the time of the commencement of the war, shall recover (recuperent) the same, in such manner as they were holding them on the day on which they lost them'. Here again, subjects only kept that which they had possessed at the point at which conflict broke out, and such property could not be lost through redress of wrongs or misdeeds committed during the conflict.[57] Similar arrangements can be seen in a range of treaties across the period 700 to 1200.[58] That peace and subsequent redress, or lack of, could leave supporters feeling aggrieved is evident from Nithard's comment on the negotiations leading up to the first division of the Frankish empire in the Treaty of Verdun in 843. In the final chapter of the *Histories*, Nithard wrote that everywhere 'dissension and struggle abound'.[59] As argued by Janet Nelson, Nithard's pessimistic view was likely coloured by his own experience of losing lands, which lay in the territories of one of the kings he did not support, and feeling that he had not been adequately compensated for this by the one he did.[60] Geary similarly argued that the reason why those recording the promises of the *Treaty of Koblenz* of 860 were so insistent they should be made in the vernacular was that to a large section of the audience – those most at risk following the peace and who had switched sides – oaths about property that they could understand were 'paramount'.[61]

Redress was clearly a divisive, if crucial, issue in transitioning societies from conflict to peace. Failure by parties to achieve redress was, furthermore, a conflict driver in that it provided an obvious justification for future conflicts. To take one example of this: a letter sent by Pope Gregory VII to the bishops of France about the money that King Philip I had 'extorted' from merchants 'who have lately assembled from many parts of the world at a certain fair in France', stating that if amends were not made it would 'give rise to infinite discord and enmities among many people'.[62] That such failure to achieve redress, coupled with lots of young men whose training and function in life was martial, was a recognised danger is evident from the fact that there are examples of attempts to maintain peace and to divert hostility and violence away from the focal point and location of dissatisfaction with redress. One of the best examples of this can be found in Norway in the midst of what is known as the civil wars period, stretching from 1130 to 1240. The contemporary *Baglar saga* describes how, in 1208, a reconciliation was effected and the Norwegian kingdom was divided into three between the two rival kings Philip and Inge, and the latter's right-hand man, Håkon – likely the real power broker in the proceedings. That the treaty, which has not survived, included an amnesty clause seems certain from the author's statement that it was agreed that 'whatever injuries have been received on either side, whether to people or goods, no one shall demand compensation, vengeance or appropriation for'.[63] The author further reports that the supporters of both kings were unhappy, because many had lost all their money or property in the war.[64] The solution, the men agreed, would be to raid the Orkneys and the Scottish isles to recuperate some of the losses incurred from the partition. The year after, in the summer of 1209, some men from both sides duly took twelve ships and set sail for the joint raid. The plan may have been a good one, but it soon went awry. According to the author of the saga, the men disagreed, were beaten soundly, and returned to Norway in disarray, only to be severely chastised by the bishops for their raiding and violence.[65]

This particular attempt at diverting violence elsewhere may have been unsuccessful, but as a concept, it was one which was tried and tested. It reflects, as an example, how successive civilisations have tried to deal with the problem of mercenaries during peace time. Hired soldiers were often left behind in the peace process, no longer entitled to compensation for losses incurred nor to wages from their employment.[66] As explored in Chapter 2, such displaced groups posed a serious threat to peace and security as they often resorted to self-help in the form of plunder when not employed, and hence they became the targets for legislation as well as condemnation from the Church.[67] Over the course of the Middle Ages, many military alliances and agreements for the hiring of mercenaries consequently came to include payment in land, which then disincentivised men from plunder and ensured an economic basis to their existence even in peace time.[68] However, some treaties concluded after conflict also tried to balance the competing demands between redress and amnesty. One of the best examples of this is the *Treaty of*

Montlouis, which concluded the conflict between King Henry II of England and his son, Henry the Young King, and his supporters in 1174. For instance, both Henry II and Henry the Young King forgave ('remisit'/'perdonavit') each other's supporters for having joined the other side, promising not to bear them any ill will or to do evil to them, and all possessions were to be held as they had been fifteen days before the outbreak of the conflict.[69] In other words, a return to status quo. At the same time, gifts of land that Henry the Young King had given, or would give, to his supporters 'for their services (pro servitio suo)' were confirmed by Henry II, showing an attempt to perhaps offset some of the effects of the amnesty clause to disincentivise further conflict.[70] An earlier example, the second *Treaty of Meerssen* (851), shows that despite having an amnesty clause cancelling material redress, the terms nevertheless required that the kings (Lothar I, Louis the German, and Charles the Bald) acknowledge their wrongdoings publicly before God.[71] This is likely a reflection of the legal dualism between Church and royal power – the two republics, as recently argued by Mayke de Jong – in the ninth century, showing the difficulty of separating the legal, political, and spiritual.[72] Indeed, the kings would have had much to gain from this offsetting of material for symbolic redress. After all, in the Middle Ages, there was no higher legal and moral authority than God, and the support of the Church hence lent added authority, legitimacy, and likely material support, to any king.

Treaties that balance the competing demands of amnesty and redress further give an insight into what war and peace meant on a very practical level. For instance, the division of the duchy of Benevento stipulated that it was lawful ('liceat') for Sikenolf, prince of Salerno, or his men, to go into the territory of Radelchis, prince of Benevento, to seek revenge against enemies to his rule without killing, burning, looting, or devastating the land. And, if it should happen that they committed such acts, the peace would remain intact if justice was done ('Et si contigerit esse factum, pax exinde non disrumpatur, se fit exinde iustitia').[73] In other words, the peace was flexible enough to distinguish between particular offences carried out by certain individuals at specific times and actual breaches of the treaty and peace concluded. A similar stipulation in a treaty between Genoa and the men of Fos of 1138 states that the latter would settle their account ('faciemus rationem') with the Genoese 'for any misdeeds (maleficiis) we have committed against them' at the end of the ten-year treaty,[74] This shows that some treaties were more clearly separating between wrongful acts which were 'criminal' and those which were regarded as warlike.[75] The former could be atoned for without breaking the terms of the treaty, and hence the peace, while the latter could not. However, just as in the *Partition of Benevento*, even breaches of the terms of the treaty were expected to be dealt with through redress rather than force, as the penultimate clause of the treaty makes clear: 'If however by unhappy chance we contravene any of the above, within 40 days of hearing from a Genoese envoy or seeing a sealed letter from the commune we shall make proportionate compensation (emendabimus tantum per tantum).'[76]

Not only do some treaties distinguish between particular wrongful acts committed under the peace concluded, but they also highlight the balancing of the competing demands of peace, amnesty, and redress as perceptions of time and space. As a start, the obvious distinction between war and peace was the point at which the oaths were sworn, with many amnesty clauses either explicitly or implicitly referring to this, by indicating a 'before' and an 'after' point at which the redress rule applied. However, some amnesty clauses show that certain offences were not bound by this time limit. The ninth-century *Partition of Benevento* seems to make a clear distinction between homicide, arson, plunder, and robbery that had been committed in the past (i.e., before the oath of peace), and for which no compensation or vengeance could be exacted, and other prior disputes ('causis anterioribus'), for which justice should be made without delay according to law.[77] The *Treaty of Montlouis*, which concluded the conflict between King Henry II of England and his sons and their supporters in 1174, has a similar clause but almost the reverse in terms of the offences covered. The treaty decreed that those who withdrew from the king and carried away chattels should not be answerable for this act ('ita quod catellis quæ asportaverunt in recessu suo non respondeant'), but for murder, treachery, or maiming of any limb they should answer according to the laws and custom of the land ('respondeant secundum judicium et consuetudinem terræ').[78] Exactly how this worked when one of the first clauses of the treaty also stipulated that both sides cancelled and forgave all displeasure against each

other's supporters promising not to do them any evil (i.e., vengeance), is not entirely clear.[79] Nevertheless, if we think of peace,
amnesty, and redress for legal wrongs as concepts that could be
plotted on a timeline, the swearing of the oaths was manifestly one
marker on it, even if certain stipulations of a treaty operated before
that marker. A second, as mentioned above, was the frequent stipulation in amnesty clauses of the return to some status quo, sometimes counted as fifteen days before the outbreak of hostilities.[80]
Again, exactly how this might have worked is unclear when, for the
majority of these treaties, we don't know exactly at what point or
how a conflict began. It is also possible that such a time limit simply
meant the point at which parties agreed that they had previously
been at peace, or the specific points at which individuals had lost
property regarded as inalienable. For instance, the emperor's oath
agreeing to the *Concordat of Worms* in 1122, stipulated the restoration of possessions seized 'from the beginning of this discord unto
this day, whether in the time of my father [Emperor Henry IV] or in
mine [Emperor Henry V]'.[81] Likewise, the *Treaty of San Salvatore
II* saw Emperor Frederick I promise the Genoese restitution for any
property or person seized by King William I of Sicily, or his men,
counted from Easter Day 1162 when the Genoese had first sought
the agreement with the emperor.[82]

The intersection of war and peace in time was not absolute and
this is further confirmed by looking at peace as a perception of space,
whereby certain areas or communities might not be covered by a
peace or they could be inside or outside it at specific times or under
specific circumstances. As explored briefly in 2011, one example
is the *Treaty of Ivry*. Concluded in 1177 between the English
and French kings, this treaty established a general peace and firm
friendship between Henry II and Louis VII, yet the disputed issues
over land and possessions in Auvergne, Chateauroux and those
in the Berry were specified to be outside the peace.[83] The expectation was that if the kings could not agree over these disputed
areas, an arbitration panel, consisting of an equal number of men
from either side, would decide.[84] Although there were attempts to
resolve matters in these areas, there was also a renewal of hostilities. Despite this, the peace seems to have remained intact and the
treaty was renewed twice in 1180, with the stipulation about the
areas exempted from peace being retained.[85] There could, in other

words, be peace and/or an amnesty declared for a ruler's lands, while at the same time conflict continued in certain areas within it – a sort of isolation of the conflict zone. That this elastic notion of peace was well established can be demonstrated from the large number of treaties with similar stipulations. For instance, the terms of the *Treaty of Toul*, concluded between the French king, Louis VII, and the Emperor Frederick Barbarossa in 1171, applied to the whole of the French kingdom but only to the part of the empire that lay between the Rhine, the Alps, and Paris ('totis terris nostris regni scilicet aut imperii infra Renum et Alpes et civitatem Parisius').[86] As this treaty dealt with the use and expulsion of mercenaries, it is hardly surprising that it applied to an area of the empire known for supplying such paid men nor is it startling that it excluded regions of the empire, such as Italy, where there was, at the time, conflict. In other words, while this was a general peace on the French side, on the imperial side, it was one which was very limited in terms of space and concept.

A more complex notion of peace is found in *II Æthelred*, dating to 994. The text states that a 'woroldfrið' (lit. world peace) had been established between the parties, but exactly what this unique Old English compound meant in time and space is unclear.[87] The clauses within the treaty certainly show that there were a number of ways of perceiving where and how the peace applied. As a start, the treaty was an extension of the terms previously obtained for certain areas – roughly covering Kent, Hampshire, and the south-west of England – by Archbishop Sigeric of Canterbury, and the ealdormen Æthelweard and Ælfric. However, this extension was not defined in space, if we perceive this as territory, but rather it applied to the English king, his people ('leodscipe') and the army ('here') of the three viking leaders; highlighting that this was a period during which kings and princes ruled over people not territory.[88] Clause 3 similarly stipulates that each man to whom the peace applied ('friðmanna') would enjoy it both on land and on water ('ge on lande ge on wætere').[89] Despite this, the treaty demonstrably also mentions specific (territorial) areas that were in or outside the peace. Clause 1.2 refers to any region ('landa') harbouring those harrying England, which would lead to it being outlawed ('utlah') by both the king and the army, while clause 3.1 states that a man, to whom the peace applies ('friðman'), who comes into an area where it does not ('unfriðland'), would still have peace for his ship and goods if the army ('here') came there ('hæbbe frið his scip 7 ealle his æhta'). The area in the first instance was evidently inhabited by the English, hence the use of outlawry, while the second instance might apply both to English or foreign districts. The latter can be seen also in the stipulations that every trading ship ('ceapscip') would have peace, even if it belonged to an area that was not included in it ('unfriðscip'), and that all men and their goods driven ashore from such ships would enjoy peace ('habban ða men frið 7 þæt hy him mid bringað') in any town to which it applied ('friðbyrig').[90] Again, what is obvious from all of these stipulations is that people, places and goods to which the peace applied were entitled to redress; those to which it did not, had no such recourse. This, furthermore, enables the historian to draw one very clear conclusion about treaties and redress; namely, that exclusion from this privilege – in whatever form – was one of the main methods of enforcement.

Enforcing an amnesty, peace, or stipulations of redress that could apply in different areas at different times or in different ways required involving multiple authorities and jurisdictions.[91] Many treaties are clear that the expectancy was that disputes between local communities were resolved locally on a continuous basis, without this breaching any overall peace and without involving the king or other individual(s), who had contracted the treaty. This is seen most clearly in the use of arbitration panels, usually drawing an equal number of men from the communities involved and mainly dealing with implementing and/or enforcing stipulations regarding redress.[92] A range of treaties further show that there could be many other ways of implementing or enforcing stipulations of redress. The *Treaty of Toul*, as an example, sets out that archbishops and bishops should use excommunication if redress for damages caused by mercenaries was not made, and that archbishops, bishops, and lords should march in arms against anyone who refused to comply.[93] The final clause of the treaty notes how to escalate things further: 'If there is a villain so powerful that it is not enough for his neighbours to reduce him, we, if he is of our subject, or the King of France, if he is subject of the king, will take revenge in person and we will march against him as soon as we are called.'[94] In other words, only when the local community could not deal with specific issues would the king be called in. This escalation in terms of enforcement and authority can be seen in a range of other treaties across the period 700 to 1200 too. For instance, treaties with arbitration panels often also have clauses showing that cases could be referred to officials, bishops, and lords, if the arbitration panel failed to agree.[95] Likewise, the tenth-century treaty between King Æthelred and the three viking leaders anticipated that if a breach of the peace ('friðbræc') took place within a town ('byrig'), the townsmen ('buruhwaru') were to deal with the matter. If they would not, the ealdorman would go there and do so, and if he would not, then the king would. If the king did not go, then that region would be excluded from the peace ('licge se ealdordom on unfriðe').[96] A similar stipulation can be found in the *Truce of Venice*, where the cities of the Lombard League and the Emperor Frederick I promised that any person, city, or place that breached the terms of the truce and failed to provide redress in accordance with the judgment of the arbitration panel, would be placed under the ban ('sub banno'), and hence excluded, but the truce as a whole would remain intact.[97] Again, what is evident from these examples is that enforcement was reliant on cooperation and collaboration between different authorities and jurisdictions, and that the ultimate enforcement was not force but rather exclusion from such cooperation and collaboration.[98] In other words, peace ensured communities and individuals were entitled to redress, and the incentive for communities to deal with local disputes was that exclusion from peace would see a return to violence with impunity, disruption to trade, exchange, and community life more generally. Most importantly, the examples discussed here show that the locus of political and legal authority in the early and high Middle Ages was polycentric, multi-layered, and rested upon the oaths of not only subjects to ruler but also the oaths of subjects and communities to adhere to a particular treaty.[99] The *Treaty of Toul*, for example, makes this link explicit by stating that adherence to the terms of the treaty had been sought not only through the oaths of those archbishops, bishops, and magnates present at the conclusion of the treaty, but also through the oaths of those absent who held authority in the particular area where the treaty applied.[100] The *Treaty of Gerberoy*, concluded between King Philip Augustus and Count Philip of Flanders in spring 1182, likewise hints at this, as Henry II of England's announcement of the reconciliation, sets out:

But because the Duke of Burgundy and the Countess of Champagne, and those allied with them were not present to conclude this peace, I should be, on the second Sunday after Easter [11 April 1182], between Senlis and Crepy-en-Valois, where they will come, so that the remaining steps may be taken to finalise this peace and ensure that it remains firm and stable.[101]

Amnesty and redress in treaties evidently express the very complex relationships between war, peace, authority, jurisdiction, and enforcement. However, the fact that redress could be set aside through an amnesty clause further highlights that there is a distinction to be made in treaties between redress for wrongs sustained during conflict or violent episodes and those which are set out for resolving such issues in the future. The vast majority of treaties deal with redress going forward and even treaties with amnesty clauses usually set out some sort of framework by which redress for wrongs could be obtained in the future. For instance, Æthelred's treaty with the viking leaders, which dismissed injuries committed before the treaty was concluded, made clear that going forward anyone robbed of their goods would have them returned and killings of both free men and slaves would be compensated.[102] In other words, to achieve peace, the slate was wiped clean, and to maintain it, the interactions between the English and those in the viking leaders' army were regulated by a similar system of compensations as that which regulated interactions between all of the king's subjects. Similarly, Llywelyn's treaty with King John's representatives stipulated that if Llywelyn or his men committed offences against the king or his men after the peace had been concluded, the king would receive amends ('emendationem recipiet') by the counsel of the representatives who had negotiated the treaty. Llywelyn would, furthermore, provide restitution for damages ('dampna restituet') caused on the king's land and punish the evildoers ('malefactoribus iustitiam faciet').[103] Whether or not these stipulations applied also to offences committed by King John and his men against Llywelyn or on Llywelyn's land is difficult to say as the copy of the agreement intended for John has not survived. This seems likely, however, as future redress was usually made on the basis of reciprocity. By contrast, the *Treaty of Adrianople* does not set out how to deal with future legal redress for wrongful acts. This is perhaps best explained by the fact that the treaty was dealing with the effects of Frederick and his army going through Byzantine lands and hence was not intended to regulate the frequent interactions of communities and the individuals within them. Nevertheless, the fact that the treaty is specific about what offences were dismissed perhaps indicates that redress could be sought for other wrongful acts. For instance, the treaty's dismissal of damages relating to 'the theft of property' would not cover damages to goods sustained by other means.[104]

Agreements that wiped the slate clean in terms of violence and injuries committed during conflict and promoted dealing with redress going forward rather than looking back, can be instructive about those, much fewer, treaties which did provide legal redress following conflict. Take for instance the *Treaty of Milan*, concluded in September 1158 between the Milanese and the German emperor, Frederick I. The text outlines that the citizens were to pay 'nine thousand marks of silver or of gold or in the coinage of the same value and worth' to the emperor or the empress or to the court 'in reparation for damages (pro emendatione iniuriarum)'. The sum was to be paid 'at fixed times: that is, a third within thirty days from the time at which this agreement is confirmed, another third within a week of the festival of the Blessed Martin [November 11], and the third part remaining in the week of Epiphany [6 January]'.[105] As the treaty came about as a result of surrender after a month-long siege, it is clear that these reparations were underpinned and enforced by military might, and that it was this that enabled Frederick to specify the very large sum and how it should be paid. Four years later, the city of Piacenza, an ally of Milan, concluded a similar treaty following its surrender in May 1162: the citizens were to pay 6,000 marks of silver, payable at specific times of the year.[106] While treaties such as these might imply that material redress following conflict was only ever provided at submissions, it is noteworthy that other submission treaties do not always follow this pattern. For instance, the treaty recording the surrender of the city of Rouen to the French king, Philip II, in June 1204 makes no mention of material redress.[107] Furthermore, treaties concluded after conflict but which are not submission treaties retain these parallel features of specified sums payable at specific times of the year. One such example is the *Treaty of Messina* of 1191, which records that in return for the French king, Philip II, releasing Richard I of England from his promise to marry Philip's sister and for relinquishing

his claim to certain properties (including the strategically significant Gisors), Richard would pay 10,000 marks of silver. This was
clearly redress for the slight to Philip's honour and the loss of the
properties, and the sum was payable along comparable lines to the
submission treaties of 1158 and 1162.[108] Nevertheless, it is clear
that the stipulation of one-sided redress presents the historian
with a number of dilemmas, one of which is the extent to which
such one-sidedness should ever be seen as redress. This is bound
up with a much larger debate among scholars, working mainly on
modern periods, on the exact legal meanings of, and differences
between, terms such as 'reparations', 'sovereign debts', 'indemnities', 'sanctions', 'restitutions', and so on, as recently summarised
by Grégoire Mallard:

> The contemporary literature on reparations separates the notions of
> reparation, debt and indemnity. Debts are normal contracts between
> creditors and debtors. Creditor and debtor are purely economic iden-
> tities, which do not preexist the loan contract and do not survive
> after that loan is paid off. In contrast, reparations are not purely
> economic contracts between interchangeable parties. Those who are
> asked to pay reparations have a moral responsibility to pay specific
> groups of people because of past misdeeds.[109]

In other words, to what extent should attempting to right a wrong
committed during a dispute or conflict be seen as something reciprocal (negotiated) rather than one-sided (imposed), as something
purely economic (debt) or as social (reparation)? That the concept
of redress for legal wrongs following conflict and the language of
this redress in modern times are conflated and linked to a range
of different ideologies, philosophies, economic policies, and laws is
perhaps most clearly shown through schemes such as those devised
in the aftermath of the Second World War. The Marshall Plan, for
instance, had the slightly controversial dual aim of aiding recovery
and reconstruction – allied aerial bombing, in particular, having
damaged cities, industrial areas, and transportation infrastruc-
ture – but also preventing the spread of communism.[110] The USSR
by contrast is often perceived as having imposed large reparations
payments on the Axis allies that were in its sphere of influence,
including East Germany, Finland, Hungary, and Romania.[111]
Evidently, a state's perception of being 'victor' or 'vanquished', and

the possibilities and problems with this, are also intertwined with how the concept and language of redress has been approached.

In the medieval period, the language of redress was often imprecise. Indeed, many of the modern English terms ('reparations', 'indemnities', 'sanctions', 'restitutions') are difficult to pin down in the, mainly Latin, treaties forming the basis of this study (hence my adoption throughout this book of the word 'redress'), and distinguishing between them or linking the terminology to specific aspects of redress, whether reciprocal or one-sided, is fraught with problems. In the *Treaty of Milan* (1158), the text is clear that the sum of 9,000 marks was to be paid 'in reparation for damages (pro emendatione iniuriarum)'.[112] Exactly what these damages were is not specified; possibly it referred simply to the slight of honour that Frederick had suffered. Several other treaties, however, show that payments for damages or injuries were often indistinct from other payments intended to buy peace, to have a ruler's mercy, to recover the costs of military campaigns, or just intended to facilitate or regulate trade in some way or another. Take for instance the treaty concluded between the Genoese and the Muslim king of Valencia in 1149. The text states that the king of Valencia, named as Boabdil but likely referring to Yusuf ibn Mardanish or his brother Ibn Mardanish, gave the Genoese 10,000 *marabotini* in order for them to 'establish and confirm peace (pa[cem fir]mant et constituunt)'.[113] The payment was to be given over two years and, in addition, the Valencian king would give 5,000 *marabotini* to the Genoese ambassador, William Lusio, who had negotiated the treaty on behalf of the city. Significantly, and certainly unusually, this treaty makes no mention of the issue of future redress for legal wrongs. Instead, the text emphasises throughout that both parties should offer peaceful treatment to each other's subjects and goods, and not behave with hostility. A slightly earlier treaty between the Genoese and the men of Fos has a similar clause, stipulating that the latter would pay 20 *minae* of corn annually in order to see to the safety and security of men from the Italian city.[114] The lack of reference to redress of any sort make these payments appear more like the tribute demanded at various point by rulers from those deemed of inferior status. However, in these instances, the payments are indistinct from the commercial interests of the Genoese, possibly reinforced by the manner in which the sums were to be paid – in gold, lengths of silk, and corn. Likewise, but almost the exact opposite in terms of language, the *Pactum Sicardi* refers to the tribute ('collatam et pristinam') that would be paid for a period of five years from July 836 by the Neapolitans to Sicard of Benevento for the peace and privileges ('ad firmandam... libertatis et pacis caritatem, per quam vos creditis illesos gubernari'). The treaty entitled Sicard to this payment even if the terms were breached before the five years were up, and the tribute owed could be recovered by seizing pledges, in the same way as was done with regards to redress for legal wrongs.[115] One could speculate then that these payments were intended to buy the type of peace referred to in the *Treaty of Artlenburg*: one that entitled the parties to redress for legal wrongs relating to commercial activities as a default.[116] Like that particular treaty, this might be confirmed in the treaty between Genoa and Fos by the detailed clauses only stipulating redress for 'maleficiis'; that is, acts such as wounding or homicide.[117] In the *Pactum Sicardi*, it can be demonstrated by the fact that merchants were the only ones from whom pledges could not be demanded ('Excepto negotiante: non habeant licentiam pignerandi').[118] Compare these treaties also to the statement in the eleventh-century *Honorantie Civitatis Papie* that an English king would pay fifty pounds of refined silver, two greyhounds, and two each of shields, lances, and swords to the court at Pavia in return for free trade and free movement of people. The author of the same document was even more explicit when he outlined a similar tribute from the Venetians: 'This tribute is called pact (Istud censsum [sic] appellatur pactum) because by it the Venetians are allowed to buy grain and wine in every market town and to make their purchases in Pavia, and they are not to suffer any injury (molestacionem).'[119]

Other treaties and diplomatic documents from the twelfth century show that the Genoese often applied a similar model of payments to parts of cities that had come into their possession through submission. For instance, following the surrender of Almería in 1147, a document was drawn up which granted the lease of the Genoese share of the city for thirty years to Otto di Buonvillano, a Genoese citizen, who in return would pay two *pallia* annually to Genoa and, after the first fifteen years, one half of Almería's import duties.[120] *Pallia* likely referred to garments or lengths of cloths, maybe even silk as in the agreement of 1149.[121] An interesting comment on this word and its link to conflict is offered much earlier in the period by Isidore of Seville. 'The word "spoils" (*spolia*),' he says, 'is from "garments" (*pallium*), as if the word were *expallia* (i.e. "unclothings"), for they are stripped away from the vanquished.'[122] Whether or not Isidore's etymology is correct is not really relevant here, but the fact that he linked the words *pallia* and *spolia* to submission is interesting as this Genoese document, though recorded almost five centuries later, was compiled in that exact context, with the payments evidently intended to be exacted from the citizens and revenues of Almería. There are several documents granting similar leases with regards to the city of Tortosa, which submitted in December 1147, and Hall and Phillips have suggested that the payments in these reflect 'the burden of the debt incurred to finance the expedition to Tortosa'.[123] In other words, these Genoese treaties and diplomatic documents show that once these cities had submitted, costs for injuries, damages, logistics, and so on were recovered from the cities concerned but administered by individuals named in the leases according to terms that are similar to what can be found in some alliances such as the *Treaty of Devol* of 1108 or the *Treaty of Dover* of 1163.[124] This similarity is, for instance, made clearer in the oath taken by Otto di Buonvillano, stating that he would keep 300 men in Almería to protect the Genoese share of the city.[125] In these instances then, payments of tribute or for commerce are used not only to recover costs or losses but also as a flexible way of extending authority and jurisdiction.[126]

There is a myriad of payments in treaties across the period 700 to 1200. For instance, the *Treaty of Azay* of 1189 records how the English king, Henry II, paid the French king, Philip II, 20,000 marks of silver ('Et rex Anglie dabit regi Franci viginti millia marcarum argenti').[127] As is so often the case, the exact nature of any injuries or grievances are not specified in the text. When Henry died just a few days later and was succeeded by his son Richard, who had been allied to the French king against his father, the treaty was renewed but on seemingly the same, or very similar, terms. The text of this renewal has not survived but the contemporary Roger of Howden records how Richard, like his father before him, now refused to concede to Philip's demands to restore to the French king Gisors and various other properties, and instead promptly promised Philip 4,000 marks 'for his expenses', in addition to the already agreed 20,000 marks.[128] However, when Howden, a few years later rewrote this episode for his *Chronica*, he added that the French king restored to Richard everything that he had taken in the war from his father, including castles and other fortified places, as well as cities, vills, and farms.[129] This subtle rewrite makes the payments appear as if they were for the purpose of reciprocal redress, despite the fact that the initial sum had been specified at Henry II's submission, as if it was a payment to have peace and mercy. By contrast, another contemporary, Ralph de Diceto, is quite clear that the original 20,000 marks paid by the English king was to compensate Philip for the great expense he had had for Châteauroux, which was situated in the midst of the conflict zone.[130] Seemingly then, Richard honoured this part of the earlier submission treaty, acknowledging the expense his ally had had in the war, and one could speculate that the additional 4,000 marks was to alleviate the blow of the refusal to restore to the French king properties such as Gisors, thereby smoothing the recognition of Richard as his father's heir to the continental Angevin lands.

Redress following conflict – unlike future redress, which is always stipulated as redress for legal wrongs – could evidently take on a number of forms in treaties, some of which are not always easily recognisable as redress. The point about the language of redress in treaties is hence an expansion of one made by Timothy Reuter many years ago that the exact differences between plunder, tribute, and gifts are not always clear but they were all part of a large-scale 'economic' circulation of goods.[131] He further commented that tribute was essentially institutionalised plunder but still it was in the first instance a *payment*.[132] Redress for legal wrongs could be added to this particular context. If we compare the evidence available in treaties to that from narrative sources, this conflation of the concept and language of redress with other payments for peace/security, tribute, plunder, and gifts becomes even clearer. For instance, the *Royal Frankish Annals* records how in 796 the duke of Friuli sent his men into Pannonia to plunder ('spoliavit') the Avars:

> The duke sent the treasure (thesaurum) of the ancient kings, which had been piled up over many centuries, to the Lord King Charles at the palace of Aachen. After receiving it and thanking God... the Lord's steward, sent Angilbert, his beloved abbot, with a large part of it to

Rome, to the threshold of the apostles. The rest he distributed among his magnates, ecclesiastic as well as lay, and his other vassals.[133]

The mention that part of this plundered treasure was sent to Rome should likely be read in context of the report in 791 that the Avars had committed wrongs against the Holy Church ('nimiam malitiam et intollerabilem... contra sanctam ecclesiam') and that emissaries had been unsuccessful in obtaining redress ('iustitias per missos impetrare non valuerunt').[134] These descriptions of self-help evidently underpin Fedele's comment about the role of reprisals.[135] However, what also emerges clearly in these narrative descriptions is that acts of self-help and reprisals were often justified on legal grounds of an initial wrongful act against the perpetrators. This then established to the reader the distinction that this was lawful redress and not reprisal or plunder, even though the terminology used to describe this in parts says something different. It is, furthermore, important to acknowledge that the terminology often reflects that annalists and chroniclers were writing within an ecclesiastical thought world in which victory – God's judgment – was seen as the best form of peace.[136] Isidore of Seville – a major influence on early medieval intellectual life – commented in his *Etymologies* that victory was 'either the killing or the complete despoiling of the enemy or both', and that such a victory was followed by peace and manifested itself in plunder (*praeda*, *manubiae*), spoils (*exuviae*, *spolia*), and booty-shares (*pars*).[137] In such a context, reprisals to obtain redress for legal wrongs were regarded as God's judgment and the terminology used to describe any payments reflects this.

The description in the *Royal Frankish Annals* does not, of course, pertain to an occasion when a treaty was concluded, but rather to its breakdown and the enforcement of its stipulations. However, many narrative descriptions of treaties concluded show similar problems of distinguishing clearly between different types of payments. To take one example, the eleventh-century chronicler Herman of Reichenau reports on how the German king, Henry III, became embroiled in a dispute with the Hungarians, after supporting their king, Peter, in the dispute over the Hungarian throne. According to Herman, in 1042 King Aba, Peter's rival on the throne, 'pillaged, burned and laid waste the territory of Bavaria on both sides of the Danube', which prompted a series of attacks and counterattacks by King Henry and the Margrave Adalbert of Austria, who was related to Peter by marriage, on the one hand, and King Aba and the Hungarians on the other. The year after, Henry seems to have prepared a larger expedition and now Aba made a treaty ('pactum') with the German king, who received 'satisfactionem, obsides, munera, regnique usque ad Litaha flumen partem accipiens'. I. S. Robinson translated this as 'reparation, hostages, gifts and the part of the [Hungarian] kingdom extending to the River Leitha'.[138] However, it is not at all clear that Herman, or Robinson, intended 'satisfactionem' to mean reparation in a material sense and, if so, the extent to which this might have been different from the gifts and the land. This is problematic when more narrative descriptions of treaties survive than actual treaty documents. While many such narrative descriptions record gifts or payments of tribute as part of the peacemaking process, it is often impossible to establish if these were gifts/tribute/payments (for peace/security/expenses/trade) or redress for whatever wrongs may have been, or might be, committed during a dispute or conflict. This is further compounded by the fact that the types of items that turn up as gifts and tributes are items which in treaties are also paid as redress: silk, gold, silver, cattle, jewels, weapons, and so on.[139] The language of redress in both documents and narratives are hence closely linked to the aims, wishes, and perceptions of the authors, their patrons, and the parties, highlighting that the various payments and concepts resulting from or caused by war and peace were a conflation of the economic, cultural, legal, and social.

While terminology and language can be revealing about the lack of distinction between redress and other interlinked concepts, they can also highlight much about the forms of actual redress in treaties. Modern international law sets out that reparation should take the form, singly or in combination, of restitution (restoration of the situation which existed before the act was committed), compensation (reparation by equivalent), or satisfaction ('an acknowledgment of the breach, an expression of regret, a formal apology, or another appropriate modality').[140] This alerts us to the fact that legal redress is not only material but also symbolic. For the medieval period the difference between material and symbolic redress is frequently expressed in the historiography of conflict resolution more generally as the difference between resolving conflicts in court through fines and compensations – a judicial or legal approach – or out-of-court settlements, often resulting in symbolic satisfaction – an extra-judicial or 'ritual' approach.[141] Gerd Althoff has examined one such symbolic satisfaction in the form of submission or ritual surrender, known as *deditio*, arguing that it was not legal norms but habits that had their place in social life. That is, it was conventions or general norms of behaviour that played a decisive role in regulating conflicts among members of the ruling class.[142] With regards to international conflicts, the attention has firmly been on symbolic redress, with many studies focusing on the symbolic gestures accompanying narrative descriptions of the conclusion of agreements.[143] However, treaties represent perhaps the clearest expression of the 'legal' aspect of international conflicts, yet stipulations within them are less clear that contemporaries distinguished between the judicial and the extra-judicial, between the material and the symbolic, in the way modern historians have. Some twelfth-century treaties seem to draw a dividing line between the two. For instance, the *Treaty of Toul* records how Frederick Barbarossa and Louis VII agreed that anyone employing mercenaries would be excommunicated until he had provided restitution according to an estimate of damage ('ad probationem suam restituat'), and, additionally, had made fitting amends to his bishop ('dignam faciat emendationem'). This difference in the language of redress is retained in the next line of the treaty stating that the archbishops, bishops, and lords would march in arms against him and ravage his land until he had provided restitution ('fuerit restitutum') and made fitting amends ('digne fuerit emendatum') to the lord of the land.[144] In both lines, the first phrasing more clearly refers to material reparations while the second plausibly referred to the symbolic aspect, with that made to the bishop meaning penance while that to the secular lord indicating *deditio* or one of the many other forms of providing symbolic redress including homage, fealty, clasping of hands, or giving/exchanging the kiss of peace.[145] Having said this, at a local level, *emendare/emendatio* could be used to indicate a fine, paid to the lord or bishop, in addition to the compensation paid to a victim.[146] It is possible that this might also have been the meaning in this treaty. Nevertheless, the last line in this section of the treaty seems to make clear that what was meant was symbolic rather than material redress when it states that he who has taken these brigands into his service cannot judge or swear in any court or in any dispute, until he has provided satisfaction for that which he has caused ('rem emendaverit').[147] The use of *emendare* rather than *restituere* here shows that it was the public gesture of acknowledging the wrong which would transition a wrongdoer from conflict to peace, enabling him to be received back into the Christian community and resume his full societal duties and rights.[148]

In the *Treaty of Toul* the language of redress then seems to make a distinction between symbolic and material redress. However, many treaties use less precise language of redress and in some treaties the language of redress had a slightly different legal (and procedural) context. For instance, the *Partition of Benevento* has a clause stipulating that those of Prince Radelchis' men who had committed homicide in the part belonging to Prince Sikenolf would be handed over to the latter. If they were unwilling to give satisfaction ('si satisfacere non fuerint ausae'), they would pay ('componam') Sikenolf 3,000 gold byzants for 'nobilibus' and for 'rusticis' they would 'pay according to the law (fiat compositio secundum legem)'.[149] That the latter part of this clause referred to material redress is evident, but the 'satisfaction' in the first part of the sentence may at first glance appear to refer to more symbolic redress. This is, for instance, how scholars dealing with dispute resolution at the lower levels of society have frequently viewed this particular word and its derivatives.[150] A careful reading, however, reveals that the expectation here was that if the person killed was 'nobilibus', satisfaction would be made with three people ('satisfaciant illud tres personae'), whosoever Sikenolf would choose, and if the killed was 'rusticis', with three people from the location where the killing had taken place ('tres personae de ipso loco, ubi homicidum fuit perpetratu'). This is unlikely to refer to making satisfaction in the sense of symbolic or material redress for committing a wrongful act, but rather it refers to the procedure of defending the accusation of having committed a wrong. In other words, the treaty anticipated that anyone accused of homicide would defend themselves with three compurgators, and if they could not, or dared not, then material redress would be made. Using the word *satisfacere* in this sense clearly follows usage in the Lombard laws, where, as an example, 'satisfaciat ad Evangelia' referred to offering an oath on the Gospels.[151]

While satisfaction has long been acknowledged as an important feature of symbolic redress at different levels of medieval society, the *Partition of Benevento* shows that it can be tricky to use the language and terminology in treaties to make a distinction between material and symbolic redress.[152] Looking beyond the issue of language, it is evident that the expectations of both material and symbolic redress in the *Treaty of Toul* reflect actual practice after conflict. To take one example, the *Treaty of Constantinople* of 945, in which the Byzantine emperor and the prince of the Rus' declares that a poor man should make amends even with the clothes on his back until he could declare he had nothing left.[153] Although this clause evidently expected payment in the material, the image presented is also reminiscent of many apology rituals, constructed to publicly shame the perpetrator. Since victims of violent behaviour had suffered publicly, the only way to even out this humiliation was to publicly shame the perpetrator too.[154] This treaty then clearly combines material with symbolic redress. A later example, the *Treaty of Milan* (1158) refers both to the money the Milanese promised to pay the Emperor Frederick I in reparation for damages ('pro emendatione iniuriarum'), and to the emperor, by the terms of the treaty, receiving the city back into his favour ('in gratiam suam recipiet') and publicly absolving the citizens from the ban ('publice a banno absolvet').[155] Similarly, in July 1189, having suffered catastrophic defeat, the English king, Henry II, renewed his homage to the French king ('rex Anglie iterum fecit homagium regi Francie'), restoring Philip as his lord ('quia ipse... reddiderat regem Francie dominum suum'), and agreed to pay him 20,000 marks of silver ('Et rex Anglie dabit regi Franci viginti millia marcarum argenti').[156] This evidence hence shows that the distinction between material and symbolic redress – frequently espoused in the historiography as the difference between the 'ritual' and 'legal' aspects of conflict resolution – is artificial. Both formed an essential part of the process of how individuals and communities transitioned from conflict to peace and can be seen in a much wider context of what, since 1945, has become known as transitional justice.[157] Much of the literature on transitional justice in the contemporary world approaches the topic from either a 'peace-building' or a 'judicial' perspective, from whether what is aimed for is retributive or restorative justice. Often, it highlights the frustration created by the imbalance between the policies and practice of transitional justice by governments and institutions, and the understanding of the key concepts of truth, justice, peace, and reconciliation at different levels by different stakeholders.[158] In essence then, these debates – whether over the transitional justice process in the contemporary or the medieval period – are frequently about enforcement and the nature and effectiveness of the 'state'.[159]

The extent to which the international legal rules may have been consistently obeyed is the most difficult part to assess, and it is a notion that goes right to the heart of the question about effectiveness or enforcement. Medieval writers were often more interested in law-breaking because obedience was not newsworthy, and indeed this is often noted also about obedience of modern-day international rules.[160] Moreover, in the ecclesiastical thought-world inhabited by chroniclers, writing providential history was the order of the day and the breaking of oaths is frequently commented upon because it was followed by divine retribution.[161] The problem with our evidence aside, we should consider carefully how useful the notion of effectiveness or enforcement is with regards to international law, because it is not the only facilitator or controller of 'state' conduct, nor is it designed to be. Indeed, the practice of international law is fundamentally linked to diplomacy, politics, and the conduct of foreign relations. Scholarly ideas about effectiveness and enforcement are often problematic because they insist that legal rules only affect behaviour when they are enforced, and they, furthermore, adopt an excessively narrow conception of law enforcement as something done violently, i.e., through the threat and exercise of physical force.[162] Hershey, to take one example, in his survey of international relations during antiquity and the Middle Ages, argued that in spite of legal forms and customary law, international relations in the early medieval period were 'mainly controlled by brute force or regulated violence'.[163] The literature on enforcement is almost unanimously focused on violence because following the Weberian theory of the state, having monopoly over violence means that dishing it out is punishment for disobedience. In the period covered by this book, while one could argue that there was a notion of the state, there was no monopoly on violence nor on authority and jurisdiction, and this has often been the linchpin of why international law cannot have existed in the Middle Ages.[164] Between 700 and 1200 there were times when certain entities (whether we think of this as kings, communities, or cities) perhaps came close to achieving the Weberian ideal, but primarily the period is best characterised as a curious nexus of competing, as well as complementing, authorities and jurisdictions; a period when the distinction between war and peace, or between the local and the international, was more blurred than usual.[165] In such a context, and quite aside from the problems with our evidence, a one-size-fit-all approach to enforcement does not work. In other words, if the only enforcement one is willing to recognise is that characterised by violence by state institutions, then international law will always look pretty ineffective.[166]

By contrast, if we perceive of enforcement through a multi-faceted perspective, accepting that any medieval polity was polycentric with many competing authorities and jurisdictions whose power to influence and cajole adherence to treaties fluctuated, it is possible to point to certain enforcement procedures, such as the loss of legal rights and privileges, i.e., exclusion from redress. Enforcement by violence was not absent, of course, but as the ruler could not be everywhere at once, nor had the capacity to wage anything near what we might think of as 'total war', a flexible approach to peace, authority, and jurisdiction enabled a ruler to pursue lots of different strategies, targeted at different levels of society or aspects of the matter in dispute at specific times. Genoa's complex relations and treaties with the rulers of Arborea are clear examples of this, as they show a myriad of enforcement strategies centred on granting/removing privileges and land, but also involved an offensive alliance (*Treaty of Ardara*) with the neighbouring ruler of Torres, Constantine, if the Arboreans failed to keep their commitments.[167] Moreover, enforcement and the transition from conflict to peace was (and is) a long process. Even violent enforcement requires moderation and other strategies for returning communities and society as a whole to peace. The various treaties concluded in the aftermath of the so-called 'great rebellion' of 1173–4, which involved not only King Henry II of England and his sons but also a whole host of other princes, and the treaties concluded as part of the Peace of Venice in 1177, reconciling the Emperor Frederick I and his allies to Pope Alexander III and his allies, are good examples of this.[168] Despite the victories of Henry II and of the Lombard League, all treaties resulting from these two instances show that the return to peace was all about balancing the competing demands of peace, amnesty, and redress across a long time span, with the *Peace of Constance* (1183) and the *Treaty of Ivry* (1177) and the *Treaty of Canterbury* (1189) highlighting that the return to formal peace in some instances took years.[169] Most importantly, thinking of enforcement as a long and multi-faceted process explains why most treaties, or the majority of terms within treaties, are forward-looking: international law was underpinned by parties' willingness to participate, to collaborate, to cooperate, and to assume obligations. This is further confirmed by the most common forms of guaranteeing treaties in the medieval period – oaths, hostages and sureties, and the fostering of peaceful relations – all of which relied on shared cross-cultural values, reinforced by social cooperation and collaboration.[170]

That enforcement did not necessarily mean violence can be seen from one of the most famous examples of conflict, namely the break-down of relations between the Mercian king, Offa, and the Frankish king, Charles the Great, in the 790s. According to the anonymous author of the *Deeds of the Abbots of St Wandrille*, Charlemagne had imposed an embargo on traders from Britain apparently after becoming annoyed over Offa's request to marry his son, Ecgfrith, to Charlemagne's daughter, Bertha.[171] The *Deeds* claims that Charlemagne 'gave the command that no-one from the island of Britain or the people of the Angles was to set foot on the shores of Gaul for the purposes of trade'.[172] The existence of the trade embargo is confirmed in the letters of Alcuin, who was a Northumbrian churchman at Charlemagne's court.[173] In 790 Alcuin wrote to the Irish monk Colcu explaining that Offa had also imposed his own embargo on traders from Francia and now 'on both sides the passage of ships has been forbidden to merchants and is now ceasing'.[174] The full impact of the dispute is not known, but as noted by Neil Middleton 'its political and commercial consequences may have been far-reaching'.[175] For instance, it was likely a factor in the introduction of a new type of coinage by Offa, and also in the reform of the Carolingian coinage, both of which have been dated to this time.[176] While we do not know how or when the embargo ended, it must have been before 796 when Charlemagne sent a very famous letter to Offa setting out a new trade treaty. This particular letter mentions both the length of the black stones, which Charlemagne was sending, and the length of the cloaks or possibly cloth, which Offa was offering to trade in return.[177] Nevertheless, what is clear is that there was an initial agreement between the two kings for merchants to trade freely and that when relations broke down, the agreement was enforced, not by violence, but by the withdrawal of the privileges to trade freely.[178] In this instance, enforcement by violence would, moreover, have provided significant logistical challenges and costs. Although no original treaty between Offa and Charlemagne survives, it is evident that the use of the trade embargo is indicative of the expected enforcement of many treaties.[179]

Any discussion of enforcement and the effectiveness of international law is likely to be controversial. It is an important discussion to have, yet it also fires wide of the mark of determining the extent to which international rules were consistently obeyed. International law could simply be considered as a 'system of law' not because it could be enforced but because it is accepted as such by the community to whom it is addressed.[180] As shown in various ways throughout this chapter, redress for legal wrongs was clearly the default mode of most treaties as well as of peace more generally. This recognition by the contracting parties of treaties, the individuals and communities named in them, is enough to show that most international rules were consistently obeyed and, therefore, that it is possible to speak of international law in the period 700 to 1200. That the acceptance of, and compliance with, international rules were linked to notions of morality, honour, and reputation is evident from the justifications used when breaking one of these rules, and it is to these we must now turn.

Notes

1 Scholars have paid significant attention to levels of compensation and injury lists in domestic laws, which have seen studies from a perspective of language, legal anthropology, material culture, medicine, and textual transmission to name but a few. For examples, see Lisi Oliver, *The Body Legal in the Barbarian Laws* (Toronto, 2011); Han Nijdam, *Lichaam, eer en recht in middeleeuws Friesland: Een studie naar de Oudfriese boeteregisters*, 2 vols. (Hilversum, 2008); Lambert, *Law and Order in Anglo-Saxon England*, especially chs. 1–2; Stefan Esders, 'Wergeld und soziale Netzwerke im Frankenreich', in *Verwandtschaft, Name und soziale Ordnung (300–1100)*, eds. Steffen Patzold and Karl Ubl (Berlin, 2014), 141–60; Helle Vogt, *The*

Function of Kinship in Medieval Nordic Legislation (Leiden, 2010), especially ch. 10.

2 James Crawford, 'The System of International Responsibility', in *The Law of International Responsibility*, eds. James Crawford, Alain Pellet, and Simon Olleson (Oxford, 2010), 20.

3 *Lamperti Monachi Hersfeldensis Opera*, ed. O. Holder-Egger, *MGH SRG*, 38 (Hanover, 1894), 80. Translation from *The Annals of Lampert of Hersfeld*, tr. I. S. Robinson (Manchester, 2015), 82.

4 Tilman Struve, 'Lampert von Hersfeld. Persönlichkeit und Weltbild eines Geschichtsschreibers am Beginn des Investiturstreits', *Hessisches Jahrbuch für Landesgeschichte*, 20 (1970), 32–142, esp. 50; Harald Dickerhof, 'Wandlungen im Rechtsdenken der Salierzeit am Beispiel der lex naturalis and des ius gentium', in *Die Salier und das Reich*, 3 vols., ed. Stefan Weinfurter (Sigmaringen, 1991), iii, 447–76, esp. 451–4. For a summary in English of Lampert's education and use of Livy, see *The Annals of Lampert of Hersfeld*, 6–9.

5 The Emperor Henry IV's oath at Canossa in 1077 was centred on a promised to do justice ('iustitiam… faciam') in complaints against him and his conduct. Gregory VII, *Registrum IV*, 12a, in *MGH Epp. sel. 2.1*, ed. E. Caspar (Berlin, 1920), 314–15. Translation in *Imperial Lives and Letters of the Eleventh Century*, tr. Theodore E. Mommsen and Karl F. Morrison (New York, 2000), 156.

6 *Treaty of Rouen* (991).

7 *Colección diplomática del Monasterio de Sahagún (857–1300)*, 4 vols., ed. J. A. Fernández Flórez (León, 1991), iv, no. 1263.

8 London, British Library Cotton Augustus II, 18. Printed as 'Letter of Wealdhere, Bishop of London, to Brihtwold, Archbishop of Canterbury (704–705)', available at http://esawyer.org.uk/charter/1428b.html [accessed: 18 October 2017]. Translation in *EHD, I*, no. 164.

9 Note that the third category will not be separately discussed in this chapter, primarily because the issues surrounding redress are those encountered also in the first category. A wider study on these 'other' in society, including slaves, based on the evidence in treaties would, however, be worth pursuing but is outside the scope of this study.

10 *AGu*, c. 2: 'gif man ofslægen weorðe… VIII healfmearcum asodenes goldes… buton ðam ceorle ðe on gefollande sit 7 heora liesengum… CC scill.'

11 *AGu*, c. 3.

12 *AGu*, c. 3.

13 *Treaty between Genoa and Pavia* (1140), cc. 4–5. The mention of money being 'brune' is a reference to the refined metal content. I am grateful to Judith Green for highlighting this to me.

14 For instance, *AGu* used considerably higher levels of compensation than Alfred's domestic laws, while *Dunsæte* uses lower than those found for comparable offenses in domestic laws.

15 *Partition of Benevento*, c. 20. Both 'nobilibus' and 'rusticis' might be umbrella terms perhaps distinguishing simply between free and unfree men. However, it is equally possible that the distinction is between the highest rank of men ('nobilibus') and everyone else, free and unfree ('rusticis'). It is also noteworthy that elsewhere in the treaty (cc. 14–15), slaves and half-free are specifically termed *servi, ancillae* and *aldii*, which corresponds more closely to what we know about social status from the laws, while others are simply referred to as 'men' (*homines*), presumably meaning all free men. On social class in Lombard society, see *The Lombard Laws*, 28–31.

16 On composition more generally, see *The Lombard Laws*, 27–8. The next sentence in the treaty makes it clear that with regards to homicide, everything should be done as decreed in the laws ('sicut in lege nostra sancitum est'). For the relevant stipulations in the Lombard laws, see *Rothair's Edict*, cc. 1–2, 10–14, 75, 129–37; *The Laws of King Liutprand*, cc. 13, 17, 20–1, 62, 92, 97, 138; *The Laws of King Ratchis*, c. 7; *The Laws of King Aistulf*, c.15.

17 *Pact between Naples and Benevento*, c. 5: 'De omnibus vero aliis causis... iudicavimus... secundum legem Romanorum aut Langobardorum...' On the juridical dualism of southern Italy, see Storti, 'Ascertainment of Customs and Personal Laws', 257–65 (esp. 258); Walter Pohl, 'Memory, Identity and Power in Lombard Italy', in *The Uses of the Past in the Early Middle Ages*, eds. Yitzhak Hen and Matthew Innes (Cambridge, 2000), 9–28; Antonella Ghignoli and François Bougard, 'Elementi romani nei documenti longobardi?', in *L'héritage byzantin en Italie (VIIIe-XIIe siècle). I. La fabrique documentaire*, eds. J.-M. Martin, A. Peters-Custot, and V. Prigent (Rome, 2011), 241–301. There is also an unpublished PhD thesis on the subject: Sonia Colafranceso, 'Interferenze e commistioni tra diritto longobardo e diritto romano-bizantino nei documenti del *Codex diplomaticus Cavensis*' (University of Chieti-Pescara, 2016).

18 E.g., *Rothair's Edict*, cc. 175, 184; *The Laws of King Liutprand*, cc. 43, 54, 73; *The Laws of King Aistulf*, c. 12.

19 E.g., *Treaty of Pavia*, c. 9, stipulating that theft is paid with four-fold compensation, which is from Justinian's *Institutes* IV.1.5. Many similarities are noted in *MGH Capit. II*, no. 233 (pp. 130–35). Cf. *Treaty of Lerici*, c. 3, between Genoa and Lucca, recording redress was to be made according to Roman law ('secundum romanas leges').

20 *Treaty of Rialto* (933), c. 2: '...qui in contra legem factum haberet, secundum sententiam pacti emendaret'.

21 *Treaty of Pavia*, c. 1. The two-fold compensation also existed in Roman law, as well as a number of early medieval laws, including the laws of Æthelberht of Kent. *Digest*, 47: 2.46,1; *Abt*, cc. 6–8.

22 *Dunsæte*, cc. 1, 1.1. As noted by Molyneaux, the period of nine days may be taken from Welsh legal tradition, as this same number dominates the so-called *Law of Hywel Dda* but has no equivalent in the English laws of the tenth or early eleventh century. *The Law of Hywel Dda. Law Texts Translated from Medieval Wales*, tr. Dafydd Jenkins (Llandysul, 1986), Bk. II, c. 6 (pp. 47, 54, 83–4, 88, 96, 101–2); Molyneaux, 'The *Ordinance Concerning the Dunsæte*', 270. On cattle-tracking, with references to both English and continental laws, see Carole Hough, 'Cattle-tracking in the Fonthill Letter', *EHR*, 115 (2000), 864–92.

23 *Dunsæte*, c. 2.2: 'Of ægðran stæðe on oðer man mot badian, bute man elles riht begytan mæge'; *Treaty of Pavia*, c. 13: 'quodsi post primum et secondam contestationem minime reddita fuerint, tunc proveniat pigneratio de loco, ubi hoc requiritur, usque dum pars parti satisfatiat; et post satisfactionem ipsa pignera reddantur'.

24 Dante Fedele, 'Indemnities in Diplomacy', in *The Encyclopedia of Diplomacy*, ed. Gordon Martel (London, 2018).

25 The evidence in treaties should here be set against the literary evidence, which often highlight amicable aspects of cross-border community relations, such as the statement in the eleventh-century German epic *Ruodlieb*: 'They went to each other's countries to purchase whatever they wanted, sometimes paying the toll and sometimes collecting it. Our girls married their men, and they gave us their daughters in marriage. They became mutual godparents and those who were not were called so.' *The Ruodlieb*, tr. Gordon B. Ford (Leiden, 1965), 17. Many studies of cross-border communities highlight such interactions. For two examples in English, see D. J. Power, *The Norman Frontier in the Twelfth and Early Thirteenth Centuries* (Cambridge, 2004), esp. 242–62; Michael Fordham, 'Peacekeeping and Order on the Anglo-Welsh Frontier in the Early Tenth Century', *Midland History*, 32 (2007), 1–18. On reprisals as justification, see Chapter 4, pp. 153–63.

26 On such arbitration panels, see Chapter 1, pp. 35–6; Chapter 5, pp. 202–4.

27 *Treaty of Gisors* (1180), c. 9. The same clause is also found in the *Treaty of Ivry* (1177), for which see Howden, *Gesta*, i, 193.

28 Other examples, with dates in brackets, include *Pactum Sicardi* (836), prol.; *Treaty of Pavia* (840), c. 17; *Cn 1027*, c. 6; *Treaty between Sergius VII of Naples and Gaeta* (1129), c. 1; *Treaty between Genoa and the men of Fos* (1138); *Treaty of San Lorenzo* (1155); *Truce of Venice* (1177); *Treaty of Novgorod* (1189x1199).

29 *Treaty of Artlenburg*, prol: '...Gutenses pacem firmam habeant, ita ut, quisquid diependii rerum suarum seu iniurie infra terminos nostri regiminis pertulerint, plenam ex iudicaria potestate nostrum iusticiam et correctionem consequantur...' Cf. *Treaty of Genoa* (1165).

30 *II Æthelred*, c. 4: 'Gyf man beo æt his æhtan bereafod, 7 he wite of hwilcum scipe, agyfe steoresman ða æhta...'

31 *Treaty of Pavia*, c. 13.

32 *LIRG*, vol. 1/2, 56: 'Si nostri homines aliquid illi vel suis abstulerunt, faciemus eis reddere vel plenariam eis faciemus iusticiam.'

33 *RPC*, 76.

34 *DD FI*, ii, 222. Note that the treaty never specifies what offence elicited such action, merely that a complaint ('queremoniam') had to be raised.

35 This link is well established for redress in domestic laws, for which see John Hines, 'Units of Account in Gold and Silver in Seventh-Century England: *Scillingas, Sceattas* and *Pæningas*', *The Antiquaries Journal*, 90 (2010), 153–73; John Hines, 'Erratum – Units of Account in Gold and Silver in Seventh-Century England: *Scillingas, Sceattas* and *Pæningas*', *The Antiquaries Journal*, 91 (2011), 397–8; Christoph Kilger, 'Silver, Land, Towns, and the Elites. Social and Legal Aspects of Silver in Scandinavia c. 850–1150', in *Nordic Elites in Transformation c. 1050–1250. Volume I: Material Resources*, eds. Bjørn Poulsen, Helle Vogt, and Jón Viðar Sigurðsson (London, 2019), 130–60. More generally, on law and materiality, but with implications for how historians might approach the study of redress, see Tom Johnson, 'Medieval Law and Materiality: Shipwrecks, Finders, and Property on the Suffolk Coast, ca. 1380–1410', *AHR*, 120 (2015), 407–32; Daniel Lord Smail, *Legal Plunder. Households and Debt Collection in Late Medieval Europe* (Cambridge, MA, 2016).

36 *II Æthelred*, cc. 5.2, 7.1.

37 E.g., *Partition of Benevento*, cc. 6, 15, 16, 21, 22.

38 *DD FI*, ii, 222–3.

39 On 'legal equals', see also Chapter 1, pp. 22–3.

40 *II Æthelred*, c. 6.1: 'Æt eallum slyht 7 æt ealre ðære hergunge 7 æt eallum ðam hearmum, ðe ær ðam gedon wære, ær ðæt frið geset wære, man eall onweig læte 7 nan man þæt ne rece ne bote ne bidde.' Note that the Latin version replaced OE 'hearmum', meaning 'injuries', for 'incendiis', here clearly referring to 'burning' or 'arson'. The close resemblance in wording of this treaty to how the author(s) of the two versions of Baglarsaga recorded the treaty of 1208 between the rival claimants of the Norwegian throne is noteworthy: 'hues skade som deris undersaatte hafde faaet paa begge sider, paa folck eller gods,

skulle ingen kræfue bod, vederlag eller opretning fore'/ 'þá skyldu hvárigir hefna, né heimta gjǫld fyrir. Svá um fjárupptektir, hvárir sem tekit hǫfðu' ('whatever injuries have been received on either side, whether to people or goods, no one shall demand compensation, vengeance or appropriation for'); *Bǫglunga Sǫgur*, ii, 117.

41 A clear outline of the problem, relating specifically to the 2012 framework for peace to end the conflict between the Colombian government forces and the Revolutionary Armed Forces of Colombia (FARC), can be found in Juan Carlos Portilla, 'Amnesty: Evolving 21st Century Constraints Under International Law', *The Fletcher Forum of World Affairs*, 38 (2014), 169–94. See also Scott W. Lyons, 'Ineffective Amnesty: the Legal Impact on Negotiating the End to Conflict', *Wake Forest Law Review*, 47 (2013), 799–842; Josepha Close, *Amnesty Serious Crimes and International Law. Global Perspectives in Theory and Practice* (Abingdon, 2019), esp. ch. 1; Michael P. Scharf, 'From the eXile Files: An Essay on Trading Justice for Peace', *Washington and Lee Law Review*, 63 (2006), 339–76, esp. 342–7; Leila Sadat, 'Exile, Amnesty and International Law', *Notre Dame Law Review*, 81 (2006), 955–1036; Heinhard Steiger, 'Peace Treaties from Paris to Versailles', in *International Law in European History. From the Late Middle Ages to World War One*, ed. Randall Lesaffer (Cambridge, 2004), 59–102, esp. 84–7; Naomi Roht-Arriaza, *Impunity and Human Rights in International Law and Practice* (Oxford, 1995).

42 Randall Lesaffer, 'Wiping the Slate Clean… for Now: Amnesty Clauses in Early-Modern Peace Treaties', available at https://opil.ouplaw.com/page/amnesty-peace-treaties (accessed 16 July 2021). Amnesty clauses have been seen as originating in the late medieval scholarship on the doctrines of just and legal war (*jus ad bellum* and *jus in bello*), themselves based on Book XIX of St Augustine's *City of God*. In light of the existence of such clauses in treaties from the earlier period, a review of this debate is now needed.

43 *Treaty of Meerssen* (851), c. 1: 'Ut omnium preteritorum malorum et contrarietatum et supplantationem ac malarum machinationum atque molitionum seu nocumentorum in invicem actorum abolitio ita inter nos.'

44 *Treaty of Koblenz*, c. 1. The annalist of Fulda seems to anticipate a similar clause with the meeting in 864 (for 865) at Tusey (near Toul), where Louis and Charles 'agreed to forgive each other (sibi mutuo dimittunt) whatever they had done as a result of human frailty or the urgings of their soldiers, thinking that the past should be forgotten'; *AF*, 62 (52). However, the *Treaty of Tusey*, as it has come down to us, does not have such a clause.

45 *The Ruodlieb*, 32.
46 *Treaty of Tudején*, c. 1: 'omnes querimonias et omnes clamores ac omnes offensas quas inter se quolibet modo usque hodie habuerunt... sibi indulgent et perdonant'.
47 *Treaty of Adrianople*, c. 1.
48 *Treaty between Llywelyn and King John's representatives*, c. 4.
49 *Historia de Expeditione*, 64–6. Translation in *CFB*, 90–2.
50 Benham, *PMA*, 188–9.
51 Pryce, *The Acts of Welsh Rulers*, 373–4
52 *Peace of Constance*, prol., c. 15.
53 *Treaty between Genoa and Narbonne*, cc. 1, 4.
54 Colombia provides a contemporary example of this, for which see Portilla, 'Amnesty', 169–71.
55 These stipulations can be found in the part of the *Treaty of Koblenz* recording the oath of Charles the Bald, for which see *MGH Capit. II*, 158.
56 On this, see the short discussion by Janet L. Nelson in ' "A King Across the Sea": Alfred in Continental Perspective', *TRHS*, 36 (1986), 53–4. The practice here seems slightly different to that summarised by Randall Lesaffer for the early modern period, for which see his 'Peace Treaties', 89.
57 Howden, *Gesta*, i, 142–3: 'Et pro malefacto vel judicio quod hactenus fecissent, eas non perdant, nec infra istos septem annos pro aliqua querimonia ulli respondeant.'
58 E.g., *Partition of Benevento* (849), cc. 18, 21; *Treaty of Montlouis* (1174) in Howden, *Gesta*, i, 77.
59 Nithard, *Histoire*, 144 (174).
60 Janet L. Nelson, 'Public Histories and Private History in the Work of Nithard', *Speculum*, 60 (1985), 271–3.
61 Geary, 'Oathtaking and Conflict Management', 247–8.
62 Gregory VII, *Registrum II*, 5, in *MGH Epp. sel.* 2.1, 130–1; *The Register of Pope Gregory VII*, 97–8. Gregory seems to have been particularly concerned about Philip I despoiling merchants and pilgrims, as evidenced also by Gregory VII, *Registrum II*, 18, 150–1; *The Register of Pope Gregory VII*, 112.
63 *Bǫglunga Sǫgur*, ii, 117. Note the similarity of this wording to that of the amnesty clause in *II Æthelred*, for which see above pp. 130–1.
64 The two versions of the saga respectively record this as that the men 'hafde mist alt deris gods oc pendinge i den feide'; 'er félausir varu ok hǫfðu þó nafnbœtr'. *Bǫglunga Sǫgur*, ii, 117–18.
65 Ibid., ii, 118–20.
66 See, as an example, William of Newburgh's comments on this issue in the middle of the twelfth century, following the conflict during

King Stephen's reign. *William of Newburgh, The History of English Affairs, Book II*, eds. P. G. Walsh and M. J. Kennedy (Oxford, 2007), 14–15 (Bk. II, cc. 1–2).

67 See Chapter 2, pp. 65–9.

68 For some examples, see *Treaty of Dover* (1163) and the accompanying document setting out the service owed for the amount of land held ('servitii... debent Henrico regi Anglorum sicut domino pro feodis que de ipso habent'; *Dip. Docs*, I, 12–13). It is possible to argue that also the *Treaty of Melfi* falls into this category as the pope promised to recognise Robert Guiscard as duke of Sicily if he managed to conquer the island, and the renewal of the alliance in the *Treaty of Ceprano* shows that this is what happened. For the text of both treaties, see *Le Liber Censuum de l'eglise romaine*, 3 vols., eds. P. Fabre and L. Duchesne (Paris, 1910), I, 422.

69 Howden, *Gesta*, i, 77. There are two noteworthy exceptions to this amnesty clause: 1) those who had been captured during the conflict and had negotiated separate agreements with Henry II, among whom was the king of Scots; 2) Henry the Young King's main ally, Louis VII of France, who is not mentioned in this treaty, and with whom no separate agreement was concluded until the *Treaty of Ivry* in 1177.

70 Howden, *Gesta*, i, 78.

71 *Treaty of Meerssen* (851), c. 7. On symbolic redress, see below pp. 00–00.

72 De Jong, 'The Two Republics', 486–500.

73 *Partition of Benevento*, c. 3. A similar clause can be found in the twelfth-century treaties of Palermo between the kings of Sicily and the city of Genoa, for which see *Treaty of Palermo* (1156), oath, c. 3; *Treaty of Palermo* (1174), c. 3.

74 *LIRG*, vol. 1/1, 23. Translation amended from Hall, *Caffaro*, 178. Fos was located near Marseille. It is possible that the cost of these offences was to be offset against the annual payments to Genoa. There are examples of such practices in dispute settlement at lower levels of society. For some examples from France, see Matthew McHaffie, 'Mercy and the Violence of Law', *The Mediaeval Journal* (forthcoming).

75 The *Treaty between Genoa and Ramon Berenguer* further makes a distinction between 'financial claims' and 'criminal cases' but both were dealt with through redress: 'hoc sit tam in pecuniariis causis quam in criminalibus'. *LIRG*, vol. 1/6, 9; Hall, *Caffaro*, 183. Cf. *Treaty of Tyre* (1190).

76 *LIRG*, vol. 1/1, 23; Hall, *Caffaro*, 178. A similar clause can also be found in the *Treaty of San Salvatore II* in *DD FI*, ii, 223.

77 *Partition of Benevento*, c. 21: 'Sed et de causis anterioribus, quas habuerunt homines utriusque partis inter se, iudicavimus exinde secundum legm et iustitiam absque omni iniusta dilatione vel fraudis argumento, except omicidio et incendio, depredatione ac zala...' See also *Partition of Benevento*, c. 19: 'De nullo homicidio vel praeda atque zala seu incendiis retroactis fiat aliqua requisitio vel vendicta per meam voluntatem.'

78 Howden, *Gesta*, i, 79.

79 Howden, *Gesta*, i, 77.

80 E.g., *Treaty of Montlouis* (1174). The Treaty of Gerberoy (1182) between King Philip Augustus and Count Philip of Flanders, which was mediated by Henry II of England, likewise sets out that those who had been dispossessed because of war should have possession of their lands as they had fifteen days before the outbreak. Gerald of Wales, *Instructions for a Ruler (De Principis Instructione)*, ed. Robert Bartlett (Oxford, 2018), 500–1.

81 *Die Urkunden Heinrichs V. und der Königin Mathilde*, eds. Matthias Thiel and Alfred Gawlik, no. 240, available at https://data.mgh.de/databases/ddhv/dhv_240.htm (accessed 16 July 2021).

82 *DD FI*, ii, 222; Hall, *Caffaro*, 199. The final treaty was concluded in June of the same year.

83 *Treaty of Ivry*, c. 3: 'Et ut inter nos amodo tollatur omnis materia discordiae, concessimus ad invicem, quod de terris et possessionibus et aliis rebus, quas quisque nostrum modo possidet, alter adversus alterum inde nihil amodo petet, excepto eo de Alvernia...; et excepto feudo de Castro Ra[d]ulfi; et excepto minutis feudis et divisis terrarum nostrarum de Berria.'

84 Ibid., c. 4.

85 *Treaty of Gisors* (1180), c. 3; Howden, *Gesta*, i, 194–6, 244–7, 250; Howden, *Chronica*, ii, 147, 198–9; *The Chronicle of Robert of Torigni, abbot of Mont St Michel*, in *Chronicles of the Reigns of Stephen, Henry II, and Richard I, vol. IV*, ed. R. Howlett (London, 1889), 274, 289–90; *Diceto*, ii, 4, 6. On *Treaty of Ivry* generally, see Benham, *PMA*, 202–4.

86 *Treaty of Toul*, c. 2.

87 For some examples of the much-debated concept of *frið*, see Christine Fell, 'Unfrið: An Approach to a Definition', *Saga-Book of the Viking Society for Northern Research*, 21 (1982–3), 85–100; Niels Lund, 'Peace and Non-Peace in the Viking Age: Ottar in Biarmaland, the Rus in Byzantium and Danes and Norwegians in England', in *Proceedings of the Tenth Viking Congress*, ed. J. E. Knirk (Oslo, 1987), 255–69.

88 *II Æthelred*, c. 1.

89 Cf. *Truce of Verneuil* (1194), in which the French king stipulated that men included in his truce were those who had been more his men than the men of the English king, Richard I, before the war, and the English king stipulated likewise for men included in his truce. Howden, *Chronica*, iii, 258.

90 *II Æthelred*, cc. 2, 2.1. Cf. *Treaty of Mallorca* (1181), c. 4, stipulating that any Genoese citizens who came to the Balearic Islands with an enemy would be treated as such by the king, despite the conclusion of this peace ('Quod si aliquis de districtu Ianue...cum aliquo de inimicis iret super ipsum et terram ejus, de eo debet sicut de inimicis rex facere'). The French translation of the Arabic text seems to define an enemy of the king as someone who is at war with the king and his subjects. Mas Latrie, *Traités de paix*, 111.

91 On the polycentric nature of medieval polities, see also Chapter 1, pp. 20–1.

92 E.g., *Treaty of Pavia*, cc. 10, 12, 19; *Dunsæte*, cc. 3.2–3.3; *Treaty of Venice*, c. 11. On arbitration panels, see Chapter 5, pp. 202–4.

93 *Treaty of Toul*, cc. 4–5.

94 Ibid., c. 8.

95 E.g., *Treaty of Pavia*, cc. 10, 12, 19, 27.

96 *II Æthelred*, c. 6.

97 *Truce of Venice*, c. 4.

98 For but a few examples of treaties (with dates) using exclusion against either individuals or specific regions/places as enforcement, see *II Æthelred* (994), c. 3.1; *Treaty between Genoa and Pavia* (1140), c. 3; *Treaty of San Salvatore I* (1162), c. 9; *Treaty of Fulda* (1173), c. 8.

99 On this, see also Padoa-Schioppa, 'Profili del diritto internazionale', 52–4.

100 *Treaty of Toul*, c. 3: 'Set archiepiscopi et episcopi et ceteri barones, qui affuerunt, quisque pro se hoc fiduciaverunt, et a reliquis archiepiscopis, episcopis, et laicis infra prescriptos terminos constitutis, qui tunc non affuerunt, eandem accepimus securitatem tali conditione...'

101 Gerald of Wales, *Instructions for a Ruler*, 500–3.

102 *II Atr* 4, 5–5.1

103 *Treaty between Llywelyn and King John's representatives*, cc. 9–10. Note that I have interpreted 'dampna' as the more neutral 'damages' rather than 'plunder' as in Pryce's edition. Pryce, *The Acts of Welsh Rulers*, 372.

104 *Treaty of Adrianople*, c. 1

105 *Treaty of Milan* (1158), c. 4. Paying at fixed times can be contrasted with stipulations of future redress, where individual claims for redress were frequently expected to be settled within a set number of days

after receiving notice of a claim. For some examples, see *Treaty between Genoa and Fos* (1138); *Treaty of Lerici* (1166), c. 33; *Treaty of Nonancourt* (1189), c. 7; *Truce of Venice* (1177) – all of which stipulated forty days. *Dunsæte* (cc. 1, 1.1) stipulated nine days, while the *Treaty of Artlenburg* (cc. 5.1–2) anticipated a year and a day. These differing time limits generally reflect those prescribed in domestic laws from the same regions, e.g., *The Law of Hywel Dda*, Bk. II, c. 6 (pp. 47, 54, 83–4, 88, 96, 101–2); *VSL*, cc. 1, 20, 33; *ESL*, Bk. I, cc. 4, 10, 33; *ESL*, Bk. II, cc. 37, 51, 55; *ESL*, Bk. III, cc. 24, 26, 54, 56, 57; *JL*, Bk. I, c. 23. On forty days as a terminus for a range of legal processes in early medieval law, see Oliver, *The Body Legal*, 38–9.

106　*Treaty of San Salvatore I* (1162), c. 6.

107　*Treaty of Rouen* (1204).

108　*Dip. Docs*, 14–15.

109　Grégoire Mallard, ' "The Gift" Revisited: Marcel Mauss on War, Debt, and the Politics of Reparations', *Sociological Theory*, 29 (2011), 226. On this debate, see also Anna Carabelli and Mario Cedrini, 'Global Imbalances, Monetary Disorder and Space: Keynes' Legacy for our Troubled World', *Intervention*, 7 (2010), 303–23; John Torpey, *Making Whole What Has Been Smashed: On Reparations Politics* (Cambridge, MA, 2006); Ariel Colonomos and Andrea Armstrong, 'German Reparations to the Jews after World War II: A Turning Point in the History of Reparations', in *The Handbook of Reparations*, ed. P. de Greiff (Oxford, 2006), 390–419; Frédéric Ramel, 'Marcel Mauss et l'étude des relations internationales: un héritage oublié', *Sociologie et sociétés*, 36 (2004), 227–45; John Torpey, ed., *Politics and the Past: On Repairing Historical Injustices* (New York, 2003). For medieval examples, highlighting similar issues, see Jocelyn Sharlet, 'Tokens of Resentment: Medieval Arabic Narratives about Gift Exchange and Social Conflict', *Journal of Arabic and Islamic Studies*, 11 (2011), 62–100, esp. 75–8.

110　There is a large literature on the Marshall Plan and its contribution to economic recovery (or not). For examples, see A. S. Millward, *The Reconstruction of Western Europe, 1945–1951* (Berkeley, 1984); Tyler Cowen, 'The Marshall Plan: Myths and Realities', in *US Aid to the Developing World*, ed. D. Bandow (Washington, DC, 1985); J. Farquharson, 'Marshall Aid and British Policy on Reparations from Germany, 1947–1949', *RIS*, 22 (1996), 361–79.

111　Adam Zwass, *The Council for Mutual Economic Assistance: The Thorny Path from Political to Economic Integration* (London, 1989), 16; B. Kuklick, *American Policy and the Division of Germany: The*

Clash with Russia over Reparations (Ithaca, NY, 1972); Mateusz Gniazdowski, 'The Problem of War Reparations: the Perspective of the Czech Republic', *The Polish Foreign Affairs Digest*, 4 (2004), 163–205;

112 *Treaty of Milan* (1158), c. 4. On this treaty and its textual variants, see Josef Riedmann, *Die Beurkundung der Verträge Friedrich Barbarossas mit italienischen Städten: Studien zur diplomatischen Form von Vertragsurkunden im 12. Jahrhundert* (Vienna, 1973), 63–72.

113 *LIRG*, vol. 1/1, 181. Translation adapted from Hall, *Caffaro*, 190. The 'marabotini' was a gold coin minted by the Muslims of North Africa and Spain. For its uses and weight, see *CDRG*, I, 206 fn. 1; Hall, *Caffaro*, 48; I. S. Robinson, *The Papacy, 1073–1198: Continuity and Innovation* (Cambridge, 1990), 270.

114 *LIRG*, vol. 1/1, 23; Hall, *Caffaro*, 178.

115 *Pactum Sicardi*, c. 2. See also c. 1 of the *Treaty between Genoa and Ramon Berenguer III of Barcelona* in 1127 where a ship that paid 10 'marabotini' was entitled to be included in the protection set out in the treaty, and c. 3 of the *Treaty of Justinopolis* (932), in which payment of 100 amphoras of wine, gave freedom of movement and entitlement to redress.

116 On the *Treaty of Artlenburg*, see above pp. 96–7. On similar issues of tribute and payments for peace in Iberia, see also Lacarra, 'Dos Tratados de paz', 123; *Treaty between Sancho IV of Navarre and al-Muktadir of Zaragoza* (1069), cc. 6, 11.

117 *LIRG*, vol. 1/1, 23; Hall, *Caffaro*, 178.

118 *Pactum Sicardi*, c. 8.

119 *Die 'Honorantie Civitatis Papie': Transkription, Edition, Kommentar*, tr. Carlrichard Brühl (Cologne, 1983), 19 (cc. 2, 4). Translation adapted from *Medieval Trade in the Mediterranean World*, tr. Robert S. Lopez and Irving W. Raymond (New York, 1955; repr. 1990), 58.

120 *LIRG*, vol. 1/1, 150; Hall, *Caffaro*, 185. An interesting comparison can be made to so-called 'commenda'/enterprise and partnership agreements. For examples, see *Medieval Trade in the Mediterranean World*, nos. 83–99. There is a large literature on these, but for two recent examples in English, see Stefania Gialdroni, '*Propter Conversationem Diversarum Gentium*: Migrating Words and Merchants in Medieval Pisa', in *Migrating Word, Migrating Merchants, Migrating Law*, eds. Stefania Gialdroni et al. (Leiden, 2020), 28–53, esp. 36–47; Anja Amend-Traut, 'Legal Structure of Early Enterprises – from *Commenda*-like Arrangements to Chartered Joint-stock Companies', in *The Company in Law and Practice: Did Size Matter? (Middle Ages to Nineteenth Century)*, eds. Dave De Ruysscher et al. (Leiden, 2017), 63–83.

121 For an overview on the different uses of silk in diplomacy and treaties, see Anna Maria Muthesius, 'Silk, Power and Diplomacy in Byzantium', in *Textiles in Daily Life. Proceedings of the Third Biennial Symposium of the Textile Society of America, September 24–26, 1992, Seattle* (Textile Society of America, 1993), available at https://digitalcommons.unl.edu/cgi/viewcontent.cgi?article=1579&content=tsaconf (accessed 16 July 2021), 101–4.

122 Isidore, *Etymologiae*, XVIII:2.8 (Barney, *Etymologies*, 360–1).

123 Hall, *Caffaro*, 185 fn. 48. Their conclusion is based on Epstein's wider discussion of the context and records, for which see his *Genoa and the Genoese*, 50–2. On the conquest of Tortosa, see also Nikolas Jaspert, ' "Capta est Dertosa clavis Cristianorum": Tortosa and the Crusades', in *The Second Crusade: Scope and Consequences*, eds. Jonathan Phillips and Martin Hoch (Manchester, 2001), 90–100.

124 For discussion of the 1163 *Treaty of Dover*, see Oksanen, *Flanders and the Anglo-Norman World*, 68–81, 92–113. *Treaty of Devol* in Anne Comnène, *Alexiade*, 4 vols., ed. and tr. Bernard Leib (Paris, 1937–76), III, 125–39. By contrast, the obligations of Alfonso VII of Léon-Castille in his treaty with Genoa specifically state that the payment of 10,000 *marabotini* was to cover the city's costs on siege engines ('pro sumptibus machinarum'). *LIRG*, vol. 1/6, 4; Hall, *Caffaro*, 179–80.

125 *LIRG*, vol. 1/1, 151: 'Transacto mense madii, tenebo homines ccc vel plus pro predicta guardia qui iurabunt predictum sacramentum et in unoquoque anno dabo censum altari Sancti Laurentii pallia II.'

126 Genoa also used alliances in a similar way, and non-payment for the military aid offered by the Genoese could result in claims for debts and further treaties for their repayments. Genoa's relations with the Sardinian rulers in the late twelfth century are clear examples, for which see *Treaty of Hyères* (1186), *Treaty between Genoa and Peter of Arborea* (1189), *Treaty of Genoa* (1198).

127 Howden, *Gesta*, ii, 70.

128 Howden, *Gesta*, ii. 74: 'In eodem colloquio Richardus dux Normannie promisit se daturum regi Francie quatuor millia marcarum esterlingorum *pro expensis suis*, et praeterea illas viginti millia marcarum quas pater ejus promisit' (emphasis added).

129 Howden, *Chronica*, iii, 4.

130 *Diceto*, ii, 63–4.

131 Timothy Reuter, 'Plunder and Tribute in the Carolingian Empire', *TRHS*, 5th ser., 35 (1985), 76–85.

132 Ibid., 87.

133 *ARF*, s.a. 796.

134 *ARF*, s.a. 791.

135 Fedele, 'Indemnities in Diplomacy'.

136 Augustine, *City of God against the Pagans*, ed. R. W. Dyson (Cambridge, 1998), 909–65.

137 Isidore, *Etymologiae*, XVIII:2.8 (Barney, *Etymologies*, 360–1).

138 *Herimanni Augiensis Chronicon*, ed. G. H. Pertz, in *MGH SS*, 5 (Hanover, 1844), 124; Herman of Reichenau, *Chronicle*, in *Eleventh-century Germany. The Swabian Chronicles*, tr. I. S. Robinson (Manchester, 2008), 74.

139 There is a huge literature on gifts and gift-giving in diplomacy. For examples, see Benham, *PMA*, 71–85; Muthesius, 'Silk, Power and Diplomacy in Byzantium', 101–4; Nicholas Drocourt, 'Les animaux comme cadeaux d'ambassade entre Byzance et ses voisins (VIIe–XIIe siècle)', *Byzance et ses périphéries: Hommage à Alain Ducellier*, eds. Bernard Doumerc and Christophe Picard (Toulouse, 2004), 67–93; Doris Behrens-Abouseif, *Practising Diplomacy in the Mamluk Sultanate: Gifts and Material Culture in the Medieval Islamic World* (London, 2016); Janet L. Nelson, 'The Role of the Gift in Early Medieval Diplomatic Relations', in *Le relazioni internazionali nell'alto medioevo: Spoleto, 8–12 aprile 2010, Settimane di studio della Fondazione Centro italiano di studi sull'alto Medioevo*, 58 (Spoleto, 2011), 225–48; Samuel Ottewill-Soulsby, 'The Camels of Charles the Bald', *Medieval Encounters*, 25 (2019), 263–92; Anthony Cutler, 'Significant Gifts: Patterns of Exchange in Late Antique, Byzantine, and Early Islamic Diplomacy', *Journal of Medieval and Early Modern Studies*, 38 (2008), 79–101.

140 ILC Articles 2001, art. 32, 34–7.

141 There is a large and complex literature on this topic. For examples, see Louis Halphen, 'La justice en France au XIe siècle', in *A travers l'histoire du moyen âge* (Paris, 1950), 175–202; Frederic L. Cheyette, 'Suum cuique tribuere', *French Historical Studies*, 6 (1970), 287–99; Stephen D. White, ' "Pactum... Legem Vincit et Amor Judicium": The Settlement of Disputes by Compromise in Eleventh-Century Western France', *AJLH*, 22 (1978); Geoffrey Koziol, *Begging Pardon and Favor: Ritual and Political Order in Early Medieval France* (Ithaca, NY, 1992), 16; Althoff, *SP*; J. G. H. Hudson, 'Court Cases and Legal Arguments in England, c. 1066–1166', *TRHS*, 10 (2000), 91–115. By contrast, Kamp has highlighted that the two concepts were not necessarily distinct to medieval people, for which see his *Friedensstifter und Vermittler*, 135–54.

142 Gerd Althoff, 'Das Privileg der *deditio*. Formen gütlicher Konfliktbeendigung in der mittelalterlichen Adelsgesellschaft', in Althoff, *SP*, 99–125; Gerd Althoff, *Die Macht der Rituale. Symbolik und Herrschaft im Mittelalter* (Darmstadt, 2003), 68–84.

143 For examples, see Benham, *PMA*, 71–113; Jean-Marie Moeglin, 'Harmiscara harmschar hochée Le dossier des rituels d'humiliation et de soumission au Moyen Age', *Archivum Latinitatis Medii Aevi*, 54 (1996), 11–65; Philippe Depreux, 'Gestures and Comportment at the Carolingian Court: Between Practice and Perception', *P&P*, 203 (2009), 57–79, esp. 66–71; Kiril Petkov, *The Kiss of Peace: Ritual, Self, and Society in the High and Late Medieval West* (Leiden, 2003); Klaus van Eickels, 'Homagium and Amicitia: Rituals of Peace and their Significance in the Anglo-French Negotiations of the Twelfth Century', *Francia*, 24 (1997), 133–40.

144 *Treaty of Toul*.

145 On these various ways of making satisfaction, see Benham, *PMA*, 90–106; Jacques Le Goff, 'The Symbolic Ritual of Vassalage', in *Time, Work and Culture in the Middle Ages*, tr. Arthur Goldhammer (Chicago, 1980), 237–87; Jean-Marie Moeglin, 'Pénitence publique et amende honorable au Moyen Âge', *Revue Historique*, 298 (1997), 225–69; Yannick Carré, *Le baiser sur la bouche au Moyen Âge* (Paris, 1992); Petkov, *The Kiss of Peace*; Alice Taylor, 'Homage in the Latin Chronicles of Eleventh- and Twelfth-century Normandy', in *People, Texts and Artefacts. Cultural Transmission in the Medieval Norman Worlds*, eds. David Bates, Edoardo D'Angelo, and Elisabeth van Houts (London, 2017), 231–51, esp. 244–5.

146 Henriette Benveniste, 'Le système des amendes pénales en France au moyen âge: une première mise en perspective', *Revue historique de droit français et étranger*, 70 (1992), 5–6.

147 *Treaty of Toul*.

148 On this aspect of *deditio*, see Gerd Althoff, 'Satisfaction: Peculiarities of the Amicable Settlement of Conflicts in the Middle Ages', in *Ordering Medieval Society. Perspectives on Intellectual and Practical Modes of Shaping Social Relations*, ed. Bernhard Jussen, tr. Pamela Selwyn (Philadelphia, 2001), 273–9; Gerd Althoff, 'Das Privileg der *deditio*', 99–125; Koziol, *Begging Pardon and Favor*, 181–7; Petkov, *The Kiss of Peace*, 10.

149 *Partition of Benevento*, c. 20.

150 On satisfaction, its link to penance and role in dispute settlement, see Rob Meens, 'Penitential Questions: Sin, Satisfaction and Reconciliation in the Tenth and Eleventh Centuries', *EME*, 14 (2006), 1–6; J. Patout Burns, 'The Concept of Satisfaction in Medieval Redemption Theory', *Theological Studies*, 36 (1975), 285–304; Althoff, 'Satisfaction', 270–84.

151 *The Laws of King Liutprand*, c. 43.

152 On the terminology, see also Domino Du Cange et al., 'Satisfacere', in *Glossarium mediae et infimae latinitatis*, ed. L. Favre (Paris,

1883–7), vol. 7, col. 316b, available at http://ducange.enc.sorbonne. fr/SATISFACERE (accessed 16 July 2021).

153 *RPC*, 76.

154 Paul R. Hyams, *Rancor and Reconciliation in Medieval England* (Ithaca, NY, 2003), 11–13.

155 *Treaty of Milan* (1158), c. 10.

156 Howden, *Gesta*, ii, 70. On the circumstances of this conflict and the treaty, see Benham, 'Writing Peace, Writing War', 273–83.

157 There is a vast literature on transitional justice in the modern world. For good introductions, see C. Baker and J. Obradovic-Wochnik, 'Mapping the Nexus of Transitional Justice and Peacebuilding', *Journal of Intervention and Statebuilding*, 10 (2016), 281–301, esp. 281–92; J. N. Clark, 'The Three Rs: Retributive Justice, Restorative Justice, and Reconciliation', *Contemporary Justice Review*, 11 (2008), 331–50; L. M. Balasco, 'Reparative Development: Re-conceptualising Reparations in Transitional Justice Processes', *Conflict, Security and Development*, 17 (2017), 1–20; K. Brown, 'Commemoration as Symbolic Reparation: New Narratives or Spaces of Conflict?', *Human Rights Review*, 14 (2013), 273–89; J. Iverson, 'Transitional Justice, Jus Post Bellum and International Criminal Law: Differentiating the Usages, History and Dynamics', *The International Journal of Transitional Justice*, 7 (2013), 413–33. On transitional justice in the medieval period, see Jenny Benham and Jamie Smith, 'Transitional Justice in the Medieval World', in *Oxford Handbook of Transitional Justice*, eds. Lawrence Douglas, Alex Hinton, and Jens Meierheinrich (Oxford, forthcoming); Jenny Benham, 'Battle Writing and the Transition from Conflict to Peace', in *Writing Battles: Medieval and Modern Perspectives on Warfare and Memory in Northern Europe*, eds. Máire Ní Mhaonaigh, Rory Naismith, and Elizabeth Ashman Rowe (London, 2020), 27–38.

158 Baker and Obradovic-Wochnik, 'Mapping the Nexus of Transitional Justice', 281–92.

159 For the Middle Ages this is clearly expressed in the work of Althoff (e.g., *Die Macht der Rituale*), whose approach and use of mainly narrative sources has been criticised by several scholars. For two examples, see Depreux, 'Gestures and Comportment', 66, 78; Jean-Marie Moeglin, ' "Performative turn", "communication politique" et rituels au Moyen Age. À propos de deux ouvrages récents', *Le Moyen Age*, 113 (2007), 393–406.

160 E.g., Jonathan Mercer's comment that 'States cannot easily get reputations for keeping promises, but can get reputations for breaking promises'. Jonathan Mercer, *Reputation and International Politics* (Ithaca, NY, 2018), 225. See also Dixon, *Textbook on IL*, 5.

161 Benham, *PMA*, 151; Benham, 'Peace, Security and Deterrence', 124–6. See also Chapter 4, pp. 148–50.

162 Hathaway and Shapiro, 'Outcasting', 257, 268–70.

163 Hershey, 'History of International Relations', 923.

164 Some scholars argue that international law, regardless of period, is unenforceable and hence not 'true' law, for which see Dixon, *Textbook on IL*, 6; Eric A. Posner, 'Do States Have a Moral Obligation to Obey International Law?', *Stanford Law Review*, 55 (2003), 1917–19. On state, authority and jurisdiction in the period 700–1200, see also Chapter 1, pp. 18–21.

165 For a good introduction to such 'legal pluralism' more generally, see Davies, 'Legal Pluralism', 805–24; William Twining, 'Normative and Legal Pluralism: A Global Perspective', *Duke Journal of Comparative and International Law*, 20 (2010), 473–518. See also comments in Chapter 1, pp. 18–21.

166 Hathaway and Shapiro, 'Outcasting', 257–8; Marc Galanter and David Luban, 'Poetic Justice: Punitive Damages and Legal Pluralism', *American University Law Review*, 42 (1993), 1401. Generally, there is a division in the literature on enforcement of international law between scholars assessing the topic in terms of 'compliance' and those thinking more in terms of 'effectiveness'. For an outline, see Laurence R. Helfer, 'The Effectiveness of International Adjudicators', in *The Oxford Handbook of International Adjudication*, 464–82.

167 *Treaty of Ardara*, c. 4: 'Quando Ianuensis consul vel consules seu legatus vel legati ascenderint in Sardineam cum galea vel galeis contra Pisanos vel ipsum Arborensem, si conventionem eis factam non observaret, tenebor eos adiuvare cum gente mea per bonam fidem...' On the treaties with Arborea, see *Treaty of Genoa* (1172, 1198), *Treaty of Hyères* (1186), *Treaty between Genoa and Peter of Arborea* (1189), *Treaty of Oristano* I–II (1192).

168 On the treaties concluded as part of the Peace of Venice, see Jenny Benham, 'The Peace of Venice (1177)', in *Encyclopedia of Diplomacy*, ed. Gordon Martel (London, 2018).

169 A summary of the ways in which Henry II dealt with the different adversaries in 1174 can be gleaned from an unpublished paper I gave at a conference at the University of St Andrews in 2011, for which see Jenny Benham, 'Law, Violence and the Practice of Political Power in England and Denmark in the Late Twelfth and Early Thirteenth Centuries', available at www.academia.edu/2506393/Law_violence_ and_the_practice_of_political_power (accessed 16 July 2021), 2–3.

170 Benham, 'Peace, Security and Deterrence', 124–31; Benham, *PMA*, 145–77; Kosto, *Hostages*, 55–62, 135–56.

171 *Gesta sanctorum patrum Fontanellensis coenobii*, eds. F. Lohier and J. Laporte (Rouen and Paris, 1936), Bk. 12, c. 2 (pp. 86–7).

172 Abbot Gervold, who sometimes acted for Charlemagne in his dealings with English kings, is described as *'procurator* of the kingdom's trade, collecting the tolls and tributes (exigens tributa et vectigalia) in various ports and cities but especially in Quentovic', and hence it is hardly surprising that he was one of those expected to enforce this embargo. *Gesta sanctorum patrum Fontanellensis coenobii*, Bk. 12, c. 2 (pp. 86–7).

173 *MGH Epp.*, IV, nos. 7, 9, 82 (pp. 32, 35, 125); S. Allott, *Alcuin of York c. A.D. 732 to 804: His Life and Letters* (York, 1974), nos. 10, 31, 39.

174 *MGH Epp.*, IV, no. 7 (p. 32); *EHD*, I, no. 192.

175 Middleton, 'Early Medieval Port Customs', 324.

176 C. E. Blunt, 'The Coinage of Offa', in *Anglo-Saxon Coins Studies Presented to F.M. Stenton*, ed. R. H. M. Dolley (London, 1961), 39–62; S. Suchodolski, 'La date de la grande réforme monétaire de Charlemagne', *Quaderni Ticinesi di Numismaticae Antichità Classiche*, 10 (1981), 399–409; Derek Chick, 'Towards a Chronology for Offa's Coinage: an Interim Study', *The Yorkshire Numismatist*, 3 (1997), revised and repr. in *The Coinage of Offa and his Contemporaries*, eds. Mark Blackburn and Rory Naismith (London, 2010), 1–3.

177 *MGH Epp.*, IV, no. 100 (pp. 145–6).

178 Cf. the *Treaty of Verona* in 983, which ended the trade embargo and conflict between the Emperor Otto II and the Venetians. On this treaty, see also Fanta, 'Die Verträge der Kaiser mit Venedig', 51–128; Wolfgang Giese, 'Venedig-Politik und Imperiums-Idee bei den Ottonen', in *Herrschaft, Kirche, Kultur. Beiträge zur Geschichte des Mittelalters. Festschrift für Friedrich Prinz zu seinem 65. Geburtstag*, ed. Georg Jenal (Stuttgart, 1993), 219–43.

179 Cf. the enforcement procedure of the World Trade Organization (WTO), which advocates non-violent enforcement, has no physical institutions that could aid enforcement, and delegates the execution of its rules to member states, which can retaliate by imposing tariffs and other protectionist measures. On this, see Petros C. Mavroidis, 'Licence to Adjudicate: A Critical Evaluation of Appellate Body So Far', in *Trade Disputes and the Dispute Settlement of the WTO: An Interdisciplinary Assessment*, ed. James C. Hartigan (Bingley, 2009), 73–90.

180 Dixon, *Textbook on IL*, 7. An attempt to problematise the issue of enforcement and obedience and the relationship to international

law more fully can be found in Posner, 'Do States Have a Moral Obligation to Obey International Law?', 1901–19. See also George W. Downs and Michael A. Jones, 'Reputation, Compliance and International Law', *The Journal of Legal Studies*, 31 (2002), 95–114; Oona Hathaway, 'Do Human Rights Treaties Make a Difference?', *The Yale Law Journal*, 111 (2002), 1935–2042; Amnon Altman, 'The Role of the "Historical Prologue" in the Hittite Vassal Treaties: An Early Experiment in Securing Treaty Compliance', *JHIL*, 6 (2004), 43–63; Helen M. Kinsella and Giovanni Mantilla, 'Contestation before Compliance: History, Politics, and Power in International Humanitarian Law', *International Studies Quarterly*, 64 (2020), 649–56, esp. 654–5; Ian Clark et al., 'Crisis in the Laws of War? Beyond Compliance and Effectiveness', *European Journal of International Relations*, 24 (2017), 319–43.

4

Justifying action: law, responsibility, and deterrence

In outlining the existence of international rules as a 'system' of law, scholars attach the utmost significance to the fact that most states do not claim that they are above the law or that international rules do not bind them.[1] It must be of some significance then that the historian of medieval Europe would be hard pushed to find examples of rulers or communities breaching treaties or international customary practices or taking action against foreign entities, groups of people, or individuals without justifying this in a legal context. As highlighted by Dixon: 'This is powerful evidence that states follow rules of international law as a matter of obligation, not simply as a matter of choice or morality. If this were not so, there would be no need for states to justify their action in legal terms when they departed from a legal norm.'[2] In modern international law, scholars tend to classify defences in the law of responsibility into two different typologies: circumstances that preclude wrongfulness (justifications) and circumstances that preclude responsibility (excuses), even though these are not exclusively legal concepts but exist also in theology and moral philosophy.[3] For the Middle Ages, separating the moral from the legal is tricky, as both wrongdoing and obligations were perceived in a religious context. Virtues and morality were believed to derive from faith itself, and those who were enemies or non-Christians were socially conceived as lawless, immoral, and as seeking conflict. Consequently, justification for action in the medieval period inevitably leads the historian to the debate over 'just war'; that is, questions over how and in what circumstances violent action was justified, and who had the authority to carry out such violence.[4] While this debate is an important aspect of justification in the medieval period, the intention with this chapter is to think about how this moral and legal discourse manifested itself in different circumstances, and demonstrate how these were used to justify breaches of treaties, customs, and general principles, that is, the three main sources of international law. This is important to do because it is circumstances that enable us to see defences to legal responsibility.

One of the clearest expressions of justifications for action can be found with the narrative of Widukind of Corvey in the mid-tenth century. Widukind reports that in the mid-tenth century the Bavarians were worn down by both internal and external armies 'for once the Hungarians departed, they were pressed by the royal army'. A truce was eventually agreed, and the various parties agreed to meet at Langenzenn in June 954 'where they would give their explanations, and where a response would be given to them'.[5] At this meeting, Widukind asserts that the king, Otto I, gave a speech outlining his reasons for the royal attacks:

'I would have endured it', he said 'if the provocation of my son and the other participants in this plot had tormented me, alone, and had not troubled the entire Christian people (totum Christiani... populum). It would have been bad enough if they only had invaded my fortresses (urbes meas...invasisset) and stripped lands (regionesque... rapuisse) from my power like thieves (more latronum), and not also sated themselves on the blood of my kinsmen and my dearest companions. Behold, I sit here bereft of sons while I suffer to have my son [Liudolf] as my greatest enemy. Behold that one, whom I loved above all, and whom I raised up from his mediocre status to the highest level and greatest honor [referring to Conrad the Red, duke of Lotharingia]. He has turned my one son against me. Even this I could have borne if they had not introduced the enemies of God and man (Dei hominumque inimici) [referring to the Hungarians] into this business. They have left my kingdom desolate, captured or killed my people, destroyed my fortresses, burned down my churches, and murdered my priests (Modo regnum meum habent desolatum, populum captum vel interfectum, urbes destructas, templa succensa, sacerdotes extinctos). The roads are now flooded with blood. The enemy of Christ now returns home, loaded down with my gold and silver with which I enriched my son and son-in-law. I cannot imagine what kind of evil, what kind of perfidy is still to come.'[6]

In response, Liudolf, the king's son, is said to have responded: 'I admit that I gathered money for those who were led against me so that they would not harm me or my dependents. If I am declared guilty in this matter, let the whole people know that I did not do this freely, but rather was forced by extreme necessity (non voluntarie, sed ultima necessitate coactum fecisse).'[7]

Neither side seems to have been convinced by these arguments as war subsequently continued until Liudolf submitted to his father in a so-called *deditio* and Otto defeated the Hungarians at the battle of the Lech in 955. Nevertheless, Widukind is an interesting example because he was writing on the cusp of the start of the Peace of God movement – often seen as the first to introduce measures under the *jus in bello* (the law(s) covering how war should be conducted) – but geographically and chronologically outside the discussions of religious, moral, and political authority of the Carolingian court circles of the late eighth and ninth centuries. Moreover, he was writing some 120 years before the revival of Roman law in the late eleventh and twelfth centuries and hence before the major developments of the just war theory of the later Middle Ages. What the exchange at the meeting at Langenzenn demonstrates very clearly are the justifications used, or at least the ones Widukind thought the parties would have used, for breaking the peace or any treaty, and for taking action, of whatever nature, against a perceived wrong by another party. As will become clear, some of these are recognisable also in modern international law, with Articles 20–25 of the International Law Commission's (ILC) Articles on the Responsibility of States for Internationally Wrongful Acts outlining the circumstances precluding wrongfulness as being consent, self-defence, countermeasures, *force majeure*, distress, and necessity.[8] Others, by contrast, are less comprehensible from a modern perspective, but nonetheless respond closely to medieval ideas and thinking about war and peace.

Above all, Otto justified his military response to his son's alliance with the Hungarians on the grounds that they were enemies of God and mankind ('Dei hominumque inimici') and a threat to the entire Christian people ('totum Christiani... populum').[9] As discussed in Chapter 2, the phrase *enemy of mankind* tended to refer to those who had committed so-called 'unemendable crimes' – e.g., arson, plundering, or robbery, flight from accusations of an 'unemendable crime', and treacherous or disloyal behaviour – or, put in another way, offences that were distinctly 'unchristian' in nature, and scholars have seen the phrase as inextricably linked to the development of the just war theory and to international criminal law.[10]

Several treaties show that parties could both acknowledge and justify their engagement in such 'unchristian' violence. For instance,
the papal privilege to Archbishop Siro of Genoa, which accompanied the *Treaty of Grosseto* of 1133, stated explicitly that these
were offences committed during the conflict between the cities of
Genoa and Pisa, and likened it to that conjured by the enemy of
mankind, i.e., the devil.[11] The phrase 'humani generis inimico' does
not appear in the *Treaty of Rouen*, concluded between the English
king, Æthelred II, and Richard I, leader of the Normans, in 991,
but it asks both parties to 'repiscerent[12] ab [hac] superstitione'.[13]
Dorothy Whitelock translated this as that they should 'recover
from their violence', while R. A. B. Mynors et al., opted for 'recover
from pagan behaviour'.[14] Clearly, what the phrase refers to is violence that was not befitting a Christian, just as the later 'enemy of
all mankind'.[15]

This notion of unchristian behaviour is epitomised in the obligation that sits at the heart of treaty- and peacemaking, namely that
agreements should be kept because one should keep one's oaths.
Treaties originating in the Iberian Peninsula are often the most specific on this issue, setting out that those breaking the oath, upon
which the treaty rested, would be regarded as traitors or as having
committed treachery. Examples include the *Treaty of Zaragoza*,
concluded in 1170 between King Alfonso II of Aragon and King
Alfonso VIII of Castile, which sets out that if either king breached
the terms he had not only committed perjury and feigned faith but
was also a knave and traitor.[16] An earlier example has been cited by
Geoffrey Koziol, who noted that those who deposed the Frankish
Emperor, Louis the Pious, in 833 justified their actions on account
of Louis being a disturber of the peace and violator of oaths by
overturning the *Ordinatio imperii* of 817 – the agreement outlining
the division of the empire between his sons and how the relations
between them should be regulated.[17] A slightly different example
can be found with the *Treaty of Jarnègues*, concluded in January
1190 between King Alfonso II of Aragon and Count Raymond
V of Toulouse. This treaty stipulates that each of those acting as
sureties in the treaty, if they failed to carry out that which they
had sworn to do in case of breaches by the count and the king,
would be a 'perjurer and traitor (perjurus et proditor)'. Moreover,
in these circumstances a claim for treachery and perjury could be

made against them in court ('ita quod de proditione et perjurio in omni curia possit appellari').[18] Here, the treaty shows that medieval treaties, and hence inter-ruler relations, did not operate solely at an abstract, 'state' or inter-ruler, level – a criticism often levied at modern international law.[19] Instead, individuals assumed personal responsibility for obligations and breaches thereof through their oaths. This is clearest, of course, in those treaties concluded between parties operating in a highly contested space where jurors, witnesses, and sureties might hold land from multiple rulers.[20] The justification of being a perjurer and traitor for failing to carry out specific treaty obligations could, in other words, result in legal action such as expulsion and/or confiscation of land and property by one ruler but not the other. Nevertheless, an individual's treacherous or unchristian behaviour did not justify the wholesale abandonment of any peace or agreement. Such notions are reinforced more generally by those treaties stating that even if the terms were not observed by some, all others who had sworn to keep the treaty would nonetheless be obligated to keep the terms.[21] An example of a treaty with such a clause is the *Treaty of Lerici*, concluded between the two Italian cities Genoa and Lucca in 1166.[22] Perhaps most importantly, the notion of sinful behaviour or violence, its connection to oaths, and the keeping thereof by all involved was not a Christian phenomenon. A single detailed example serves to prove the rule. The sanction clause of the *Treaty of Mallorca* (1188), concluded between the Genoese and the king of Mallorca, states that it had been agreed according to the law of all men ('secundum legem omnium hominum') – perhaps a nod to the general principle of *pacta sunt servanda* or to a notion of *ius gentium* – and that a breach of the terms would be an offence against God ('et qui contra fecerit Deum offendet').[23] Quite simply, breaking any oath to keep the terms of a treaty made the perpetrator an enemy of all mankind.

Breaking oaths, plainly, was a serious moral, cultural, and legal matter. Given freely, the oath acted as consent that an agreement had been entered into and that obligations would be adhered to.[24] Canon law stipulated that oaths exacted under duress had no validity, hence most treaties tended to include a statement that oaths and promises had been made voluntarily, and/or in good faith without fraud or evil intent. Alterations to the terms of agreements, however, could be made without breaking the oath, and the circumstances within which this could be done are usually stipulated in the text. The common phrase in treaties that neither contracting party would consent to the making or ending of peace, or a truce, or renewal of hostilities with a third party without the wish (*voluntas*) or consent (*consensus*) of the other is an example of this.[25] Many specific stipulations that parties anticipated might require modification related to redress, and the majority of these are to be found in treaties involving at least one party from Italy. For instance, requests to delay or to void a claim for redress required consent from the injured party, i.e., the individual or group of individuals making the claim, while to amend the timeframe for providing justice consent was required at the level of the contracting party – the ruler or ruling council whose subject had made the claim.[26] None of these circumstances suspended the underlying obligation or right in the treaty, but were temporary measures to deal with particular circumstances. That not all requests to alter the terms of treaties were granted seems likely. At the end of the first *Pact of Arichis*, the compiler of the manuscript added a historical comment, noting that shortly after it was concluded (in c. 784), the Neapolitans transgressed the treaty and did not want to live according to what had been stipulated. 'We,' says the compiler, referring to the Beneventans, 'in no way consented to it.'[27] Presumably this was intended to show that the Beneventans, led by Arichis, had not consented to whatever alterations to the treaty the Neapolitans had asked for, and so justified subsequent action of whatever nature. This particular comment on a late eighth-century treaty is the clearest example that in the period c. 700–1200 there was an understanding of the principle *volenti non fit iniuria* (to a willing person, no injury is done), set out in Justinian's *Digest* – the principle that sits at the heart of the justification of consent in more modern times.[28] The manuscript of this treaty originating in southern Italy and the lack of comparative examples in other treaties may, however, say more about the anonymous commentator and his cultural and social background than it does about any justifications in international law in this period.[29]

One recurring connection between consent and wrongdoing in the period examined here, relates to compulsion, and, unsurprisingly, given the ecclesiastical nature of many such sources, it is frequently seen in narrative descriptions. In the eleventh century, the

chronicler Herman of Reichenau recorded how Andreas had been
set up as king of Hungary in opposition to Emperor Henry III's
preferred claimant, Peter, and how he sent envoys to the emperor
upon hearing that the latter planned a large expedition to Hungary
to avenge his preferred candidate. According to the chronicler,
Andreas claimed that he had been 'compelled by the Hungarians to
accept the kingship, exculpating himself from the injuries inflicted
on Peter (regnum se ab Ungariis coactum suscepisse confirmans, de
Petri sese iniuriis excusans)'.[30] A modern reader might, of course,
see in Henry's military expedition a threat that was not less of a
compulsion than anything Andreas had, supposedly, been subjected
to in taking the throne. However, the whole point of the consen-
sual nature of oaths was evidently not the wider circumstances in
which they were sworn, e.g., coercion by a more powerful neighbour, but rather that there was an acknowledgement on both sides
of having consented to enter into any agreement. In this case, the
chronicler seems to imply that Andreas acknowledged the wrongful
acts and injuries against Peter, but that the lack of consent was a
circumstance that precluded responsibility for his actions – it was
an excuse rather than a justification.[31]

Consent was a crucial issue, and breaches of it had consequences
in this life and beyond. The whole point of designating someone
as an *enemy of mankind* – as someone that had broken an oath
and therefore acted in an unchristian manner – was that this justified any action against them as self-defence.[32] Isidore of Seville
linked the right to self-defence to natural law (*ius naturale*) in his
Etymologies when he asked:

> What is natural law? Law is either natural, or civil, or of peoples
> (gentium). Natural law is common to all nations (nationum), and,
> because it exists everywhere by the instinct of nature, it is not kept
> by any regulation. Such is... the repulsion of violence by force
> (violentie per vim repulsio). These and similar things are never unjust
> (injustum) but are natural and equitable.[33]

This notion of justification for action had been inherited from
Greek and Roman writers, such as Cicero, according to whom
a fundamental precept of natural law was the instinct for self-
preservation and, as an extension of this, the right of self-defence.
To defend oneself – as a natural inclination – was a just act, as was

defending one's associates.[34] In the early eleventh century, at latest, it is evident that this notion was used for practical measures to regulate and limit violence at lower levels of society, with Burchard of Worms' well-known law for the *familia* (household) at Worms setting out that defending one's own life, as well as one's goods and family was a lawful justification for killing another person.[35] By time we get into the twelfth century, some of these notions, mixed with Augustine's emphasis on 'just wars avenge injuries (iusta bella ulciscuntur iniurias)', became enshrined in Gratian's *Decretum*.[36] As recently summarised by Rory Cox, to clarify what made a war just, Gratian cited the definitions of Isidore and Augustine and offered his own synthesis: 'A just war is that which is waged from an edict, and in which injuries are avenged.' This definition, according to Cox, 'blended both the Isidorian emphasis on authority and self-defence with the Augustinian emphasis on punitive action'.[37] That these ideas were prevalent among those in the twelfth century writing about rulers and their deeds is evident from, to take one example, Otto of Freising. Otto records how the Emperor Frederick I proceeded against the city of Milan on grounds of having the authority to face 'anything that may threaten the security of the Roman empire'. He further noted that Frederick had a just cause for war ('iustam… belli causam') since the city had been revealed 'as rebellious against lawful authority (legittimo imperio rebelles)' and that his men would engage in warfare 'not from greed or cruelty, but eager for peace, that the insolence of the wicked maybe restrained, and that the good may be fittingly rewarded'.[38] Charles Mierow, the modern editor and translator of Freising's *Gesta Friderici imperatoris*, noted that Gratian's *Decretum* likely lay behind this statement.[39] Whatever the case, it is obvious that Otto considered self-defence a justification for violent action by a legitimate authority.

The justification of self-defence can be matched very easily against specific obligations in many treaties. One of the clearest examples can be found with the alliance between the cities of Genoa and Pisa in 1140. Clause seven of this treaty stipulated that neither side would conclude any peace or truce, nor renew the war, without the say so of the consuls of either city or without any injury having been made to them.[40] Any action was hence only justified if it was preceded by an initial offence having been committed against one or the other of the cities. Another example, the *Treaty of Mallorca* (1181) between the city of Genoa and Ishak-ibn-Mohammed, governor ('alfachinus') of the Balearic islands, stipulated that neither side would carry any hostility to the other and that those who contravened this would be proceeded against according to the law and faith.[41] The justification of self-defence further extended to one's allies, with *The Treaty of San Salvatore II* (1162), as an example, making clear that the Emperor, Frederick I, would 'inflict a just retribution (vindictam inde et justiciam faciemus)' on anyone doing violence to his Genoese allies or their property. Furthermore, the obligation of loyalty between subject and emperor included the expectation of defending the latter's allies if they were attacked, thereby drawing in the assistance of surrounding lords and cities for the Genoese.[42] That such stipulations were not merely a twelfth-century phenomenon is evident from the *Treaty of Tusey*, in which the two Frankish kings, Louis the German and Charles the Bald, each promised to preserve and defend not only his own family but also that of the other, if he died. That this was tied to the concept of loyalty through the oath is clear in that the treaty likens any failure in this duty as a denial of faith, making the perpetrator worse than an infidel – an enemy of mankind.[43]

Designating someone as an *enemy of mankind* additionally meant condemning that person's deeds and its results; the plunder, robbing, and stealing of lands and goods, the murder of priests and other non-combatants, and the burning of churches, as Widukind records Emperor Otto complaining.[44] Taking action against any such deeds committed at a time when a treaty was in force is usually referred to as 'reprisals' in the historiography because they were aimed at compensating damage or injury to an individual or to property, and were usually perceived as violent seizures of property to achieve this. Paddeu, in discussing the origins of reprisals as an institution, notes that they were essentially private in character, carried out by private, and often the injured, citizens, with authorisation of their sovereign in the form of letters of reprisals.[45] Dante Fedele has similarly argued that to be considered a 'reprisal' an act 'had to meet a series of stringent conditions'. These were laid down to ensure that 'acts of unjustified violence were not committed under the pretext of reprisals, thus provoking counter-reprisals and resulting in chaos'. According to Fedele, regulations led to reprisals being legitimated by public authorities and thus becoming a true legal institution under which a citizen who suffered an injury in a foreign territory and did not obtain redress from local courts could ask his own government for protection; if the latter could not resolve the dispute, it would provide the injured person with a letter of reprisal which gave him the right to seek satisfaction by acting personally against the citizens of the other country and their goods – if those citizens found themselves in the territory to which the injured party belonged.[46]

What is evident from this is that the development of reprisals as an institution was interlinked with the development of the debate over who had legitimate authority to carry out violence.[47] It further shows that reprisals are almost indistinguishable from the issue of redress for legal wrongs, such as compensation for damages to merchant goods or reparations for injuries suffered during violent conflict.[48]

We can see this in one example of how reprisals were intended to work. In November 1186, the French king, Philip II, found out that some men had been killed and wounded in a local skirmish on the border between Normandy and France, and that at least one perpetrator had fled to the count of Poitou, who was also the son of the English king. Deeming this to be a breach of a treaty concluded, Philip then seized all the English king's men – clergy as well as laymen – and their goods, who could be found within his dominions ('omnes qui invenirentur in terra sua de terra regis Angliae, sive clerici sive laici, ipsi et eorum catalla caperentur'). Henry II, likewise, ordered his bailiffs in Normandy and other territories to seize all of Philip's men and their goods ('Similiter ballivi regis in Normannia, et in aliis terris suis transmarinis, fecerunt de hominibus regis Francie, et de catallis eorum, ubicunque inveniri poterant in terra regis Angliae'). Shortly afterwards, however, Philip released those seized and their goods, on the advice of his followers, at which Henry promptly did the same ('Sed paulo post... rex Franciae fecit omnia reddi; et similiter ballivi regis Angliae libere abire permiserunt homines regis Franciae cum catallis suis').[49] Whether or not the original breach was resolved through the payment of compensation for those injured or killed is not known. The English chronicler Roger of Howden merely records that the English and French king had made a truce shortly before this incident, promising to keep the peace until the next Feast of Saint Hilary, i.e., 13 January 1187.[50] The truce seems to have held despite this incident and at some point, there was a proposal to prolong the agreement until Easter and it seems this was done as the next meeting between the kings didn't take place until April 1187. Hence, we could speculate that the issue over the injured and killed men may have been satisfied in some way, or that the issue formed part of the ongoing discussions for a more permanent peace. Either way, what this incident shows is that this was a reprisal enacted by royal order in response to a breach of the agreement concluded shortly before the incident took place. Reprisals then, while a justification for action, were essentially a method of enforcement intended to achieve redress for legal wrongs, to get the parties back around the negotiating table or to do both.[51]

The evidence for the diplomatic dealings of the English king, as also for many of the Italian cities, is particularly rich in the late twelfth century, and a myriad of similar incidents to that of 1186 can be found within various narratives and can be cross-checked with texts of treaties, oaths, laws, and financial records.[52] Recreating a similar picture for other entities or rulers and other time periods is much more difficult. In particular, it is worth noting that the period 700 to 1200 is one where the terminology and practice of reprisals, such as that 'private' aspect based on authorised letters anticipated by Fedele and Paddeu, cannot always be found in the evidence across all (or even any) geographical areas.[53] While it is not possible to entirely overcome this problem with the evidence, what we can be certain about, as noted by Fedele, is that some earlier treaties had stipulations that effectively allowed reprisals within certain limits. An example of this is the second clause of the ninth-century *Pactum Sicardi*, which stipulated that the Neapolitans were to pay Sicard, prince of Benevento, tribute each year, as they had done in the past, but, in case this payment ceased before the end of the five-year term of the treaty, Sicard could seize pledges from the Neapolitans ('nos licentiam habeamus... pignerare') to recover the amount due.[54] If the Neapolitans objected, they would be subject to the enormous fine of 3,000 Beneventan (gold) solidi, as well as military operations for the repayment by force.[55] Again, reprisals were clearly used as one of many strategies of enforcement as well as deterrence.[56] Other treaties, by contrast, had stipulations that effectively prevented reprisals being used as justifications for action.[57] For instance, the Treaty of Pisa concluded in 1126 between that city and the citizens of Amalfi sets out that if any Amalfitan ships, or if one of its men, were with the Pisans or within their territory and offended or injured them, the Amalfitans, their property, and their ships would still be safe and secure and would suffer no violence or injury.[58]

Finding examples of what might be reprisals is relatively easy at a time when writers justified similar acts carried out by rulers and communities, such as tribute-taking, plundering, raiding, or besieging. Indeed, as commented by Stephen Neff, the line between war and reprisals was frequently illusory.[59] The difficulty lies in pinning down such warlike acts as justified acts that had been undertaken in response to a breach of an obligation or an unlawful act as specified in a source of international law; a treaty, a general principle of law, or a custom. One good example, which makes explicit reference to an international rule, is found in a letter sent by the Emperor Frederick Barbarossa to his son Henry in 1189 during the Third Crusade. The letter explains how Frederick and his forces occupied and plundered towns, castles, and villages in retaliation for offences committed by the Byzantine emperor, Isaac II, contrary to the terms of a treaty concluded between them. Frederick had decided to take the land route to the Holy Land and relied on the treaty concluded with Isaac for safe conduct and provisions, but the letter sent to his son outlines that as soon as Frederick and his forces reached the frontiers of the Byzantine empire, they were attacked, deprived of promised provisions, and discovered that their envoys had been captured. Frederick depicted Isaac's offences as being ones against the honour of all Christians, as well as against himself and his envoys, describing the latter as having been thrown into prison 'naked (detrudi)'; that is, dispossessed of any clothing or items that showed their social status. According to Frederick, with these acts, the Byzantine emperor had not only breached the treaty between them but also the international rules guiding the treatment of envoys ('contra ius universarum nationum et legatorum').[60] Here, is a reference to a notion of international law beyond that in treaties. In fact, this general principle of law, on the inviolability of envoys, was one that was frequently commented on even in the earlier Middle Ages, and which, like that of *pacta sunt servanda*, was also a customary rule, the consistent practice of which is evident across several thousand years.[61] In fact, the chronicler recording the letter detailing these events subsequently says that the imprisonment of the envoys 'was a crime unheard of for many centuries', which was not necessarily true but an indication that contemporaries felt such behaviour was out of the ordinary as well as unlawful.[62]

According to the letter that Frederick sent to his son, the envoys were eventually returned less 'two thousand marks of their money', but although the Byzantine emperor was said to be prepared to keep the obligations he had made in the treaty, Frederick had 'no trust any more in the oaths... of the Greeks'.[63] Consequently, Frederick urged his son to send a request for aid to a number of Italian cities, asking them to prepare to attack Constantinople by sea in the spring of 1190, while Frederick and his forces attacked it by land. In addition, Henry was to enlist the moral support of all the empire through prayers, as well as ask the pope to encourage the people of God against the 'enemies of the Cross, and especially the Greeks'.[64] What is evident from the letter, and also from subsequent events, is that Frederick considered not only his reprisals to be justified acts but also that they were simply one type of justified acts among a multi-pronged strategy. This included asking for redress, continued negotiations with a range of different parties (alliance building), reprisals in the form of destruction and seizure of goods and occupation of territory, as well as making plans for resuming formal hostilities and war.[65] When scholars look at the effectiveness of diplomacy and treaties in the medieval period, they often assume that any hostile act was a renewal of war. However, judging by the evidence presented in the *Historia*, and elsewhere in this chapter, we should be careful in taking such a simplistic approach. It is evident that throughout this incident and beyond, Frederick expected Isaac to still perform the obligations he had agreed to in the treaty. In other words, the treaty was still in force and Frederick's reaction could be seen as a measure of coercion intended to pressure Isaac into stopping what was considered unlawful behaviour. Frederick was not necessarily interested in achieving redress – as in the reprisals of Philip of France discussed above – but rather the aim was to ensure that there was no repetition of Isaac's wrongful behaviour so that the journey towards Jerusalem could continue. This is clearly shown in that it was not until several weeks later, after several rounds of negotiations had failed, that Byzantine envoys were sent back to Constantinople with a formal declaration of war ('denuntiatione belli') – a unilateral termination of the treaty which can be seen as yet another form of reprisal.[66] Indeed, it seems clear that Frederick's sustained pressure and various strategies eventually brought the Byzantine emperor to 'belated penance (sera penitentia)', as the chronicler describes it, and the treaty was reconfirmed and eventually recorded as the *Treaty of Adrianople*.[67] Analysing justifications for action, such as reprisals, are hence important in allowing the historian to think about medieval diplomacy and the ideals and practice of war and peace in a more nuanced way.[68] The nature of the medieval evidence makes this a tricky endeavour with different aspects of a chain of events often becoming lost in the mists of time. Indeed, the late date of this incident may leave the historian to wonder if these sorts of sustained reprisals took place in, say, the eighth or ninth centuries. There is a definite example with the Frankish king's expedition into Italy in 756, during which he besieged and surrounded the Lombard king, Aistulf, and conquered the city of Ravenna, after the Lombard breached the promises regarding the rights of St Peter that he had made in the treaty of 755. Following these reprisals, Aistulf then handed over the properties listed in the treaty.[69] It would make perfect sense if other similar reprisals took place in the eighth and ninth centuries, because it is not always desirable to terminate a treaty and recommence hostilities, but exact evidence is often missing.

If we look at the history of reprisals in more modern times – or countermeasures, as they have become termed in contemporary international law – it is possible to find a number of measures and practices that are not necessarily linked to seeking compensation or reparation for injuries but that, nonetheless, can be linked to the concept of reprisals as a justification in the medieval evidence.[70] Paddeu, in her recent survey of reprisals and countermeasures, lists some of the other actions in that category as being non-payment of debts, pacific blockades, temporary occupation of territory of the target state, withholding of performance of obligations, and unilateral termination of treaties. Two of these measures could be seen with the example of Frederick Barbarossa above, but among the others, measures such as blockades, embargoes, and sanctions provide the most plentiful examples from the period 700 to 1200. As with other reprisals, there is no consistent or exact terminology to distinguish these measures, and although they were usually of an economic kind and intended to prohibit trade or navigation, or to detain foreign ships and/or men, they often also had a political, or even military, objective, making them tricky to separate from what we might think of as 'economic warfare'. Moreover, the measures could be targeted or more general.[71] One of the most well-known, and earliest, examples is the embargo imposed by Charlemagne and Offa banning each other's merchants, their ships and goods, following the breakdown of negotiations, supposedly, over a marriage alliance between their children. As discussed in Chapter 3, in this case, we can be confident that the embargo should be considered as a reprisal and was part of a more general termination of the friendship and treaty between the two kings, even though the exact breach is unclear and no written treaty survives. It is also evident that the embargo effectively did what such reprisals were supposed to do: cease the unlawful behaviour and encourage the parties back around the negotiating table.[72] A second example, from the early eleventh century, demonstrates a similar trajectory of events. According to Wipo, upon the entry of Conrad II into Italy to claim the kingdom, the citizens of Pavia were denied his peace and protection on account of having razed the royal palace in the city upon the death of Emperor Henry II. Despite repeated efforts, the two parties failed to come to a satisfactory agreement, and so Conrad began significant reprisals against the citizens, including plundering, laying waste to fields, cutting off vines, and, in particular, by stopping shipping by river and banning the exchange of goods. These reprisals continued for two years, until the citizens complied with all his orders.[73] As with the embargo between Offa and Charlemagne, there can be no doubt that these economic measures were reprisals against a perceived breach of faith and agreement. What is perhaps less clear is the extent to which Pavia, in 1026–7, should be regarded as an entity with some ability to act independently. A similar issue surrounds a later example, emanating from the newly created kingdom of Sicily in the early twelfth century. Shortly after his coronation in 1130, Roger II of Sicily demanded that the Amalfitans hand over certain fortifications and at their refusal, Roger refused to accept their fealty to him ('a fidei suae consortio dissociavit').[74] In response to this breach of the agreement between them, Roger then sent the 'Grand Emir George, a man most faithful to the king' to blockade Amalfi from the sea 'so that he could capture any Amalfitan who might be at sea and prevent aid from anywhere else coming by that same route'.[75] This is an interesting example because just four years earlier Amalfi had concluded a treaty with the Pisans, showing that, at that point, it had some ability to act independently. Roger's concern to incorporate them into his new kingdom was likely driven, in parts, by the desire to supress anyone attempting to exercise such authority, as well as a wish to profit from controlling the Amalfitan trade. This incident thus highlights many of the complex issues involved in thinking about international law in the medieval period, because not only is the issue between reprisals and war quite blurred, but so is also the line between conflict within an entity as opposed to between entities. It is in other words, an incident that shows competing authorities, claims, and justifications. That our knowledge of this incident is written from the perspective of the party that eventually came out on top is evident from the description of the resolution of the conflict. With the king and his forces having first blockaded and then seized a number of Amalfitan towns, the inhabitants of the city asked for new peace terms: Roger received all that he wanted and returned the victor.[76] Alexander of Telese implied, within, as noted by Graham Loud, fairly 'conventional monastic parameters', that Roger restored peace and order to southern Italy, where a number of individuals and communities, including Amalfi, had risen against a rightful and divinely appointed authority thereby breaching the bonds of faith and committing perjury.[77]

Separating measures, like blockades, from strategies of economic war more generally is often then dependent on the nature of our evidence. Yet it is also in showing the ambiguities of competing authorities, claims, and justifications that we can more clearly see the plurality of law and how it was practised in different situations. In particular, it is often with economic reprisals that we can see complementing strategies of secular and ecclesiastical law and authority to ensure success. Peter Clarke, in his 2007 study of interdict in the thirteenth century, demonstrated that temporal sanctions were frequently used to coerce recalcitrant entities. He notes, for instance, that in dealing with those Italian city communes defying interdict, Pope Innocent III wrote off to several princes and other cities asking them to confiscate the goods of merchants from affected cities, to hold their merchants and goods, and/or to introduce trade embargoes against those cities – all intended to hit at the source of the cities' power. Moreover, although compliance was reliant on cooperation from secular powers, 'commercial and territorial rivalries between Italian cities provided an incentive to comply'.[78] Stefan Stantchev has similarly highlighted that the main employer of embargoes in the later medieval period was the papacy, though arguing that these were mostly against powers outside the Christian west.[79] Looking beyond the papacy and also solely trade bans, that both secular and ecclesiastical authorities were engaged in similar economic tactics on other occasions is apparent through a range of evidence. Apart from the trade embargo of Offa and Charlemagne in the 790s, we know that Charlemagne also used similar measures in dealing with Venice. This can be seen in a letter from Pope Hadrian to Charlemagne, dated 787x791, which outlines that the pope had responded to the king's order to expel Venetian merchants from Ravennan lands and that Hadrian himself had instructed the archbishop of Ravenna to confiscate Venetian goods and estates.[80] In another example, from the 970s, the Byzantine emperor, John Tzimiskes, sent envoys to the doge and bishops of the Venetians threatening to set their ships, men, and cargo on fire unless the Venetians stopped trading in lumber and weapons with those Muslim territories that were hostile to Byzantium. According to the Venetian document recording the implementation of this ban, John was not appealing to a breach of any obligation in a treaty but rather to the fact that such commerce was an act against all Christian people.[81] This same justification can be seen in a similar ban by the Genoese in 1151.[82] These examples highlight that justifications of self-defence and reprisals were frequently intertwined, and certainly couched in the same language of moral, religious wrongdoing. Measures suspending trade in various ways, or the movement of particular groups of people, to aid or facilitate war against non-Christians and Christians alike can, furthermore, frequently be seen in domestic legislation as well as treaties in the period 700–1200. As with most economic measures, some were general, such as the ban on selling Lombard slaves to Muslims in the *Pactum Sicardi*, while others were more specific, such as the ban on Lombard merchants trading with Romans during times of war in the *Laws of King Aistulf* or the exporting of horses overseas unless it was a gift in the laws of the English king, Athelstan.[83]

That embargoes on trading various items to specific entities or peoples were not entirely successful, however, is evident, for instance, through the 1201 letter of a Tunisian divulging to his Pisan friend that the smuggling of steel was rife.[84] Even the Venetians, after declaring that they would heed the embargo of the Byzantines in the 970s, suggested that some men from the area were so poor that they would be granted a license to carry logs and spars to certain Muslim regions, though reportedly not larger timbers for shipbuilding.[85] Such evidence led Stantchev to argue in 2012 that 'just as during the early Middle Ages there was law but there were no lawyers… so too there were embargoes as legislated realities, as export control systems, but not as relevant and frequently applied policy tools, except maybe – and the stress is on maybe – in the Byzantine empire'.[86] However, these conclusions are perhaps premature for two reasons. First, Stantchev's short study, and also its expansion in monograph form, starts off on the wrong premise by examining how measures such as embargoes were used to control and regulate trade more generally. In other words, Stantchev was looking for restrictions, regulations, and enforcement thereof on a frequent basis. This might work for the evidence and context of the later period, but for that before 1200, the evidence of treaties, which Stantchev did not examine, show that the most desirable state of affairs between entities in times of peace was unimpeded movement of goods and people.[87] In such a context it does not seem at all surprising that the evidence for implementation and enforcement of measures such as embargoes is scarce because they were aimed at wrongdoing (e.g., plundering, killing of non-combatants, enslavement) and intended to be sharp and short-term, thereby coercing the other party to cease their wrongdoing or to recover redress for injuries. The fact that these measures tend to be justified in some way or another, or that they emerge during specific times of hostile action, simply highlights that many were intended as reprisals not 'policy tools' for regulating trade generally.[88] It is curious that Stantchev did not consider the relationship between embargoes and economic reprisals – or put in a different way, the relationship between economic warfare and peace – despite acknowledging that embargoes were both 'a legal and a moral discourse' and linking the concept to its modern equivalents and to international law.[89] Second, studying embargoes and other such measures in the period before 1200 requires a different approach than simply looking at legislation. The evidence presented here on reprisals in the period before 1200, as also demonstrated in Clarke's study on the thirteenth century, highlight that both the Church and secular rulers understood how to use and implement different practical instruments of law in various ways at different points to justify and to enforce action between different authorities or political entities. Piecing this together fully for the earlier medieval period, however, requires an examination of a cross-section of all the available evidence, and a clear understanding of what to look for – it is work that deserves a study of its own, or even several such studies.[90]

That justifications of self-defence and reprisals in the period 700 to 1200 were interlinked and drew on wider religious and cultural ideas and social practices is evident. Justifications can also be tied very closely to the principles and practices of a ruler's responsibility towards himself, his family and immediate supporters, but also more widely, towards his people and the entity they inhabited (whether kingdom, duchy, or city). This is frequently expressed in the justification known as necessity. In the ILC Articles on the Responsibility of States for Internationally Wrongful Acts, necessity is perceived as unpredictable or extraordinary circumstances that may require 'the adoption of measures departing from the normally applicable law in order to protect basic values and fundamental interests'.[91] Paddeu has concluded that, unlike justifications such as self-defence or countermeasures, necessity cannot claim a long history.[92] This is despite the fact that the functions that the concept of necessity play in law are frequently described through two Latin maxims that originate in medieval canon law: *necessitas non habit legem* (necessity has no law) and *necessitas facit legem* (necessity makes law).[93] Nevertheless, Paddeu highlights that terminology and a shifting development of the concept and of state responsibility mean that it is tricky to trace the concept before the Early Modern period and writers such as Grotius.[94] It has been argued that from at least the seventeenth century, the concept of necessity seems to have been linked to those rights that were 'inherent' in statehood, e.g., right to self-preservation, independence, equality, respect, and commerce.[95] However, as a consequence of all states having these 'inherent rights, the idea of necessity became described as a conflict of interests or of rights.[96] To deal with this problem, in modern international law, the criteria which a state must meet is that there must be 'a grave and imminent danger' against which a state is safeguarding an 'essential' interest.[97] Nevertheless, that the justification of necessity remains a highly contested area of international law would seem a fair assessment of the available legislation, literature, and case history.

For the period 700 to 1200, Franck Roumy's study on the origin and dissemination of the phrase *necessitas non habit legem* has shown that the concept of necessity (*necessitas*) as a justification can be found in a range of literature across the early medieval period, even if the exact phrase did not standardise until the late twelfth century.[98] With regards to relations between rulers and treaties, the Latin word *necessitas* is usually linked to other legal justifications, such as self-defence – which is how it often occurs also in later historical periods.[99] Widukind's description of events at Langenzenn in June 954 shows this link between necessity and self-defence clearly, when Otto I's son, Liudolf, is said to have first responded, 'I admit that I gathered money for those who were led against me so that they would not harm me or my dependents' – a justification of self-defence. In the next sentence Liudolf then continues: 'If I am declared guilty in this matter, let the whole people know that I did not do this freely, but rather was forced by extreme necessity (non voluntarie, sed ultima necessitate coactum fecisse).'[100] Widukind implies that there was a notion of a distinct but linked legal category of necessity, and that it trumped the justification of self-defence. Widukind does not elaborate on the circumstances of this 'necessity', though they perhaps fit the modern notion of grave and immediate danger, making it tricky to determine the reason why necessity might trump self-defence or link it specifically to those 'inherent' rights of statehood – self-preservation, independence, equality, respect, and commerce – in the way that commentators on international law have done in later periods. The notion of those 'inherent' rights of statehood, which scholars usually trace to the Early Modern period and the treaties that made up the Peace of Westphalia in 1648, can, of course, be traced to some extent in the period 700 to 1200. For instance, the rights of self-preservation, independence, and equality were frequently asserted by rulers and medieval writers, and are certainly evident in customary practice. This can be seen most clearly through the study of those places where rulers met to negotiate and conclude treaties. As I argued in 2011, both treaties and narrative evidence frequently record that rulers met at locations regarded as the border at that particular time in order to preserve their equality of status, whether perceived or real.[101] Furthermore, that such meetings were recognised as an important characteristic of independent rulership is evident from the existence of claims to meet other rulers on border sites by those with no clear customary practice of this. For instance, according to one early twelfth-century chronicler, when the English king, William II, in 1093 asked Malcolm, king of Scots, to come to his court at Gloucester, the king of Scots refused saying he would meet William only somewhere on the frontier between their kingdoms ('in regnorum suorum confiniis'), and do justice to him in accordance with the judgment of the chief men of both kingdoms ('rectitudinem facere… secundum judicium primatum utriusque regni').[102] Although Malcolm claimed that this had been the customary practice, the evidence for this is scant.[103] In the early thirteenth century, the Welsh prince, Llywelyn ap Iorwerth, made a similar claim to the regents of Henry III of England, but again without any clear precedents.[104] A curious piece of evidence comes from the so-called laws of Hywel Dda – nominally the laws of a tenth-century Welsh king but compiled in the twelfth and thirteenth centuries – showing that one of the most serious offences was killing a man 'during a meeting on the border with another Welsh ruler'.[105] What this piece of evidence again highlights is the existence of the concept and a recognition that meetings on border sites was the ideal rulers aspired to even if no, or little, evidence of the practice existed. In short, what all of this evidence on meeting places demonstrates is that there was in the earlier Middle Ages a notion of what historians of later periods have regarded as the 'inherent' rights of statehood. What none of this evidence does is connect these rights to the justification of necessity.

Some scholars have seen a connection between necessity and the rights of state in the literature of the Carolingian renaissance, primarily through the phrase *necessitas et utilitas*, and variations thereof, which also turns up in treaties and documents regulating relations between rulers.[106] The *Ordinatio imperii* of 817, outlining the relations within the Frankish Empire and between its constituent kingdoms and their rulers, notes how Louis the Pious' oldest son, Lothar, as emperor, would have oversight of all interactions and diplomacy with foreign rulers. His brothers, Louis, king of Bavaria, and Pippin, king of Aquitaine, would deal with embassies concerning matters of lesser consequence, but should 'never fail to inform their eldest brother how matters stand within their own territories, so that he may be found always alert and prepared to do anything that the need and profit (necessitas et utilitas) of the kingdom shall demand'.[107] This seems to imply that *necessitas et utilitas* – described as 'reasons of state' by Elisabeth Magnou-Nortier – could be used as justifications for action.[108] Here, it seems likely that again, the justification of necessity demonstrated the expectation that a king should use his resources for the defence of the kingdom – preserving its very existence.[109] That the defence of the kingdom against invasion was such a necessity that it involved everyone to preserve its existence is, furthermore, outlined in the *Treaty of Meersen* (847). The announcement of Charles the Bald instructs his men, 'in whosoever's kingdom he is', to go with their lord to the army or to whatever other royal need ('utilitatibus') there might be, 'unless, God forbid, an invasion of the kingdom of such a kind takes place, which they call *lantweri*, that all people of that kingdom proceeds as a collective (communiter) to repel it.'[110] Similarly, the first clause of the *Treaty of Tusey*, concluded in 865 between Louis the German and Charles the Bald, set out that the terms would be set forth 'out of fraternal need (necessitates fraterne)'.[111] There is nothing to explain exactly what 'fraternal need' might have meant, but the brothers were seemingly justifying their alliance against their nephews Lothar II and Emperor Louis II – the sons of their deceased older brother, Emperor Lothar I. This is made clearer in the third clause which explains the pressing need to defend and protect the church and kingdom which God had entrusted to them.[112] There is a clear Christian moral tone to this treaty, depicting certain kings as the defenders of a community of faithful against other rulers and their supporters, whose wicked deeds and inability to keep their sworn agreements rendered them, effectively, an enemy of mankind – the standard justification for action.[113] Most ninth-century Frankish treaties have similar language and justifications.

The *Treaty of Fouron*, concluded in 878 between the two Frankish kings Louis the Stammerer and Louis the Younger, serves as a typical example with the second clause declaring: 'If the pagans or false Christians (pagani sive pseudochristiani) rise up against one of us... each... should help his fellow-ruler wherever... necessary (necesse)...'[114]

Ninth-century Frankish treaties are not the only ones to explicitly link the justification of necessity to self-defence of a particular Christian community. By the twelfth century, it is possible to see this through a range of treaties and related diplomatic and legal documents, including some surrounding the expedition and conquest of Almería, in modern Spain, in the 1140s. For instance, the decision granting the lease of the Genoese share of the city for thirty years to Otto di Buonvillano, a Genoese citizen, contains the following justification: 'The consuls [of Genoa] announced this legal decision because they have taken the city of Almería for the glory of God and of the whole of Christendom and have decided to retain control over it in response to the pressing requirements of the Christians (summa necessitate Christianorum).'[115] Here, the justification clearly plugged into the wider cultural and religious contexts of the crusades and crusading ideas, because, as noted by Nikolas Jaspert, some contemporary narrative sources describe the expedition to Almería 'as part of a general struggle against Islam'.[116] It is interesting to note, however, that the treaties of alliance concluded with Alfonso VII, king of León-Castille, and Ramon Berenguer IV, count of Barcelona, for the purpose of the conquest of Almería and Tortosa, contain no references to the need of Christians nor to the necessity of defending them.[117] More commonly, for the whole period, treaties frequently invoked necessity to explain why one party might defend another by acting against a third party, regardless of religious differences. The *Treaty of Dover* (1163), as an example, listed necessity ('ante necessitatem') as the main reason why the English king might summon his Flemish ally and his men to fight the king's enemies.[118] The treaty of 1073 between Sancho IV, king of Navarre, and al-Muktadir, ruler of Zaragoza, stipulates this responsibility and its justification clearly: if al-Muktadir needed help ('necesse hauerit adiutorium') in some parts (of his territory?), he could ask Sancho to come to his aid with his men. That any requests came at a high price is indicated by the fact that under such circumstances, Sancho could demand such hostages ('ostaticos') as he chose from al-Muktadir, and it seems likely that this is the condition that hints fully at the meaning of necessity.[119]

That necessity as a justification can be linked to self-defence as one of the fundamental functions and responsibilities of a ruler is hardly surprising. Yet necessity as a justification also had other applications in the early medieval period. One of the best examples can be found with the late ninth-century treaty between the West Saxon king, Alfred, and Guthrum, king of the people in East Anglia. The final clause of the treaty states that 'if it happens that from necessity (neode) any one of them wishes to have traffic with us, or we with them, for cattle or goods, it is to be permitted on condition that hostages shall be given as a pledge of peace and as evidence so that one may know no fraud is intended'.[120] Here, necessity as a justification recognised the importance of commerce to their kingdoms and to individual communities but also the right of each king to control it – a mutual recognition of rulership. This treaty seemingly renders the Latin *necessitas* into Old English with a similar conceptual meaning as can be seen among Frankish writers of the same period. We can see this link more clearly in the conceptualisation of necessity (*necessitas*) and utility (*utilitas*) in the wider literature of Carolingian reform, setting out the ethical dimensions of Christian leadership with abbots ensuring the stability and peace of their community by assuming responsibility for relations with the outside world. Necessity was a justification for action while utility provided the basis for distinguishing between business (legitimate action), commerce (a private activity), and usury (a forbidden act).[121] Transposing these ideas into government, the king was to be to his subjects as the abbot was to his monks.

The treaty between Alfred and Guthrum seemingly then provides an example that commerce and the economy could form part of the essential interests of entities for the purpose of justification. The link to how this is conceptualised in Frankia in the same period is interesting, and perhaps an in-depth study of the concept and terminology of necessity in vernacular evidence, e.g., Old English *nid* in its variant forms, would be useful to clarify the matter.[122] In any case, it is difficult not to view the usage of necessity in this treaty in a context of Alfred's educational reforms; a programme of reforms that included the translation of Latin texts into Old English.[123]

We know that Alfred certainly travelled to Rome twice as a young boy and that on at least one of those journeys he was also a guest at the west Frankish court of Charles the Bald – one of the intellectual centres of Europe at the time. During his reign, he further invited scholars and ecclesiastics to his own court in a conscious effort to revive learning, and he translated and commented on several Latin texts himself.[124] Hence, it is not entirely fanciful to expect that Alfred may have gained a clear understanding of how the ethical dimensions of business and commerce could be conflated to encompass the needs of ruler, kingdom, and the individuals within it. Viewed in this context, the treaty between Alfred and Guthrum – which survives only as a copy of a West Saxon version – is a highly crafted document linking the ideology and practice of kingship. Most importantly, for this study at least, all of this connects the usage of the Old English term for necessity in this treaty – a source of international law – to one of those 'inherent rights' – commerce – that scholars of the history of international law usually associate only with later periods.

The treaty between Alfred and Guthrum provides an early example of commerce as one of the essential interests of medieval entities for the purpose of justification. Similar examples are not abundant. One later example can be found among the diplomatic documents emanating from Genoa. In the 1150s, Genoa raised taxes and sold off a range of landed interests and commercial rights around the Mediterranean, and one document records how the city leased its possessions in Acre in the Latin kingdom of Jerusalem to two brothers of the Embriaco family – one of the leading families of Genoa. In return, one of the brothers, Ugo, paid the Genoese consuls 100 *librae* 'in magna necessitate', which Hall and Philips have translated as 'because of their pressing need' – likely referring to the city's financial crisis caused by rising debts from the campaign against Tortosa in 1148.[125] Evidently, treaties and related diplomatic documents highlighting necessity as a justification for action links it in some way to the functions and expectations of the ruler – their 'essential' interests, if you like. Defending his people and territory against attacks from external and internal threats was the primary expectation, though, as the examples from the reign of Alfred in the ninth century and Genoa in the mid-twelfth century show, it could extend to trade and commerce to ensure the prosperity of an entity. Whether or not the element of exceptional or unexpected circumstances surrounded such justifications of necessity is perhaps more doubtful.[126] The number of examples is certainly small and usually linked to the performance of some specific obligation. As mentioned above, one example of this is the requirement in the *Treaty of Meersen* (847) that all men should turn out to defend the kingdom in case of a sudden invasion.[127] In the *Treaty of Fouron* of 878 Louis the Stammerer and Louis the Younger undertook to 'unite in every way possible (coniungere omnimodis)' at a future meeting involving also Carloman (Karlmann) and Charles the Fat, the brothers of Louis the Younger. This obligation should hold even if the latter's brothers did not turn up, 'unless by chance such an unavoidable need (necessitas) arises as to make that quite impossible'.[128] Similarly, the *Treaty of Antioch* of 1127, a confirmation of privileges in that city granted by Prince Bohemond II to the Genoese, noted that if anyone offended against the rights granted and brought a complaint to Bohemond, he would give the Genoese redress or mediation, unless he was 'reasonably prevented'. Here, the English translation by Hall and Phillips does not fully convey the justification retained in the Latin: 'nisi impeditus rationabili necessitate fuerim (unless prevented by a reasonable necessity)'.[129] The exact circumstances of the necessity is not defined – perhaps it truly meant something unexpected – but certainly, and similar to the treaty between Alfred and Guthrum, the most notable difference compared to the evidence from most treaties and from narratives such as that of Widukind in the tenth century, is that this justification is not explicitly linked to self-defence.

Necessity in the period 700 to 1200 does not emerge as 'the most often employed possibility to derogate from treaty obligations'.[130] In the period before 1200, necessity was primarily linked to the justification of self-defence without that notion of there being 'a grave and imminent danger' against which the ruler protected an 'essential' interest. Although, there are some exceptions to this, such as the ninth-century treaty between Alfred and Guthrum or the *Treaty of Antioch* (1127), we should not be surprised by this recourse to the justification of self-defence because it, as explained above, could be strongly contextualised within an ecclesiastical, philosophical, and hence moral and ultimately legal discourse. Nevertheless, the idea of necessity resulting from a 'grave and imminent danger' can be connected to another justification, which in modern international law is known as *force majeure*: 'the occurrence of an irresistible force or of an unforeseen event, beyond the control of the State, making it materially impossible in the circumstances to perform the obligation'.[131] Emperor Conrad II's biographer, Wipo, provides evidence of this connection in his report of the arrival of Normans in southern Italy, commenting that they had been 'compelled by some necessity or other' to flock together into Apulia.[132] Exactly what such necessities might have been is left to the reader's imagination: a common theme in the evidence. More usefully, we find it in the *Treaty of Devol*, in which Bohemond of Antioch acknowledged a prior treaty with the Byzantine emperor, Alexius Komnenus, saying 'that agreement, in consequence of certain unexpected events, has since been violated'. The text of the treaty helpfully adds that this precluded the emperor from making any claims against Bohemond by relying on that agreement, thereby aptly explaining the legal function of justifications in international law.[133]

The evidence may not always be specific about what these unexpected events or necessities were, but they are usually grouped into two clear categories: natural and man-made disasters. These can be seen with one of the earliest surviving Venetian *commenda* – a sort of investment contract or loan for overseas commercial ventures.[134] Dating to August 1073, the text of this particular contract reveals how Giovanni Lissado received an investment of £200, with which he acquired shares in a ship sailing to Thebes to make some profits for himself and the investor on the (undefined) goods. But, 'if all these goods are lost because of the sea or of people (Et si... a mare vel a gente supertotum istud habere perditum fuerit)' then neither party should ask for anything from the other.[135] Here, are two examples of *force majeure*, and that the first was a storm at sea seems evident; in other words, a natural disaster. What might be intended with 'people (gente)' can be perhaps be debated, but that it related to something man-made seems clear; here, likely piracy.[136] These same two categories can be found also in an early eleventh-century letter by a Jewish trader who had settled and married in Egypt, and who, on one of his journeys, had suffered shipwreck. The letter reveals that his wife had received, prior to his departure, a conditional bill of divorce, to enable her to marry again in case he died on one of his travels, by acts of God or men, without leaving an eyewitness of this.[137] Neither of these examples are drawn from a treaty – a source of international law   yet, it is apparent that these two categories are retained in many treaties and narratives describing treaties through the two phrases 'act of God' (*impedimentum Dei*) – a force of nature – and 'clear/material/unavoidable impediment' (*certum/ evidente/inevitabili impedimentum*) – a man-made force or event.[138] How treaties interpreted and implemented these two categories, however, depended on geographical area, as we shall see.

That 'acts of God' related to natural disasters, such as storms at sea, is obvious from the fact that the phrase occurs mainly in treaties involving maritime cities or in relation to obligations to undertake sea journeys. For instance, the *Treaty of Genoa I* (1146), by which the Genoese and Alfonso of Leon-Castile allied for the purpose of the military expedition to Almería, states that Alfonso promised to set off on the journey and remain with the army 'subject to any reasonable over-riding cause placed in our way by God (*Dei impedimento*) or by agreement between them and ourselves'.[139] Similarly, the Genoese committed to undertake the journey and stay with the expeditionary force 'unless we are prevented from coming by some just impediment imposed by God (*nisi remanserit iusto Dei impedimento*)'.[140] A second example, Philip II of France's treaty with the Genoese for the transport of his force to the Holy Land in 1190, sets out that the French king 'will cross the sea from the city of Genoa this coming summer; or if he is not able to travel through some act of God or for whatever reason (*aliquo iusto Dei impedimento vel quacumque de causa*), his generals who will make the crossing on his orders will start the voyage from Genoa'.[141] It seems likely, but not certain, that the 'act of God' also in this example referred to a storm at sea. Anna Komnena, in reporting on the war between the Byzantines and the Norman leader of southern Italy, Robert Guiscard, in the early 1080s, likewise comments that Robert had been thwarted by storm and shipwreck, 'the wrath of God', confirming that connection.[142] It can also be explained by the large number of treaties, involving at least one maritime party, that include clauses relating to shipwreck and redress resulting from such events. In particular, treaties tend to grant exemptions from the usual custom of shipwreck, which allowed the ruler or the inhabitants of a particular area to seize that which washed ashore from any wreck.[143] For instance, the *Treaty of Acre*, concluded in 1124 between the representatives of King Baldwin II of Jerusalem and the Venetians, sets out: 'If any Venetian shall be shipwrecked, he shall not suffer loss of any of his property. If he dies in the shipwreck, the property which he leaves shall be sent back to his heirs or to other Venetians.'[144] Other Venetian treaties with the princes of Outremer seem to have replicated at least the first part of that clause, e.g., the treaty with Bohemond III of Antioch of 1167.[145] In 1132, the inhabitants of Narbonne promised to the Genoese, as a concession for injuries done to them, not to avail themselves of their right to shipwreck if a Genoese ship was lost in their territory.[146] Similarly, in 1184 Count Raymond V of Toulouse and his allies promised to 'lead, defend and conduct (regere, defendere, gubernare)' the Genoese and their goods 'through both shipwreck and sound [waters] (tam naufragos quam sanos)' across the areas where they held authority, and to restore fully any losses. Any claims for redress should be settled within one month unless impeded by an act of God or by legitimate delays of indulgence ('iusto Dei impedimento aut pro dilationibus legitime indulgendis').[147] The 911 *Treaty of Constantinople* between the Rus' and the Byzantines has similar stipulations. If a ship was wrecked or detained by storms, then the Rus' were to conduct the men and their goods safely to Byzantine territory if the event took place in 'foreign lands' or near Byzantine shores. If, however, it took place near the shore of the Rus', then whatever of the ship's cargo was retrieved would be sold, and the amount received would be paid back to the owner upon request or when a Rus' next visited Constantinople.[148] By contrast, the ninth-century *Pactum Sicardi* notes about shipwreck that only if it happened because of the fault of the men onboard would the goods be returned to the owner.[149] In other words, an act of God precluded wrongfulness against breaches of the obligations in the treaty, and hence would not generate legal redress for injuries resulting from that event. Only loss resulting from human intervention carried liability and resulted in redress.[150] In a different example, the exact nature and understanding of the exemption from the right to shipwreck seem to be different in the two versions of the treaty. The Latin version of the *Treaty of Mallorca* (1181) sets out that if any Genoese ship suffered shipwreck, the inhabitants of the Balearic Islands would recover the men and their goods from the wreck and restore to them that which belonged to them, 'except in the case of money lying at the bottom [of the sea]'.[151] The Arabic version, however, seems to have stipulated only that survivors could freely recover what belongings they found in the sea or on the beaches.[152] The reason for this discrepancy in the two versions is not entirely clear. Nonetheless, what is interesting in these examples is that domestic customary practices regarding shipwreck could be set aside with reference to another legal principle; that contained within a treaty.

If storms at sea, and shipwreck as a result of such an event, were justified as acts of God, it is also obvious that other natural disasters could befall medieval societies, and that such events would then preclude wrongfulness in case a treaty obligation was not carried out. One can imagine that such natural disasters could include earthquakes, floods, wildfires, droughts, or epidemics of infectious disease. However, if they did, finding exact evidence to demonstrate this is nigh on impossible.[153] Treaties usually do not specifically define acts of God outside the evidence pertaining to storms at sea.[154] By contrast, narrative sources, such as chronicles and letters, certainly mention such occurrences but without specifically connecting them to treaties or breaches thereof.[155] Natural disasters, of course, have been disrupting human life and interactions between communities occasionally from their very beginning; hence, specification was perhaps unnecessary.[156] Yet, it also seems logical that with commerce being one of the most common reasons for interactions, storms at sea were those acts of God where specificity was particularly needed because they were the most frequently occurring such events. One perspective is offered by the *Treaty of San Salvatore II*, which records that the Genoese would support Frederick in his efforts to conquer the kingdom of Sicily by providing a naval force from 1 September 1162 or during the whole of May the year after. If, however, the emperor would be unable to set out with his own land force by May, 'through some just and obvious impediment (iusto et evidenti impedimento)', he committed to inform the Genoese of the new date and as long as this fell between 1 May and 1 September, they would mobilise their force and 'not subsequently abandon his army unless a reasonable and manifest obstacle stands in the way through divine intervention (Dei impedimentum), or by authority of the emperor or his trusted ambassador'.[157] This seems to imply that only the Genoese obligations could be impeded by

acts of God (*impedimentum Dei*), while implying that any impediment ('iusto et evidenti impedimento') of Frederick would have
been of a different kind, presumably involving human intervention.
This is despite the fact that natural disasters might affect any ruler
or entity at any point.

The exact nature of any impediments that might have delayed
Frederick Barbarossa's expedition is not divulged, but what some
such impediments were can be gleaned from descriptions of
agreements and negotiations in narrative sources. Emperor Henry
IV wrote a letter to Duke Álmos in 1096, urging the latter to intercede on Henry's behalf with Coloman, king of Hungary. Henry
suggests that Coloman had been unable to do justice to Henry for
injuries suffered, because of 'his own necessities (suas necessitates)'.
It seems clear that Henry was referring to either war or rebellion of
some sort, as Henry further notes that Coloman had recently 'gotten
out of his straits with a victorious right hand (victrici dextera suas
angustias recuperavit)'.[158] Evidence from treaties tends to be less
clear on the exact nature of these unexpected but major events, but
often include the expectancy that once they had been overcome,
the obligation should still be carried out.[159] For instance, when
Emperor Henry IV swore his famous oath to Pope Gregory VII at
Canossa in 1077, he promised that if a 'concrete obstacle (certum
impedimentum)' would hinder him or the pope from bringing about
justice to the complaints from German ecclesiastics and magnates,
he would be prepared to do it when that obstacle had been overcome.[160] In another example, the *Ordinatio imperii* of 817 outlines
that each royal brother with the title of king should visit their
oldest brother (the emperor) once a year. But 'if it happens that
one of them is prevented from coming by an unavoidable necessity (inevitabili necessitate impedimentum)', he should inform the
oldest brother of this.[161] The *Treaty of Benevento* (1156) likewise
set out that the king of Sicily undertook to pay the papacy 1,000
schifati a year, 'unless by chance some impediment shall intervene
(nisi forte impedimentum aliquod intervenerit)'. That this referred
to some unexpected event that the king would be able to overcome
is clear from the expectation that once this impediment no longer
applied the payment would have to be paid in full.[162] It is tempting
to hazard a guess that at least in the last two examples, the unexpected impediment also referred to war or rebellion.

It is possible that the reason why the nature of acts of God but not other unexpected impediments tend to be defined should be explained with reference to Roman law, as it contained a number of different *casi*, including fortuitous event (casus fortuitus), *force majeure* (vis major), fatal damage (damnum fatale), and divine force (vis divina).[163] This would partially also explain why the majority of the examples discussed so far originate with parties in Italy or Byzantium, and most of them also date to the twelfth century – the period of renewed, widespread study of Roman law. Only the *Ordinatio imperii* of 817 and Henry IV's letter to Duke Álmos of the late eleventh century would seem to be exceptions to those two factors. All of this then might indicate that there was no concept of *force majeure* in other parts of Europe in the period 700–1200.

A different way of looking at the evidence in treaties from the rest of Europe is to start with the *Treaty of Worms*. This treaty was concluded in June 1193 between the Emperor Henry VI and Richard I of England, then in the emperor's captivity. Among other things, the text outlines the safe conduct of the huge ransom for Richard, and as such, it is a treaty that we might expect to contain a clause of *force majeure*, given the obligation to deliver the ransom and the logistical challenges this presented. However, the treaty stipulates that the English king held responsibility for the money if it was lost while transported through his territories, while Richard's captor, Emperor Henry VI, likewise, bore responsibility if the money was lost within the empire.[164] One way of looking at this stipulation is to argue, though admittedly from an absence of evidence, that there would be no need to specify that Richard and Henry held liability for the loss of money, unless a concept existed that precluded liability in certain circumstances. In fact, many treaties from the rest of Europe tend to be specific about liability or responsibility, possibly indicating imprecision, rather than absence, in both the terminology and the concept.[165] According to the *Treaty of Dover* (1101), Count Robert of Flanders would serve King Henry I of England 'unless he stays at home on account of a demonstrable illness of body, of the loss of his land, of a military summons from Philip, king of the French, or of a summons issued by the emperor of the Romans'.[166] This particular treaty was guaranteed by a number of sureties, who in the case of default by the count of Flanders promised to pay a set sum each to the English king within 120 days. In case a surety died, he would be replaced, and if the money was lost at sea, there would be a respite of forty days to replace it.[167] Like the *Treaty of Worms*, there seems to be a recognition that a natural disaster was a possibility, but this did not justify non-performance of the obligation to pay. Unlike treaties from Italy and Byzantium, where two categories of what we might think of as *force majeure* emerge more clearly, in these two treaties there seems to be only a single category, which made no distinction between the justification *force majeure* and lawful excuses of a more procedural nature. The *Treaty of Dover* (1101) even uses the same terminology as that of English law in noting that if Count Robert defaulted on account of the aforesaid lawful excuses ('si comes R. defuerit propter aliquam predictorum exoniarum'), six of those nominated as sureties would lead the promised soldiers in his stead.[168] The Latin term *essonium/exonium* – an essoin; that is, an excuse for non-appearance – is usually perceived as an excuse for non-appearance in court but in the treaty used to denote the non-appearance of the Flemish count in the service of the English king.[169]

Lawful excuses are more commonly indicated through phrases such as *iustum/legale impedimentum*, and for treaties it seems clear that they covered both lawful excuses and unexpected events such as natural disasters or wars, i.e., *force majeure*. For instance, the *Treaty of Tudején*, an alliance agreed in 1151, shows that if Alfonso VII of Léon and Castile was unable to aid the count of Barcelona, Ramon Berenguer III, to acquire Murcia on account of illness or a just and known impediment ('iustum et cognitum impedimentum'), the count, if he managed to acquire the city and its kingdom, would still hold them from Alfonso.[170] Illness is regarded as a lawful excuse across most legal systems, while the other impediments are not defined and could evidently cover any, and all, other circumstances.[171] The *Treaty of Logroño* (1176), in which the kings of Navarre and Castile agreed to refer their dispute to the English king for arbitration, stipulates that if the envoys of either king failed to turn up to hear Henry II's decision, that ruler would automatically forfeit his suit. According to the text, lawful excuses could be made for any who had been detained on the road by death, illness, or captivity; the first two of which frequently appear as lawful excuses in domestic laws, while the third was such an event that might be considered *force majeure*.[172] The fact that circumstances such as illness or death are known lawful excuses (*iustum/legal impedimentum*) provides another way of ascertaining that treaties emanating in Italy frequently distinguished between such excuses and those impediments that should be considered under the category of man-made *force majeure*. For instance, those treaties that exclusively use the phrase 'lawful excuse/impediment' tend to do so in what one might consider to be a court setting, and the matter frequently concerned claims of legal redress. We can see this clearly in the *Peace of Constance*, the final peace settlement between the cities of the Lombard League and the Emperor Frederick I concluded in 1183. The text records that in cases of disputes heard by the emperor's officials, the decision had to be given within two months unless 'the case has been deferred by reason of some legal hindrance (iusto impedimento) or by the consent of both parties'.[173] The *Treaty of Antioch* (1101) likewise shows how Tancred, the regent of Antioch, in the event anyone lodged a complaint against the Genoese, agreed to provide redress within thirty days of receiving the complaint, 'unless I am prevented by a lawful impediment (per legale impedimentum remanserit). I [Tancred] will then make amends within another 30 days after such a lawful impediment has passed unless the matter is waived with the consent of the plaintiff (transacto impedimento infra alios triginta dies emendare faciam nisi per eius parabolam remanserit).'[174] Similar clauses about promises to satisfy claims for injuries, unless the case had been deferred by some lawful impediment can be found also in the *Treaty between Genoa and Pavia* (1130), and the *Treaty of Milan* (1158).

Force majeure as a justification precluding wrongfulness is a difficult concept to trace in the period 700–1200. The terminology is varied and interlinked with concepts commonly found in domestic law, including excuses/delays and accidents, and also with other justifications in international law, e.g., necessity. It is easy to imagine, as an example, that the notion of *force majeure* as a man-made unexpected event/force is in the period before c. 1050 subsumed in the justifications of necessity and self-defence, thereby explaining the fewer examples of *force majeure* from that period. Moreover, it is not always clear that when these unexpected events or forces occurred that there was an expectancy of non-performance of obligations or a lack of liability or responsibility. Instead, as shown above, many treaties are specific in outlining arrangements for how an obligation or responsibility should still be adhered to even in the face of severe and unexpected events. Some of these problems and possibilities are evident also in later historical periods, and even in modern international law. Paddeu has shown, for instance, how different domestic legal systems and terminology surrounding *force majeure* has shaped the modern interpretation and use of it.[175] For the period 700–1200 it is also the defence for action that appears closest to being mainly a legal issue, not a legal and moral issue.

The defences for action investigated here have, for purpose of brevity, been fewer than those listed in Articles 20–25 of the International Law Commission's (ILC or Commission) Articles on the Responsibility of States for Internationally Wrongful Acts.[176] Nevertheless, each show in different ways the blurring of private and public, domestic and international, war and peace, and, significantly, the moral and the legal in the period 700 to 1200. These are issues that go right to the heart about the debate over justifications in international law also in the modern period and show one important difference between the medieval and the modern. Treaties in the medieval period were personal undertakings by rulers (or ruling councils) and their followers on behalf of all subjects or citizens. These had a moral as well as a legal responsibility for which they were personally accountable, in this life and the next, through the oaths sworn.[177] By contrast, critics of modern international law point out that 'wrongdoing is the behavior of a general category known as "states" and is not the behavior of morally responsible human beings. It therefore obscures the fact that breaches of international law are attributable formally to the legal persons known as states but morally to the human beings who determine the behaviour of states'.[178] Allott further argues that aspects of international law, such as international crimes, where individual responsibility is attached, is one for which the collective responsibility of the 'state' would be more appropriate: 'The most heinous international behavior will not be discouraged by attaching liability to individual human beings if it has the effect of removing legal and moral liability from the whole society which makes such behavior possible and for whose benefit the behaviour may well be carried out.'[179]

What Allott, and others, in essence highlight is the difficulty of weighing legal responsibility, whether through obligations and rights outlined in treaties or through conduct in war, against enforcement of that responsibility. Justifications, in other words, preclude wrongfulness. That there was a concept of this also in the period 700 to 1200 is evident from the fact that action against other rulers or communities is always justified in a legal, and thereby moral, context. It is harder to explain such justification away, than simply acknowledging that there was a concept of international rules in the Middle Ages. Importantly, justifications show that deterrence and enforcement of responsibility required a multi-pronged approach to resolving disputes between rulers. One such will be explored in the next chapter.

Notes

1 Dixon, *Textbook on IL*, 5.
2 Ibid.
3 Paddeu, *Justification*, 8–9; Crawford, *State Responsibility*, 274–7.
4 On this, see Russell, *The Just War*; Cox, 'The Ethics of War', 99–121.
5 Widukind, *RGS*, Bk. III, cap. 31 (p. 118): '...rationis dandae et responsionis reddendae.' English translation from Widukind, *Deeds*, 116.
6 Widukind, *RGS*, Bk. III, cap. 32 (pp. 118–19); Widukind, *Deeds*, 117.
7 Widukind, *RGS*, Bk. III, cap. 32 (p. 119); Widukind, *Deeds*, 118.
8 https://legal.un.org/ilc/texts/instruments/english/draft_articles/9_6_2001.pdf (accessed 16 July 2021), art. 20–5.
9 Widukind, *RGS*, Bk. III, cap. 32 (pp. 118–19); Widukind, *Deeds*, 117.
10 For this discussion and references to relevant literature, see Chapter 2, p. 58. See also Elisabeth Magnou-Nortier, 'The Enemies of the Peace: Reflections on a Vocabulary, 500–1100', in *The Peace of God: Social Violence and Religious Response in France around the Year 1000*, eds. Thomas Head and Richard Landes (Ithaca, NY, 1992), 60, 67–8. On the use of similar justifications in other historical periods, see Sonja Schillings, *Enemies of All Humankind. Fictions of Legitimate Violence* (Hanover, NH, 2017); Jenny S. Martinez, *The Slave Trade and the Origins of International Human Rights Law* (Oxford, 2012); Christian Boudignon, ' "How am I to Love the One Who Hates Me?" Love for One's Enemy, Persecution and Human Rights in Maximus the Confessor', in *The Quest for a Common Humanity: Human Dignity and Otherness in the Religious Traditions*

of the Mediterranean, ed Matthias Morgenstern (Leiden, 2011), 199–218; Helen M. Kinsella and Giovanni Mantilla, 'Contestation before Compliance: History, Politics, and Power in International Humanitarian Law', *International Studies Quarterly*, 64 (2020), 649, 652.

11 *CDRG*, I, 78. The phrase occurs in a similar context also in the pope's arbitration of 1188 in the conflict over Sardinia between the same two cities, for which see *CDRG*, ii, 333.

12 *Sic* in MS. for *resipiscerent*.

13 Chaplais, *EDP*, 37.

14 *EHD*, I, no. 230; WM, GRA, I, 278–9. See also Du Cange et al., 'Superstitio'. Cf. J. Tolan, '*Lex alterius*: Using Law to Construct Confessional Boundaries', *History and Anthropology*, 26 (2015), 59.

15 A letter from Pope Gregory VII to the archbishop of Rheims, asking him to restrain the violent actions and extortions of King Philip I against foreign merchants, makes the link between unchristian violence and the enemy of mankind clear. Gregory VII, *Registrum II, 32*, in *MGH Epp. sel. 2.1*, 168. Clause 18 of the *Partition of Benevento*, concluded in the mid-ninth century, likewise speak of the barbaric ('barbaricum'), i.e., plunder, arson and killings, that had arisen between the two parties.

16 *Treaty of Zaragoza*, in González, *El reino de Castilla*, 251–2: 'si ego… hoc quod supra scriptum est non attendero, ex tunc sim periurus, fide mentitus, proditor et aleuosus' (repeated for each king). On such clauses in Iberian treaties, see also Adam Kosto, *Making Agreements in Medieval Catalonia. Power, Order and the Written Word, 1000–1200* (Cambridge, 2001), 121–4. Similar phrasing occurs also in *Liber Feudorum maior: Cartulario real que se conserva en el Archivo de la Corona de Aragon*, 2 vols., ed. Francisco Miquel Rosell (Barcelona, 1945–7), nos. 6, 34, 522 and 601. My thanks to Adam Kosto for pointing me in the direction of these. Non-Iberian examples can be found with the *Treaty of Gaeta* (1029), in Martin, *Guerre*, 223; and the announcement of Tassilo's final submission in 794, according to which he had shown himself to be 'a betrayer of his faith (fraudator fidei suae)' in *MGH Capit. I*, no. 28, c. 3.

17 Koziol, *The Peace of God*, 12; *MGH Capit. II*, no. 197, c. 2 (p. 54).

18 *Treaty of Jarnègues*, c. 12.

19 For one well-known critique of modern international law, highlighting this issue, see Allott, 'State Responsibility', 13–15. See also discussion below, pp. 179–80.

20 Generally, on this problem, see Klaus van Eickels, 'Um 1101: Wo man im Mittelalter zwei Herren dienen konnte – und welche Folgen

dies hatte', in *Die Macht des Königs: Herrschaft in Europa vom Frühmittelalter bis in die Neuzeit*, ed. Bernhard Jussen (Munich, 2005), 165–78.

21 For a discussion of what such clauses can tell us about how peace operated in time and space, see Chapter 3, pp. 106–11.

22 *Treaty of Lerici*, c. 32: 'Et si aliquis Lucensis consul vel consules, potesta vel potestates aliquod predicte conventionis capitulum, quod absit, non observaverit, nichilominus omnem aliam suprascriptam conventionem firmam tenebo.'

23 *Treaty of Mallorca* (1188), c. 11. It is worth noting that the text has survived in a Latin and an Arabic version. The 1181 treaty between the same parties had a similar clause, declaring that whosoever contravened the terms would be guilty of an offence that was against religion. *Treaty of Mallorca* (1181), c. 8.

24 E.g., *AGu*, prol.; *Treaty between Sancho IV of Navarre and al-Muktadir of Zaragoza* (1069); *Treaty of Messina* (1127); *Treaty of Portovenere* (1149, 1169); *Treaty of Constantinople* (1169); *Treaty of Zaragoza* (1170); *Treaty of Najac-de-Rouergue* (1185), cc. 1–2; *Treaty of Messina* (1190), oath; *Treaty of Genoa I* (1190).

25 Examples include *Treaty of Melfi* (1059); *Treaty of Devol* (1108); *Treaty between Genoa and Pavia* (1130); *Treaty between Genoa and Fos* (1138); *Treaty of Portovenere* (1149); *Treaty of Sahagún* (1158); *Treaty of San Salvatore II* (1162); *Treaty of Pavia* (1162); *Treaty of Najac-de-Rouergue* (1185).

26 Examples include *Treaty between Genoa and Raymond of Toulouse, Sancho of Provence, William of Forcalquier*, c. 1; *Pact of Milan and Piacenza* (1156), c. 6; *Treaty of Genoa* (1165), c. 18.

27 Martin, *Guerre*, 180: 'nullo modo consensimus ei illud'.

28 For a clear analysis of this particular defence in modern international law, see Cliff Farhang, 'The Notion of Consent in Part One of the Draft Articles on State Responsibility', *Leiden Journal of International Law*, 27 (2014), 55–74. More widely, see also Michelle Madden Dempsey, 'Victimless Conduct and the Volenti Maxim: How Consent Works', *Criminal Law and Philosophy*, 7 (2013), 11–27, esp. 12–14; Paddeu, *Justification*, 131–4; Crawford, *State Responsibility*, 283–9.

29 For discussion of this treaty, its manuscript and historical context, see Martin, *Guerre*, 8–11, 78–82.

30 *Herimanni Augiensis Chronicon*, 127; *Eleventh-century Germany*, 82.

31 There is debate over the exact difference(s) between excuses and justifications in international law, with scholars acknowledging that many defences could be both. For examples of the literature, see Paddeu, *Justification*, 10, 12; Vaughan Lowe, 'Precluding

Wrongfulness or Responsibility: A Plea for Excuses', *EJIL*, 10 (1999), 405–11; Crawford, *State Responsibility*, 274–84.

32 As a non-Christian comparator, it is worth noting that this is specifically set out in Muslim law, for which see *The Islamic Law of Nations*, 247–9.

33 Isidore, *Etymologiae*, V:4.1–2. Translation from Barney, *Etymologies*, 117.

34 Cox, 'The Ethics of War', 103. Cicero, *On Duties*, 1:11, 13, 35, 39–41; 3:99.

35 Burchard of Worms, *Lex familiae*, c. 30.

36 On Augustine, see Russell, *The Just War*, 18–20.

37 Cox, 'The Ethics of War', 110.

38 *Gesta Friderici*, 202–3; Otto of Freising, *The Deeds of Frederick Barbarossa*, tr. C. C. Mierow (Toronto, 1994), 205.

39 *The Deeds of Frederick Barbarossa*, 205 fn. 87. See also *Decretum*, C.23 q.1 c.6; C.23 q.2 c.1; C.23 q.3 c.1.

40 *Treaty between Genoa and Pavia* (1140), c. 7: 'Et non faciemus inde pacem neque guerram recretam neque treguam nisi per parabola consulum utriusque civitatis vel illius cui iniuria facta fuerit.'

41 *Treaty of Mallorca* (1181), cc. 1–5, 8. Note that, judging by the French and Italian translations of the Arabic version of the treaty, this hostility is expressed with slight differences in the Latin and Arabic versions of the text.

42 *DD FI*, ii, 223; Hall, *Caffaro*, 199.

43 *Treaty of Tusey*, c. 4; *DD FI*, ii, 223.

44 Widukind, *RGS*, Bk. III, cap. 32 (pp. 118–19); Widukind, *Deeds*, 117.

45 Paddeu, *Justification*, 228.

46 Dante Fedele, 'Indemnities in Diplomacy'. See also Thomas Heebøll-Holm, *Ports, Piracy and Maritime War: Piracy in the English Channel and the Atlantic, c. 1280–c. 1330* (Leiden, 2013), 131–52; René de Mas Latrie, *Du droit de marque ou droit de représailles au moyen-âge* (Paris, 1875), 11–22.

47 These ideas are perhaps best highlighted and summarised in the twelfth century through Gratian's *Decretum*, and in the thirteenth century through the *Summa Theologiae* of the philosopher Thomas Aquinas. *Decretum*, C.23; Thomas Aquinas, *Summa Theologiae*, part 2–2, q. 40, art. 1. That regulations limiting private reprisals existed much earlier is clear from, as an example, ninth-century capitularies for the Frankish kingdoms, e.g., 'Capitulary of Quierzy, 857', cc. 9–10.

48 On redress and reprisals, see Chapter 3, pp. 95–6, 117–18; Heebøll-Holm, *Ports, Piracy and Maritime War*, 149–51; Marie-Claire Chavarot, 'La pratique des lettres de marque d'après les arrêts du parlement

(xiie-début xve siècle)', *Bibliothèque de l'école des chartes*, 149 (1991), 51–4; Ganshof, *MA*, 312; Mas Latrie, *Du droit de marque*, 8–9.

49 Howden, *Gesta*, i. 354–5; Howden, *Chronica*, ii, 315.

50 The text of this treaty does not survive merely Howden's narrative account. Howden, *Gesta*, i. 353; Howden, *Chronica*, ii, 315.

51 On this, see also Chapter 3, pp. 95–6. Paddeu makes a similar point about reprisals in more modern times, for which see Paddeu, *Justification*, 247–9.

52 One other example is the seizure of sureties by Richard I in 1196 following the treaty of Louviers. For a brief discussion, see Benham, *PMA*, 169–70. In the later period, the evidence of reprisals is most plentiful from Italian cities, such as Genoa or Venice, or areas trading with them. Chavarot, 'La pratique des lettres de marque', 54–5; Mas Latrie, *Du droit de marque*, 5.

53 Thomas Heebøll-Holm and Marie-Claire Chavarot have shown that in northern Europe, letters of marque and reprisals were established in the period just beyond that covered by this book, and only became common from the fourteenth century onwards. Heebøll-Holm, *Ports, Piracy and Maritime War*, 131–48, 155–60; Chavarot, 'La pratique des lettres de marque', 55–6. See also Mas Latrie, *Du droit de marque*, 12–22; Ganshof, *MA*, 311–14.

54 *Pactum Sicardi*, c. 2.

55 Ibid., c. 2: 'vel si ante pignus steteritis de istis supradictis capitulis, componere nobis debeatis secundum vestram promissionem auri solidos Beneventanos numero tria milia, et insuper per scamaratores seu cursas et publicum exercitum oppressionem facere usque ad nostram satisfactionem.'

56 Grygiel has described reprisals as traditional but ineffective acts of deterrence. Grygiel, 'The Primacy of Premodern History', 15–16. At the lower levels of society, these types of acts are often considered self-help, which has generated a large debate among scholars over the nature of feud and legitimate authority in medieval society. For examples of this large historiography, see Joseph Schmitt, *Die Selbsthilfe im römischen Privatrecht* (Erlangen, 1868); Josef Semmler, 'Eine Herrschaftsmaxime im Wandel: Pax und Concordia im karolingischen Frankenreich', in *Frieden in Geschichte und Gegenwart* (1985), 24–34; Gerhard Dilcher, 'Fehde, Unrechtsausgleich und Strafe im älteren langobardischen Recht: Eine Skizze', in *Hoheitliches Strafen in der Spätantike und im frühen Mittelalter*, ed. Jürgen Weitzel (Cologne, 2002), 27–45; John Hudson, 'Feud, Vengeance and Violence in England from the Tenth to the Twelfth Centuries', in *Feud, Violence and Practice: Essays in Medieval Studies in Honor of*

Stephen D. White, eds. Belle S. Tuten and Tracy L. Billado (Farnham, 2010), 29–53; John D. Niles, 'The Myth of the Feud in Anglo-Saxon England', *Journal of English and Germanic Philology*, 114 (2015), 163–200.

57 Fedele, 'Indemnities in Diplomacy'.

58 *Treaty of Pisa* (1126), c. 5: 'Similiter, si aliqua vestra navis, una aut plures, vel si aliquis vester homo, unus aut plures, apud nos fuerint cum aliquibus rebus et forsitan vestri homines offenderint nos vel nostros homines in aliquibus locis vel partibus, vestri tamen homines et eorum res seu navigia eorum apud nos secura et salva erunt eis, et non faciemus aliquam violentiam eis nec patiemur aut consentiemus ut fiat neque in personis neque in rebus eorum.'

59 S. C. Neff, *War and the Law of Nations* (Cambridge, 2005), 215. See also Magnou-Nortier, 'The Enemies of the Peace', 71–2.

60 *DD FI*, iv, 304: 'in contumelian creatoris et crucis scandalum, cui militabant, iussit captivari et fame sue minus consulens contra ius universarum nationum et legatorum ignominiose in carcerem iussit detrudi. Talibus auditis universus crucis exercitus infremuit et postmodum civitates, castella, vicos depopulari atque occupare non cessavit, quoadusque imperator Constantinopolitanus magnificentie nostre legate cum magno honore ad nos redituros litterarum suarum tenore nobis significavit.' Translation in *CFB*, 69, 71.

61 *Digest*, 50:7.18: 'Si quis legatum hostium pulsassit, contra jus gentium id commissum esse existimatur, quia sancti habentur legati.' This was adapted in Isidore, *Etymologiae*, V:6. For the practice in antiquity, see examples in Bederman, *International Law in Antiquity*, 106–20. For a few medieval examples, invoking this principle or breaches thereof, see *The Decree of King Childebert*, c. 8.6; *Ripuarian Laws*, c. 68(65).3; *Treaty of Pavia* (840), c. 18; *The Law of Hywel Dda*, 5; Gregory VII, *Registrum IV*, 12a, in *MGH Epp. sel. 2.1*, 315; *Gesta Friderici*, 174–5.

62 *Historia de Expeditione*, 47; *CFB*, 75.

63 *DD FI*, iv, 304; *CFB*, 71.

64 *DD FI*, iv, 305; *CFB*, 72.

65 On this continued issue and events, see *Historia de Expeditione*, 45–58; *CFB*, 72–84. For a different example of a similar multi-pronged strategy of reprisals, see the documents surrounding the so-called 'Golden Inscription' in Hall, *Caffaro*, 207–12.

66 *Historia de Expeditione*, 58; *CFB*, 84. For another example of termination of treaty as a reprisal, see *Treaty of Devol*, c. 1. On the topic generally, see Paddeu, *Justification*, 236; Derek Bowett, 'Treaties and State Responsibility', in *Le droit international au service de la paix, de*

la justice et du développement, Mélanges Michel Virally (Paris, 1991), 137–15, L. A Sicilianos, 'The Relationship between Reprisals and Denunciation or Suspension of a Treaty', *EJIL*, 1 (1993) 341–59, esp. 344–5.

67 *Historia de Expeditione*, 60–1, 64–6; *CFB*, 87, 90–2. A complementary account of these events can also be found in the *Historia Peregrinorum*, in *Quellen zur Geschichte des Kreuzzuges Kaiser Friedrichs I*, ed. A. Chroust, *MGH SRG* n.s., 5 (Berlin, 1928), 127ff.

68 A point similarly made, but in a more theoretical context, by Jehangir Y. Malegam, 'Suspicions of Peace in Medieval Christian Discourse', *Common Knowledge*, 21 (2015), 236–52, esp. 237–8, 251–2.

69 *ARF*, s.a. 755–6; *LP*, i, 452–3.

70 On the history of reprisals and the re-naming of these to the more 'neutral' countermeasures, see Paddeu, *Justification*, 225–44.

71 On defining these terms, see Stefan Stantchev, 'The Medieval Origins of Embargo as a Policy Tool', *History of Political Thought*, 33 (2012), 374–7.

72 *Gesta sanctorum patrum Fontanellensis coenobii*, Bk. 12, c. 2 (pp. 86–7); *MGH Epp.*, IV, nos. 7, 9, 82 (pp. 32, 35, 125); Allott, *Alcuin of York*, nos. 10, 31 39. For discussion of this incident, see Chapter 3, pp. 125–6.

73 *Gesta Chuonradi II Imperatoris*, in *Die Werke Wipos*, ed. H. Bresslau, *MGH SRG*, 61 (Hanover, 1915), cc. 7, 12 (pp. 33–4).

74 *Alexandri Telesini Abbatis Ystoria Rogerii Regis Siciliae atque Calabriae atque Apulie*, ed. Ludovica de Nava (Rome, 1991), Bk. II, c. 7; Alexander of Telese, *History of King Roger*, in *Roger II and the Creation of the Kingdom of Sicily*, tr. Graham A. Loud (Manchester, 2012), 80. On urban resistance to the new Sicilian king in this period, see Francesco Calasso, 'La città nell'Italia meridionale durante l'età Normanna', *Archivio Storico Pugliese*, 12 (1959), 18–34; Paul Oldfield, 'Urban Government in Southern Italy, c.1085–c.1127', *EHR*, 122 (2007), 579–608, esp. 581–4; D. Matthew, *The Norman Kingdom of Sicily* (Cambridge, 1992), 31–53.

75 *Alexandri Telesini Abbatis Ystoria Rogerii Regis*, Bk. II, c. 8: 'mare, iussu eiusdem regis, sollicitus secus Amalfiam circumgirando observare studet, si forte amalfitanorum aliquos pelagus peragrantes capere posset; et ne forte quilibet alii undecumque per equora accedentes, eis opitula[tu]ri sucurrerent.' Translation from *Roger II*, 80.

76 *Alexandri Telesini Abbatis Ystoria Rogerii Regis*, Bk. II, c. 9–11; *Roger II*, 80–1.

77 Graham A. Loud, 'Introduction', in *Roger II*, 52–3.

78 Peter D. Clarke, *Interdict in the Thirteenth Century: A Question of Collective Guilt* (Oxford, 2007), 182–3.

79 Stantchev, 'The Medieval Origins of Embargo', 398. For a fuller study of this, see Stefan Stantchev, *Spiritual Rationality: Papal Embargo as Cultural Practice* (Oxford, 2014).

80 'Codex Carolinus', ed. W. Gundlach, in *MGH Epp.* III (Berlin, 1892), no. 86 (pp. 622–3).

81 *Storia documentata di Venezia. Tomo 1*, ed. S. Romanin (Venice, 1853), 373: '...et terribiliter minantes per gloriosissimi Imperatoris verbum, ut se (nec?) de tali lignamine barbaris adjutorium preberent, quae ad dignitatem imperii, et Christianum populum fuissent (sic) naves cum hominibus, et sumptis, quod invenirent igne cremare facerent.' English translation in *Medieval Trade in the Mediterranean World*, 333–5. On acts against the entire Christian people, see also Widukind, *RGS*, Bk. III, cap. 32 (p. 118); Widukind, *Deeds*, 117.

82 *LIRG*, vol. 1/1, no. 151 (p. 223): 'Hanc vero laudem suprascripti consules fecerunt quoniam cognoverunt hoc esse servicium Dei et omnium Christianorum et comunis Ianue.'

83 *Pactum Sicardi* (836), c. 3; *Laws of King Aistulf*, c. 4; *II Athelstan*, c. 18. For other examples, see *Codex Iustinianus*, ed. P. Krueger (Berlin, 1915), 4.41:1–2; *Treaty between Genoa and Fos* (1138), c. 6; 'Capitulary of Mantua, 781', c. 7; *Lex Frisionum*, XVII:5, available at www.keesn.nl/lex/lex_en_text.htm (accessed 16 July 2021); *The Visigothic Code: (Forum judicum)*, ed. S. P. Scott (Boston, 1910), Bk. XI, Title III: 3–4; 'General Capitulary of Thionville, 806', c. 7 (p. 248); 'Capitulary of Herstal, 770', c. 20. On trade references in the laws of early medieval Europe, the essential study is Harald Siems, *Handel und Wucher im Spiegel frühmittelalterlicher Rechtsquellen* (Hanover, 1992).

84 *I diploma arabi del R. Archivio Fiorentino: testo originale con la traduzione letterale e illustrazioni, vol. 1*, ed. M. Amari (Florence, 1863), 51–2.

85 *Storia documentata di Venezia. Tomo 1*, 374–5.

86 Stantchev, 'The Medieval Origins of Embargo', 383.

87 On the nature and purpose of peace, see Chapter 3, pp. 97–9, 105–11, 115–19.

88 Cf. *Treaty of Pavia* (715), which demonstrably is an attempt to regulate trade. For the context, see Hartmann, *Zur Wirtschaftsgeschichte Italiens*, 74–90; Gasparri, 'The First Dukes and the Origins of Venice', 16–18.

89 Stantchev, *Spiritual Rationality*, 1–2; Stantchev, 'The Medieval Origins of Embargo', 399.

90 A longer study of reprisals as an institution in the period before 1200 might better draw out the comparisons and contrasts with later practices. The sample of evidence provided here certainly shows that there is a significant corpus of material to examine. Mas Latrie commented on the origins of the practice in this period, but without examining any of this available evidence. *Du droit de marque*, 3–11.

91 Tarcisio Gazzini, Wouter G. Werner and Ige F. Dekker, 'Necessity across International Law: An Introduction', *Netherlands Yearbook of International Law*, 41 (2010), 3–4. See also Diane A. Desierto, *Necessity and National Emergency Clauses: Sovereignty in Modern Treaty Interpretation* (Leiden, 2012), 2; Paddeu, *Justification*, 334–5.

92 Paddeu, *Justification*, 338. See also the overview by Desierto, *Necessity and National Emergency Clauses*, 63–9.

93 Paddeu, *Justification*, 335; Desierto, *Necessity and National Emergency Clauses*, 63–6.

94 Paddeu, *Justification*, 338–43.

95 Arrigo Cavaglieri, *I diritti fondamentali degli stati nella Società Internazionale* (Padua, 1906), 24

96 Paddeu, *Justification*, 366–8; Crawford, *State Responsibility*, 305–6.

97 *ILC Responsibility of States for Internationally Wrongful Acts* (2001), available at https://legal.un.org/ilc/texts/instruments/english/draft_articles/9_6_2001.pdf (accessed 16 July 2021), art. 21.1(a); Gazzini et al., 'Necessity across International Law', 4; Dixon, *Textbook on IL*, 265; Crawford, *State Responsibility*, 307–13.

98 Franck Roumy, 'L'origine et la diffusion de l'adage canonique *Necessitas non habet legem* (VIIIe–XIIIe s.)', in *Medieval Church Law and the Origins of the Western Legal Tradition. A Tribute to Kenneth Pennington*, eds. Wolfgang P. Müller and Mary E. Sommar (Washington, DC, 2006), 301–19.

99 On this, see Paddeu, *Justification*, 350–63.

100 Widukind, *RGS*, Bk. III, cap. 32 (p. 119); Widukind, *Deeds*, 118.

101 Benham, *PMA*, 21–37, esp. 32–5. For a wider view across the whole medieval period, see also Werner Kolb, *Herrscherbegegnungen im Mittelalter* (Frankfurt, 1988); Voss, *Herrschertreffen*.

102 *The Chronicle of John of Worcester*, iii, 64–5.

103 No full study of the period before 1154 has currently been completed. On the meeting places between the English and Scottish kings in the late twelfth century, see Benham, *PMA*, 51–6.

104 *Calendar of Ancient Correspondence concerning Wales*, ed. J. G. Edwards (Cardiff, 1935), 2. On this request and meetings between Welsh and English rulers, see Benham, *PMA*, 44–51.

105 *The Law of Hywel Dda*, 5.

106 On *necessitas* and *utilitas* and their link to concepts of 'state', see F. M. Powicke, 'Presidential Address: Reflections on the Medieval State', *TRHS*, 4th ser., 19 (1936), 5–7. See also the outline in Alan Harding, *Medieval Law and the Foundations of the State* (Oxford, 2002), 38–42.

107 *Ordinatio imperii*, c. 8: '…semper ad senioris fratris notitiam perferre non neglegant, ut ille semper sollicitus et paratus inveniatur ad quaecumque necessitas et utilitas regni postulaverit.' English translation from B. Pullan, *Sources for the History of Medieval Europe* (Oxford, 1966), 40.

108 Magnou-Nortier, 'The Enemies of the Peace', 62–3, 65.

109 Susan Reynolds, *Before Eminent Domain. Toward a History of Expropriation of Land for the Common Good* (Chapel Hill, NC, 2010), 22; Powicke, 'Reflections on the Medieval State', 7.

110 *Treaty of Meersen* (847), announcement of Charles the Bald, c. 5: 'Et volumus, ut cuiuscumque nostrum homo, in cuiuscumque regno sit, cum seniore suo in hostem vel aliis suis utilitatibus pergat; nisi talis regni invasio, quam lantweri dicunt, quod absit, acciderit, ut omnis populus illius regni ad eam repellendam communiter pergat.' On this specific necessity, see Walter Goffart, ' "Defensio Patriae" as a Carolingian Military Obligation', *Francia*, 43 (2016), 21–39.

111 *Treaty of Tusey*, c. 1.

112 *Treaty of Tusey*, c. 3: '…ut ecclesia et regnum, quod Deus in manus progenitorum nostrorum adunavit et nobis misericordia sua commisit, in nostro tempore necessariam defensionem et tuitionem et honorem atque soliditatem habeat.'

113 On necessity as a justification protecting the interests of the international community as a whole in the modern period, see Desierto, *Necessity and National Emergency Clauses*, 105. On enemies of mankind across historical periods, see also Jennifer Pitts, 'Empire and Legal Universalisms in the Eighteenth Century', *AHR*, 117 (2012), 92; Liliana Obregón, 'The Civilized and the Uncivilized', in *OHHIL*, 930.

114 *Treaty of Fouron*, c. 2. See also *Treaty of Meersen* (851), c. 3; Oath of Louis the German at Koblenz (860), in *MGH Capit. II*, 154–5.

115 *LIRG*, vol. 1/1, 150: 'Hanc vero laudem isti consules fecerunt quoniam ad honorem Dei et tocius Christianitatis civitatem Almarie ceperunt et summa necessitate Christianorum eam retinere decreverunt.' Hall, *Caffaro*, 185. On this document, see also Chapter 3, pp. 115–16. The *Treaty of Naples* (1191) has a similar clause, but it is not specifically connected to necessity. *LIRG*, vol. 1/2, 29.

116 Jaspert, ' "Capta est Dertosa clavis Cristianorum" ', 91. On this issue, see also Giles Constable, 'The Second Crusade as Seen by

Contemporaries', *Traditio*, 9 (1953), 213–79; Jason T. Roche, 'The Second Crusade, 1145–49: Damascus, Lisbon and the Wendish Campaigns', *History Compass*, 13 (2015), 599–609.

117 Constable has highlighted that Caffaro, who was an eyewitness, in recording Genoese attacks on other Muslim areas is similarly silent on any religious motivation. Constable, 'The Second Crusade as Seen by Contemporaries', 235.

118 *Treaty of Dover* (1163), cc. 2, 4, 8.

119 *Treaty between Sancho IV of Navarre and al-Muktadir of Zaragoza* (1073), c. 6: 'Iterum si Almuctadir uille necesse hauerit adiutorium in aliquas partes, et requisierit suum amicum regem dominum Sancium ut per suum corpus metipsum cum suos barones ei adiubet, accipiat ille rex tales ostaticos de eo quales elegerit et uadat in suo adiutorio.' It is noteworthy that the intention was that the hostages would be returned once the obligation to provide aid had been fulfilled (c. 9). On hostages in Iberian agreements, see Kosto, *Hostages*, 9–16, 130–56; Kosto, *Making Agreements*, 124–33.

120 *AGu*, c. 5. English translation from *EHD, I*, no. 34.

121 Jean-Pierre Devroey, 'Monastic Economics in the Carolingian Age', in *The Cambridge History of Medieval Monasticism in the Latin West*, eds. Alison I. Beach and Isabelle Cochelin (Cambridge, 2020), 472–3.

122 David Pratt has shown that *utilitas* and *necessitas* were used in Alfred's reign in Latin and Old English literature, and likely betray Carolingian influences. Most of his examples and analysis of 'need' in various ways connect to defence against external and internal enemies, including impact on trade and commerce, but the usage in the treaty, or in other time periods, is not specifically discussed. David Pratt, *The Political Thought of King Alfred the Great* (Cambridge, 2007), 173–4, 206–7, 280–1, 288, 290–4, 305–6, 341–2.

123 For examples, see *Bischofs Wærferths von Worcester Übersetzung der Dialoge Gregors des Grossen*, ed. Hans Hecht (Leipzig, 1900), 1; David Yerkes, 'The Full Text of the Metrical Preface to Wærferth's Translation of Gregory', *Speculum*, 55 (1980), 513; *Asser's Life of King Alfred*, ed. W. H. Stevenson (Oxford, 1904), c. 77. On the reforms more generally, see Paul Booth, 'King Alfred versus Beowulf: The Re-Education of the Anglo-Saxon Aristocracy', *BJRL*, 79 (1997), 44–9; Pratt, *The Political Thought of King Alfred the Great*, 115–66; Janet L. Nelson, 'Alfred of Wessex at a Cross-roads in the History of Education', *History of Education*, 6 (2013), 697–712.

124 *Asser's Life of King Alfred*, cc. 8, 11, 24–5, 74, 76–8, 87–9, 106. For one example of Alfred's own writings, see *King Alfred's West-Saxon*

Version of Gregory's Pastoral Care, 2 vols., ed. Henry Sweet (London, 1871–2), i, 6–7

125 *LIRG*, vol. 1/1, 241; Hall, *Caffaro*, 194 and fn. 75. On this financial crisis, see Epstein, *Genoa and the Genoese*, 51–2; E. H. Byrne, 'Genoese Trade with Syria', *AHR*, 25 (1920), 196–7.

126 A letter, widely disseminated in the Middle Ages, from Pope Leo I in the fifth century, in which necessity was linked to great danger ('in temporis necessitates et periculi urgentis'), shows that this aspect of necessity was certainly known among ecclesiastical writers, such as Hincmar of Rheims. *De divortio Lotharii regis et Theutbergae reginae*, ed. Letha Böhringer, *MGH Concilia 4*, Supplementum 1 (Hanover, 1992) 216; *The Divorce of King Lothar and Queen Theutberga. Hincmar of Rheims's De Divortio*, tr. Rachel Stone and Charles West (Manchester, 2016), 253. On this letter, see Roumy, 'L'origine et la diffusion', 304–5.

127 *Treaty of Meersen* (847), announcement of Charles the Bald, c. 5.

128 *Treaty of Fouron*, c. 6: 'nisi forte talis inevitabilis necessitas evenerit, pro qua id fieri nullatenus possit.' Note English translation amended slightly from that of Janet L. Nelson in *The Annals of St-Bertin*, 214–15.

129 *LIRG*, vol. 1/2, 153; Hall, *Caffaro*, 171. The phrase is retained in the renewal of 1169 by Bohemond III. *LIRG*, vol. 1/2, 158.

130 Binder, 'Stability and Change', 916.

131 *ILC Responsibility of States for Internationally Wrongful Acts*, art. 23. For a detailed discussion of what this entails, see *'Force Majeure' and 'Fortuitous Event' as Circumstances Precluding Wrongfulness – Survey of State Practice, International Judicial Decisions and Doctrine – Study Prepared by the Secretariat* (Topic: State responsibility), A/CN.4/315, Yearbook of the International Law Commission, vol. II(1), 1978, available at https://legal.un.org/ilc/documentation/english/a_cn4_315.pdf (accessed 16 July 2021), 66–71.

132 *Gesta Chuonradi II Imperatoris*, c. 17 (p. 37): 'Nortmannis, qui de patria sua, nescio qua necessitate compulsi, in Apuliam confluxerunt...'

133 *Treaty of Devol*, c. 1.

134 There is a large literature on these contracts. For examples, see G. Astuti, *Origini e svolgimento storico della commenda fino al secolo XIII* (Milan, 1933); John H. Pryor, 'Mediterranean Commerce in the Middle Ages. A Voyage under the Contract of Commenda', *Viator*, 14 (1983), 132–94; Hassan S. Khalilieh, *Admiralty and Maritime Laws in the Mediterranean Sea (ca. 800–1050): The Kitāb Akriyat Al-Sufun Vis-a-vis the Nomos Rhodion Nautikos* (Leiden, 2006).

135 *Documenti del commercio veneziano nei secoli XI-XIII, vol. I*, eds. R. Morozzo della Rocca and A. Lombardo (Rome, 1940), 12. English translation from *Medieval Trade in the Mediterranean World*, 177. On shipwreck and *commenda* contracts, see Khalilieh, *Admiralty and Maritime Laws in the Mediterranean Sea*, 224–6.

136 Cf. correspondence of 1201 between a Tunisian and a Pisan referring to the capture of merchant ships by pirates. *I diploma arabi del R. Archivio Fiorentino*, 60.

137 *Letters of Medieval Jewish Traders*, tr. S. D. Goitein (Princeton, NJ, 2015), no. 71 (pp. 316, 318–19).

138 On the terminology in modern times, see *'Force majeure' and 'Fortuitous event'*, 68–9. For a summary of recent moves away from this traditional division, see Jill M. Fraley, 'Re-examining Acts of God', *Pace Environmental Law Review*, 27 (2010), 669–90.

139 *Treaty of Genoa I* (1146), Alfonso's obligations, c. 2: 'nisi remanserit iusto Dei impedimento aut consilio eorum et nostrum'. The English translation by Hall and Philips (Hall, *Caffaro*, 179) disguises that the phrase is exactly the same as that stipulated in the Genoese obligations below.

140 *Treaty of Genoa I* (1146), Genoese obligations, c. 3. This same justification is repeated in the *Treaty of Genoa II* (1146), c. 4. A similar clause can be found also in the *Treaty of Portovenere* (1149, 1169), c. 7.

141 *LIRG*, vol. 1/6, 13; Hall, *Caffaro*, 219. Also the Genoese obligations mention this, for which see *CDRG*, ii, 367.

142 *The Alexiad*, bk. 4, c. 2 (p. 137).

143 The customs on shipwreck do not seem to have been written down until the thirteenth century across most of Europe. For examples, see *Las Siete Partidas, Volume 4: Family, Commerce, and the Sea: the Worlds of Women and Merchants (Partidas IV and V)*, ed. Robert I. Burns (Philadelphia, 2000), 1079; *JL*, III:63; *SL*, c. 165. For a useful study, see Edda Frankot, *Of Laws of Ship and Shipmen: Medieval Maritime Law and its Practice* (Edinburgh, 2012).

144 *Treaty of Acre* (1124), c. 6: 'Si vero aliquis Veneticorum naufragium passus fuerit, nullum de suis rebus patiatur dampnum. Si naufragium mortuus fuerit, suis heredibus aut aliis Veneticis res sue remanentes reddantur.'

145 *Treaty of Antioch* (1167), c. 3.

146 *Treaty between Genoa and Narbonne* (1132), c. 3.

147 *Treaty between Genoa and Raymond of Toulouse, Sancho of Provence, William of Forcalquier*, prol, c. 1.

148 *RPC*, 67.

149 *Pactum Sicardi*, c. 13.

150 According to Fraley, this reflects the traditional doctrine of act of God in tort, contract, and insurance law, i.e., the event has to be caused exclusively by forces of nature without any human action or interference to preclude liability and hence legal redress for damages. Fraley, 'Re-examining Acts of God', 673–6.

151 *Treaty of Mallorca* (1181), c. 5: 'Alfachinus vero conventionem legato et preceptum generale fecit ut... navis aliqua Ianuensium vel de districtu Ianuensium in aliqua prescriptarum insularum naufragium patcretur, quod homines sui eos salvarent naufragos et eorum bona nec inde auferrent vel minuerent, set quicquid inde habere possent, restituerent. Excepto si de pecunia que iacet in fundo...'

152 Frédéric Bauden, 'Due trattati di pace conclusi nel dodicesimo secolo tra i Banū Ġāniya, signori delle isole Baleari, e il commune di Genova', in *Documentos y manuscritos árabes del occidente musulmán medieval*, ed. Nuria Martínez de Castilla (Madrid, 2010), 55.

153 Most treaties that include this justification tend to do so without any specification as to the nature of any act of God. E.g., *Treaty of Genoa* (1165), c. 18; *Pact between Milan and Piacenza* (1156), c. 6.

154 According to Binder this is the case also with acts of God in the earliest records of them in English domestic law, with both Binder and Rundall asserting that the phrase first appears in the records of the sixteenth century. Denis Binder, 'Act of God? Or Act of Man? A Reappraisal of the Act of God Defense in Tort Law', *Review of Litigation*, 15 (1995), 5; M. T. Rundall, 'Act of God as a Defense in Negligence Cases', *Drake Law Review*, 25 (1975–1976), 754. See also Fraley, 'Re-examining Acts of God', 672–3.

155 As an example, Otto of Freising comments that the Milanese surrendered to Frederick Barbarossa in 1158 under compulsion of famine, pestilence, and the sword, but the treaty makes no mention of this nor how, or if, it might prevent the Milanese from carrying out their obligations. *Gesta Friderici*, 218 (III:45).

156 On *force majeure* as a general principle of law across time and space, see Federica Paddeu, 'A Genealogy of Force Majeure in International Law', *The British Yearbook of International Law*, 82 (2012), 384–7.

157 *DD FI*, ii, 224: 'non relinquet exercitum eius nisi iustum et evidens Dei impedimentum intercesserit... vel licentia domini imperatoris aut eius certi missi...' Translation adapted from Hall, *Caffaro*, 200.

158 *Die Briefe Heinrichs IV*, ed. Carl Erdmann, in *MGH Deutsches Mittelalter. Kritische Studientexte*, 1 (Leipzig, 1937), no. 23 (p. 33); *Imperial Lives and Letters of the Eleventh Century*, 171. Mommsen and Morrison (fn. 105) suggest the victories referred to dealing with 'marauding bands' returning from the First Crusade.

159 Christina Binder has similarly argued about modern international law that 'a successful invocation of *force majeure* or necessity does not permanently affect the treaty relationship but only temporarily excuses non-performance while the circumstance in question subsists', showing the endurability of this rule. Binder, 'Stability and Change', 920.

160 Gregory VII, *Registrum IV*, 12a, in *MGH Epp. sel. 2.1*, 315; *Imperial Lives and Letters of the Eleventh Century*, 156.

161 *Ordinatio imperii*, c. 4.

162 *Treaty of Benevento* (1156), c. 13.

163 For discussion of these, see F. M. de Robertis, *La responsabilità contrattuale nel diritto romano dalle origini a tutta l'età postclassica* (Bari, 1996), 136–44.

164 Howden, *Chronica*, iii, 216. A similar stipulation can be found in the tenth-century treaty concluded between the Byzantine emperor and the Emir of Aleppo, for which see *Treaty of Aleppo*, c. 21.

165 It is worth noting, for instance, that aside from acts of God and man-made impediments, some domestic laws describe similar unexpected events as 'accidents'.

166 *Treaty of Dover* (1101), c. 4: 'Si non remanserit propter monstrabilem sui corporis infirmitatem, vel terrae suae amissionem, vel Lodovici regis Francorum expeditionis summonitionem, vel propter Imperatoris Romani summonitionem…' This excuse is repeated almost word for word in clause 13, concerning service in Normandy.

167 *Treaty of Dover* (1101), c. 17: 'Et si aliquis ex illis obsidibus mortuus fuerit… comes alium equivalentem in loco eius… restaurabit… Et si in mari perdiderint, habebunt respectum per xl dies, ad restaurandam pecuniam.'

168 *Treaty of Dover* (1101), c. 17.

169 On essoins in English law at end of twelfth century, see *EHD*, ii, nos. 48–9; *Glanvill*, 14–17; *Pleas before the King or his Justices 1198–1202. Volume I*, ed. D. M. Stenton (London, 1953), 153–4. For discussion, see J. G. H. Hudson, *The Oxford History of the Laws of England. Volume II, 871–1216* (Oxford, 2012), 588–91; J. Boorman, 'The Sheriffs of Henry II and the Significance of 1170', in *Law and Government in Medieval England and Normandy. Essays in Honour of Sir James Holt*, eds. George Garnett and John Hudson (Cambridge, 1994), 255–75.

170 *Treaty of Tudején*, c. 8: 'Si, vero, imperator propter infirmitatem aut iustum et cognitum impedimentum, in quo nullus dolus interesset, predictum comitem adiuvare non posset, nullum ex hoc imperator

paciatur incomodum, sed de quantocumque comes adquirere poterit, de Murcia et eius regno, ita habeat per imperatorem...'

171 The most common lawful excuses in domestic laws tend to be death, illness, absence in king's service or overseas or on pilgrimage. Insanity also appears as a lawful excuse to betrothals. For a few examples from the laws, see *Digest*, 23:1.8, 40:7.4; *Pactus Legis Salicae*, in *MGH LL nat. Germ.* 4:1, ed. K. A. Eckhardt (Hanover, 1962), c. 76; *Glanvill*, 14–17; *SL*, cc. 83, 146.

172 Howden, *Gesta*, i, 140; Howden, *Chronica*, ii, 122.

173 *Peace of Constance*, c. 10.

174 *Treaty of Antioch* (1101), c. 3; Translation adapted from Hall, *Caffaro*, 170.

175 Paddeu, 'A Genealogy of Force Majeure in International Law', 387–93.

176 They are outlined as being consent, self-defence, counter-measures, *force majeure*, distress, and necessity. https://legal.un.org/ilc/texts/instruments/english/draft_articles/9_6_2001.pdf (accessed 16 July 2021), art. 20–5.

177 See also Benham, 'Peace, Security and Deterrence', 124–30. A more detailed study of consent as a justification is in development.

178 Allott, 'State Responsibility', 13–14.

179 Ibid., 15.

5

Resolving disputes: arbitration, mediation, and third-party intervention

When direct negotiations failed, or disputes were particularly violent, tricky to resolve, or prolonged, third parties could intervene or be asked to intervene. Much work has been done by historians on third-party intervention in disputes at the lower levels of society across the whole of the medieval period and across most geographical areas.[1] Most notably, Hermann Kamp's important 2001 study *Friedensstifter und Vermittler im Mittelalter* differentiates between mediators and arbitrators. Mediators, Kamp argued, were those who intervened in a dispute by helping to bring about a settlement acceptable to all parties. An arbitrator, by contrast, was given the power by both parties to decide on and impose a settlement.[2] In an international context, there have been many studies on direct negotiations and mediation for the period 700–1200; indeed, we can be confident that most medieval treaties came into being as a result of these two methods.[3] Arbitration, by contrast, historians have seen as a late-medieval phenomenon, pointing towards its use by, among others, the towns of the Hanseatic League to settle any differences that arose between them with regards to trade.[4] In fact, arbitration seems to have suffered a similar fate to the history of international law generally, namely that scholarly treatment of the subject often jumps from the Greek and Roman periods to the late medieval period, without mentioning developments in the intervening 800 or so years.[5] This chapter will aim at bridging this gap in the current historiography, thinking about the extent to which we can identify arbitration as an established legal practice – an institution, if you like – that came with a specific set of rules, terminology, and procedures, and was distinct from mediation and other third-party interventions. This is important to do because one of the requirements of international law is that it had the function to resolve 'disputed questions of fact and law'.[6]

In the twelfth century, that international arbitration was distinct from mediation can be shown, first and foremost, through the resultant documentation. The best example of this is the arbitration by Henry II of England in 1177 in the dispute over various territorial claims and rights between kings Alfonso VIII of Castile and Sancho VI of Navarre.[7] We are unusually well informed about this arbitration and the surrounding documents thanks to the English historian and royal clerk Roger of Howden, who recorded the process in strict chronological order in his *Gesta Regis Henrici Secundi*. Howden begins by stating how envoys of the two Iberian kings turned up at Henry II's court, then residing in Windsor, and showed Henry the *Treaty of Logroño* (1176) outlining that Alfonso and Sancho had agreed to submit their dispute to Henry's arbitration.[8] The English king subsequently summoned a council to London, where the envoys began to present the claims of the kings. Finding it difficult to understand the words of the envoys, however, Henry asked for all their 'claims, charges and allegations' to be reduced to writing and gave them three days in which to do so.[9] On the fourth day, the council reconvened and now the envoys presented their cases together with letters and treaties recording the process so far. The documents presented included pedigrees of the kings of Castile, Navarre, and Aragon; the claims of Sancho and Alfonso; and the *Treaty of Fitero*, concluded in 1167, which Sancho's envoys alleged had been broken.[10] Having heard and seen the claims and documents, and secured oaths from the envoys for the observance of any decision, King Henry made his award after deliberating with the assembled council and a notification (the *Treaty of London*) was drawn up announcing it.[11] That this sequence of events and accompanying documents was not an English phenomenon, can be ascertained from an example originating in northern Italy and dating to 1188, when Pope Clement III arbitrated the disputes between the Genoese and the Pisans over land, resources and authority in Sardinia. Unlike the English example, however, it does not have a chronicler contextualising the events and the documents.[12] The *Annals of Genoa* merely record that in 1188 Pope Clement restored peace ('pax facta fuit mediante domno apostolico Clemente') after war broke out in 1187, when the Pisans broke their oath and attacked Genoese merchants, their goods and properties in Sardinia, expelling them from the *iudicatus* (kingdom) of Cagliari.[13]

One of the main things that the sequence of events retold by Roger of Howden shows is that both the narrative and the documents indicate that significant importance was attached to procedure.[14] Arbitration was a formal process with specific requirements and expectations that had to be expressed both orally and in writing. One such requirement was that the parties had to agree to submit the matter to arbitration. David W. Rivkin has noted that arbitrators 'derive their authority from the parties who appointed them, and they are called up only to resolve the dispute between those parties'.[15] This statement is as true of modern arbitration as it was of medieval arbitration.[16] In the twelfth century, the notion that parties had to agree to submit their dispute to arbitration was set out in Gratian's collection of canon law, known as the *Decretum*, which drew on Justinian's *Digest* and detailed that arbiters differed from ordinary judges in that their power came only with the consent of the litigants, i.e., *arbiter ex compromisso*.[17] The first sentence of the *Treaty of Logroño* (1176) sets this requirement out clearly – 'This is the treaty and agreement (pactum et conventio) made... for submitting the disputes (de querelis) between them [the kings of Castile and Navarre] to the judgment of the king of England (judicio regis Anglie)' – while the second clause stated that each king had given sureties that he would accept and fulfil ('accipiat et compleat') Henry's judgment ('judicium').[18] Another example can be found with the *Treaty of Dover* (1110), which sets out that if either the count of Flanders, Robert, or the English king, Henry I, breached the terms of the treaty, the count of Boulogne would decide who had made the breach. Count Eustace was expected to decide this from the terms in the written treaty, which would be brought to a meeting in Boulogne if the claim of a breach was made by the English king, or to Dover if the claim was brought by the count of Flanders. The violator then had to make amends for the breach within forty days.[19] Again, the treaty shows that there was a clear strategy for resolving any future conflict or breaches of the terms of the treaty through arbitration, and that this process started with an agreement on such a strategy. Whether or not cases were always submitted for arbitration as a joint statement, as in 1110 and 1177, is less clear. In 1188, the citizens of Genoa and Pisa certainly took oaths on separate occasions, agreeing to abide by any peace that the pope would broker. That the pope's authority to arbitrate rested on these individual oaths is confirmed in a subsequent announcement of Pope Clement III that he had instructed two papal legates to draw up the treaty, which would have to be accepted and observed, without further discussion.[20] In the *Treaty of Grosseto*, 1133, Pope Innocent II likewise ordered the cities of Genoa and Pisa, on the strength of the oaths they had taken both to the pope and to his envoys, that they would set aside all conflict and observe the peace concluded.[21] This shows agreement to adhere to any decision, but without divulging exactly how or in what circumstances these oaths were taken. Other cases echo this by indicating that it was not how the request was submitted but rather that both parties did submit it. In one example, the rivals, Svein and Cnut, asked successive German kings to intervene in their conflict over the Danish throne.[22] Two letters from the contemporary collection of Abbot Wibald of Stablo and Corvey show that in 1151 both Svein and Cnut wrote to King Conrad III requesting his aid in the conflict. Their approach to this task is interesting, however, in that neither directly asked Conrad to arbitrate in their dispute, but rather requested by other means that he would decide in their favour.[23] Sven asked Conrad, as a 'father', to preserve a son's honour against those who tried to rise up to destroy it, while Cnut appealed to Conrad's sense of justice to take pity on a man in exile, who had been bereft not only of his kingdom but also his patrimony.[24] One of the things that this highlights is that the historian cannot use terms such as judgment or decision (*judicatio, judicium, arbitrium*) to ascertain whether a case is being arbitrated or not, in particular for those instances (which is most) where the full range of documents has not survived or, possibly, was never made in the first place.[25] In fact, in the dispute between the Danish rivals, we can only ascertain that this matter was arbitrated by the fact that Conrad's successor on the German throne, Frederick I, made an award that is known only from a charter recording Frederick's privileges to the abbey of Corvey. This charter shows that both Svein and Cnut were present at a diet at Merseburg in May 1152, and the first two witnesses of the charter are listed as 'Svein, king of the Danes, who in that same place received the kingdom from the hand of the lord king. Cnut, another Dane, who in that same place withdrew [his claim] to the kingdom at the hand of the lord king.'[26] What is remembered in this charter is the physical act – the ritual if you like – by which the judgment was enacted and it is not by accident that it appears in a charter to Corvey because the abbot was Wibald, who, as explained above, also preserved the letters that the two claimants had previously written to the German king.

Whether or not these few examples show that the revival of Roman law was seeping into conflict resolution between kings and changing or formalising previous procedures is very difficult to say. Only in the case between Genoa and Pisa of 1133 can we link the practice very clearly to the revival of Roman law, because we know that one of the negotiators and draughtsman of the documents surrounding the arbitration was Aimery (also referred to as Haimeric), the papal chancellor. Kenneth Pennington has shown that Aimery not only had a great interest in arbitration, asking his friend Bulgarus (one of the most important teachers of Roman Law in Bologna) to detail in his treatise how to differentiate between an arbitration and a suit brought before a judge in court, but also that one papal letter from the same period as the treaty, drafted by the chancellor, contained significant references to Bulgarus' treatise and had glosses with citations to Justinian's *Digest* and the *Codex*.[27]

Outside of twelfth-century examples, the surviving evidence is often not clear enough to say how parties submitted their dispute to arbitration and hence it is tricky to differentiate between arbitration, mediation, and more general appeals to a third party to act as a judge in which only one side might to be prepared to accept any decision.[28] For instance, when Charlemagne in 796 wrote to Offa, king of the Mercians, regarding the exiles that had sought shelter in the Frankish kingdom, he stated that he had sent them to Rome 'so that their case may be heard and judged (*audita causa illorum judicaretur*) in the presence of the apostolic lord and your distinguished archbishop..., so that fair judgment (*aequitatis judicatio*) may do what pious intercession (*pietatis intercessio*) could not'.[29] The letter further acknowledges that the two kings had different opinions on the matter, but it does not explicitly state that Offa and Charles had agreed to approach the pope, even if this seems likely.[30] Some forty years later, in the narrative of Nithard, there is clear evidence of agreement to refer certain matters in dispute to a third party but the circumstances and the language used make it difficult to think of these instances as arbitration. Nithard, likely an eyewitness to some of the events recorded, stated how, in March 842, the two brothers, Charles the Bald and Louis the German, attempted to settle the issue over the kingdom that had previously belonged to their brother, Emperor Lothar, whom they had recently defeated and driven into exile. Nithard is very specific in stating that first it seemed to the brothers that they should 'submit the matter to bishops and priests'.[31] A short while later, having received a proposal from Lothar regarding the division of the Frankish kingdoms between the three brothers, Charles and Louis submitted also this to a council of bishops and priests who gave their consent, called for emissaries, and granted Lothar's request.[32] After some further negotiations, the three brothers eventually met at Koblenz in October 842 and a further matter, relating to the nature of the oaths in the agreements and perjury, was referred for a decision to a council of churchmen.[33] Of particular interest in these instances is the fact that the third party was not an individual but a council, showing communal involvement in and engagement with diplomatic negotiations, which mirrors the 'collective judgment' of arbitration cases and dispute settlement at lower levels of society.[34] Indeed, it would appear that in the examples given by Nithard, the idea of submitting matters to a council of churchmen was more along the lines of a consultation for how to proceed than an attempt to judge a specific issue in the dispute between the kings. Nithard's use of the verbs *conferre* and *referre*, both of which can mean 'to consult' or 'to refer/report to', seems to back this up, as does the fact that in the case of the first example, the disputed issues were not necessarily concerning relations between the kings and their kingdoms but rather within them.

Having said this, it might also be relevant that at least one of the treaties intended to divide the Frankish kingdoms and regulate the relations between each of its kings (who were all brothers) anticipated intervention in case of disputes, and the text makes it clear that this was an escalation in the dispute resolution process. The tenth clause of the *Ordinatio imperii* of 817 describes that a particularly recalcitrant brother (i.e., a ruler over one of the Frankish kingdoms), who oppressed churches and poor men or behaved in a tyrannical way, would be summoned by the other two brothers and the common decision of all ('communi omnium sententia') would determine what would be done about him.[35] Arguably, this is what happened to Lothar and the matter was decided through his defeat at the Battle of Fontenoy in 841. The issues that remained to be settled, i.e., how to divide his kingdom and its resources, were then put to the arbitration panel of their advisers, as Nithard records.[36] The idea of submitting matters in dispute to arbitration seems implicit in the *Ordinatio* but indeed so is also the consent of the brothers in question as the document was issued by their father Louis the Pious. Thus, at best, what we have evidence of here is the potential of future consent to submit disputes to arbitration rather than actual agreement by the contracting parties to do so.

A useful comparison to Nithard's examples can be found with two examples from Anglo-Saxon England. The first is that found in the early eighth-century letter of Wealdhere, bishop of London. In this letter, Wealdhere writes about the attempts to establish peace between the East and West Saxon rulers stating that they had agreed 'by common consent (communi consensione)' to assemble, together with other bishops, abbots, and councillors, at the place called Brentford, and 'having summoned a council there, should determine the causes of all dissensions (ibi adunato concilio omnium dissimultatum causæ determinarentur)...' and if anyone is shown to have offended 'he shall make amends with rightful compensation (recta emendatione satisfaciat)'.[37] The second example, from the *Ordinance of Dunsæte*, shows a similar concern with resolving disputes. Parts of the *Ordinance* stipulate how to deal with disputes over cattle theft between the English and the Welsh, highlighting in particular the use of sureties and their seizure in case of forfeiture. Clauses 3.2 and 3.3 anticipate that whether such measures were just or not would be decided by a group of six 'lahmen' from either side. If the judgment of the group was wrong they, in turn, would forfeit their property or have to admit they knew no better.[38] These examples were not about consultation but rather they show a clear resemblance to those arbitration panels that are frequently found within treaties in the twelfth century. Such arbitration panels were usually devised to settle outstanding issues – thereby allowing a peace to be made while at the same time deferring parts of the conflict – or they were intended to provide a framework for how to resolve disputes going forward – aimed at a local level and concerning daily, or at least regular, interactions between the subjects of both parties. For instance, the *Treaty of Ivry* (1177) and the renewal of it in 1180 (*Treaty of Gisors*) both set out that three bishops and three magnates on either side would investigate the rights and claims in dispute in the Berry, and that future disputes over the dominions of the English and French kings would also be settled by this arbitration panel. Whatever the panel decided the kings promised to hold firm.[39] In another example, the *Treaty of Najac-de-Rouergue*, Richard, count of Poitou (later better known as Richard I of England), and Alfonso II, king of Aragon, set out that any disputes that broke out would be settled by two honest men from either side.[40] Two was also the number of arbiters on each side in the *Truce of Verneuil* of 1194. These arbiters, according to the text, should specifically deal with issues of redress within forty days, and if there were any disputes over their decision, the papal legate in France, Cardinal Melior, would decide.[41] The *Truce of Venice*, 1177, similarly decreed that appointed men from the cities of both the Lombard League and the Emperor Frederick I were to investigate and settle claims of infringements of the terms within forty days, and a similar arrangement was made in the *Treaty of Venice* for outstanding issues between the pope and the emperor.[42] This latter example, furthermore shows that mediation and arbitration operated in tandem because those appointed to this panel were called 'mediatores' but they were expected to determine ('terminent') claims and disputes through a judgment ('juditio') – i.e., arbitration – or through an agreement ('concordia') – i.e., mediation.[43] No treaty from the period before 1100 explicitly had arbitration panels such as these, even though the descriptions in Wealdhere's letter and in the *Ordinatio imperii* indicate that the concept existed. Perhaps the closest similarity can be found with a statement in the third *Treaty of Meersen* (870) that areas where the parties could not agree would be divided according to whatever the *missi* of the kings determined to be most just ('secundum quod communes nostri missi rectius invenerint').[44] A second possibility is afforded by the *Treaty of Pavia* (840), and its subsequent renewals in the ninth and tenth centuries. Several clauses specifically mention the use of judges who were to make swift decisions in disputes over a range of issues regulating the relations between the Venetians and the mainlanders, i.e., those living in the Italian kingdom.[45] In many ways these stipulations are similar to the expectations of the arbitration panels in treaties from the twelfth century or the role of the *missi* in 870. It is further evident that this arrangement was different from other forms of dispute resolution as Lothar's *missi* might also be called upon to provide justice, which looks more like a process of appeal than an arbitration – 'a last resort', as argued by G. V. B. West.[46] Nevertheless, these treaties clearly set out how these panels were specifically appointed to resolves disputes between parties, showing a concept of the principle of *arbiter ex compromisso*.

From all of these early examples, we might conclude that while there was a notion of the principle of *arbiter ex compromisso*, even when this appears more as a form of consultation, the idea of arbitration as a process to resolve international disputes was not well developed in this period.[47] Having said this, in most of the early examples, the Church emerges as a third party whose semi-independence in conflicts was assumed. This clearly speaks to the Church as a supranational institution in this early period whose moral guidance and sanction of matters relating to both war and peace was an essential part of conflict resolution. It is relevant that in at least one of the examples from Nithard, the specific issue referred for a decision related to oaths, which was a matter for the Church.[48] In such a context, the blurring between consultation and arbitration does not seem so strange, and may also highlight that the Church in such cases drew its authority from the consent by both parties to intervene as well as from canon law more generally. Its ability to arbitrate in more secular matters in dispute, however, may have been less certain and may have required more explicit consent from the disputants. Moreover, it is important to not lose sight of the nature of the early evidence, which comes from a range of different documents and narratives, and the difficulties that this brings. Many writers describe the same event or process in different ways, using varied language. Hence, it is extremely difficult to rule out that what was lacking, among some writers, was knowledge of the precise legal terminology and definitions relating to arbitration and its processes rather than the actual practice itself. Nevertheless, and despite the meagre early evidence, if we're attempting to find a working framework of international arbitration, the act of agreeing to submit matters in dispute to a third party must be seen as a requirement in this process, because the third party had no authority or jurisdiction other than that explicitly given by the two disputants.

A second indicator and expectation of arbitration concerns the judgment, decision, or award. As the evidence before 1100 does not always separate clearly between international arbitration, mediation, and more general appeals to a third party, it is difficult to hazard a guess at the process surrounding judgments or decisions. From the evidence for the twelfth century, however, one thing immediately stands out, namely that parties could ask for the decision they eventually received. In 1152, the letters by Svein and Cnut are revealing as to Frederick I's decision in the dispute over the Danish kingdom. Svein's letter intimated that as king he would recognise the overlordship of the German king as a good and dear son at a meeting of Conrad's choosing.[49] By contrast, Cnut's letter pointed out that he had not only lost his realm – thereby clearly acknowledging that he was not the rightful king – but also his paternal inheritance, which lay on the island of Zealand – presumably hinting that it was inalienable.[50] Consequently, as noted in the charter to Corvey, Frederick awarded the kingdom to Svein and Cnut renounced his claim. Although we have no official documents that say whether Cnut received his paternal inheritance as he had asked, narrative evidence would indicate that this was the case. The near contemporary *Gesta Friderici* states that Cnut received 'certain provinces' after abdicating his royal title.[51] Helmold, whose *Chronicle of the Slavs* was written shortly after 1177, does not state what Cnut received merely that he was subjected to Svein ('eidem hominio subactis').[52] Saxo Grammaticus, writing the contemporary section of the *Gesta Danorum* shortly after 1184/5, specifically names Cnut's share as Zealand and, like the author of the *Gesta Friderici*, notes that he received it on condition that he renounced his claim to the royal title.[53] Overall, these narratives seem pretty close to the evidence found in the Corvey charter and in Cnut's letter.

In the arbitration of 1177, Henry II adjudicated that both sides were to have restored to them the territory that the other party had seized and that restitution for revenues lost would be paid to Sancho of Navarre.[54] This was what Alfonso and Sancho had themselves asked for through their envoys in the claims made both orally and in written form to the English king, and Howden specifically noted in Henry's summing up of the case that neither side offered a rebuff or denial to the claims of the other.[55] All of this may make it seem as if, by the time we get into the later twelfth century, arbitration was always predetermined. However, a close reading of the documents and the procedure envisaged would argue against this. For instance, Alfonso VIII was not awarded the redress for losses on land devastated by plunder and fire during the conflict, which he asked for in his claim.[56] Furthermore, the *Treaty of Logroño* makes it clear that if the envoys of either king failed to turn up to hear Henry's decision, that ruler would automatically forfeit his suit, which of course reflects the rules of litigation more generally across the medieval West.[57] Furthermore, Roger of Howden records how both kings had also sent two champions who would decide the matter by single combat if it proved necessary, showing both that the eventual award was not predetermined and that there was an expectancy that Henry II could ask for the dispute to be decided in this way.[58] That contemporaries thought that this was a recognised way to settle disputes between kings is evident from a large number of literary and narrative sources. For instance, when later chroniclers wrote about how the West Saxon Edmund Ironside and the Dane Cnut made peace by dividing the English kingdom between them in 1016, some preferred to give the impression that the two kings had in fact fought a judicial duel to settle their dispute over the throne.[59] In the thirteenth century Matthew Paris even made a depiction of this in his *Chronica Maiora*.[60] Settling disputes between rulers by single combat was evidently a topos in medieval literature, and Howden's insistence on this feature in 1177 is one of the very few instances of this playing a seemingly feasible part of the process of international arbitration. Roger of Howden's evidence is worthy of some credence – as one of Henry II's itinerant justices he was well versed with legal procedures – even though we cannot rule out that he might have inserted a feature that was current in England or at least in England's literary circles.[61] Another thing that is noteworthy about the use of judicial duels is that even at lower levels of society it is often explicitly linked to arbitration. For instance, Widukind of Corvey, in recording the conflicts over inheritance law in the German kingdom in the tenth century, stated that Otto I ordered an assembly at Steele in May 938 where it was decided that the matter should be investigated and decided by judicial arbitration ('ut causa inter arbitros iudicaretur debere examinari'). Once there, however, Otto thought better of this plan and ordered the matter to be decided by gladiators ('gladiatores').[62] What is evident is that although parties were expected to ask, or at the very least hint, at the judgment they wanted and would find acceptable, other means of getting a decision were possible. For best results, however, one can certainly imagine that heeding what had been requested was prudent.

The judgment, whether predetermined or not, should also make us consider what this tells us about the existence of international law more generally in the medieval period. Dixon argues that arbitration in the contemporary world 'is concerned with the rights and duties of the parties under international law and a settlement is achieved by the application of this law to the facts of the case'.[63] However, in the absence of a systematic comment on what international law was in the earlier medieval period, what law was any arbitrator supposed to try a case against? This is not entirely easy to answer but there are a few options. In 1177, Henry might for instance have relied on customary practice and precedents in other treaties. There are a plethora of earlier divisions of lands and rights, including the well-known *Treaty of Verdun* or the partition of the English kingdom between Edmund Ironside and Cnut of 1016, both of which Henry or at least some of his ecclesiastical advisers could reasonably be expected to have known about.[64] Gerald of Wales certainly thought that Henry had assembled all those skilled in law, in addition to the wisest of men, to the meeting where the case was presented.[65] However, Henry had personal experience of other strategies for resolving contested claims to specific regions or even whole kingdoms. Consider for instance how Henry succeeded to the English throne after a protracted conflict with King Stephen. The first clause of the *Treaty of Westminster* declared that King Stephen had established Henry, then duke of Normandy, as his successor in the kingdom, while Henry, in turn, promised to be faithful to Stephen as king for the remainder of his life.[66] Furthermore, as duke of Normandy, Henry tried several strategies when it came to resolving the dispute with the French king over the Vexin and the castle of Gisors, including contracting marriage alliances that would see a future descendant of both kings inherit the land in dispute.[67] It is evident from this that in deciding the Iberian case of 1177, Henry would not have been short of precedents from other treaties and agreements; in other words, he could, if nothing else, draw on two of the most important sources of international law.

A second option in 1177 could have been to turn to domestic laws and practices surrounding the inheritance of land. This could perhaps explain why in 1177 both parties submitted royal pedigrees and outlined how they had come into possession of the disputed territory. Of course, for lots of reasons, such a recourse would have been tricky and therefore possibly unlikely. However, there is possible evidence of such usage in 1152 when Frederick I arbitrated between the rival candidates Svein and Cnut. Saxo comments that Svein asked that his father's estates on Zealand, as his private property, be exempted from the award of the island to Cnut. As this was customary in German law, the proviso was supposedly granted.[68] It is not really relevant here whether or not this actually took place in this precise manner, but rather that Saxo, and presumably his audience, thought that parties could draw on domestic law in resolving aspects of international disputes. In any case, it is evident from treaties too, as shown above, that settling disputes over claims to land through legal inheritance was often the framework within which dispute resolution operated and it was more a question of negotiating a way by which this could happen. More generally, it seems likely that one of the most used principles in making an award in arbitration was to eliminate that nothing was procedurally wrong. This certainly explains why in 1177 Alfonso and Sancho provided summaries of their royal descent and how they had come into possession of the disputed lands – they needed to show that they could substantiate and justify their claims.[69] It also explains why Howden describes the process in such a meticulous manner, recording the documents supplied, the names of witnesses and envoys, the swearing of oaths, the champions, and the fact that failure to turn up to the hearing would result in the forfeiture of the case.[70] Recording procedure thus not only ensured that the arbitration had taken place in the correct manner, thereby eliminating loopholes or justification for breaching the eventual judgment, but also provided a basis for the arbitrator to make a decision. That this makes sense and was a concept that would have been understood by all parties is clear from the fact that dispute settlement and the operation of justice more generally within medieval polities relied on this same principle. For instance, in her 1986 article on

Carolingian dispute settlement, Janet L. Nelson showed that a certain Agintrude lost her property case because her title of purchase had not been corroborated properly in that it lacked 'attestations of specified witnesses'.[71] Similarly, just with reference to wounding in England and Scandinavia in the twelfth and early thirteenth centuries, it is clear that both laws and records of cases have significant focus on how to bring cases to court, the number of witnesses, how to inspect wounds, the time prescribed for making a claim for compensation, and so on.[72] Indeed, it has often been observed that much of medieval law – whether domestic, canon, or Roman – was procedural.[73] From the evidence presented then it is apparent that if we are looking for law against which the facts of a case could be applied in making any decision, there are several options, or combinations of options. And, as arbitration always took place in circumstances in which men, lay and clerical, acted as advisers, we can be reasonably sure that resorting to legal principles and law in making any award was usual and expected, even in international arbitration, because, as argued in Chapter 4, these were not always necessarily distinct from observed practices, from ideas about how to behave, and from notions of honour and shame.[74]

Of course, law was only one factor an arbitrator had to consider in making a judgment. Political, economic, and cultural factors could also play a part, but they are often harder to tease out or to show in a quantifiable way because we rarely have evidence of any party's motivation or intent. For instance, when some contemporary commentators thought that Henry had gone down 'the middle way' in making his decision in 1177, we could speculate that such factors would have played a part.[75] This is because the English king was hardly an independent arbiter and showing to both Sancho and Alfonso that he had acted fairly would likely have ensured smoother relations with two rulers with whom he shared dynastic, cultural, territorial, and economic connections.[76] Such a principle of equity and fairness seems to have been in play during other arbitrations too. The arbitration of Pope Innocent II between Genoa and Pisa of 1133, in which the pope ordered the two cities to refrain from war and discord, pay reparations, and set up an arbitration panel for resolving any future disputes, should be seen in the context of a papal bull issued to Bishop Siro of Genoa on the same day (20 March). This bull outlines the conflict between the two cities and the violence committed, which made them an enemy of all mankind ('humani generis inimico') – an expression linked to just war theory and international criminal law.[77] The solution was to raise Siro and his see from a bishopric to an archbishopric and divide equally the jurisdiction over the sees on the disputed island of Corsica between the archbishops of Genoa and Pisa, with each receiving three sees.[78] The conflict over the control of Corsica had begun in earnest in 1118, when Pope Gelasius II confirmed the primacy of the archbishop of Pisa over the church in Corsica, which had originally been granted by Pope Urban II in 1092. The Genoese appealed in 1120 and were partially successful when Pope Calixtus II in 1121 issued a bull revoking Pisa's right to consecrate bishops on Corsica, reverting it to the papacy. An unsuccessful appeal by the Pisans followed in 1123, but just three years later another pope, Honorius II, reinstated the Pisan archbishopric's rights. In 1130, Innocent II brokered a truce, which held until the arbitration of 1133.[79] From all of this it appears that the arbitration of 1133 in fact had two judgments; one ordering the division of the jurisdiction over the Church in Corsica, and a second ordering the two cities to refrain from violence and to make peace. The fact that this was done across two separate documents make the two issues appear non-related but the bull, referring to the conflict, make it clear that they were one and the same. This shows the difficulties of separating political and economic factors from legal and religious ones in this period. Furthermore, as the two cities had gone through several stages of papal appeals interspersed with warfare, but without any clear winner, this seems a likely reason why Pope Innocent took a middle option, making both sides compromise while each at the same time received or retained something. According to Gerald of Wales, this was how Henry II had also dealt with the arbitration between the kings of Castile and Navarre: 'each should give something and retain something, and neither side suffer any excessive loss of land'.[80] Equity and fairness reigned. Indeed, it seems, as Frederic Cheyette observed about Languedoc arbitration practices before 1250, that the idea was not to apply objective rules but rather to ensure that 'both parties should be satisfied'.[81] Despite this, it is impossible not to consider the wider context of events in the Mediterranean when it comes to the 1133 arbitration. Innocent's own troubles with the anti-pope Anacletus II and his supporter King Roger of Sicily meant that diverting Genoa and Pisa's interests and naval strength from their own conflict over Corsica to support Innocent's cause must at least have been a consideration factoring into his award.[82] Thus political, religious or economic factors were relevant, even if, as in the modern world, they, of themselves, cannot be seen to have affected the outcome.[83]

A final indicator, and indeed requirement, in the process of arbitration was the notification of the decision – the arbitration treaty. Treaties achieved by mediation or by direct negotiations are never issued by those who had negotiated them but always survive in texts issued by one or both of the contracting parties, i.e. the rulers or communities involved. Here, there is a clear and distinct difference between these two forms of dispute resolution and arbitration. In 1177, the notification was preserved as a letter in Henry II's name addressed to both Alphonso VIII of Castile and Sancho VI of Navarre, which outlined the claims and the process of arbitration as well as Henry's judgment – we can call it the *Treaty of London* from the location where Henry held the assembly at which he made the judgment.[84] Similarly, the *Treaty of Grosseto* is the surviving notification of the arbitration between the cities of Genoa and Pisa by Pope Innocent II.[85] The fact that an arbitration treaty is made in the name of the person who arbitrated the case seems logical as it was essentially the third party who guaranteed the award. Such arbitration treaties show a remarkable consistency in format across the period investigated here, although the overall number is extremely small, and they are also similar to such notifications of arbitrations at the lower levels of society.[86]

A notification of the arbitration between the Danish rivals by Frederick Barbarossa has not survived, but there seems no reason to doubt that one was made. Saxo Grammaticus wrote with the full knowledge of the resolution of the conflict in 1157 and that the eventual winner was neither Svein nor Cnut but Valdemar, later known as 'the Great'. He also wrote at a time when the Danish king had asserted his independence from the German king and hence memories of any intervention in the dispute over the kingdom were significantly manipulated and blamed on the two unsuccessful candidates. Despite this, it would be tricky to deny that documents, such as the initial letters to Conrad III, were the basis of Saxo's narrative, because he conflates and counters even minute points in them. For instance, Saxo notes that Frederick reminded Svein that they 'were old friends and companions-in-arms' and invited him to a conference, which echoes Svein's letter to Conrad reminding him of his service in his household and his request for a conference at a location of Conrad's choice.[87] Similarly, Saxo states that Frederick tried to impose his judgment on Svein by threatening to send an imperial force with Cnut to Denmark if he did not comply, which is similar to Cnut's request for the German king to restore his rights with a 'sharp sword'.[88] Hence, there seems no reason to doubt that when Saxo records the decision, he relied upon the testimony of someone who had seen (or heard) the arbitration treaty. Apart from recording that Svein would be the rightful king under the overlordship of the emperor while Cnut received Zealand, he notes that the estates of Svein's father on Zealand would be exempted from Cnut's portion, and that the terms would be enforced by military means and an assurance that certain subjects would go over to the other side in case of breaches.[89] The last of these features is one common to very many other treaties too.[90] Indeed, the way in which Saxo retells the whole sequence of events is similar to the format of other arbitration treaties in that it details how the request for an intervention was sought, the journey to Merseburg, the large number of magnates present, the accusations and claims, and finally the decision and its approval by the parties.

The fact that arbitration treaties are issued in the name of the third party allows us to identify the earliest arbitration treaty for which a text has survived into the modern period, namely the *Treaty of Rouen* (991). This treaty is a notification in the name of Pope John XV detailing the reconciliation and peace agreement of 991 between King Æthelred II and Richard I, duke of Normandy, or the *marquis* as he is referred to in the letter. The document outlines how, having heard of the hostilities between Æthelred and Richard, Pope John sent his legate, Bishop Leo of Trevi, to the two rulers with letters admonishing them to put aside their hostility. First, he visited England, where he met the king on Christmas Day 990 and gave him the pope's letters. After consulting with his witan, the king agreed to make peace with Richard and sent Bishop Æthelsige of Sherborne, Leofstan son of Ælfwold, and Æthelnoth son of Wigstan to Normandy with the legate. After peacefully receiving the pope's warning and hearing of the decision of Æthelred and his court, Richard confirmed the peace on the condition that if any of their people, or they themselves, were to commit any wrong against the other, it should be atoned for with fitting compensation. The peace was to remain forever and was confirmed at Rouen on 1 March by the oaths of both parties, that is the three envoys on behalf of Æthelred and Bishop Roger of Lisieux, Rodulf son of Hugh, and Tursten son of Turgis on behalf of Richard. A postscript then adds that neither ruler was to receive the men or enemies of the other without the latter's seal.[91] Much like the *Treaty of Grosseto*, the decision centred on establishing peace between the parties and finding a way for them to avoid future conflict, but there is no indication as to the actual issue in dispute. Scholars have speculated that it might have related to the final statement of the notification – that neither side was to receive the men or enemies of the other without some form of identification – but there are no additional documents or contemporary references to this treaty or the conflict in the narrative evidence that allows us to confirm this.[92] In addition, the lack of additional information surrounding this arbitration means that we don't know if it was preceded by other negotiations, which is possible, nor how the parties agreed to the arbitration. Possibly, the statement in the treaty that Æthelred 'concessit' – a word which confusingly can mean 'to allow, assent to, concede, agree' or even 'to grant' – peace and then sent his envoys with the papal legate to Normandy, where the peace was agreed by the leader of the Normans, should be seen as an indication of both parties agreeing to abide by the decision. In any case, this notification is very significant as it is the lone such pre-1100 document – one that survives as a copy made within ten to fifteen years of the original – and it is hence our only solid evidence, before the revival of Roman law in the twelfth century, that arbitration could be a solution to international disputes and not just a strategy to resolve future conflicts as in the case of arbitration panels within treaties.[93]

What has emerged from this discussion about the expectations and requirements of arbitration is that in its full manifestation, international arbitration might have been relatively rare. We only have three incidents that meet all of the requirements outlined above – the Italian cases of 1133 and 1188, and the Iberian case of 1177. A fourth arbitration, the Anglo-Norman case of 991, likely meets all of them but the lack of contextual evidence hinders our interpretation of it. One other case, the Danish one of 1152, can be reconstructed from narrative evidence even though the final notification, i.e., the treaty, has not survived. There are also a handful of incidents which look like arbitrations but that, in the end, were resolved by different means. One such example is the dispute over exiles and fugitives between Charlemagne and Offa: a case which was clearly never resolved. Although Alcuin wrote to Offa during the spring of 796 that Charlemagne had sent his envoys and the exiles into the presence of the pope and the archbishop of Canterbury – the latter might have been the Mercian king's representative at the papal court – Offa died in July of that same year, thereby ending the dispute and any mandate for arbitration.[94] Another example can be found with the dispute over the so-called 'Golden Inscription', which set out the legal rights of the Genoese in the kingdom of Jerusalem. A series of letters between 1167 and 1186 outlines the appeal to the pope for the restoration of these rights and how successive popes pressured the kings of Jerusalem to restore them, before Pope Urban III in 1186 proposed that the matter should be put to arbitration ('justicie') and even wrote to the proposed arbiters: the archbishop of Nazareth and the masters of the Templars and the Hospitallers.[95] However, political events meant that the dispute was eventually not resolved through arbitration. Instead, the rights were restored after the fall of Jerusalem in 1187 when the remnants of the Frankish settlements in the Holy Land needed friendlier relations with the Genoese and their fleet.[96]

Scholars have often asserted that international arbitration was frequent by the twelfth century. For instance, Ganshof's influential study on the history of international relations in the Middle Ages asserted that arbitration became the most widespread (peaceful) method of settling conflicts in the twelfth century.[97] Similarly, Gary B. Born has argued that after a decline during the late Roman period, international arbitration saw a surge in the medieval period, even though he admits that the picture is incomplete and, indeed, his own study only lists late medieval examples.[98] Kamp argued that arbitration became more prominent after the Gregorian reform, when popes were keen to impose settlements, and he sees this development as deriving from the extension of the papacy's power in the eleventh and twelfth centuries.[99] However, Kamp's observation allows us to see that there is a confusion in the current historiography between international arbitration and appeals to the papacy for a judgment in a dispute. An appeal to the pope was an attempt to achieve a judgment to end all disputes, and, as observed by Kamp, there is no doubt that they became more frequent after the Gregorian reform. The papacy was the court supreme in the Middle Ages, which, according to Ullmann, from the mid-twelfth century onwards had a body of law capable of being administered and applied, and which could reasonably anticipate the enforcement of its decisions by virtue of the fact that canon law was universal and hence rulings applied to all Christians.[100] In the earlier period, this concept was less developed even though the writings of Pope Leo I (440–61) provided his successors with a concept of authority, which 'made the pope the ultimate earthly judge, who could himself be judged by no one save God'.[101] However, as I argued in 2011, and shown through two well-known examples, despite the theory of papal jurisdiction, the practice 'by no means involved simply the issuing of papal commands followed by local obedience to such commands'.[102] Furthermore, as evidenced from the dispute between Genoa and Pisa over Corsica, where appeals resulted in counter appeals until the arbitration of 1133, such papal decisions could be reversed with the arrival of a new pope. Hence, and because appeals were frequently one-sided and not based on the principle of *arbiter ex compromisso*, attempts to compel rulers to accept papal judgments were fraught with difficulties.[103] It is also evident that the papacy itself saw arbitration as different to ordinary judgments, because both sides had to agree to submit their dispute to arbitration, and this, presumably, made it more likely that the parties would abide by any decision.[104] This was likely why Pope Urban III in 1186, following decades of the papacy failing to enforce the successful appeal of the Genoese with regards to their rights in the kingdom of Jerusalem, wanted the parties to submit the dispute to arbitration. Urban's instructions to the proposed arbiters were very clear: they were to 'bring this dispute to its due end, with no scope for further delay through appeal'.[105] In other words, arbitration in many ways was the ultimate appeal procedure, seemingly not reversible, and, as a consequence, rarer than historians have acknowledged. Although scholars often confuse appeals to the papal court as arbitration, the evidence seems unequivocal that the two were not the same.[106] While they were both third-party interventions, they were not both arbitrations. Nevertheless, that arbitration by the twelfth century was well-known and widely practised is clear from the large body of evi dence of arbitration panels in treaties, and within such a context, arbitration as a viable strategy intended to resolve disputes between rulers does not look out of place even if the surviving records of this are very sparse. Perhaps most importantly, there evidently were two competing strands of arbitration in medieval Europe; one borne out of Christian and Roman doctrine, and another borne out of customary practices, i.e., decisions by peers. Although both strands had the express consent of the parties as their basis, it is the second strand that appear more established with clear procedures and processes understood by all parties, as demonstrated by the evidence from arbitration panels as well as the Danish case of 1152 and the Iberian case of 1177.

Having methods and strategies for resolving conflicts is one thing, quite another is the extent to which these included the cap-ability and willingness to enforce the resulting judgments and treaties. The question, of course, is exactly how to measure this from the evidence available between 700 and 1200? Enforcement is often intertwined with success and, as I argued in 2011, this is a subjective measurement that alters depending on a person's perspective at any one time.[107] Scholars writing about this issue frequently comment on the unwillingness of parties to keep agreements made or adhere to the decisions of arbitrators and on the inability of arbitrators and other guarantors to enforce it. For instance, both Luis Corral and Charles Tindal-Robertson have argued that neither Alfonso VIII of Castile or Sancho VI of Navarre showed any inclination to abide by the judgment proclaimed by Henry II in 1177 and that sub-mitting their dispute was primarily a diplomatic card to be played in order to delay matters.[108] Tindal-Robertson further noted that the real problem arising from the litigation was that there was no means of enforcing it in the absence of strong royal power. In other words, scholarly expectation is frequently that enforcement should be something achieved by force (often violent) by a state-like power in case of non-compliance. However, often this view has arisen out of a fundamental misunderstanding as to what arbitration is and what it does. Henry II's notification sets this out clearly when it says that his award would terminate the dispute but that in addition to the award, 'by this present writing', he commanded Alfonso and Sancho to 'establish peace between you and faithfully observe it in the future'.[109] In other words, the judgment may have terminated parts of the dispute but this was not the same as establishing peace. This is backed up by other aspects of the decision. For instance, only the most recent conquests of lands were subject to Henry's judgment while previous, outstanding claims were disregarded.[110] Hence, when the two parties following this arbitration continued hostilities dispersed with negotiations for the next two years before a peace was concluded in 1179, this may not necessarily have been because the arbitration was unsuccessful but because peace has to be negotiated and the personal enmity between the two kings set aside. This should not come as a surprise to anyone and must be seen in a much broader context of dispute settlement across the medieval West, where scholars such as Stephen D. White, have observed that 'a judgment could sometimes end a dispute between two parties; it could not establish peace between them'.[111] Moreover, Esther Pascua has rightly pointed out the complicated cross-border rela-tionship at the heart of the eventual peace treaty, which underlines that Henry II's decision was never abandoned but adapted. In the *Treaty of Logroño* (1179), Sancho VI of Navarre had to submit to Alfonso VIII of Castile some of the property awarded to him in 1177. The Castilian king, in turn, was to give them to three named men, who were originally from Navarre but had become vassals of the Castilian king, and these also had to take an oath of loyalty to Sancho.[112] The idea was clearly to tie the castles and those holding them closer to both kings – an adapted compromise, which is not inconsistent with Henry's award.[113]

We can see a similar pattern with regards to the 1152 arbitration by Frederick I. Despite the fact that the conflict over the kingdom continued and that at some point a third claimant, Valdemar, appeared on the scene, all subsequent attempts at establishing peace adhered to the two principles set out by Frederick in 1152: Svein was to have the title of king and Cnut was to have Zealand.[114] An eventual agreement was reached in 1157, which divided the kingdom in three with each rival having the title king and importantly, in the division, Cnut retained Zealand.[115] Saxo, in commenting on this agreement, further implies that Cnut was less than the other two by virtue of having the third choice and Zealand having been disregarded by Svein and Valdemar, which could be interpreted as adhering to Frederick's decision.[116] Of course, in the end, this agreement did not establish peace either, because Svein swiftly killed Cnut at the feast of Roskilde, after which Valdemar killed Svein at the Battle of Grathe Heath and proclaimed himself sole king as Valdemar I.[117] Again, the arbitration of 1152 was not intended to establish peace between the parties but rather to give each what they could prove they were entitled to or what neither objected to. Subsequent agreements and events show that the basic premise of the decision was adhered to, presumably because it was underpinned by established rights and practices in terms of inheritance and possession, even if peace proved elusive.[118]

Both the example of 1152 and that of 1177 were arbitrations by and for peers: a ruler arbitrating in a dispute between other rulers. As such, the arbitrator was expected to enforce his decision not by force but by persuasion, cooperation, and collaboration, using the full extent of his familial, social, and economic links with the various stakeholders.[119] This is obvious if we consider the reasons why Henry II and Frederick I were chosen as arbiters in the first place. The English king was certainly not an independent third party in 1177. His daughter Eleanor was married to Alfonso VIII of Castile, who is referred to in the notification as Henry's 'dearly beloved son'. Sancho is similarly referred to as the 'uncle' of Alphonso, emphasising both the actual and the spiritual familial connections between the three kings.[120] As duke of Aquitaine, Henry was also the neighbour to King Sancho VI of Navarre, who, in the early 1170s had also been present at a peace conference at Limoges together with the count of Toulouse and the king of Aragon. The latter of whom was also a party in the *Treaty of Logroño*, by which Alphonso and Sancho agreed to submit their dispute to arbitration.[121] Henry was thus familiar with some of the rights, claims, lordships, and disputes of the three Iberian kings and was likely chosen for this particular reason. In fact, his role was clearly that of a friend (again, borne out in the notification), performing those two fundamental functions of aid and counsel.[122] However, he was not just any friend, as Henry had been chosen to arbitrate ahead of his French counterpart, and the arbitrating king is portrayed both in the documents and in narratives covering the events of 1177 as more of a 'special friend', even though not explicitly described as such.[123] Similarly, in 1152, we know that one of the claimants to the Danish throne, Svein, had spent time at the German court. Indeed, Svein's letter to King Conrad III requesting his aid in the conflict over the Danish throne reminded the German king of this sojourn at the court. However, Conrad passed away shortly after this letter was written and was succeeded by Frederick Barbarossa, who seems to have taken up the case almost immediately. Saxo Grammaticus likely tells us why when he recalls that Frederick was a 'socio militiae' of Svein – that is his 'military buddy' – indicating that the two had been in the household of Conrad III. Clearly then, the special friend – the arbitrating king – was never an independent party and he was expected to exercise the full extent of his various relationships with the disputing parties, and their supporters, in order to implement the judgment.[124] As noted by Kamp, because these various relationships and links overlapped again and again, it was difficult to escape such pressure.[125] This is not to say that enforcement by violent means was not one way in which this could be done. Cnut's letter, likely written around the same time as that of Svein – indicating again that both parties have to agree to submit their claims to an arbiter – appealed to Conrad's sense of justice and goodness as a Christian prince. However, couched in the humility, Cnut was also asking for a judgment at the point of a 'sharp sword', if necessary.[126]

By contrast to the above examples of arbitration, it is evident that there are significant differences between arbitrations by and for peers and those effected by the papacy, as in 1133 and 991. Both arbitration treaties have survived as records that ordered the parties to conclude and observe peace. In the case of the arbitration between the Genoese and the Pisans, the actual decision over the dispute – the raising of the see of Genoa to an archbishopric and the division of ecclesiastical authority on Corsica – was contained in a separate document and we should consider that this may also have been the case in 991, although no such document now survives. Here, the arbitrations achieved both a judgment and a peace. Possibly the pope was with this exercising his right as the highest peacemaker on Earth or it was because the matters in dispute centred on issues that fell under ecclesiastical jurisdiction.[127] If the latter, this means that scholars currently have misinterpreted the historical context of the 991 arbitration, which is nearly always seen as a dispute over the Normans harbouring viking raiders, not any ecclesiastical matter.[128] In any case, based on current evidence – meagre though it is – papal arbitration seems to have differed from peer arbitration by providing both a judgment in the matter of dispute and the conclusion of peace. Looking at enforcement strategies furthermore brings the differences between mediation and peer arbitration on the one hand and papal arbitration and papal appeals on the other into sharper focus, because, as noted above, the pope had the ability to enforce his decisions in very tangible, if not always successful, ways: by using interdict and excommunication.[129] We might think that the papacy's ability to enforce international shame and exclusion through excommunication or inflict sanctions through the use of interdict was not likely to be conducive to peace, but the arbitration of 1133 and the peace achieved persisted, for the most part, and was reinforced through alliances between the two cities over the next two decades.[130] Likewise, the treaty of 991 seems to have remained intact until the death of the Norman leader, Richard I, in 996, and the peace was reinforced subsequently through a marriage alliance between the English king and Emma of Normandy in 1002, the daughter of Richard I and sister of Duke Richard II.

From the evidence presented, it is possible to draw a few tentative conclusions about how international dispute resolution worked in the period before 1200. All arbitrations seem to have been a last option, after the failure of protracted conflict, negotiations, and treaties. Peer arbitration was a way to achieve a decision over a limited issue and probably it was a 'softer' option, less alienating than an appeal to the papacy. Papal arbitration was the ultimate decision and peace treaty, likely only effected over ecclesiastical matters, and fully enforceable through interdict and excommunication by the fact that it rested on the parties' own agreement to submit their dispute to arbitration. It seems probable that this also made it a rare option. However, the possibility of achieving a judgment in a dispute made appeals to the papacy commonplace, even though such decisions, by virtue of their one-sidedness, were more difficult to enforce. Bearing all of this in mind then, it is hardly surprising that the vast majority of treaties in the period 700 to 1200 were achieved by direct negotiations or mediation.

According to Article 2(3) of the first chapter of the United Nations Charter, all members 'shall settle their international disputes by peaceful means in such a manner that international peace and security, and justice, are not endangered'.[131] In the Middle Ages, there was no rule setting this out explicitly, but nevertheless there seems to have been an underlying principle of this in international conflicts. Looking at diplomatic negotiations across the early and central Middle Ages, a pattern emerges whereby hostility and conflicts could generate direct negotiations, mediation, and appeals, with the first two being the most likely to lead to a treaty. However, they could also lead to an appeal to the pope, which usually resulted in further mediation and negotiations before any treaty was concluded. In addition, the appeal could result in a judgment, but not, by itself, in a treaty or in arbitration. Direct negotiations and mediation could lead to arbitration, which in turn ended with a judgment in the form of the arbitration treaty. The pattern is similar, if extended, to what scholars have observed about dispute settlement more generally. For instance, Jón Viðar Sigurðsson has shown that conflict on Iceland usually resulted in direct negotiations or mediation, which could result in either an agreement or arbitration, the latter of which also ended with an agreement.[132] The options for dispute resolution, at whatever level, were hence both intertwined and complementary. Most importantly, as Dixon has observed also of the contemporary world, the methods were cumulative and did not operate in isolation.[133] There can thus be no doubt that rulers and communities had well-developed methods and strategies for settling disputes between them peacefully, thereby fulfilling one of the central obligations of international law.[134]

Notes

1 For examples, see Gerd Althoff, 'Compositio. Wiederherstellung verletzter Ehre im Rahmen gütlicher Konfliktbeendigung', in *Verletzte Ehre. Ehrkonflikte in Gesellschaften des Mittelalters und der Frühen Neuzeit*, eds. Klaus Schreiner and G. Schwerhoff (Cologne, 1995), 63–76; Per Andersen et al., eds., *Law and Disputing in the Middle Ages* (Copenhagen, 2013), 123–36, 165–80; White, 'Pactum… Legem', 281–308; William I. Miller, 'Avoiding Legal Judgment. The Submission of Disputes to Arbitration in Medieval Iceland', *AJLH*, 28 (1984), 95–134.

2 Kamp, *Friedensstifter und Vermittler*. From the thirteenth century, a distinction also came to be made between *arbiter* and *arbitrator*, with the former deciding according to law and formal procedure while the latter decided according to justice and without formal procedure. On the distinction between the concepts, see K.-H. Ziegler, 'Arbiter, Arbitrator und Amicabilis Compositor', *Zeitschrift der Savigny-Stiftung für Rechtsgeschichte*, 84 (1967), 376–81; Linda Fowler, 'Forms of Arbitration', in *Proceedings of the Fourth International Congress of Medieval Canon Law*, ed. S. Kuttner (Vatican City, 1972), 133–47.

3 For examples, see Benham, *PMA*, 74–9, 202–9; Chaplais, *EDP*, 1–74; Ganshof, *MA*, 4–5, 36, 37, 126–7, 128, 131–2, 136–7; Andrew Gillet, *Envoys and Political Communication in the Late Antique West, 411–533* (Cambridge, 2003), 174–90, 230–69; Nicolas Drocourt, 'Passing on Political Information between Major Powers: The Key Role of Ambassadors between Byzantium and some of its Neighbours', *Al-Masaq: Journal of the Medieval Mediterranean*, 24 (2012), 91–112; Ecaterina Lung, 'Barbarian Envoys at Byzantium in the 6th Century', *Hiperboreea Journal*, 2 (2015), 35–52, esp. 45–7; Ottewill-Soulsby, 'The Camels of Charles the Bald', 263–92, esp. 264–6; Tansen Sen, 'In Search of Longevity and Good Karma: Chinese Diplomatic Missions to Middle India in the Seventh Century', *Journal of World History*, 12 (2001), 1–28.

4 Gary B. Born, *International Arbitration: Cases and Materials* (Alphen, 2011), 4; Justyna Wubs-Mrozewicz, 'The Late Medieval and Early Modern Hanse as an Institution of Conflict Management.' *Continuity and Change*, 32 (2017), 67–70; Stuart Jenks, 'Friedensvorstellungen der Hanse (1356–1474)', *Vorträge und Forschungen: Träger und Instrumentarien des Friedens im hohen und späten Mittelalter*, 43 (1996), 405–39.

5 For examples, see David W. Rivkin, 'The Impact of International Arbitration on the Rule of Law', *Arbitration International*, 29 (2013), 330; Henry S. Fraser, 'Sketch of the History of International Arbitration', *Cornell Law Review*, 11 (1926), 191; Moeglin, *Diplomatie*, 703–18.

6 Dixon, *Textbook on IL*, 5.

7 On this arbitration, see F. Luis Corral, 'Alfonso VIII of Castile's Judicial Process at the Court of Henry II of England: An Effective and Valid Arbitration?', *Nottingham Medieval Studies*, 50 (2006), 22–42; C. Tindal-Robertson, 'Peacemaking in Medieval Léon and Castile, c.1100–1230', unpublished PhD thesis (Exeter, 2014), 112–14.

8 Howden, *Gesta*, i, 139–43.

9 '...petitiones et calumnias et allegationes...'. Howden, *Gesta*, i, 145–6.
10 Howden, *Gesta*, i, 145–50. Note that in the *Chronica*, the two treaties are given first, as if he thought these documents had pre-eminence, after which Roger recorded the written claims of the two kings. Howden, *Chronica*, ii, 122–5.
11 A number of other contemporaries also commented on this event, for which see Gerald of Wales, *Expugnatio Hibernica*, Bk. II, ch. 31 (pp. 222–3); Walter Map, *De Nugis Curialium. Courtiers' Trifels*, tr. M. R. James, revised by C. N. L. Brooke and R. A. B. Mynors (Oxford, 1983), 508–11; *Diceto*, i, 418–20.
12 The case can be followed through its documentary records, for which see *CDRG*, ii, nos. 172–5.
13 *Annali Genovesi*, ii, 24–5.
14 By contrast, King and Le Forestier argued that the procedural aspects of arbitration in the Middle Ages were ad hoc, for which see Henry T. King Jr. and Marc A. Le Forestier, 'Papal Arbitration: How the Early Roman Catholic Church Influenced Modern Dispute Resolution', *Dispute Resolution Journal*, 52 (1997), 79 fn. 31.
15 Rivkin, 'The Impact of International Arbitration on the Rule of Law', 328.
16 Ganshof concluded that this was the only principle of arbitration worth citing. Ganshof, *MA*, 152.
17 *Decretum*, C.2 q.6 c.33; *Digest*, 1:4.8.
18 Howden, *Gesta*, i, 140.
19 *Dip. Docs*, 7.
20 *CDRG*, ii, 333: 'universitatis vestre sub debito iuramenti quod nobis prestitistis mandamus atque precipimus quatenus mandata que predicti cardinales super omnibus et singulis capitulis ex parte nostra vobis indixerint, sicut ex ore nostro prolata succipitais et inviolabiliter sine contradictione qualibet observatis'. For the oath of the Genoese, see *CDRG*, ii, 322–32.
21 *Treaty of Grosseto*, c. 1. It might be relevant that the *Annals of Genoa* recorded for the year 1130 that Pope Innocent II concluded a truce between the Genoese and the Pisans 'with many oaths undertaken on both sides, until the pope should return from France'. *Annali Genovesi*, i, 26. See also the similar statement in *LP*, ii, 381. On this arbitration, see also Werner Maleczek, 'Das Frieden stiftende Papsttum im 12. und 13. Jahrhundert', *Vorträge und Forschungen: Träger und Instrumentarien des Friedens im hohen und späten Mittelalter*, 43 (1996), 260–2.
22 On the wider context, see Odilo Engels, 'Friedrich Barbarossa und Dänemark', *Vorträge und Forschungen*, 40 (1992), 371–3.

23 *Dip. Dan*, I:2, nos. 103–4. On Wibald's letter collection and its date, see Timothy Reuter, 'Gedenküberlieferung und -praxis im Briefbuch Wibalds von Stablo', in *Der Liber Vitae von Corvey*, 2 vols., eds. Karl Schmid and Joachim Wollasch (Wiesbaden, 1989), ii, 161–77; Timothy Reuter, 'Rechtliche Argumentation in den Briefen Wibalds von Stablo', in *Papsttum, Kirche und Recht im Mittelalter: Festschrift für Horst Fuhrmann zum 65. Geburtstag*, ed. Hubert Mordek (Tübingen, 1991), 251–64.

24 *Das Briefbuch Abt Wibalds von Stablo und Corvey*, 3 vols., ed. Martina Hartmann, *MGH Briefe der deutschen Kaiserzeit*, 9 (Hanover, 2012), ii, no. 314 (p. 666): 'Convenit igitur paternitati vestre filii honori providere et si qui ad nostri destructionem emerserint, eorum temeritatem compescere'; ibid., ii, no. 315 (p. 668): 'Privati igitur non solum regno verum eciam patrimonio, Christo et vobis conquerimur, ut iusticia dictante nobis exulibus condescendatis et compatiamini.'

25 This reflects other studies of arbitration, showing terminology to be a determining factor but not necessarily a decisive one. For two examples, see Kamp, *Friedensstifter und Vermittler*, 14–27; Jón Viðar Sigurðsson, 'The Role of Arbitration in the Settlement of Disputes in Iceland c. 1000–1300', in *Law and Disputing in the Middle Ages*, 123–32.

26 'Sueno rex Danorum, qui ibidem regnum suscepit de manu domni regis. Knut alter Danus, qui ibidem regnum in manu domni regis refutauit.' *Dip. Dan*, I:2, no. 110.

27 Kenneth Pennington, 'The Jurisprudence of Procedure', in *The History of Courts and Procedure in Medieval Canon Law*, eds. Wilfried Hartmann and Kenneth Pennington (Washington, DC, 2016), 127–9.

28 For similar observations at lower levels of society, see Born, *International Arbitration*, 4; Kamp, *Friedensstifter und Vermittler*, 143; Susan Reynolds, *Kingdoms and Communities in Western Europe 900–1300*, 2nd edn. (Oxford, 1997), 26.

29 *MGH Epp.*, IV, no. 100, p. 145. English translation from Allott, *Alcuin of York*, 52.

30 A letter from Alcuin to Offa similarly confirms that Charles had sent envoys to the pope for a judgment but divulges no further details about the process. *MGH Epp.*, IV, no. 101.

31 Nithard, *Histoire*, IV:1 (165): 'Et quidem primum visum est, ut rem ad episcopos sacerdotesque... conferrent.'

32 Ibid., IV:3 (168): 'Verumtamen solito more ad episcopos sacerdotesque rem referent... Quibus cum undique... consentiunt, legatos convocant, postulate concedunt.'

33 Ibid., IV:5 (171): 'Et hoc quoque ad conferendum episcopis commissum.'

34 Janet L. Nelson, 'Dispute Settlement in Carolingian West Frankia', in *The Settlement of Disputes in Early Medieval Europe*, eds. Wendy Davis and Paul Fouracre (Cambridge, 1986), 58–60; Reynolds, *Kingdoms and Communities*, 23–6. On the role of community and consensus in diplomacy more generally, see also Benham, 'Peace, Security and Deterrence', 124–9.

35 *Ordinatio imperii*, c. 10.

36 Nithard, *Histoire*, IV:1 (165).

37 Sawyer, *Anglo-Saxon Charters*, in its revised form available online as the 'Electronic Sawyer' (www.esawyer.org.uk), S1428b. English translation adapted from *EHD*, i, no. 164.

38 *Dunsæte*, cc. 3.2–3.3.

39 Howden, *Gesta*, i. 192; Howden, *Chronica*, ii, 144–5; *Treaty of Ivry* (1180), cc. 3–6.

40 *Treaty of Najac-de-Rouergue*, c. 4: 'et predicta etiam discordia per duos de probis hominibus utriusque partis bona fide et sine dilacione pacificaretur'.

41 Howden, *Chronica*, iii, 259.

42 *DD FI*, iii, 208; *Treaty of Venice*, c. 11. Similar stipulations can be found in other Italian treaties, e.g., *Treaty of Grosseto* (1133), *Treaty of Montebello* (1175).

43 *Treaty of Venice*, c. 11.

44 *MGH Capit. II*, 194–5.

45 *Treaty of Pavia*, cc. 10, 12, 19. It is noteworthy that the term 'arbitrium', which later came to refer to a judgment in arbitration, is used in this particular treaty. For the context, see West, 'Communities and *pacta*', 376–9.

46 *Treaty of Pavia*, c. 27. West, 'Communities and *Pacta*', 379. Jennifer Davis has similarly commented on the ability of *missi* to 'evaluate and, when necessary, replace' judges. Jennifer R. Davis, 'A Pattern for Power: Charlemagne's Delegation of Judicial Responsibilities', in *The Long Morning of Medieval Europe*, eds. Jennifer R. Davis and Michael McCormick (Aldershot, 2008), 240.

47 Kamp similarly concluded that mediation and arbitration were not conceptually distinct until the twelfth century, for which see his *Friedensstifter und Vermittler*, 135, 143, 185, 217–18.

48 K.-H. Ziegler, 'From *foedera pacis* to *foedera paces*', in *Peace Treaties and International Law*, 150.

49 *Dip. Dan*, I:2, no. 103. The language here is similar to how the relationship between the Pope and the Holy Roman Emperor is often described in their agreements. For examples, see *Treaty of Venice* (1177) and *Treaty of Constance* (1153).

50 *Dip. Dan*, I:2, no. 104. On these events, see Jenny Benham, 'The Context of Peacemaking', in *The Nordic Civil Wars*, eds. Hans Jacob Orning, Jón Viðar Sigurðsson, and Kim Esmark (forthcoming 2022).

51 *Gesta Friderici*, 106.

52 *Helmold von Bosau Slawenchronik*, ed. B. Schmeidler, revised by H. Stoob (Darmstadt, 1973), c. 73 (pp. 254–5).

53 Saxo, *GD*, ii, 1034–5. This is echoed by *Knytlingasaga*, for which see *Danakonunga sögur: Skjöldunga saga, Knýtlinga saga, Ágrip af sögu Danakonunga*, ed. Bjarni Guðnason (Reykjavik, 1982), c. 109; *Knytlingasaga: The History of the Kings of Denmark*, tr. Hermann Pálsson and Paul Edwards (Odense, 1986), 150. In the early thirteenth century, Arnold of Lübeck commented that Cnut's son, Bishop Valdemar of Slesvig, was a very rich man 'not only from his episcopal revenues, but from the great patrimony that he had inherited from his father', possibly confirming that this patrimony was what had been awarded by Frederick and that this was because it was inalienable. *Arnoldi Chronica Slavorum*, ed. G. H. Pertz, *MGH SRG*, 14 (Hanover, 1868), 111 (III:22); *The Chronicle of Arnold of Lübeck*, ed. Graham A. Loud (Abingdon, 2019), 131.

54 Howden, *Gesta*, i, 153; Howden, *Chronica*, ii, 130.

55 Howden, *Gesta*, i, 147–9, 152; Howden, *Chronica*, ii, 125–9.

56 Howden, *Gesta*, i, 148; Howden, *Chronica*, ii, 126.

57 The treaty shows that lawful excuses could be made for any who had been detained on the road by death, illness, or captivity, but there was no provision if they all failed to turn up. Howden, *Gesta*, i, 140; Howden, *Chronica*, ii, 122. For examples of failure to turn up to a hearing and thereby forfeiting a claim, see *Glanvill*, 14–17; *JL*, Bk. III, c. 50; *ESjL*, Bk. III, c. 21; *Digest*, 23:1.8, 40:7.4.

58 '…duo strenuissimi viri… ad suscipiendum duellum in curia regis Anglie, si adjudicatum fuerit.' Howden, *Gesta*, i, 139. The *Chronica* has the same but Howden has replaced 'strenuissimi viri' with 'milites'. Howden, *Chronica*, ii, 120.

59 *Henry, Archdeacon of Huntingdon, Historia Anglorum*, tr. Diana Greenway (Oxford, 1996), 360–1; Walter Map, *De Nugis Curialium*, 424–7. By contrast, William of Malmesbury thought that single combat had been proposed but that the matter was settled by the treaty dividing the kingdom. WM, *GRA*, i, 316–19.

60 CCCC MS 26, fo. 160.

61 That settling disputes through single combat was accepted practice in England at the time is evident from the contemporary *Glanvill*, 172–3. On similar practices in dispute settlement, see White, 'Pactum… Legem', 295, 298; Hudson, *The Oxford History of the Laws of England*, 327–8, 598–600. On *judicium dei* more generally, see Robert Bartlett, *Trial*

by Fire and Water: The Medieval Judicial Ordeal (Oxford, 1986), 103–26. That it had a long literary tradition and link to international agreements and arbitration is evident in the *Iliad* in the story of the treaty between Greeks and Trojans on deciding the war through single combat between Menelaus and Alexander. *Iliad*, ll. 3320–472.

62 *Widukind RGS*, Bk. II, cap. 10 (p. 74); Widukind, *Deeds*, 70. This incident can also be found in the work of Sigebert of Gembloux, s.a. 942 and in the version of that work copied by Diceto in his *Abbrevationes Chronicorum*. *Diceto*, i, 146. Again, the great interest in arbitrations may show their rarity. Cf. judicial duels in *Thietmari Merseburgensis Episcopi Chronicon*, ed. J. M. Lappenberg (Hanover, 1889), III:9 (p. 59); *Gesta Chuonradi II Imperatoris*, c. 33 (pp. 52–3).

63 Dixon, *Textbook on IL*, 293.

64 That the 1016 division was well-known in twelfth-century court circles is evident from the large number of writers that commented on it, for which, see Benham, 'Battle Writing and the Transition from Conflict to Peace', 29–31. On partitions in treaties, see Chapter 1, pp. 36–7.

65 Gerald of Wales, *Expugnatio Hibernica*, Bk. II, ch. 31 (pp. 222–3).

66 *Treaty of Westminster*, c. 1.

67 For an overview with texts and references to documents, see L. Landon, *The Itinerary of King Richard I* (London, 1935), 219–34.

68 Saxo, *GD*, ii, 1034–5 and fn. 66.

69 Many modern commentators have similarly observed that disputes over territory frequently involve appeal to history. Surya P. Sharma, *Territorial Acquisition, Disputes and International Law* (The Hague, 1997), 265–6; Kevin Y. L. Tan, 'The Role of History in International Territorial Dispute Settlement: The Pedra Branca Case (Singapore v Malaysia)', in *Asian Approaches to International Law and the Legacy of Colonialism: The Law of the Sea, Territorial Disputes and International Dispute Settlement*, eds. Jin-Hyun Paik, Seok-Woo Lee, and Kevin Y. L. Tan (London, 2012), 152–83.

70 That envoys failing to turn up to hearings or negotiations could have consequences is evident from the negotiations between King John and Pope Innocent III in 1213, for which see Benham, *PMA*, 121.

71 Nelson, 'Dispute Settlement', 59.

72 Jenny Benham, 'Wounding in the High Middle Ages: Law and Practice', in *Wounds in the Middle Ages*, eds. Cordelia Warr and Anne Kirkham (Farnham, 2014), 220–43.

73 E.g., John Hudson's 2012 survey of English law to 1216 shows that there was an increased focus on procedure across the period, which reflects the contemporary evidence. Hudson, *The Oxford History of the Laws of England*, 66–92, 303–32, 574–626. See also Paul Hyams,

'Henry II and Ganelon', *Syracuse Scholar*, iv (1983), esp. 27–34; Per Andersen, *Legal Procedure and Practice in Medieval Denmark* (Leiden, 2011), 130–92; Benham, 'Wounding in the High Middle Ages', 220–43; Nicholas Karn, *Kings, Lords and Courts in Anglo-Norman England* (Woodbridge, 2020).

74 Chapter 4, pp. 145–80. For similar observations about arbitrations in the Languedoc in the eleventh to the thirteenth centuries, see Cheyette, '*Suum cuique tribuere*', 288–9.

75 Gerald of Wales, *Expugnatio Hibernica*, Bk. II, ch. 31 (pp. 222–3).

76 See below, pp. 216–17.

77 On 'enemy of all mankind', see Chapter 2, p. 69; and Chapter 4, pp. 147–9.

78 *LIRG*, vol. 1/2, 13–14 (no. 282).

79 *LIRG*, vol. 1/2, nos. 280–1. For a summary, see Stanton, *Medieval Maritime Warfare*, 119–21; Epstein, *Genoa and the Genoese*, 40–2, 46. For a longer study, see Raoul Colonna de Cesari-Rocca, *Recherches sur la Corse au Moyen âge: Origine de la rivalité des Pisans et des Génois en Corse, 1014–1174* (Genoa, 1901).

80 Gerald of Wales, *Expugnatio Hibernica*, Bk. II, ch. 31 (pp. 222–3).

81 Cheyette, 'Suum cuique tribuere', 293.

82 Stanton, *Medieval Maritime Warfare*, 121.

83 Dixon, *Textbook on IL*, 293.

84 Howden, *Gesta*, i, 151–4.

85 *CDRG*, i, no. 64.

86 Nelson, 'Dispute Settlement', 56–7; Cheyette, '*Suum cuique tribuere*', 291–6.

87 *Dip. Dan*, I:2, no. 103; Saxo, *GD*, ii, 1034–5.

88 *Dip. Dan*, I:2, no. 104; Saxo, *GD*, ii, 1034–5.

89 Saxo, *GD*, ii, 1034–7.

90 On this, see Chapter 1, pp. 31–2.

91 For the best Latin version, see Chaplais, *EDP*, 37–8; H. Zimmermann, *Papsturkunden 896–1046*, 3 vols. (Vienna, 1984–9), I, no. 307. Translation in *EHD, I*, no. 230.

92 A useful outline of the historiography is available in Bauduin, 'La papauté, les Vikings et les relations Anglo-Normandes', 202–6.

93 For a full discussion of this treaty and its context, see Benham, 'The Earliest Arbitration Treaty?', 189–204.

94 *MGH Epp*, IV, no. 101. Compare also nos. 92–3, the first of which contains instructions to Charlemagne's envoy, and the second the Frankish king's letter congratulating the new pope, Leo III, on his election and wishing for the agreements between them to be renewed. There is no mention of the exiles or the arbitration.

95 *LIRG*, vol. 1/2, nos. 311–13, 316–21. Translation in Hall, *Caffaro*, 207–11. There is a large literature on this inscription. For a good summary, see Benjamin Z. Kedar, 'Again, Genoa's Golden Inscription and King Baldwin I's Privilege of 1104', in *Chemins d'outre-mer. Etudes d'histoire sur la Méditerranée médiévale offertes à Michel Balard*, eds. Damien Coulon et al. (Paris, 2004), 495–502. See also Elena Bellomo, *The Templar Order in North-West Italy (1142–c.1330)* (Leiden, 2008), 49–50; Hall, *Caffaro*, 24–8.

96 *LIRG*, vol. 1/2, nos. 330–1, 333–6, 342–3.

97 Ganshof, *MA*, 152. Henry S. Fraser's assertion that arbitration did not exist prior to the twelfth century because 'war was the rule rather than the exception', requires little discussion although it is worth mentioning that he noted the lack of a comprehensive study on the topic for the Middle Ages. Fraser, 'Sketch of the History of International Arbitration', 191.

98 Born, *International Arbitration*, 4.

99 Kamp, *Friedensstifter und Vermittler*, 215–17.

100 Walter Ullmann, 'The Medieval Papal Court as an International Tribunal', repr. in *The Papacy and Political Ideas in the Middle Ages* (London, 1976), 356–62.

101 Kathleen G. Cushing, 'Papal Authority and its Limitations', in *Oxford Handbook of Medieval Christianity*, ed. John H. Arnold (Oxford, 2014), 517–19.

102 Benham, *PMA*, 186; Cushing, 'Papal Authority and its Limitations', 517.

103 Evident during the conflict between Emperor Henry IV, the anti-king Rudolf, and the papacy in the 1070s, when several narratives show the reluctance of the kings to allow the pope to decide the matter of the kingship. For one example from 1078, see *Die Chroniken Bertholds von Reichenau und Bernolds von Konstanz*, ed. I. S. Robinson, MGH SRG n.s., 14 (Hanover, 2003), 420.

104 For this, see above p. 198.

105 '…causam ipsam sublato appellationis obstaculo fine debito terminetis.' *LIRG*, vol. 1/2, no. 317. Translation in Hall, *Caffaro*, 210.

106 According to Linda Fowler, this distinction is clear in canon law, for which see her 'Forms of Arbitration', 142–4.

107 Benham, *PMA*, 201–10.

108 Corral, 'Alfonso VIII of Castile's Judicial Process', 38; Tindal-Robertson, 'Peacemaking in Medieval Léon and Castile', 112–14.

109 '…scripto praesenti mandamus ut pacem inter vos firmetis et in perpetuum fideliter observetis.' Howden, *Gesta*, i, 153; Howden, *Chronica*, ii, 130.

110 Howden, *Gesta*, i, 153–4; Howden, *Chronica*, ii, 130; Tindal-Robertson, 'Peacemaking in Medieval Léon and Castile', 112; Corral, 'Alfonso VIII of Castile's Judicial Process', 35.

111 White, 'Pactum... Legem', 300. This is also expressed in legal texts, such as *Leges Henrici Primi*, cc. 49.5a, 57.1a. Cf. Dixon's comments that the scope of Art. 2(3) of the United Nations Charter is that 'states should settle disputes peacefully, not that they should *settle* them', showing that the jurisdiction of most international courts and tribunals is not compulsory. Dixon, *Textbook on IL*, 286. Cf. Hermann Kamp, 'Vermittlung in der internationalen Politik des spaten Mittelalters', in *Frieden stiften. Vermittlung und Konfliktlösung vom Mittelalter bis heute*, ed. Gerd Althoff (Darmstadt, 2011), 98–123, esp. 98–9.

112 Pascua, 'South of the Pyrenees', 115–16; *Treaty of Logroño* (1179) cc. 1–9.

113 Moeglin and Péquignot agree with this assessment, stating that the *Treaty of Logroño* of 1179 set out peace along similar lines to the arbitration of 1177. Moeglin, *Diplomatie*, 706.

114 *Dip. Dan*, I:2, no. 110.

115 Saxo, *GD*, ii, 1034–7, 1086–9; *Danakonunga sögur*, c. 112 (*Knytlingasaga*, 154); *Helmold von Bosau Slawenchronik*, c. 85 (pp. 302–3).

116 Saxo, *GD*, ii, 1086–9.

117 Ibid., ii, 1088–93, 1110–11

118 On this, see Benham, 'The Context of Peacemaking'. Battles, another form of judgment, can be contextualised in the same way, as they were frequently followed by months of military activity and negotiations before the conclusion of peace but without altering the fundamental award of victory. The battle of Fontenoy 841, eventually leading to the division at Verdun in 843, is one example, and the battle of Legnano 1176, leading to the peace conference in Venice in 1177, another. For this, see Benham, 'The Peace of Venice (1177)'; Benham, 'The Treaty of Verdun, 843'.

119 On collective responsibility and the role of community, see Benham, 'Peace, Security and Deterrence', 123–9.

120 Howden, *Gesta*, i, 151–2.

121 Howden, *Gesta*, i, 143;

122 On friends, see Chapter 1, pp. 29–31; Benham, *PMA*, 103–5. On political, familial, and cultural considerations behind the choice of arbitrator in more recent periods, see Bennett Ostdiek and John Fabian Witt, 'The Czar and the Slaves: Two Puzzles in the History of International Arbitration', *AJIL*, 113 (2019), 563–4.

123 Walter Map records that 'it was from old time the custom of all realms to choose the court of France and prefer it to all others; but now our court, that of our king, has been deservedly preferred to all...' Map is likely exaggerating but probably also hinting at the reputation of the pre-eminence of Charlemagne's court in twelfth-century literary circles, showing where he thought any international arbitration would have been solved previously. Walter Map, *De Nugis Curialium*, 508–11.

124 The role and function of the arbitrator here mirrors that of the mediator as can be seen in domestic dispute settlement. For examples, see Cheyette, '*Suum cuique tribuere*', 291–5; White, 'Pactum... Legem', 300.

125 Hermann Kamp, 'Soziologie der Mediation aus historischer Perspektive', *Zeitschrift für Rechtssoziologie*, 36 (2016), 142.

126 *Dip. Dan*, I:2, no. 104.

127 Kamp, *Friedensstifter und Vermittler*, 217.

128 For a summary of the context, see Benham, 'The Earliest Arbitration Treaty?', 190–4.

129 We should not equate this difference to the later differentiation in canon law between *arbiter* and *arbitrator*, because, while both peer and papal arbitration were done according to formal procedures, in making judgments, law was sometimes used but so was also a more general sense of justice. See above, pp. 205–11.

130 See *Treaty of Portovenere* (1149, 1169).

131 *Charter of the United Nations*, Ch. 1, Art. 2(3), available at www.un.org/en/about-us/un-charter/chapter-1 (accessed 16 July 2021).

132 Sigurðsson, 'The Role of Arbitration', 130, Figure 1. See also Y. Bongert, *Recherches sur les cours laïques du Xe au XIIIe siècle* (Paris, 1949), 98–111.

133 Dixon, *Textbook on IL*, 287.

134 Ibid., 286.

Conclusion

It is possible to conceive of international law in Europe 700–1200. By exploring the content of treaties and by comparing this to domestic law and customs, it is possible to see a framework of international rules that reflects the interactions and issues arising from those interactions across centuries of practice. Peaceful relations between entities was a goal that could be pursued in many different ways, and rulers frequently did so using well-known institutions (e.g., arbitration, expulsion, and redress), a plethora of customs and legal practices (e.g., amnesty, reprisal, and consent), and a combination of domestic and international legal instruments and diplomatic documents (e.g., treaties, laws, and letters). Rulers, their supporters, and whole communities not only considered themselves bound by this 'system', such as it was, but they also bear testament to its success, however small, as evidenced by its frequent and sustained use throughout the medieval period.[1] The four ways of evidencing this framework of international law, although formulated by scholars to aid understanding and study of modern international law, is clearly born out of that practice developed over centuries. This is not to argue that international law was the same in the medieval period as in the contemporary world, or that we should draw a straight line of development between these different periods. Rather, it is to say that many of the challenges surrounding war and peace – how to transition from conflict to peace; how to ensure friendly relations and smooth commerce; how to protect the rights and status of people and goods in foreign lands or during conflict; how to resolve disputes; how to create deterrence – are largely the same.[2] The details of how challenges have been resolved (or not), of course, differ according to circumstances, historical and cultural context – this is as we would expect. The polycentric nature of power and the legal pluralism of medieval Europe mean that the details of the international rules in the period 700 to 1200 were frequently subject to competing, as well as complementing, terminologies, strategies, and methods of application.[3] Yet, it is often also these nuances and plurality that show the principles of the framework at their clearest.

Treaties are an expression of the right to determine law, and as such they are also in some ways frozen in the times and circumstances in which they were concluded. We might use this to explain the instability of peaceful relations in medieval Europe, and the futility of an international law lacking a written universal doctrine and based on the notion of *pacta sunt servanda*.[4] However, medieval treaties are complex documents, often perceived as several texts aimed at different audiences or with different purposes, and our knowledge can be significantly hampered by how and in what circumstances a particular document or text has survived. Moreover, treaties frequently contained a combination of obligations, rights, and measures; some of which dealt with specific problems, others of which made promises for the future, and others yet again recorded customary practices of longer standing. Treaties and their terms could be determined and interpreted by recognised institutions (e.g., the Church, assemblies, arbitration panels), there were rules governing their conclusion (e.g., canon law, customs), and they created legally binding obligations and rights (e.g., as seen through justifications). Treaties as sources of international law then reflected a complex mix of religious and legal doctrine, customary practices, as well as circumstance. By virtue of being written down, they also set precedent, and as such, are a significant comment on what medieval rulers and their followers thought that international law was in this period.

The four ways of evidencing international law in the period 700 to 1200 demonstrate the challenges faced in ensuring peaceful relations, as well as some of the solutions. Displacement of people was, and continues to be, one of the most enduring threats to peace and security. Expulsion was both a cause and a result of displacement, and that it was regularly practised throughout the whole period cannot be in doubt. The reasons for expulsion show consistency across time and space – heinous crimes – and dealing with it clearly required a multi-pronged approach involving all levels of society, and both domestic and international institutions at different times in the process: to identify such individuals or groups; to work towards integrating or reintegrating them in the community; or to simply expel them in the first place. The extent to which these measures were successful in meeting the challenge of displacement – like international law as a whole – largely depend on how we balance the various details of the process at specific points in time but also on what we think that international law is and what it should do.[5]

Redress for legal wrongs stood at the heart of achieving peaceful relations in the medieval period. It is the international rule most consistently obeyed as well as the rule participants most wanted to obey or be seen to obey. Set out as promises for the future, clauses of redress provided proof of intention and of an ability to shoulder obligations; that is, that the ruler and his close followers had the means to provide redress.[6] However, perhaps the best way to see that redress for legal wrongs was the international rule most consistently obeyed is to look to amnesty: a denial of redress, which had to be specifically stipulated. Even then, it was almost always followed by concessions of some sort – material or symbolic – and a promise of redress for wrongs going forward. In an age when rulers primarily ruled over people, an inability or an unwillingness to provide redress for a legal wrong was a denial of justice and hence of peace that struck at the heart of their own office as rulers.[7] This explains why the line between providing redress, giving gifts, and taking tribute is often porous, with the exact nature frequently depending on the type of source and the vantage point of the compiler of that source at a particular point in time. Redress for legal wrongs was, and is, an immensely complex task to get right. It required balancing lots of factors, and often pitted different aims, rights, authority, and jurisdiction of various individuals, communities, or sections of society against each other at different times in the peace process. As a consequence, it was a task underpinned by parties' willingness to participate, to collaborate, to cooperate, and to assume obligations. That these were all intimately linked to notions of morality, honour, and reputation is evident from the justifications for actions in breaching treaties or customary rules, showing that the practice and doctrine of international law were closely intertwined. In short, then, redress explains well the purpose and function of international law in the period 700–1200.

It has been said that international rules are 'rarely enforced, but usually obeyed'.[8] The question of compliance in international law has always been a much-debated issue. For the medieval period, it has usually been approached from the doctrinal perspective of what scholars tend to call the *respublica Christiana*; that is, that medieval Europe was a religious, cultural, juridical, and maybe even political unity. An idea that the political entities of the Latin West took part in a hierarchical and, through Roman and canon law, legal whole under the, albeit theoretical, leadership of the pope and the emperor. Treaties were similarly considered to have validity through the Christian oath, which was a sacrament and subject to the authority and jurisdiction of the Church.[9] However, while this conceptualisation is a main part of the story of international law in the medieval period, it is also one that was only just emerging in its full sense by the time this study ends in 1200. The Christianisation, or re-Christianisation, of Europe was still an ongoing project; the revival of Roman law and development of canon law, which began in the late eleventh century, had not yet reached the heights it did with writers like Aquinas in the thirteenth century; and the notion of a 'Europe' under the dual leadership of pope and emperor, even a theoretical one, is mainly traceable to particular times and individuals. Furthermore, and going beyond the idea of a Christian whole, it is evident that the oath was a cross-cultural and cross-religious concept, and both written treaties and narrative descriptions thereof bear witness to the fact that many treaties were concluded with other non-Christian rulers and entities that were multi-cultural. Thinking about compliance to international rules in medieval Europe hence requires an approach that does not ignore the doctrine yet also goes beyond it.

Justifications highlight that medieval rulers had a surprisingly large arsenal of 'enforcement' methods. Ensuring that the inter-national rules were obeyed required multi-pronged strategies, some of which excluded (e.g., expulsion, excommunication, denial of redress), others coerced in violent (e.g., seizure of men, goods, and property, occupation of territory, counter-piracy) as well as non-violent ways (e.g., alliance-building, unilateral termination of treaty, appeals), or a bit of both (e.g., embargoes, blockades).[10] Rulers and their followers at times went to extreme lengths to ensure that they were perceived to have provided opportunities for redress and that they were keeping to obligations and hence to peace. Not every hostile act in the medieval period was an instigation or a renewal of war, and there were countless ways of achieving deterrence. We should be careful not to dismiss such efforts as weak and lacking in effectiveness, because such strategies, in fact, show the great complexity involved in negotiations surrounding war and peace, and a need to read our evidence with significant care. Medieval deterrence and enforcement strategies were multi-faceted, flexible, and, while following particular principles, tended to be tailored to the circumstances – the kind of strategic approach scholars often argue is needed to meet contemporary demands because 'one-size fits all' solutions are no longer viable.[11] The polycentric nature and legal pluralism of medieval Europe as well as the nature of warfare before 1200 – dominated by the raid – explain the strategies employed, as does the balance with the demands of redress, and with the duties and function of rulership. The international rules mattered, as did obedience, but even with the best will in the world, such circumstances and contexts cannot demand successful obedience to every rule all the time. Likely, however, the rules were obeyed often and successfully enough.

Negotiations were an essential aspect of the many strategies to ensure peaceful relations, deterrence, obedience to the rules, and even enforcement. Indeed, that medieval rulers and communities had well-established methods to resolve disputes over fact and law cannot be in doubt. Many studies have highlighted the importance of direct negotiations, for instance, at meetings between rulers, and the strategic, symbolic, and practical role these played in medieval diplomacy, or the role of individuals or groups of individuals in brokering settlements of differing kinds.[12] Arbitration, however, brings the many issues surrounding international law into sharp focus. It exemplifies the legal pluralism of medieval Europe in the division between papal arbitration and papal appeals on the one hand, and peer arbitration on the other. Papal arbitration was underpinned by the universal doctrine and law applying to all Christians, while peer arbitration relied largely on customary practices and precedent. Nevertheless, while both papal and peer arbitration were what we might think of as legal processes with clear procedures and outcomes, neither was immune to political, economic, and cultural factors. Social networks among rulers (or ruling councils) mattered, as treaties with undefined obligations demonstrate, and indeed this is brought out in great clarity in any dispute resolutions involving a third party.[13] Arbitration further exemplifies the disparity between the universality of the international rules advocated and enforced by the Church and the polycentric nature of legal and political power evident in peer arbitration. The latter is seen clearly in the fact that it is arbitration panels within treaties that emerge as the most frequently used strategy to resolve disputes of fact and law in the period 700 to 1200. These were aimed primarily at dealing with local, intra-community disputes, perhaps most commonly over redress, and often neither transgressions of stipulations nor the methods of compliance and enforcement involved the rulers who had contracted the treaty. Such arrangements demonstrate further that at a practical level, peace itself was modular, as were many of the obligations in the treaties concluded. Consent by rulers as well as their followers – lay and ecclesiastical – underpins such notions, as indeed it does dispute resolution generally, regardless of whether this is employed through direct negotiation, mediation, or arbitration.[14]

There were developments and adaptations in the framework of international law across time and space between 700 and 1200. The development of canon law and the revival of Roman, and later natural, law was a game-changer in many ways, as several scholars have argued, and can perhaps be particularly seen in how terminology of legal practices and concepts becomes more consistent towards the end of the period investigated. However, there were other economic, political, and cultural developments too and it is perhaps not wise to pinpoint the exact reason for particular changes in practice (or even terminology) over time, especially because of the uneven distribution of our evidence. It can even be difficult to say if there were genuine changes in legal practice or if the nature of our evidence simply makes it seem that way. Clauses dealing with redress for legal wrongs serve as a good example. In early treaties, such clauses are often concerned with the rights and status of people – who committed what act, against whom, in what circumstance, and who was liable to pay. More occasionally, clauses mention movables, and very rarely they involve land, usually that which was inalienable. By the end of the twelfth century, clauses of redress tend to be less concerned about the status of people, and the violent acts for which redress could be sought are less frequently specified and commonly set out using umbrella terms such as 'criminal deeds', 'injuries', or 'damages.' Property, however, became an increasingly defined driver of redress in twelfth-century treaties; that is, redress for injury or damage to movables, land, or buildings. The increased focus on property is hardly surprising and well known in medieval history more generally. It reflects, for instance, increased territorialisation across the period, with a multiplication and diversification of settlements and settlement patterns (including greater urbanisation), and many scholars have commented that property became an increasing focus also in domestic law and justice.[15]

Diversifications in how to achieve compliance to treaties in particular circumstances further show this change. As I noted in 2011, sureties became an increasing feature of treaties concluded by the English kings in the twelfth century, and by the last decade of that century, property (real surety) usually accompanied personal sureties, i.e., the person who promised to hand himself into captivity if the treaty was breached.[16] This variation seems to have been specifically developed between adversaries, such as the kings of England and France, who were frequently in conflict with each other and where both sides – kings as well as supporters – could draw upon different familial, economic, legal, and social bonds.[17] It is no accident that those named as sureties in such treaties tended to be those whose support was fiercely contested and/or whose property was located in a disputed area; that is, the practice reflects circumstances in which balancing the different demands of redress were particularly difficult. Even then, treaties concluded in periods of more intense conflict are more likely to have such arrangements (e.g., *Treaty of Louviers*).[18] However, this particular variation of treaties containing both personal and real sureties does not seem to have survived the loss of most of the English king's continental lands in 1204. Subsequent Anglo-French treaties, if they have sureties, do not contain a combination of real and personal sureties. For instance, the Treaty of Paris (1259) has no named sureties, and, in case of breaches, these promised only to 'help the king of France and his heirs against us [the king of England] and our heirs until this thing is sufficiently amended in the opinion of the court of the king of France'.[19] This shows that some practices were created or adapted for very specific circumstances and lapsed when those no longer applied. In short, the details of international law as seen in treaties could adapt to social and economic, political and cultural changes. The framework of international law, by contrast, did not: redress was still a fundamental aspect of it.

What about the wider, global medieval context? Alas, a universal international law based around Christian doctrine is difficult to transpose across a global Middle Ages, whereas a framework of international rules based on interactions between rulers, communities, and entities that aimed at solving similar challenges of war and peace might be expected to yield some commonalities. There are a number of ways to approach this, but here, a single comparative example will be used to demonstrate the possibilities. The example in question is the so-called 'uncle-nephew' pillar, which stands outside the oldest Tibetan Buddhist temple, now known as the Jokhang.[20] It was erected in 823 but records the treaty of 821/2 between the Chinese emperor Mu-Tsung (r. 820–4) of the Tang dynasty and the Tibetan king, Tritsuk Detsen, better known as Relpachen (r. 815–38). This example has been deliberately chosen, because, unlike with the Islamic world, there is no evidence of diplomatic contacts between Chinese rulers and those of the Latin West in the ninth century. The text of the treaty is recorded in both Chinese and Tibetan on the west face of the pillar. The east face contains an edict (or announcement) by the Tibetan king, which sets out the background to the treaty and the king's authority over the Indians, the Arabs, and the Turks, while the north and south faces contain a list of names of the signatories and witnesses to the treaty; the Tibetans on the north and the Chinese on the south face.[21] The text on the pillar is now largely illegible but scholars have reconstructed it with the help of rubbings obtained in the fifteenth and the eighteenth centuries.[22]

Even a cursory glance at the various texts that make up this treaty enables the historian to draw out some interesting points of comparison and contrast. As a start, the edict, or announcement, by the Tibetan king on the east face of the pillar, which outlines the background and justification for the treaty, does not look entirely dissimilar to the capitulary that accompanies the *Treaty of Savonnière* in 862, which sets out the historical context from the perspective of the West Frankish king Charles the Bald, or to the description of the papal involvement in the *Treaty of Rouen* of 991.[23] Furthermore, it will come as no surprise that just like any European treaty in the period 700 to 1200, the text of this agreement also invokes divine sanction through oaths: 'May we invoke the Three Jewels, the various saints, the sun and the moon, and the planets and stars as witnesses. Having been declared by the solemn words, after the animals have been sacrificed and the oath has been sworn, the treaty is made.'[24] The two rulers further affixed their seals, it was signed and witnessed by their officials and close followers, and the treaty document was preserved in the treasury; all of which are frequently seen in treaties in Europe throughout the period 700–1200.[25] More surprisingly perhaps, is the appearance of a clause on criminals/exiles, who should be returned, or the stipulation that violation through reprisals or similar did not amount to a breach of the treaty; that is, it was a justification.[26] Again, these are easily recognisable from the majority of European treaties before 1200.

One of the most interesting clauses in the Chinese-Tibetan treaty relates to safe conduct:

> The emissaries from either side, having followed the old route in proceeding on the journey, shall be in accordance with the former custom. Between the two, China and Tibet, they will change horses at Tsangkunyok and meet the Chinese at Tsezhengchek, below which (i.e. to the east) the Chinese shall honor them (i.e. provide them with the necessary supplies for their journey and their sojourn in China). They [will] meet the Tibetans at Tsengshuhywan, above which (i.e. to the west) the Tibetans shall honor them.[27]

No document from the ninth century tells us exactly how safe conducts were carried out in practice in Europe, but at the end of the twelfth century, it was outlined in great clarity in a letter of King Richard I of England, dated to April 1194. In this letter, the English king set out that the king of Scots, William the Lion, should have the same escorts ('conductus') in going to, and returning from, Richard's court, as previous Scottish kings, namely:

> that the bishop of Durham and the sheriff and barons of Northumberland will come to him [William] at the frontier of his realm (in finibus regni), and receive him there and take him to the [river] Tees. There the archbishop of York, and the sheriff and barons of Yorkshire will come to him, receive him and take him to the bishopric of Lincoln. There the bishop of Lincoln, and the sheriff and barons of the shire will come to him, and receive him, and take him through their territory, and so in turn the bishops and the sheriffs of the shires through which he goes, until he arrives at our [Richard's] court.[28]

European treaties do not often refer to safe conduct, but there is a plethora of narrative descriptions from across the period 700–1200 that confirms the practice. For instance, the Danish historian Saxo Grammaticus recalls the journey of Valdemar I, king of Denmark, to the huge gathering at Saint-Jean-de-Losne in 1162, which was intended to discuss and settle conflict between the Emperor Frederick I and Pope Alexander III. According to Saxo, Valdemar travelled to the limits of his kingdom, which was the river Eider, where he was met by Count Adolph of Holstein who escorted him to Bremen, the extent of his duties. Here, the Danish king was met by Archbishop Hartwig, who provided hospitality but also acknowledged that it was his duty to provide the Danes with an escort to the meeting, not merely a guide.[29] An earlier example can be found in a letter by the Christian missionary bishop Bruno of Querfurt to the German king Henry II in the early eleventh century. The letter records how Bruno set off to conclude an agreement with the Pechenegs – a nomadic people living between the Don and the Danube rivers – and that while in the land of the Rus', he was given an escort by Prince Vladimir of Kiev and his army to the farthest boundary of the latter's kingdom.[30] In the tenth century, the Frankish annalist Flodoard of Rheims records how the English king Athelstan in 936 sent his nephew Louis – an exile at Athelstan's court – to Francia with bishops and other faithful men. According to Flodoard, the Frankish magnates met Louis on the beach at Boulogne-sur-Mer, as both sides had agreed with oaths, before he was conducted to Laon for his coronation as king of the West Franks.[31] In 808, Eardwulf, king of the Northumbrians, who had been driven from his throne, went to Rome, and on his return to Northumbria, he was provided with an escort by Pope Leo III and the Emperor Charlemagne. One of those forming part of this escort, a deacon by the name of Aldulf, was captured by pirates on his return journey, and had to be ransomed by the Mercian king, Cenwulf, before he could return to Rome.[32] What is evident from all of these examples is that providing safe conduct – a physical escort – to rulers and envoys was a general principle of law, as well as a customary rule, the consistent practice of which is evident across time and space. Moreover, the practice of safe conduct went beyond the rule on the inviolability of envoys, in that often, certain individuals held responsibility for providing provisions, and for escorting and guiding the foreign dignitary to a specific meeting place – often regarded as a border of some sort – where the duty was assumed by someone else [33] Evidently, many international rules do not appear to be exclusively Western or European. This study has aimed to provide a clearer understanding of what international law was in medieval Europe; the challenge remains for someone better qualified than this medievalist to place it in a broader global context.

Genuine interdisciplinary or comparative work across time and space is very difficult to do, frequently because of boundaries created by languages and scholarly traditions. The challenge of how to transition from conflict to peace is one example. One aspect of this is what is referred to as transitional justice in the modern world, and which centres on the gross violations of human rights with the specific aims to ensure accountability; promote truth and memory about past violations; provide justice and remedies to victims; ensure social cohesion, nation-building, ownership, and inclusiveness; and to prevent the recurrence of conflict and future violations. Scholars working on these issues tend to see the emergence of the field in the 1980s and the 1990s during the political transitions that took place in Latin America and Eastern Europe, though some traces its history to 1945 and the trials at Nuremberg following the Second World War.[34] As the medieval period lacks codification of human rights and international law, among other foundations of transitional justice, and no sub-field of medieval studies or even medieval conflict resolution refers to transitional justice, it is easy to appreciate why this has been the case. However, it is possible to take a broader interpretation of law and justice, and to explore how the various practices of transitional justice were adapted to societies very different from our own, and to what success. As shown throughout this study, while there was no international law of human rights as such, there were widely understood concepts within Christianity and medieval culture generally creating notions of just behaviours, e.g., the idea of 'enemy of mankind' or the large corpus of both ecclesiastical and secular legislation to limit such a perpetrator's actions.[35] These, in turn, stimulated the use of methods such as apology, memorialisation, reparation, and arbitration in response to violations. Though 'true democracy' was never the goal, these approaches encouraged social cohesion, inclusion, and collaboration between former enemies, precipitating peace. The study of all of these practices are thriving for the medieval period, yet few historians refer to this as the study of transitional justice, instead preferring to focus on overarching terms such as dispute or conflict resolution or on very focused terminology of particular practices as they appear in the medieval evidence, e.g., 'deditio' (ritual surrender), to avoid anachronism. Yet specificity also divides scholarly disciplines and communities even where closer contacts would be beneficial to truly draw out what pertains to a particular chronological period or geographical region.

The methodology adopted in this study has drawn significantly on historiographies, the methodologies and theoretical frameworks of scholars of historical periods other than the medieval. One reason for this, as mentioned in the introduction, is that works examining international legal practice, including that in treaties, across any historical period are significantly fewer than those exploring doctrine. In fact, understanding the function, role, and theory behind particular aspects of treaties, e.g., amnesty or necessity, in the period 700 to 1200 would have been impossible without recourse to how scholars have theorised and approached international law in other periods. It is important to recognise that our picture of international law, and indeed, of peace, security, and deterrence more generally in medieval Europe before 1200 is still woefully inadequate. Lots of questions about how conflict and conflict resolution was regulated remain unanswered, and in particular, the ways and means by which peace was secured and maintained. As highlighted by John Watkins in 2008, partly the reason for this incomplete picture is the nature of our sources, but partly it is because a scholarly tradition in which a cross-disciplinary approach to the study of medieval international relations, such as that which has broadened the discussion of diplomatic issues for later historical periods, is only slowly emerging. He observed that scholars 'writing on anything from strategic negotiations and treaty-making to the cultural impact of shifting political configurations in the premodern period could benefit from reading bodies of IR theory that explicitly challenge the state-based assumptions currently dominating the field', as well as from intellectual exchanges with those working within art history, the history and philosophy of science and technology, English and the modern languages, comparative literature, gender studies, rhetoric, and cultural studies.[36] Indeed, this gap in our knowledge has become more evident over the past two decades with the renewed interest among the scholarly community working on more recent history and events in how conflicts were resolved in a period before fully-fledged nation states. In such a context, realigning the medieval historiography on many aspects of international law, conflict resolution, and diplomacy with its more modern counterparts is essential. This study has attempted to provide a new starting point for investigating and thinking about international law in the medieval period, but essentially the harder work begins now. It is certainly hoped that many of the issues raised in this study provoke future debate and research.

The history of the period 700–1200 in Europe is frequently characterised as one in which wars were fought without norms moderating its conduct and in which treaties confirmed the outcome of conflict rather than representing compromise at the negotiating table. Both characterisations are demonstrably wrong. We can perceive of international law in medieval Europe, but, as many recent events and history will tell us, having law, physical institutions, enforcement methods, and even deterrence does not create long-lasting or successful peaceful relations with every state or political actor forever. As shown in various ways throughout this study, success is about perspective, and it is the recognition that there are other ways of perceiving international law – even if they seem unworkable and less successful than our own – that enables us to understand what it might have entailed in medieval Europe.

Notes

1 For the symbolic and communal aspect of international law and peacemaking, see also Benham, 'Peace, Security and Deterrence', 124–34.
2 For similarities in domestic laws across time and space, see also Nelson, 'Dispute Settlement', 60; Maurizio Lupoi, *The Origins of the European Legal Order* (Cambridge, 2000).
3 Cf. Stewart and Kiyani's characterisation that modern trials for international crimes involve a complex dance between international and domestic criminal law, 'the specificities of which vary markedly from one forum to the next'. Stewart and Kiyani, 'The Ahistoricism of Legal Pluralism', 393.

4 Binder, 'Stability and Change', 909–10; Grygiel, 'The Primacy of Premodern History', 14–15.

5 For some of the factors needed to judge success, see Benham, *PMA*, 201–12.

6 Cf. the notion of the generous ruler, which is a characteristic of rulership more generally as evidenced through a range of medieval evidence. For examples and a discussion, see Benham, *PMA*, 73–6.

7 On the importance of justice, see Isidore, *Etymologiae*, ii:24.6. Scholars are unanimous that a prime role of a medieval prince, regardless of religion, was to provide justice. For examples of the literature, see A. K. S. Lambton, 'Justice in the Medieval Persian Theory of Kingship', *Studia Islamica*, 17 (1962), 91–119; Kershaw, *Peaceful Kings*, ch. 4; Timothy Reuter, 'Mandate, Privilege, Court Judgment: Techniques of Rulership in the Age of Frederick Barbarossa', in *Medieval Polities and Modern Mentalities*, ed. Janet L. Nelson (Cambridge, 2006), 413–31; Smita Sahgal, 'Situating Kingship within an Embryonic Frame of Masculinity in Early India', *Social Scientist*, 43 (2015), 3–26, esp. 4–5, 17–18; Fritz Kern, *Kingship and Law in the Middle Ages* (New York, 1970).

8 Koh, 'Why do Nations Obey International Law', 2603.

9 Ziegler, *Völkerrechtsgeschichte*, 97, 107–11, 120–7, 133–7; Steiger, *Die Ordnung der Welt*, 710; Koh, 'Why do Nations Obey International Law', 2604–5.

10 On similar observations about modern international law, see Abbott and Snidal, 'Hard and Soft Law', 425.

11 Patrick M. Morgan, 'The State of Deterrence in International Politics Today', *Contemporary Security Policy*, 33 (2012), 103; Williamson Murray and Peter R. Mansoor, *Hybrid Warfare: Fighting Complex Opponents from the Ancient World to the Present* (Cambridge, 2012), esp. chs 1 and 11; Alexander Lanoszka, 'Russian Hybrid Warfare and Extended Deterrence in Eastern Europe', *International Affairs*, 92 (2016), 175–95, esp. 190–5. On deterrence and enforcement linking to concept of peace in the medieval period, see Malegam, 'Suspicions of Peace', 236–52. See also Benham, 'Peace, Security and Deterrence', 132–4.

12 For summary and references to the literature, see Chapter 5, p. 196.

13 On this, see also Benham, *PMA*, 36; Benham, 'Peace, Security and Deterrence', 129–31.

14 Dixon, *Textbook on IL*, 286; Jin-Hyun Paik, 'Globalisation and International Adjudication', in *Asian Approaches to International Law*, 29–32. See also Yoshifumi Tanaka, *The Peaceful Settlement of International Disputes* (Cambridge, 2017), chs 1, 2, 4, and 5; C. M.

Chinking, 'Third-Party Intervention before the International Court of Justice', *AJIL*, 80 (1986), 195 531.

15 One of the most useful descriptions of this transformation is still Robert Bartlett's *The Making of Europe. Conquest, Colonization and Cultural Change 950–1350* (London, 1994). On property becoming a prominent feature also in domestic law, see Frederic L. Cheyette, 'Giving Each His Due', in *Debating the Middle Ages*, eds. Lester K. Little and Barbara H. Rosenwein (Oxford, 1998), 170–79, esp. 172–3; Hudson, *The Oxford History of the Laws of England*, 487–9, 576, 676–8; Matthew McHaffie, 'Law and Violence in Eleventh-century France', *P&P*, 238 (2018), esp. 30–41.

16 For examples of treaties with sureties, see *Treaty of Dover* (1101, 1110, 1163), *Treaty of Falaise* (1174), *Treaty of Messina* (1191), *Treaty of Louviers* (1196). For discussion, see Benham, *PMA*, 165–71; Benham, 'Peace, Security and Deterrence', 127–9; Kosto, *Making Agreements*, 97–100

17 Kosto, *Hostages*, 156.

18 On the surety arrangements in the *Treaty of Louviers*, see D. J. Power, 'L'aristocratie Plantagenêt face aux conflits capétiens-angevins: l'exemple du traité de Louviers', in *Noblesses de l'espace Plantagenêt (1154–1224)*, ed. Martin Aurell (Poitiers, 2001), 121–37.

19 *EHD*, iii, 378–9.

20 For an introduction to the pillar, the texts and the historical background, see Fang-Kuei Li, 'The Inscription of the Sino-Tibetan Treaty of 821–2', *T'oung Pao*, 44 (1956), 3–24. See also the short introduction by Gray Tuttle in 'The Chinese-Tibetan Treaty of 821–822', in *Sources of Tibetan Tradition*, eds. Kurtis R. Schaeffer et al. (New York, 2012), 76–7.

21 For the various texts in the original language and in modern English, see H. E. Richardson, 'The Sino-Tibetan Treaty Inscription of A.D. 821/823 at Lhasa', *The Journal of the Royal Asiatic Society of Great Britain and Ireland*, 2 (1978), 137–162. The west-side text can also be found in 'The Chinese-Tibetan Treaty of 821–822', in *Sources of Tibetan Tradition*, 77–8.

22 Richardson, 'The Sino-Tibetan Treaty Inscription', 137–9.

23 Ibid., 144–6; *MGH Capit. II*, no. 243 (pp. 159–63); *EHD*, I, no. 230.

24 *Sources of Tibetan Tradition*, 78; Richardson, 'The Sino-Tibetan Treaty Inscription', 154.

25 Richardson, 'The Sino-Tibetan Treaty Inscription', 154; *Sources of Tibetan Tradition*, 78. For two examples of treaties kept in the royal treasury, see 'Capitulary of Frankfurt, 794', c. 3; *Treaty of Benevento* (1156), c. 13.

26 Richardson, 'The Sino-Tibetan Treaty Inscription', 153–4; *Sources of Tibetan Tradition*, 77–8.

27 *Sources of Tibetan Tradition*, 77; Richardson, 'The Sino-Tibetan Treaty Inscription', 154.

28 *Anglo-Scottish Relations 1174–1328*, 10.

29 Saxo, *GD*, ii, 1198–1203.

30 *Epistola Brunonis ad Henricum regem*, ed. Jadwiga Karwasinska, *Monumenta Poloniae Historica* series nova, 4,3 (Warsaw, 1973), 97–106.

31 *Les annales de Flodoard*, 63.

32 *ARF*, s.a. 808–9.

33 *Anglo-Scottish Relations 1174–1328*, 10–11; *Sources of Tibetan Tradition*, 77; Richardson, 'The Sino-Tibetan Treaty Inscription', 154. On meeting places and borders, see Benham, *PMA*, 21–37.

34 Paige Arthur, 'How "Transitions" Reshaped Human Rights: A Conceptual History of Transitional Justice', *Human Rights Quarterly*, 31 (2009), 326; Ruti G. Teitel, 'Transitional Justice Genealogy', *Harvard Human Rights Journal*, 16 (2003), 70; Iverson, 'Transitional Justice, Jus Post Bellum and International Criminal Law', 415. On transitional justice in other historical periods, see Gary J. Bass, *Stay the Hand of Vengeance: The Politics of War Crimes Tribunals* (Princeton, NJ, 2000); Jon Elster, *Closing the Books: Transitional Justice in Historical Perspective* (Cambridge, 2004).

35 For examples of the literature, see John Gillingham, 'Surrender in Medieval Europe – an Indirect Approach', in *How Fighting Ends: A History of Surrender*, eds. Holger Afflerbach and Hew Strachan (Oxford, 2012), 55–72; James W. Houlihan, '*Lex Innocentium* (697 AD): Adomnán of Iona – Father of Western *jus in bello*', *International Review of the Red Cross*, 101 (2019), 715–35; Quinton-Brown, 'The South, the West, and the Meanings of Humanitarian Intervention in History', 514–33. See also Chapter 2, p. 69; Chapter 4, pp. 147–9.

36 John Watkins, 'Toward a New Diplomatic History of Medieval and Early Modern Europe', *Journal of Medieval and Early Modern Studies*, 38 (2008), 5–6.

Appendix: List of treaties

Introduction

The list that follows is of some 200 treaties from the period c. 700–1200, which have formed the basis of this study on international law. They represent a selection of the available evidence from the period. The criteria of this selection are outlined briefly in the introduction and more fully in Chapter 1.

Name and date of treaties

As far as possible, treaties have been listed in alphabetical order using first and foremost the place where they were concluded, when the text has indicated this. Where the text supplies specific additional details, such as 'in the palace', these have been explained in the endnotes. Some texts carry no place, but where there is good narrative evidence of a treaty having been concluded in a particular place, this has been used. A similar approach has also been taken to dates.

In cases where several treaties have been concluded in the same place, a date has been placed in brackets, in this list as in the main text, so that the reader can distinguish which treaty is referred to. In those exceptional cases, where two or more treaties were concluded in the same place in the same year, a Roman numeral after the name has been used, e.g., *Treaty of Genoa I.*

Where no place can be securely deduced, the treaty has been listed as 'between' the contracting parties.

Names and titles of parties

Because treaties are often a statement of, or claim to, what princes ruled over, as far as possible the titles of the contracting parties have been given as they are recorded in the text of the treaty. Specific explanations, where relevant, have been placed in endnotes. There is one significant exception: as is common also in Frankish capitularies of this period, the kings have no titles in the treaties, and are throughout the texts usually only referred to by their names and 'lord'. It is also worth noting that Lothar II was king of the so-called 'middle kingdom', which in the tenth century became known as *Regnum Lotharii*, i.e., kingdom of Lothar or Lotharingia. This designation has been used in square brackets in the list for convenience, even though anachronistic, in the same way the kingdoms of other Frankish rulers have also been indicated.

In some cases where a particular treaty has been concluded by a named representative, as given in the text, this has also been indicated in the list.

Printed editions and translations

Throughout I have tried to indicate every treaty where a translation or partial translation of the text exists. Such translations are in some cases rather old and not always entirely satisfactory, but these have been included to make the evidence accessible to non-specialists and students. In some cases, there are several printed editions of the same treaty text. The aim has been to attempt to refer to the best edition of each text, but in cases where one edition has the text divided into clauses but the best text does not, both have been listed so that easy reference can be made to particular clauses in the main analysis.

List of treaties

Key: abp. (archbishop); c. (count); d. (duke); k. (king)

Name of Treaty	Printed edition	Parties and date
II Æthelred	*Die Gesetze*, I, 220–5. Translation in *EHD*, I, 401–2.	994 Æthelred II, k. of the English Olaf, Josteinn and Guthmund Steitason, leaders of the army
Concordat of Worms	'Pax Wormatiensis cum Calixto II', in *MGH Const. I*, no. 107 (pp. 159–60) for promise of Henry V; no. 108 (pp. 160–1) for promise of Callixtus. A newer edition of Henry's promise can be found with *Die Urkunden Heinrichs V. und der Königin Mathilde*, eds. Matthias Thiel and Alfred Gawlik, no. 240, available at https://data.mgh.de/databases/ddhv/dhv_240.htm	1122 Callixtus II, pope Henry V, emperor
Division of the Realm	'Regni Divisio' in *MGH Capit. II*, 21–4.	831 Louis (the Pious), emperor Pippin, k. of Aquitaine Louis (the German), k. of Bavaria Charles (the Bald), k. of Alemannia
Division of the Realms	'Divisio regnorum' in *MGH Capit. I*, 126–30. Translation in *Charlemagne: Translated Sources*, 251–5.	806 Charles, emperor, k. of the Franks and of the Lombards Louis (the Pious), k. [of Aquitaine] Pippin, k. [of Italy and Bavaria] Charles, k. [of Frankia, Burgundy and Alemannia]

Dunsæte	*Die Gesetze*, I, 374–9.	Undated but likely 10th–early 11th century Two border communities
Oath of Canossa[1]	Gregory VII, *Registrum IV*, 12a, in *MGH Epp. sel.* 2.1, 314–15. Translation in *Imperial Lives and Letters of the Eleventh Century*, 156.	1077 Henry IV, emperor[2] Gregory VII, pope
Oaths of Strasbourg	Nithard: *Histoire*, 103–9. Translation in *Carolingian Chronicles*, 162–3.	842 Charles (the Bald), k. [of West Frankia] Louis (the German), k. [of East Frankia]
Oath of Berengar I of Italy to Angiltrude	*MGH Capit. II*, no. 231.	898 Berengar I, k. of Italy Angiltrude, widow of Emperor Guy III (Wido) of Spoleto
Ordinatio imperii (817)	*MGH Capit*, I, no. 136 (pp. 270–3). Translation in Pullan, *Sources for the History of Medieval Europe*, 38–42.	817 Louis (the Pious), emperor, k. of the Franks Lothar, co-emperor Louis (the German), k. of Bavaria Pippin, k. of Aquitaine
Pact of Arichis I[3]	Martin, *Guerre*, 179–80.	784?[4] Arichis II, prince of Benevento [no name], 'iudex'[5] of the Neapolitans

(continued)

Name of Treaty	Printed edition	Parties and date
Pact of Arichis II	Martin, *Guerre*, 182–3.	784–7? Arichis II, prince of Benevento Neapolitans
Pact between Louis the Pious and Pope Paschal I	'Pactum Hludowici Pii cum Paschali pontifice', in *MGH Capit. I*, no. 172 (pp. 352–5).	817 Louis (the Pious), emperor Paschal I, pope
Pact between Naples and Benevento (936)	Martin, *Guerre*, 217–19.	936 John III, d. of Naples Landulf I, prince [of Benevento] Atenulf II, prince [of Benevento] Atenulf III, prince [of Benevento]
Pact between Philip of Swabia and Philip II of France	*MGH Const. II*, 1–2. A partial English translation is available in *A Sourcebook for Medieval History*, eds. Oliver J. Thatcher and Edgar Holmes McNeal (New York, 1905), 227–8.	1198 Philip II, k. of the Franks Philip [of Swabia], k. of the Romans
Pactum Sicardi	*MGH LL*, iv, ed. G. H. Pertz (Hanover, 1868), 216–21.[6] See also revisions of this text in Martin, *Guerre*, 185–99. A partial English translation is available in *Medieval Trade in the Mediterranean World*, 33–5.	836 Sicard, p. of the Lombard people Andrea II, *magister militum*[7] of Naples John, bishop-elect of Naples

Partition of Benevento	Martin, *Guerre*, 201–15.[8]	848x849 Radelchis I, prince [of Benevento] Sikenolf, prince of Salerno
Peace of Constance (1183)	*DD FI*, iv, no. 848 (pp. 68–77). A partial English translation is available in *Medieval Italy: Texts in Translation*, eds. Katherine L. Jansen et al. (Philadelphia, 2009), 61–3.	1183 Frederick I, emperor Henry VI, k. of the Romans (son of the emperor) The cities of the Lombard League
Treaty of Aachen	'Pactiones Aquenses' in *MGH Capit.* II, 192. Translation in *The Annals of St-Bertin*, 166.	870 Charles (the Bald), k. [of West Frankia] Louis (the German), k. [of East Frankia]
Treaty of Acre[9] (1124)	*UHSRV*, I, no. 40 (pp. 79–89, text pp. 84–9). The confirmation of 1125 is available in same volume no. 41 (pp. 90–4). Translation in *A History of Deeds Done beyond the Sea. Volume 1*, ed. Emily Atwater Babcock and A.C. Krey (New York, 1943), 552–6.	1124 Domenico Michiele, d. of the Venetians Baldwin II, k. of Jerusalem, through his representatives Warmund, patriarch of Jerusalem; William de Bury, constable of the king; and Payens, chancellor of the king[10]
Treaty of Acre[11] (1190)	*LIRG*, vol. 1/2, no. 332 (pp. 183–9). Translation in Hall, *Caffaro*, 140–2.	1190 Genoa, represented by Guidone Spinola Guy, k. of the Latins in Jerusalem[12] Sibylla, queen

(*continued*)

Name of Treaty	Printed edition	Parties and date
Treaty of Adrianople	*Historia de expeditione*, 64–6. Translation in *CFB*, 90–2.	1190 Frederick I, emperor Isaac II, emperor
Treaty of Agreda	González, *El reino de Castilla*, no. 449 (pp. 770–1)	1186 Alfonso VIII, k. of Castile Alfonso II, k. of Aragon
Treaty of Anagni	*DD FI*, iii, no. 658 (pp. 161–5). A partial English translation is available in *A Sourcebook for Medieval History*, 197–9.	1176 Frederick I, emperor, through his representatives Alexander III, pope, through his representatives
Treaty of Andeli	*EMDP*, ii, no. 243 (pp. 466–7).	1197 Richard I, k. of England Baldwin IX, c. of Flanders
Treaty of Antioch[13] (1098)	*CDRG*, I, nos. 7–8 (pp. 11–13). The first document is Bohemond's grant of privileges in Antioch, while the second is the Genoese obligations. Translation in Hall, *Caffaro*, 169–70.	1098 Bohemond I, lord[14] Genoa
Treaty of Antioch (1101)	*CDRG*, I, no. 12 (pp. 16–18). Translation in Hall, *Caffaro*, 170.	1101 Tancred[15] Genoa
Treaty of Antioch[16] (1127)	*LIRG*, vol. 1/2, no. 337 (pp. 152–4). Translation in Hall, *Caffaro*, 171–2.	1127 Bohemond II, prince of Antioch Genoa

Treaty of Antioch (1167)	*UHSRV*, I, no. 61 (pp. 148–50)	1167 Bohemond II, prince of Antioch [not specified], d. of the Venetians[17]
Treaty of Antioch (1169)[18]	*LIRG*, vol. 1/2, no. 340 (pp. 157–60). Translation in Hall, *Caffaro*, 172–3.	1169 Bohemond III, prince of Antioch Genoa
Treaty of Ardara	*LIRG*, vol. 1/2, no. 409 (pp. 377–9). For the Genoese ratification, see same volume, no. 410 (pp. 380–2).	1191 Constantine, 'iudex'[19] of Torres Genoa
Treaty of Arles[20]	*CDRG*, ii, no. 7 (pp. 16–17); *LIRG*, vol. 1/2, no. 366 (pp. 256–7).	1165 Ramon Berenguer II, c. of Provence Genoa
Treaty of Artlenburg	*Urkunden Heinrichs des Löwen, part I*, ed. K. Jordan (Leipzig, 1941; repr. 1957), no. 48 (pp. 68–70)	1161 Henry the Lion, d. of Saxony The Gotlanders
Treaty of Azay	Howden, *Gesta*, ii, 70–1.	1189 Henry II, k. of England Philip II, k. of France

(*continued*)

Name of Treaty	Printed edition	Parties and date
Treaty of Bamberg	'Pactum cum Benedicto VIII', in *MGH Const. I*, no. 33 (pp. 65–70).	1020 Henry II, emperor Benedict VIII, pope
Treaty of the Basilica of Cosmas and Damian[21]	*CDRG*, I, no. 31 (pp. 38–40). Translation in Hall, *Caffaro*, 103–5.	1120 Genoa The 'fideles' of Pope Calixtus II
Treaty of Benevento (1073)	Gregory VII, *Registrum I*, 18a, in *MGH Epp. sel.* 2.1, 30–1. Translation in *The Register of Gregory VII*, no. 1.18a (pp. 20–1).	1073 Gregory VII, pope Landulf VI, prince of Benevento
Treaty of Benevento (1156)	*MGH Const. I*, no. 413 (pp. 588–90). Translation in *The History of the Tyrants of Sicily by "Hugo Falcandus"*, 1154–69, tr. G.A. Loud and Thomas Wiedemann (Manchester, 1998), 248–52.	1156 William I, k. of Sicily Adrian IV, pope
Treaty of Bonn (921)	'Pactum cum Karolo Rege Franciae Occidentalis', in *MGH Const. I*, 1–2. There is a partial English translation in Grewe, *The Epochs of International Law*, 77.	921 Charles the Simple, k. of the West Franks Henry I, k. of the East Franks

Treaty of Burgo San Genesio[22]	*MGH Const. I*, no. 214 (pp. 302–4); for the oath of the consuls of Lucca, see *DD FI*, ii, no. 375 (pp. 239–41).	1162 Frederick I, emperor, through his representative Rainald von Dassel, abp. of Cologne and arch-chancellor Lucca
Treaty of Canterbury	*Anglo-Scottish Relations 1174–1328*, no. 2 (pp. 6–8).	1189 Richard I, k. of the English William I, k. of Scotland
Treaty of Capua	Gregory VII, *Registrum I*, 21a, in *MGH Epp. sel.* 2.1, 35–6. Translation in *The Register of Gregory VII*, no. 1.21a (pp. 25–6).	1073 Gregory VII, pope Richard, prince of Capua
Treaty of Castel San Giovanni	'Pactum cum Venetis', in *MGH Const. I*, no. 378 (526–30).	1197 Henry VI, emperor and k. of Sicily Enrico Dandolo, d. of Venetians
Treaty of Ceprano	*Le Liber Censuum*, I, 422.	1080 Robert Guiscard, d. of Apulia, Calabria and Sicily Gregory VII, pope
Treaty of Constance (1153)	*DD FI*, i, nos. 51–2 (pp. 85–9). Translation in *A Sourcebook for Mediæval History*, 179–80.	1153 Frederick I, k. of the Romans Eugene III, pope

(*continued*)

Name of Treaty	Printed edition	Parties and date
Treaty of Constantinople (911)	RPC, 65–8.	911 Oleg, Grand Prince of Rus' Leo VI, emperor Alexander, co-emperor Constantine, co-emperor
Treaty of Constantinople (944)	RPC, 73–7.	944 Igor, Grand Prince of Rus' Romanos I, emperor Constantine, co-emperor Stephen, co-emperor
Treaty of Constantinople (992)	*I trattati con Bisanzio, 992–1198,* eds. M. Pozza and G. Ravegnani (Venice, 1993), no. 1 (pp. 21–5); UHSRV, no. 17 (pp. 36–9).	992 Basil II, co-emperor Constantine VIII, co-emperor Peter Orseolo II, d. of Venetians
Treaty of Constantinople (1169)	LIRG, vol. 1/2, no. 352 (pp. 183–9). Translation in Hall, *Caffaro,* 204–7.	1169 Genoa Manuel Komnenos, emperor
Treaty of Correggio Verde[23]	*Die Urkunden Lothars III. und der Kaiserin Richenza,* ed. E. von Ottenthal and H. Hirsch (Berlin, 1927), no. 97 (pp. 151–6).	1136 Lothar III, emperor Pietro Polani, d. of the Venetians
Treaty of Cremona	CDRG, II, no. 111 (pp. 243–5).	1177 Venice Genoa

Treaty of Devol	Anne Comnène, *Alexiade*, 4 vols., ed. and tr. Bernard Leib (Paris: 1937–76), III, 125–39 (bk. XIII, ch. 12). Translation in *The Alexiad*, 424–34.	1108 Alexios I Komnenos, emperor Bohemond I, prince of Antioch
Treaty of Dover (1101)	*Dip. Docs*, no. 1 (pp. 1–4). Translation in E. van Houts, 'The Anglo-Flemish treaty of 1101', *ANS*, 21 (1998), 169–74.	1101 Henry I, k. of the English Robert II, c. of Flanders
Treaty of Dover (1110)	*Dip. Docs*, no. 2 (pp. 5–7).	1110 Henry I, k. of the English Robert II, c. of Flanders
Treaty of Dover (1163)	*Dip. Docs*, no. 3 (pp. 8–12). Translation in Oksanen, *Flanders and the Anglo-Norman World*, 264–9.	1163 Henry II, k. of the English Thierry, c. of Flanders Philip, c. and heir [to Flanders]
Treaty of Falaise	*Anglo-Scottish Relations 1174–1328*, 2–11.	1174 Henry II, k. of England William I (the Lion), k. of Scots
Treaty of Fitero (1167)	Howden, *Gesta*, i, 149–50.	1167 Alfonso VIII, k. of Castile Sancho VI, k. of Navarre

(*continued*)

Name of Treaty	Printed edition	Parties and date
Treaty of Fouron	*Hludowici iunioris et Hludowici Balbi conventio Furonensis*, in *MGH Capit. II*, no. 246 (pp. 168–70). Translation in *The Annals of St-Bertin*, 213–15.	878 Louis (the Stammerer), k. Louis (the Younger), k.
Treaty of Fulda	*DD FI*, iii, no. 602 (pp. 86–7).	1173 Frederick I, emperor Philip, c. of Flanders
Treaty of Gaeta	Martin, *Guerre*, no. 6 (pp. 222–3).	1029 Sergius IV, d. of Naples and 'magister militum' John V, consul and d. of Gaeta Emilia, duchess of Gaeta[24] Sicelgaite[25] The people of Gaeta[26]
Treaty of Galliate[27]	*DD FI*, I, no. 94 (pp. 156–60).	1154 Frederick I, k. of the Romans Domenico Morosini, d. of the Venetians
Treaty of Genoa I (1146)	*LIRG*, vol. 1/6, nos. 932 (pp. 3–6). For the Genoese obligations, see same volume no. 933 (pp. 6–7). Translation in Hall, *Caffaro*, 179–82.	1146 Genoa Alfonso VII, emperor of Spain[28]
Treaty of Genoa II (1146)	*LIRG*, vol. 1/6, no. 934 (pp. 8–11). Translation in Hall, *Caffaro*, 182–3. For the obligations of Ramon Berenguer, see *LIRG*, vol. 1/2, no. 297 (pp. 62–9).	1146 Genoa Ramon Berenguer IV, c. of Barcelona

Treaty of Genoa (1164)	*LIRG*, vol. 1/2, no. 382 (pp. 317–22).	1164 Genoa Barisone II, k. of Sardinia
Treaty of Genoa (1165)	*CDRG*, II, nos. 8–9 (pp. 17–22; 22–7). The ratifications are published as nos. 12–13 in same volume (pp. 29–39).	1165 Genoa Rome
Treaty of Genoa (1168)	*LIRG*, vol. 1/2, no. 388 (pp. 331–3).	1168 Genoa Barisone II, k. of Sardinia
Treaty of Genoa (1172)	*LIRG*, vol. 1/2, no. 385 (pp. 327–31).	1172 Genoa Barisone II, k. of Arborea
Treaty of Genoa (1174)	*LIRG*, vol. 1/2, no. 362–3 (pp. 231–44).	1174 Raymond V, c. of Toulouse Genoa
Treaty of Genoa (1186)	*LIRG*, vol. 1/2, no. 407 (pp. 373–5). For Genoese obligations, see same volume no. 408 (pp. 375–7).	1186 Barisone II, 'iudex' of Torres Genoa
Treaty of Genoa I (1190)	*LIRG*, vol. 1/6, no. 935 (pp. 11–14). The Genoese obligations are available in *CDRG*, ii, no. 192 (pp. 366–8). Translation of the French obligations in Hall, *Caffaro*, 218–20.	1190 Philip II, k. of the Franks, through his representative Hugh, d. of Burgundy Genoa

(*continued*)

Name of Treaty	Printed edition	Parties and date
Treaty of Genoa II (1190)	*LIRG*, vol. 1/2, no. 353 (pp. 189–92). Translation in Hall, *Caffaro*, 221–2.	1190 Philip II, k. of the Franks Genoa
Treaty of Genoa (1192)	*CDRG*, III, no. 11 (pp. 25–6).	1192 Genoa Alessandria
Treaty of Genoa[29] (1198)	*LIRG*, vol. 1/2, no. 395 (pp. 347–50).	1198 Hugh de Bassio, son of Hugh de Bassio[30] Genoa, represented by Alberto de Mandello
Treaty of Gerberoy[31]	Gerald of Wales, *Instruction for a Ruler*, 500–3.	1182 Philip II, k. of France Philip d'Alsace, c. of Flanders
Treaty of Gisors (1160)	*Recueil des actes de Henri II, roi d'Angleterre et duc de Normandie concernant les provinces françaises et les affaires de France*, 2 vols., ed. L. Delisle, revised by E. Berger (Paris, 1916), I, no. 141 (pp. 251–3); L. Landon, *The Itinerary of King Richard I* (London, 1935), 221–2.	1160 Louis VII, k. of France Henry II, k. of England
Treaty of Gisors (1180)	*Rec. des actes de Philippe Auguste*, i, no. 7 (with division into clauses); Howden, *Gesta*, I, 247–9; Howden, *Chronica*, ii, 198–9. Translation in *The Annals of Roger de Hoveden*, 2 vols., ed. H.T. Riley (London, 1853), i, 521–3.	1180 Philip II, k. of the Franks Henry II, k. of the English

Treaty	Source	Date / Parties
Treaty of Le Goulet	*EMDP*, II, no. 288 (pp. 615–17); Howden, *Chronica*, iv, 148–51. Translation in *The Annals of Roger de Hoveden*, ii, 508–12.	1200 John, k. of England Philip II, k. of the Franks
Treaty of Gravina	'Tancredi regis pactum cum Coelestino III', in *MGH Const. I*, no. 417 (pp. 593–4). The oaths are in same volume, nos. 416, 418 (pp. 592–3, 595).	1192 Tancred, k. of Sicily Celestine III, pope
Treaty of Grosseto	*CDRG*, I, no. 64 (pp. 76–7).	1133 Pope Innocent II (arbiter) Genoa Pisa
Treaty of Hyères	*LIRG*, vol. 1/2, nos. 396 (pp. 350–4).	1186 Arenburg, queen of Arborea Genoa
Treaty of Ivry[32] (1177)	Howden, *Gesta*, i; 191–6; Howden, *Chronica*, ii, 144–6. Translation in *The Annals of Roger de Hoveden*, I, 464–6. A version, based on the French exemplar, is also available in Gerald of Wales, *Instruction for a Ruler*, 460–7.	1177 Henry II, k. of England Louis VII, k. of Franks
Treaty of Jarnègues[33]	*Actes concernant les vicomtes de Marseille et leur descendants*, ed. H. De Gérin-Ricard (Monaco, 1926), no. 288 (pp. 81–3).	1190 Alfonso II, k. of Aragon Raymond V, c. of Toulouse

(continued)

Name of Treaty	Printed edition	Parties and date
Treaty of Justinopolis[34] *(932)*	*UHSRV*, I, no. 10 (pp. 5–10).	932 Peter Candiano, d. of Venetians Justinopolis
Treaty of Justinopolis (977)	*UHSRV*, I, no. 15 (pp. 31–5).	977 Peter Orseolo I, d. of Venetians Sicard, c. of Justinopolis
Treaty of Koblenz	'Hludowici, Karoli et Lotharii II. Conventus apud Confluentes', in *MGH Capit. II*, no. 242 (pp. 152–8). For translation of the oath of Louis, see *The Annals of Fulda*, 47.	860 Charles (the Bald), k. [of West Frankia] Louis (the German), k. [of East Frankia] Lothar II, k. [of Lotharingia]
Treaty of Lerici[35]	*CDRG*, II, no. 14 (pp. 40–7).	1166 Genoa Lucca
Treaty of Liège	'Hlotharii et Karoli Conventus Leodii Habitus', in *MGH Capit. II*, no. 207 (pp. 76–8).	854 Lothar I, emperor Charles (the Bald), k. [of West Frankia]
Treaty of Lodi	*ACM*, nos. 53–4 (76–81).	1167 Lodi Milan Bergamo Cremona Brescia Mantua

Treaty of Logroño (1176)	Howden, *Gesta*, i, 140–3; Howden, *Chronica*, ii, 122–4. Translation in *The Annals of Roger de Hoveden*, i, 441–4.	1176 Alfonso VIII, k. of Castile Sancho VI, k. of Navarre
Treaty of Logroño (1179)	González, *El reino de Castilla*, no. 321 (pp. 532–7).	1179 Alfonso VIII, k. of Castile Sancho VI, k. of Navarre
Treaty of London	Howden, *Gesta*, I, 151–4; Howden, *Chronica*, ii, 129–31. Translation in *The Annals of Roger de Hoveden*, i, 449–51.	1177 Henry, k. of England (arbiter) Alfonso VIII, k. of Castile Sancho VI, k. of Navarre
Treaty of Louviers[36]	*Dip. Docs*, no. 6 (pp. 16–18). Published with divisions into clauses in *Rec. des actes de Philippe Auguste*, II, no. 517 (pp. 53–7).	1196 Richard I, k. of England Philip II, k. of the Franks
Treaty of Lucca[37]	*CDRG*, II, no. 174 (pp. 334–9). For the oaths agreeing to the arbitration, see same volume no. 172 (pp. 321–32). The pope's order to adhere to decision is no. 173 (p. 333).	1188 Clement III, pope (arbiter), through his papal legates the cardinal priests Peter of Santa Cecilia and Sifrid of Santa Maria in Via Lata Genoa Pisa

(*continued*)

Name of Treaty	Printed edition	Parties and date
Treaty of Mallorca (1181)	Latin text: *CDRG*, II, no. 133 (pp. 271–3). For French translation of Arabic text, see Mas Latrie, *Traités de paix*, 109–113; for Italian translation of Arabic text, see Frédéric Bauden, 'Due trattati di pace conclusi nel dodicesimo secolo tra i Banū Ġāniya, signori delle isole Baleari, e il commune di Genova', in *Documentos y manuscritos árabes del occidente musulmán medieval*, ed. Nuria Martínez de Castilla (Madrid, 2010), 51–6.	1181 Genoa, through its representative Rodoan de Mauro Ishak-ibn-Mohammed, governor ('Alfachinus') of the Balearic islands
Treaty of Mallorca (1188)	Latin text: *CDRG*, II, no. 177 (pp. 341–4). For Italian translation of the Arabic text, see Bauden, 'Due trattati di pace', 70–4.	1188 Genoa, through its representative Nicholas Lecanozze Abu Mohammed Abd-Allah, k. of Mallorca[38]
Treaty of Mantes	Howden, *Chronica*, iii, 217–20; *EMDP*, II, no. 287 (pp. 613–15). Translation in *The Annals of Roger de Hoveden*, ii, 298–301.	1193 Richard I, k. of England, through his representatives Philip II, k. of France
Treaty of Meerssen (847)	'Hlotharii, Hludowici et Karoli conventus apud Marsnam primus', in *MGH Capit. II*, no. 204 (pp. 68–71). For a partial English translation of the 'announcement' of Charles the Bald, see *A Sourcebook for Mediaeval History*, 360–1.	847 Lothar, [emperor] Louis (the German), [k. of East Frankia] Charles (the Bald), [k. of West Frankia]

Treaty	Source	Date and parties
Treaty of Meerssen (851)	'Hlotharii, Hludowici et Karoli conventus apud Marsnam secundus' in *MGH Capit. II*, no. 205 (pp. 72–4). Translation in *The Annals of St-Bertin*, 70–3.	851 Lothar, [emperor] Louis (the German), [k. of East Frankia] Charles (the Bald), [k. of West Frankia]
Treaty of Meerssen (870)	'Divisio regni Hlotharii II', in *MGH Capit. II*, 193–5. Translation in *The Annals of St-Bertin*, 168–9.	870 Louis (the German), k. [of East Frankia] Charles (the Bald), k. [of West Frankia]
Treaty of Melfi	*Le Liber Censuum*, I, 422. Translation in B. Tierney, *The Crisis of Church and State: 1050–1300* (Toronto, 1988), 44.	1059 Robert Guiscard, d. of Apulia and Calabria Nicholas II, pope
Treaty of Messina[39] (1127)	G. Filippi, 'Patto di pace tra Ruggiero II Normanno e la Citta di Savona', *Archivio storico per le provincie napoletane*, 14 (1889), 753–7.[40]	1127 Roger, d. of Sicily and Calabria Savona
Treaty of Messina (1190)	Howden, *Gesta*, ii, 133–5. For the oath of the sureties, see Howden, *Gesta*, ii, 136. Translation in *The Annals of Roger de Hoveden*, ii, 164–6.	1190 Richard, k. of England Tancred, k. of Sicily
Treaty of Messina (1191)	*Dip. Docs*, no. 5 (pp. 14–15).	1191 Richard I, k. of England Philip II (Augustus), k. of the Franks

(*continued*)

Name of Treaty	Printed edition	Parties and date
Treaty of Metz	'Hludowici et Karoli Pactiones Mettenses', in *MGH Capit. II*, no. 245 (pp. 167–8).	867 Louis (the German), [k. of East Frankia] Charles (the Bald), [k. of West Frankia]
Treaty of Milan (1158)	*Gesta Friderici*, 221–4. Translation in Otto of Freising, *The Deeds of Frederick Barbarossa*, 220–3.	1158 Frederick I, emperor Milan
Treaty of Milan (1196)	*ACM*, no. 194 (pp. 272–9).	1196 Milan Como
Treaty of Montebello[41]	*DD FI*, iii, no. 638 (pp. 135–8).	1175 Frederick I, emperor Cities of the Lombard League
Treaty of Montferrand	Howden, *Gesta*, i, 36–41. A summary of the terms in English can be found in *The Annals of Roger de Hoveden*, i, 362–8.	1173 Henry II, k. of England Humbert III, c. of Maurienne
Treaty of Montlouis	Howden, *Gesta*, i, 77–9; Howden, *Chronica*, ii, 67–9. Translation in *The Annals of Roger de Hoveden*, i, 386–8.	1174 Henry II, k. [of England] Henry (the Young King), k. [of England] Richard[42] Geoffrey

Treaty of Najac-de-Rouergue (1185)	R. Benjamin, 'A Forty Years War: Toulouse and the Plantagenets, 1156–96', *Historical Research*, 61 (1988), 283–5.	1185 Alfonso II, k. of Aragon Richard, c. of Poitou and son of the king of England
Treaty of Naples	*CDRG*, iii, no. 2 (pp. 4–12); *LIRG*, vol. 1/2, no. 286 (pp. 28–34). For a partial English translation, see Hall, *Caffaro*, 203.	1191 Henry VI, emperor Genoa
Treaty of Nonancourt (1189)	*Rec. des actes de Philippe Auguste*, i, no. 287 (with division into clauses); *Diceto*, ii, 73. For German translation, see A. Cartelliere, *Philipp II August. König von Frankreich*, 4 vols. (Leipzig, 1899–1906), ii, 92–3.	1189 Richard I, k. of England Philip II, k. of the Franks
Treaty of Novgorod	Swedish translation in *Sveriges traktater med främmande magter. Första delen 822–1335*, ed. O. S. Rydberg (Stockholm, 1877), no. 52 (pp. 106–8); German translation in *Hansische Urkundenbuch. Band I*, ed. Konstantin Höhlbaum (Halle, 1876), no. 50 (pp. 26–7).	c. 1199 Jaroslaw, prince of Novgorodians Germans[43] Gotlanders
Treaty of Oribuela	'Treaty of Tudmir', in *Reading the Middle Ages: Sources from Europe, Byzantium, and the Islamic World*, 79.	c. 713 Theodemir,[44] c. of Murcia[45] Abd al-Aziz, leader of Muslim forces in Spain
Treaty of Oristano I	*LIRG*, vol. 1/2, no. 393 (pp. 342–4).	1192 Hugh I, k. of Arborea Genoa

(continued)

Name of Treaty	Printed edition	Parties and date
Treaty of Oristano II	*LIRG*, vol. 1/2, no. 403 (pp. 367–9). For oath of the king, see same volume no. 404 (pp. 370–1).	1192 Peter, k. of Arborea[46] Genoa
Treaty of Orvieto	*MGH Const. I*, no. 325 (pp. 464–5).	1186 Henry VI, k. of the Romans Hugh III, d. of Burgundy[47]
Treaty of Pavia (715)	Peter Classen, *Politische Verträge des frühen Mittelalters* (Germering, 1966), no. 19 (pp. 54–5).	715 (or 730)[48] Liudprand, k. of the Lombards Comacchio, represented by the priest Lupicino, the *magister militum* Bertarene and the 'comites' Mauro and Stefano
Treaty of Pavia (840)	*Pactum Hlotharii I*, in *MGH Capit. II*, no. 233 (pp. 130–5).	840 Lothar I, emperor Peter, d. of the Venetians
Treaty of Pavia (1162)	*DD FI*, ii, no. 357 (p. 204).	1162 Frederick I, emperor Pisa
Treaty of Pavia (1175)	*CDRG*, II, no. 101 (pp. 227–31).	1175 Genoa Pisa

Treaty of Palermo (1156)	Main text in *CDRG*, I, no. 279 (pp. 339–41). For the oath of William I, see *Guillelmi I. Regis Diplomata*, ed. H. Enzensberger (Cologne, 1996), no. 17 (p. 48); *CDRG*, I, no. 280 (pp. 341–2). For the oath of the Genoese, see *CDRG*, I, no. 282 (pp. 344–9).	1156 William I, k. of Sicily Genoa
Treaty of Palermo (1174)	*CDRG*, II, no. 94 (pp. 202–4).	1174 William II, k. of Sicily Genoa
Treaty of Péronne	*Rec. des actes de Philippe Auguste*, ii, no. 621.	1200 Philip II, k. of Franks Baldwin IX, c. of Flanders
Treaty of Piacenza (1167)	*ACM*, no. 55 (82–3). For the draft articles of the treaty (agreed in Cremona) and the oaths of the citizens of Milan, Bergamo and Cremona, see *ACM*, nos. 50–2 (pp. 73–6).	1167 Milan Bergamo Mantua Cremona
Treaty of Pisa	F. Bonaini, 'Due carte pisano-amalfitane', *Archivio storico italiano*, 3rd ser, 8 (1868), 5–7.	1126 Pisa Amalfi
Treaty of Portovenere (1149)	*CDRG*, I, no. 195 (pp. 243–7).	1149 Genoa Pisa

(*continued*)

Name of Treaty	Printed edition	Parties and date
Treaty of Portovenere (1169)	CDRG, II, no. 48 (pp. 99–102).	1169 Genoa Pisa
Treaty of Ravenna	'Pactum Karoli III', in MGH Capit. II, no. 236 (pp. 138–41).	880 Charles (the Fat), k. Urse, d. of the Venetians
Treaty of Rialto[49] (933)	UHSRV, I, no. 11 (pp. 11–16).	933 Peter II Candiano, d. of Venice Wintherius, margrave[50] of Istria
Treaty of Rialto[51] (1145)	UHSRV, I, no. 48 (pp. 105–7).	1145 Peter Polani, d. of Venetians Justinopolis
Treaty of Rome (824)	'Constitutio Romana', in MGH Capit. I, no. 161 (pp. 322–4).	824 Lothar I, emperor (Louis the Pious, emperor)[52] Eugenius II, pope
Treaty of Rome (962)	Die Urkunden der deutschen Könige und Kaiser. Erster Band. Die Urkunden Konrad I, Heinrich I und Otto I, ed. T. Sickel (Hanover, 1879–84), no. 235 (pp. 322–7).	962 Otto I, emperor John XII, pope
Treaty of Rome (967)	Die Urkunden der deutschen Könige und Kaiser. Erster Band. Die Urkunden Konrad I, Heinrich I und Otto I, no. 350 (pp. 478–83).	967 Otto I, emperor Venice

Treaty	Source	Date and parties
Treaty of Rouen (991)	Chaplais, *EDP*, pp. 37–8. Translation in *EHD*, I, no. 230.	991 John XV, pope (arbiter), through his legate Leo of Trevi Æthelred, k. of the West Saxons[53] Richard I, marquis[54] [of the Normans]
Treaty of Rouen (1204)	*Rec. des actes de Philippe Auguste*, ii, no. 803 (pp. 379–81).	1204 Peter de Preaux, and other knights ('milites') Robert, the mayor Jurors ('jurati') and commune of Rouen Philip II, k. of France
Treaty of Sahagún	González, *El reino de Castilla*, no. 44 (pp. 80–2).	1158 Sancho III, k. of Toledo and Castile Ferdinand II, k. of Léon and Galicia
Treaty of Salò	'Pactum Berengarii I' in *MGH Capit. II*, no. 238 (pp. 143–7).	888 Berengar, k. [of Italy] Peter, d. of the Venetians
Treaty of Sant Feliu de Guíxols[55]	*Liber maiolichinus de gestis pisanorum illustribus*, ed. C. Calisse (Rome, 1904), appendix 1 (pp. 137–40).	1113 Pisa Ramon Berenguer III, c. of Barcelona
Treaty of San Lorenzo[56]	*LIRG*, vol. 1/1, no. 181 (pp. 262–4). Translation in Hall, *Caffaro*, 195–6.	1155 Manuel Komnenos, emperor Genoa

(continued)

Name of Treaty	Printed edition	Parties and date
Treaty of San Salvatore I	*DD FI*, ii, no. 362 (pp. 212–14).	1162 Frederick I, emperor Piacenza
Treaty of San Salvatore[57] *II*	*DD FI*, ii, no. 367 (pp. 220–25). A partial translation in Hall, *Caffaro*, 196–203.	1162 Frederick I, emperor Genoa
Treaty of Santa Maria de Vineis	For the Genoese promise, see *CDRG*, II, no. 131 (pp. 266–8). For the promise of the city of Alessandria, see same volume no. 132 (268–70).	1181 Genoa Alessandria
Treaty of Sardinia	*LIRG*, vol. 1/2, no. 415 (pp. 392–4)	1168 Peter, 'iudex' of Cagliari Barisone, II, 'iudex' of Arboreans
Treaty of Savonnières	'Hludowici, Karoli et Hlotharii II conventus apud Saponarias', in *MGH Capit. II*, no. 243 (pp. 163–5)[58]	862 Louis (the German), k. [of East Frankia] Charles (the Bald), k. [of West Frankia] Lothar II, k. [of Lotharingia]
Treaty of Seligenstadt	*DD FI*, iv, no. 970 (pp. 248–51).	1188 Frederick I, emperor Alfonso VII, k. of Castile
Treaty of Silistra	*RPC*, 89–90.	971 John Tzimiskes, emperor Sviatoslav I, prince of Rus'

Treaty	Source	Date and parties
Treaty of St-Quentin	'Karoli II et Hlotarii II conventus apud Sanctum Quintinum', in *MGH Capit. II*, no. 268 (pp. 293–5).	857 Charles (the Bald), [k. of West Frankia] Lothar II, [k. of Lotharingia]
Treaty of Toul (1171)	*DD FI*, iii, no. 575 (pp. 46–7).	1171 Frederick I, emperor Louis VII, k. of Franks
Treaty of Tarvisio	'Pactum cum Venetis', in *MGH Const. I*, no. 72 (121–4).	c. 1095 Henry IV, emperor Vitale Faliero, d. of the Venetians
Treaty of Tudején	*Liber Feudorum Maior*, ed. F. Miquel Rosell, 2 vols. (Barcelona, 1945), I, no. 29 (pp. 39–42).	1151 Alfonso VII, 'emperor of Spain' [k. of Léon and Castile] Sancho, son of Alfonso Ramon Berenguer IV, c. of Barcelona
Treaty of Tunis	Mas Latrie, *Traités de paix*, 23–6.	1157 Pisa, represented by Archbishop Villanus Abu Abd Allah ibn Khorasan, emir of Tunis
Treaty of Tusey	'Hludowici et Karoli Pactum Tusiacense', in *MGH Capit. II*, no. 244 (pp. 165–7).	865 Louis (the German), [k. of East Frankia] Charles (the Bald), [k. of West Frankia]
Treaty of Túy	*Colección diplomatica del monasterio de Sahagún*, 7 vols., ed. J. A. Fernández Flórez (Léon, 1988–97), IV, no. 1263.	1137 Alfonso VII, k. of León Alfonso, k. of Portugal

(continued)

Name of Treaty	Printed edition	Parties and date
Treaty of Tyre (1187)	*LIRG*, vol. 1/2, no. 330 (pp. 135–7). Translation in Hall, *Caffaro*, 215–16.	1187 Genoa The barons of the kingdom of Jerusalem
Treaty of Tyre (1189)	*LIRG*, vol. 1/2, no. 342 (pp. 160–1).	1189 Bohemond III, prince of Antioch Genoa
Treaty of Tyre[59]	*LIRG*, vol. 1/2, no. 331 (pp. 137–40). Translation in Hall, *Caffaro*, 215–16.	1190 Genoa Conrad of Montferrat, lord of Tyre
Treaty of Tyre (1192)	*LIRG*, vol. 1/2, no. 334 (pp. 144–6). Translation in Hall, *Caffaro*, 223–4.	1192 Genoa, through its representative William Riccio Conrad of Montferrat, lord of Tyre
Treaty of Valenciennes	'Hlotharii et Karoli Conventus Valentianas', in *MGH Capit. II*, no. 206 (pp. 75–6).	853 Lothar I, [emperor] Charles (the Bald), [k. of West Frankia]
Treaty of Venice I (1177)	*DD FI*, iii, no. 687 (pp. 202–6). Translation in E. F. Henderson, *Select Historical Documents of the Middle Ages* (London, 1896), 425–30.	1177 Frederick I, emperor Alexander III, pope
Treaty of Venice II (1177)	*Chronicon Romualdi Salernitani*, ed. C. A. Garufi (Citta di Castello, 1935), 291–2.	1177 Frederick I, emperor William II, k. of Sicily

Treaty of Venice III (1177)	DD FI, iii, no. 695 (pp. 218–22).	1177 Frederick I, emperor Sebastian Ziani, d. of Venice
Treaty of Verona (983)	Die Urkunden der deutschen Könige und Kaiser. Zweiten Bandes erster Theil. Die Urkunden Otto des II (Hanover, 1888), no. 300 (pp. 352–6). The announcements are in same volume, nos. 298–9 (pp. 350–2).	983 Otto II, emperor Tribuno Menio, d. of Venetians
Treaty of Verona (1111)	MGH Const. I, no. 102 (152–6).	1111 Henry V, emperor Ordelafo Faliero, d. of Venetians
Treaty of Westminster (1153)	Regesta Regum Anglo-Normannorum, 3 vols., eds. H. A. Cronne and R. H. C. Davis (Oxford, 1968), iii, no. 272.	1153 Stephen, k. of England Henry, d. of Normandy
Treaty of Windsor	Howden, Gesta, I, 102–3; Howden, Chronica, II, 84–5. Translation in The Annals of Roger de Hoveden, i, 402–4.	1175 Henry II, k. of England Rory, k. of Connacht
Treaty of Worms	Howden, Chronica, iii, 215–16. Translation in The Annals of Roger de Hoveden, ii, 296–7.	1193 Henry VI, emperor Richard I, k. of England

(continued)

Name of Treaty	Printed edition	Parties and date
Treaty of Würzburg	*Historia de expeditione*, 103–5.	1193 Henry VI, emperor Leopold, d. of Austria
Treaty of York	Howden, *Gesta*, I, 96–9; Howden, *Chronica*, II, 80–2. Translation in *The Annals of Roger de Hoveden*, i, 398–401.	1175 Henry II, k. of England William I, k. of Scots
Treaty of Zaragoza	Gonzalez, *El reino de Castilla*, no. 147 (pp. 251–3).	1170 Alfonso VIII, k. of Castile Alfonso II, k. of Aragon
Treaty between Alfred and Guthrum	*Die Gesetze*, i, 126–8. Translation in *EHD*, I, 380–1.	880x890 Alfred, king of the West Saxons Guthrum, king of the people in East Anglia
Treaty between Baldwin of Jerusalem and Genoa	*LIRG*, vol. 1/1, nos. 60–1 (pp. 98–102). The first document is the oath of the Genoese, the second, the terms and obligations of the king. Translation in Hall, *Caffaro*, 174–6.	1104 Baldwin I, k. of Judaea and Jerusalem Genoa
Treaty between Barisone II of Arborea and Barisone II of Torres	*LIRG*, vol. 1/2, no. 390 (pp. 335–7). For the oaths of Barisone of Torres and the Genoese mediator, see no. 391 of the same volume (pp. 337–8).	1168 Barisone II, 'iudex' of Arborea Barisone II, 'iudex' of Torres

Treaty between Bertrand of Saint-Gilles and Genoa	LIRG, vol. 1/1, no. 119 (pp. 182–3). Translation in Hall, *Caffaro*, 176–7.	1109 Bertrand, c. of Saint-Gilles[60] Genoa
Treaty between Charlemagne and Offa of Mercia	MGH Epp., IV, no. 100 (pp. 145–6). Translation in *EHD*, I, no. 197.	796 Charles, k. of the Franks and the Lombards Offa, k. of the Mercians
Treaty between Coloman of Hungary and Venice	*UHSRV*, I, no. 29 (pp. 65–6).	1098x1101 Coloman, k. of the Hungarians Vitale I Michiele, d. of Venetians
Treaty between Emperor Frederick I and Ramon Berenguer IV of Barcelona and Ramon Berenguer II of Provence	DD FI, ii, no. 378 (pp. 243–5). The investiture of Ramon Berenguer II with Provence is no. 382 (pp. 248–51) of same volume.[61]	1162 Frederick I, emperor Ramon Berenguer IV, c. of Barcelona Ramon Berenguer II, c. of Provence

(continued)

Name of Treaty	Printed edition	Parties and date
Treaty between Genoa and Antibes	*LIRG*, vol. 1/1, no. 18 (pp. 28–9).	1138 Genoa Antibes
Treaty between Genoa and Alfonso II of Aragon	*LIRG*, vol. 1/2, no. 293 (pp. 54–7).	1167 Genoa Alfonso II, k. of Aragon
Treaty between Genoa and Barisone II of Torres (1166)	*LIRG*, vol. 1/2, no. 405 (pp. 371–2).	1166 Barisone II, 'iudex' of Torres Genoa
Treaty between Genoa and Boabdil of Valencia[62]	*LIRG*, vol. 1/1, no. 118 (pp. 180–1). Translation in Hall, *Caffaro*, 190–1.	1149 Genoa, represented by William Lusio 'Boabdil'.[63] k. of Valencia
Treaty between Genoa and Fos	*LIRG*, vol. 1/1, no. 14 (pp. 22–3). Translation in Hall, *Caffaro*, 177–8.	1138 Genoa Fos
Treaty between Genoa and Fréjus	*LIRG*, vol. 1/1, no. 16 (pp. 25–6).	1138 Genoa Fréjus

Treaty between Genoa and Hyères	LIRG, vol. 1/1, no. 17 (pp. 27–8).	1138 Genoa Hyéres
Treaty between Genoa and Lucca	CDRG, I, no. 238 (pp. 287–8).	1153 Lucca Genoa
Treaty between Genoa and Marseille	LIRG, vol. 1/1, no. 15 (pp. 23–5).	1138 Genoa Marseille
Treaty between Genoa and Narbonne	CDRG, I, no. 62 (pp. 73–5).	1132 Genoa Narbonne, through representatives of Viscount Aimery, Archbishop Arnold and the people of the city
Treaty between Genoa and Pavia (1130)	CDRG, I, no. 56 (pp. 66–7).	1130 Genoa Pavia
Treaty between Genoa and Pavia (1140)	CDRG, I, no. 105 (pp. 124–6).	1140 Genoa Pavia

(continued)

Name of Treaty	Printed edition	Parties and date
Treaty between Genoa and Peter of Arborea	*LIRG*, vol. 1/2, no. 397 (pp. 354–5). For the oaths, see same volume nos. 398–9 (pp. 356–9); the initial undertaking is no. 401 (pp. 361–3) and the confirmation no. 402 (pp. 364–6).	1189 Peter, k. of Arborea Genoa
Treaty between Genoa and Ramon Berenguer III of Barcelona	*CDRG*, I, 46 (pp. 55–7)	1127 Ramon Berenguer III, c. of Barcelona Genoa
Treaty between Genoa and Raymond of Toulouse	*LIRG*, vol. 1/2, nos. 360–1 (pp. 226–30).	1171 Raymond V, c. of Toulouse Genoa
Treaty between Genoa and Raymond of Toulouse, Sancho of Provence, William of Forcalquier	*LIRG*, vol. 1/2, no. 365 (pp. 253–5).	1184 Raymond V, c. of Toulouse Sancho, c. of Provence William IV, c. of Forcalquier Genoa

Treaty between Genoa and Tortona	1138 Genoa Tortona	LIRG, vol. 1/1, no. 23 (pp. 35–6).
Treaty between Llywelyn and the representatives of King John (1201)	1201 John, k. of England, through his representatives Llywelyn ap Iorwerth[64]	The Acts of Welsh Rulers 1120–1283, no. 221 (pp. 371–3).
Treaty between Milan and Piacenza	1156 Milan Piacenza	ACM, nos. 35–6 (pp. 55–6). The first document is the obligations of the Milanese and the second the obligations of Piacenza.
Treaty between Mu-Tsung of China and Tritsuk Detsen of Tibet	821/2 Mu-Tsung, Tang emperor of China Tritsuk-Detsen, emperor of Tibet	Richardson, 'The Sino-Tibetan Treaty Inscription', 137–162; Sources of Tibetan Tradition, 77–8.
Treaty between Pisa and Abu-Yusuf-Yakub of the Almohads	1186 Pisa Abu-Yusuf-Yakub al-Mansur, emir of the Almohads	For Italian translation of the Arabic original, see Mas Latrie, Traités de paix, 28–30.

(continued)

Name of Treaty	Printed edition	Parties and date
Treaty between Sancho IV of Navarre and al-Muktadir of Zaragoza (1069)	J. M. Lacarra 'Dos Tratados de paz y alianza entre Sancho el de Peñalén y Moctadir de Zaragoza (1069 y 1073)', in *Homenaje a Johannes Vincke*, 2 vols. (Madrid, 1962–3), i, 131–3.	1069 Sancho IV 'of Peñalén', k. of Pamplona[65] 'Almuktadir bille', [k.] of Zaragoza[66]
Treaty between Sancho IV of Navarre and al-Muktadir of Zaragoza (1073)	Lacarra 'Dos Tratados de paz', 133–4.	1073 Sancho IV 'of Peñalén', k. of Pamplona 'Almuctadir uille', [k.] of Zaragoza
Treaty between Sergius VII of Naples and Gaeta	Martin, *Guerre*, no. 7 (pp. 224–5).	1129 Sergius VII, d. of Naples and 'magister militum' The people of Gaeta[67]
Treaty between Venice and Byzantium (1082x1092)	*I trattati con Bisanzio, 992–1198*, no. 2 (pp. 37–43); UHSRV, I, 51–4.	1082x1092[68] Alexios I Komnenos, emperor [not known], d. of the Venetians

Treaty between Venice and Byzantium (1147)	*UHSRV*, I, no. 51 (113–24).	1147 Manuel I Komnenos, emperor [not specified][69] d. of the Venetians
Treaty between Venice and Byzantium (1187)	*UHSRV*, I, nos. 70–2 (pp. 179–203).	1187 Isaac II Angelos, emperor Orio Mastropiero, d. of the Venetians
Truce of Aleppo (969)	*The Truce of Safar A.H. 359. December–January 969–970*, ed. Wesam Farag (Birmingham, 1977), 4–7.	969 Nikephoros II Phokas, emperor, through his representative Petros Qarquya, emir of Aleppo
Truce of Venice (1177)	*DD FI*, iii, no. 689 (pp. 207–8). For edition with clauses, see *ACM*, no. 110 (pp. 151–3).	1177 Frederick I, Emperor The cities of the Lombard League
Truce of Verneuil[70]	Howden, *Chronica*, iii, 257–60. Translation in *The Annals of Roger de Hoveden*, ii, 329–32.	1194 Richard I, k. of England Philip II, k. of France

[1] Only the oath of Henry IV survives from this controversial event, but it can be compared with Pope Gregory VII's account of it in a letter sent to the archbishops and bishops across Europe, for which see Gregory VII, *Registrum IV*, 12, in *MGH Epp. sel. 2.1*, 312–14.

[2] The text simply refers to Henry as king, but different versions of the oath in different manuscripts and textual traditions use 'imperator' (emperor) and 'rex Teutonicorum' (king of the Germans), the latter clearly intended as an insult by Gregory's supporters.

3 In dealing with the so-called 'Pactum' of Arichis, I am convinced by, and have followed, the analysis of Jean-Marie Martin, showing that this document is, in fact, two. Martin, *Guerre*, 9–11.

4 On the date, see Martin, *Guerre*, 78–82.

5 It is difficult to know exactly who or what this referred to. The term 'iudex' can be translated directly as 'judge' and it is possible that this is what it meant. However, it may also have indicated a ruler or governor of the city. Cf. 'iudex' of Arborea/Cagliari.

6 Additional information on the treaty can be found in the *Chronicon Salernitanum. A Critical Edition with Studies on Literary and Historical Sources and on Language*, ed. Ulla Westerbergh (Stockholm, 1953).

7 This phrase is usually translated as 'master of the soldiers', and certainly indicated the military leader of the duchy of Naples ('ducati Neapolitani'), hence why modern historiography tends to refer to him, and other Neapolitan leaders, as 'duke' (*dux*). Later treaties tend to be explicit about the link between the two titles: 'dux atque magister militum' Martin, *Guerre*, 223–4.

8 Additional information on the treaty can be found in the *Chronicon Salernitanum. A Critical Edition with Studies on Literary and Historical Sources and on Language*, ed. Ulla Westerbergh (Stockholm, 1953).

9 The treaty is frequently referred to as 'Pactum Warmundi' after the negotiator Warmund, patriarch of Jerusalem. The text is clear, however, that it was concluded at Acre ('apud Acron').

10 King Baldwin II was in captivity during the conclusion of the treaty but the long prologue is clear that his representatives concluded it based on earlier proposals by the king ('…eiusdem regis Balduini promissiones secundum litterarum suarum et nuntiorum prolocutiones…'). Furthermore, c. 9 sets out that the king would ratify the treaty if he was released from captivity, or in the event he was not and a new king was elected, ratification of these terms would be a condition for the elevation to the throne. In the event, it was the former that came true and the treaty was confirmed by Baldwin II in 1125.

11 The text notes that the treaty was concluded 'in obsidione Acconensi', that is, during the siege of Acre. The treaty was subsequently confirmed in Jaffa in 1191 at the request of King Richard I of England. *LIRG*, vol. 1/2, no. 333 (pp. 142–3).

12 The text calls him 'king of the Latins in the holy city of Jerusalem (in sancta civitate Ierusalem rex latinorum)'. Cf. *Treaty between Baldwin of Jerusalem and Genoa* (1104); *Treaty of Acre* (1124)

13 The two different documents and obligations that make up this treaty do not mention the place. The grant of privileges mentions that it was enacted on 14 July 1098, only two weeks after the city had fallen to the crusaders, and that it was sealed and signed by Bohemond himself with the Genoese representatives as witnesses. There seems no reason to doubt that this took place at Antioch, the authority over which was at this time disputed between Bohemond and Raymond of Toulouse – a fact mentioned in the Genoese commitments. On the historical context, see Thomas S. Asbridge, *The Creation of the Principality of Antioch 1098–1130* (Woodbridge, 2000), 34–7.

14 Neither text gives Bohemond a title other than 'lord' (*dominus*), although the grant of privileges calls him 'son of Robert Guiscard duke of Apulia.'

15 Tancred has no title in the text, which has a much-debated history, for which see *CDRG*, i, 16–17. He was the regent of Antioch during the captivity of Bohemond I.

16 The text is clear that this agreement was made 'in camera domini patriarche Antiochie (in the chamber of the lord patriarch of Antioch)'.

17 The text refers to the doge but without specifically naming one. Judging by the date, this was Vitale II Michiele.

18 There was an additional renewal of this agreement in 1144 (*LIRG*, vol. 1/2, no. 338), which I have not listed separately here because the text simply confirmed the previous grants without outlining the actual terms or privileges.

19 Medieval Sardinia consisted of four independent entities (*iudicati*) – Arborea, Gallura, Cagliari, and Torres – each with a ruler called *iudex* (judge). Note, however, that some treaties also refer to each of these rulers as king (*rex*).

20 The text specifically notes it was concluded in the chapel of the palace.

21 The text states 'Actum est hoc ante ecclesiam Sanctorum Cosme et Damiani in Silice', identifiable as the Basilica of Cosmas and Damian located in the Forum of Vespasian in Rome, also known as the Forum of Peace. On this church in the twelfth century, see Pier Luigi Tucci, *The Temple of Peace in Rome* (Cambridge, 2017), 695–732.

22 Near the town of San Miniato on the Via Francigena, i.e., the pilgrim route from France to Rome. It is now an archaeological site. According to the text, the treaty was concluded in 'domo Rambotti', the house of Rambotto.

23 Near the north Italian town of Guastalla, as the text states: 'Viridi Coreggia prope Wartstallum'.

24 Wife of Duke John III of Gaeta (978–1008), who assumed the regency of her grandson, Duke John V, in c. 1025. On the historical context, see Patricia Skinner, *Family Power in Southern Italy. The Duchy of Gaeta and its Neighbours, 850–1139* (Cambridge, 1995), 151, 173, 273–4.

25 Sister of Sergius IV of Naples and wife of Duke John IV of Gaeta (993–1011/12).

26 'Gagetanos magnes et mediocres', lit. 'Gaetans great and ordinary', which a little later in same document become 'Gaietanos maiores et minores', lit. 'Gaetans great and small'.

27 The treaty specifies it was written 'in territorio Novariense in obsidione castri Galliate'; that is, in the province of Novara during the siege of Galliate.

28 In the text Alfonso claims to be 'Hyspaniarum imperator' but more realistically he was king of León-Castille.

29 The text states the treaty was concluded 'actum Ianue, in publico parlamento', i.e., at the public assembly of the city.

30 The text gives no title to Hugh but the reference to him being the son of Hugh de Bassio is a recognition of him reclaiming the viscourty of Besalú in the principality of Catalonia. Elsewhere in treaties with Genoa, he is referred to as Hugh I, king (or judge) of Arborea.

31 The actual text of this treaty has not survived, but its terms can be gleaned from the announcement of the English king, who mediated the agreement. Here, as also in the main text, I indicate this fact by not italicising the title of the treaty. The treaty was confirmed in the same year at a meeting at La Grange Saint Arnoul and then renegotiated in 1185 at Boves, but neither text has survived.

32 It is worth noting that Ralph de Diceto gives the place for this treaty as Nonancourt, the ford at which was a well-known meeting place between the kings but a location that is some 14 miles from Ivry.

33 Text states: 'Acta fuerunt apud Gernicam insulam'; that is enacted on the island of Jarnègues, which is situated in the river Rhône between Tarascon and Beaucaire.

34 Identified as the modern Slovenian city of Koper (It: Capodistria).

35 The text states that the treaty was enacted 'in loco Lerici prope ubi dicitur Sancto Georgio iuxta portum ipsius loci', likely referring to St George's church (not to be confused with the current, sixteenth-century church) in the town of Lerici.

36 The dating clause of the treaty states that it was concluded between Gaillon and Vaudreuil (*Dip. Docs.*, 18), but the contemporary chronicler Roger of Howden states that it had been agreed that the parties would meet at Louviers, roughly between the two locations, or the feast of St Hilary (13 January) to confirm the treaty. Howden, *Chronica*, iii, 305. On how Anglo-French treaties record meeting places, see Benham, *PMA*, 23.

37 On the place and date, see short summary of the manuscripts by Imperiale di Santangelo in *CDRG*, ii, 334.

38 The first line of the treaty gives his Arabic title, 'Emir', but elsewhere in the document he is referred to as 'king of Mallorca'.

39 The text states that the Savonese came to Roger 'cum ipse resideret in cappella palatii sui messane', that is, while he was sitting (holding court?) in the chapel of his palace at Messina.

40 Abulafia, *The Two Italies*, 65–70, has a discussion and corrections of the text as given by Filippi.

41 The text of the treaty notes that it was concluded 'in territorio Papie, in campo subtus Montebellum inter exercitum imperatoris et Lonbardie'; that is, in the territory of Pavia, in a field beneath Montebello between the army of the emperor and that of Lombardy.

42 Only Henry the Young king among Henry II's sons is referred to by any title in the text.

43 The Germans and the Gotlanders referred to in the text are groups of merchants.

44 Named in the Arabic original as 'Tudmir', hence the traditional name of the treaty.

45 The text of the treaty states that the terms applied to seven cities: Orihuela, Valentilla, Alicante, Mula, Bigastro, Ello, and Lorca.

46 This treaty, concluded at the same time as that with Hugh I, recognised Peter as co-ruler of Arborea.

47 The text refers to Hugh as being the duke of Dijon (*dux Divionensis*), a reference to the capital and commercial centre of the dukedom of Burgundy.

48 On the two possible dates of this treaty, see comments by Massimo Montanari, 'Il capitolare di Liutprando: note di storia dell'economia e dell'alimentazione', in *La Civiltà Comacchiese e Pomposiana dalle origini preistoriche al tardo medioevo* (Bologna, 1986), 461 fn. 1.

49 The document notes that this treaty was 'acta vero Rivoalto', i.e., drawn up at Rialto, the central part of what eventually turned into the city of Venice, which was located on an islet and included the ducal palace and the basilica of St Mark. 'Venice' in this early period was often synonymous with the whole region/duchy rather than the city. For this, see Luigi Andrea Berto, *The Political and Social Vocabulary of John the Deacon's 'Istoria Veneticorum'* (Turnhout, 2013), 141–5.

50 The text refers to him as 'marchio'.

51 According to the text, this agreement was concluded in the court of the Venetian doge ('actum est in curia domini nostri Petri Polani ducis') in 'Rivoalto'. Unlike the tenth-century treaties with Justinopolis, it is evident that this was a significant extension of Venetian power, with the first clause setting out that the citizens owed fealty to the duke and the church of St Mark, and the location of where it was done emphasises this.

52 Louis is named in the text of the oath, presumably because he was the senior emperor, but narrative sources are clear that Lothar dealt with the conflict and concluded the treaty. *ARF*, s.a. 823–4. For the context, see O. Bertolini, 'Osservazioni sulla Constitutio Romana e sull Sacramentum Cleri et Populi Romani dell'anno 824', in his *Scritti scelti di storia medioevale*, 2 vols., ed. O. Banti (Livorno, 1968), II, 705–38.

53 The text refers to Æthelred as king of the West Saxons ('Saxonum Occidentalium regis'), though historians tend to think of him as king of the English.

54 The text calls Richard *marchio* (marquis), perhaps best translated, in practical terms, as 'leader' of the Normans.

55 Sant Feliu de Guíxols in the district of Gerona, north of the city of Barcelona, for which see Silvia Orvietani Busch, *Medieval Mediterranean Ports. The Catalan and Tuscan Coasts, 1100 to 1235* (Leiden, 2001), map 1.

56 The text sets out that it was concluded in the church of San Lorenzo in Genoa.

57 Referring to the monastery of San Salvatore in Pavia, 'in the emperor's palace', according to the text, which also adds that this took place 'after the destruction of Milan and the "deditio" (surrender) of Brescia and Piacenza', i.e., after 11 May 1162. *DD FI*, ii, 225. A treaty with Cremona was concluded at San Salvatore a couple of days later (*DD FI*, ii, no. 369), which describes San Salvatore as located outside the gates of the city of Pavia ('extra portas civitatis Pavia') and divulges that this was the site of the emperor's chapel ('capella'). Two weeks later, the imperial court had moved on to Savignano near the city of Modena, where a treaty was concluded with the city of Ravenna (*DD FI*, ii, no. 372)

58 It is worth noting I have taken a different view of this treaty to the *MGH* editors, namely that the 'capitulary' that accompanies the announcements cannot be considered part of the treaty, other than to give a historical context from the perspective of Charles the Bald. For the context of how the documents were drawn up, see *AB*, s.a. 862.

59 The text specifically says the treaty was concluded 'in hospicio Bernardi de Templo', i.e. in the house of Bernard of the Temple. The treaty was renewed with some small amendments by Henry de Troyes (count of Champagne), lord of Tyre, in 1192, for which see *LIRG*, vol. 1/ 2, no. 335 (pp. 146–9).

60 The text refers to Bertrand as count of Saint-Gilles, a nod to his claim to the county of Toulouse, for which see Kevin James Lewis, *The Counts of Tripoli and Lebanon in the Twelfth Century: Sons of Saint-Gilles* (Abingdon, 2017), 7, 28–9. The terms of the treaty make it clear that the agreement related specifically to Bertrand's lands in Tripoli and surrounding area.

61 This second document was concluded at Turin, but the text of the treaty does not carry any indication of place. Frederick's charters indicate that he was near Piacenza on 27 July and in the area of Turin by 6 August, and the treaty was concluded at some point before 1 August.

62 The treaty records that the Genoese ambassador came with the document and the seal to the king of Valencia 'here in this place', but the name of this place is not identified.

63 The text refers to 'Boabdele Mahometo filius Saide', which likely referred to the governor of Valencia, Yusuf ibn Mardanish, or his brother Ibn Mardanish. See Hugh Kennedy, *Muslim Spain and Portugal. A Political History of al-Andalus* (London, 1996), 194–5.

64 The text reads 'Ieulinus filius Ioruert'; that is, Llywelyn, son of Iorwerth. There is no mention of any specific title, but that Llywelyn ruled over Gwynedd in north Wales is certain.

65 As per text. More commonly referred to as the kingdom of Navarre, which was centred on the city of Pamplona.

66 The text refers to him as 'Almuktadir bille', that is Ahmad ibn Sulayman al-Muqtadir, often simply referred to as Moctadir or al-Muqtadir, who ruled the *taifa* (independent Muslim principality) of Zaragoza. Note that the Latin text does not refer to his title, although contemporary chroniclers call him *rex* (king). Perhaps implied by the Arabic bi-llah, rendered in the text as 'bille', meaning 'with/through God', and seemingly corresponding to the Latin 'Dei Gratia' (by the grace of God).

67 'populo Gaietano'.

68 The date of this treaty has been much debated. For two examples, see Thomas F. Madden, 'The Chrysobull of Alexius I Commenus to the Venetians: the Date and the Debate', *JMH*, 28 (2002), 23–41; Peter Frankopan, 'Byzantine Trade Privileges to Venice in the Eleventh Century: The Chrysobull of 1092', *JMH*, 30 (2004), 135–60.

69 The text does not specify but if the date is correct then the doge must have been Pietro Polani, who was doge until 1148.

70 More accurately, the text records that the truce was concluded at a meeting between Verneuil and Tillière, on the river Avre, for which, see map 2 in Benham, *PMA*, 34.

Bibliography

Manuscripts

Cambridge, Corpus Christi College, MS 26
London, British Library Cotton Augustus II
Paris, Archives nationales, AE/II/199
Paris, Bibliothèque nationale de France, MS Lat. 9654
Rome, Vatican Library, MS Vat. Lat. 4982

Primary sources

Actes concernant les vicomtes de Marseille et leur descendants, ed. H. De Gérin-Ricard (Monaco, 1926)
The Acts of Welsh Rulers 1120–1283, ed. Huw Pryce (Cardiff, 2005)
Alexandri Telesini Abbatis Ystoria Rogerii Regis Siciliae atque Calabriae atque Apulie, ed. Ludovica de Nava (Rome, 1991)
The Alexiad of Anna Comnena, tr. E. R. A Sewter (London, 1969)
Allott, S., *Alcuin of York c. A.D. 732 to 804: His Life and Letters* (York, 1974)
Anglo-Scottish Relations 1174–1328: Some Selected Documents, ed. E. L. G. Stones (London, 1965)
Annales Bertiniani, ed. G. Waitz, *MGH SRG*, 5 (Hanover, 1883)
Annales Fuldenses, ed. F. Kurze, *MGH SRG*, 7 (Hanover, 1891)
Annales Regni Francorum, ed. F. Kurze, *MGH SRG*, 6 (Hanover, 1895)
Annali Genovesi di Caffaro e de' suoi continuatori, 4 vols., eds. L. T. Belgrano and Cesare Imperiale di Sant'Angelo (Rome, 1890–1929)
The Annals of Fulda, ed. Timothy Reuter (Manchester, 1992)
The Annals of Lampert of Hersfeld, tr. I. S. Robinson (Manchester, 2015)
The Annals of Roger de Hoveden, ed. H.T. Riley, 2 vols. (London, 1853)
The Annals of St-Bertin, ed. Janet L. Nelson (Manchester, 1991)
Anne Comnène, *Alexiade*, 4 vols., ed. and tr. Bernard Leib (Paris, 1937–76)

Arnoldi Chronica Slavorum, ed. G. H. Pertz, *MGH SRG*, 14 (Hanover, 1868)

Asser's Life of King Alfred, ed. W. H. Stevenson (Oxford, 1904)

Gli atti del commune di Milano, ed. C. Manaresi (Milan, 1919)

Augustine, City of God against the Pagans, ed. R. W. Dyson (Cambridge, 1998)

Bibliotheca rerum germanicarum, tomus secundus: Monumenta gregoriana, ed. P. Jaffé (Berlin, 1865)

Bischofs Wærferths von Worcester Übersetzung der Dialoge Gregors des Grossen, ed. Hans Hecht (Leipzig, 1900)

Bǫglunga Sǫgur, 2 vols., ed. Hallvard Magerøy (Oslo, 1988)

Bonaini, F., 'Due carte pisano-amalfitane', *Archivio storico italiano*, 3rd ser., 8 (1868)

Das Briefbuch Abt Wibalds von Stablo und Corvey, 3 vols., ed. Martina Hartmann, *MGH Briefe der deutschen Kaiserzeit*, 9 (Hanover, 2012)

Die Briefe Heinrichs IV, ed. Carl Erdmann, in *MGH Deutsches Mittelalter. Kritische Studientexte*, 1 (Leipzig, 1937)

The Burgundian Code, tr. Katherine Fischer Drew (Philadelphia, 1972)

Caffaro, Genoa and the Twelfth-Century Crusades, tr. Martin Hall and Jonathan Phillips (Farnham, 2013)

Calendar of Ancient Correspondence concerning Wales, ed. J. G. Edwards (Cardiff, 1935)

Carolingian Chronicles, tr. B. W. Scholz (Ann Arbor, 1972)

Chronica Magistri Rogeri de Hovedene, 4 vols., ed. W. Stubbs, Rolls Series, 51 (London, 1868–71)

The Chronicle of Arnold of Lübeck, ed. Graham A. Loud (Abingdon, 2019)

The Chronicle of John of Worcester, 3 vols., ed. R. R. Darlington and P. McGurk (Oxford, 1995–98)

The Chronicle of Magnus of Reichersberg, in *The Crusade of Frederick Barbarossa*, tr. Graham Loud (Farnham, 2010)

The Chronicle of Robert of Torigni, abbot of Mont St Michel, in *Chronicles of the Reigns of Stephen, Henry II, and Richard I, vol. IV*, ed. R. Howlett (London, 1889)

Chronicon Romualdi Salernitani, ed. C. A. Garufi (Citta di Castello, 1935)

Die Chroniken Bertholds von Reichenau und Bernolds von Konstanz, ed. I. S. Robinson, *MGH SRG* n.s., 14 (Hanover, 2003)

Classen, Peter, *Politische Verträge des frühen Mittelalters* (Germering, 1966)

Codex Iustinianus, ed. P. Krueger (Berlin, 1915)

Codice diplomatico della repubblica di Genova, 4 vols., ed. C. Imperiale di Santangelo (Rome, 1936–42)

Colección diplomática del Monasterio de Sahagún (857–1300), 4 vols., ed. J.A. Fernández Flórez (León, 1991)

Councils and Synods, with Other Documents Relating to the English Church. I, A.D. 871–1204, 2 vols., eds. D. Whitelock, M. Brett, and C. N. L. Brooke (Oxford, 1981)

The Crusade of Frederick Barbarossa, tr. Graham Loud (Farnham, 2010)

Danakonunga sögur: Skjöldunga saga, Knýtlinga saga, Ágrip af sögu Danakonunga, ed. Bjarni Guðnason (Reykjavik, 1982)

The Danish Medieval Laws, eds. Ditlev Tamm and Helle Vogt (London, 2016)

Danmarks gamle landskabslove med kirkelovene, 8 vols., eds. Johannes Brøndum-Nielsen et al. (Copenhagen, 1926–51)

Decrees of the Ecumenical Councils, vol. 1, ed. Norman P. Tanner (Washington, DC, 1990)

Decretum Magistri Gratiani, ed. Emil Friedberg, *Corpus Iuris Canonici*, I (Leipzig, 1879)

The Deeds of Frederick Barbarossa, tr. C. C. Mierow (Toronto, 1994)

The Digest of Justinian, 4 vols., ed. T. Mommsen, tr. Alan Watson (Philadelphia, 1985)

I diploma arabi del R. Archivio Fiorentino: testo originale con la traduzione letterale e illustrazioni, vol. 1, ed. M. Amari (Florence, 1863)

Diplomatarium Danicum, vol. 1, parts i–vii, ed. C. A. Christensen (Copenhagen, 1975–93)

Diplomatic Documents Preserved in the Public Record Office, 1101–1279, ed. P. Chaplais (London, 1964)

The Divorce of King Lothar and Queen Theutberga. Hincmar of Rheims's De Divortio, tr. Rachel Stone and Charles West (Manchester, 2016)

Documenti del commercio veneziano nei secoli XI-XIII, vol. I, eds. R. Morozzo della Rocca and A. Lombardo (Rome, 1940)

Documenti sulle relazioni delle citta Toscane coll'oriente Cristiano e coi Turchi, ed. Giuseppe Müller (Florence, 1879)

Du Cange, Domino et al., *Glossarium mediae et infimae latinitatis*, ed. L. Favre (Paris, 1883–7), available at http://ducange.enc.sorbonne.fr/ (accessed 16 July 2021).

Dudo of St Quentin, *History of the Normans*, tr. Eric Christiansen (Woodbridge, 1998).

Eleventh-century Germany. The Swabian Chronicles, tr. I. S. Robinson (Manchester, 2008)

English Historical Documents. Volume I, c. 500–1042, ed. D. Whitelock, 2nd ed. (London, 1979; repr. 1996)

English Historical Documents. Volume II 1042–1189, eds. D. C. Douglas and G. W. Greenaway, 2nd edn. (London, 1981; repr. 1996)

English Historical Documents, Volume 3: 1189–1327, ed. Harry Rothwell (London, 1996)

English Medieval Diplomatic Practice Part I, 2 vols., ed. Pierre Chaplais (London, 1982)

Epistola Brunonis ad Henricum regem, ed. Jadwiga Karwasinska, Monumenta Poloniae Historica series nova, 4,3 (Warsaw, 1973)

Epistolae Merowingici et Karolini Aevi, Tomus I, ed. E. Dümmler, *MGH Epp*. III (Berlin, 1892)

The Etymologies of Isidore of Seville, tr. Stephen A. Barney et al. (Cambridge, 2006)

Filippi, G., 'Patto di pace tra Ruggiero II Normanno e la Citta di Savona', *Archivio storico per le provincie napoletane*, 14 (1889)

Flodoard, *Historia Remensis ecclesiae*, eds. J. Heller and G. Waitz, *MGH SS*, 13 (Hanover, 1881)

Formulae Merowingici et Karolini aevi, ed. K. Zeumer (Hanover, 1886)

The Formularies of Angers and Marculf: Two Merovingian Legal Handbooks, tr. Alice Rio (Liverpool, 2008)

The Fourth Book of the Chronicle of Fredegar with its Continuations, tr. J. M. Wallace-Hadrill (London, 1960)

Geoffrey Malaterra, *De rebus gestis Rogeri Calabriae et Siciliae comitis et Roberti Guiscardi ducis fratris eius*, 2nd edn., ed. Ernesto Pontieri, Rerum Italicarum Scriptores 5:i (Bologna, 1925–8)

Gerald of Wales, *Instructions for a Ruler (De Principis Instructione)*, ed. Robert Bartlett (Oxford, 2018)

Gerald of Wales, *Expugnatio Hibernica: The Conquest of Ireland*, eds. A. B. Scott and F. X. Martin (Dublin, 1978)

Die Gesetze der Angelsachsen, 3 vols., ed. Felix Liebermann (Halle, 1903–16)

Gesta Regis Henrici Secundi Benedicti Abbatis, 2 vols., ed. W. Stubbs, Rolls Series, 49 (London, 1867)

Gesta sanctorum patrum Fontanellensis coenobii, eds. F. Lohier and J. Laporte (Paris, 1936)

Guillaume de Pouille, *La geste de Robert Guiscard*, ed. M. Mathieu (Palermo, 1963)

Guillelmi I. Regis Diplomata, ed. H. Enzensberger (Cologne, 1996)

Hansische Urkundenbuch. Band I, ed. Konstantin Höhlbaum (Halle, 1876)

Heinrici Chronicon Lyvonie, ed. W. Arndt, in *MGH SS*, 23 (Hanover, 1874; repr. Stuttgart, 1986)

Henderson, E.F., *Select Historical Documents of the Middle Ages* (London, 1896)

Henry, Archdeacon of Huntingdon, Historia Anglorum, tr. Diana Greenway (Oxford, 1996)

Helmold von Bosau Slawenchronik, ed. B. Schmeidler, revised by H. Stoob (Darmstadt, 1973)

Herimanni Augiensis Chronicon, ed. G. H. Pertz, in *MGH SS*, 5 (Hanover, 1844)

Hincmar of Rheims. *De divortio Lotharii regis et Theutbergae reginae*, ed. Letha Böhringer, *MGH Concilia* 4, Supplementum 1 (Hanover, 1992)

Historia de Expeditione Friderici Imperatoris, in *Quellen zur Geschichte des Kreuzzuges Kaiser Friedrichs I*, ed. A. Chroust, *MGH SRG* n.s., 5 (Berlin, 1928)

The Historical Works of Master Ralph de Diceto, 2 vols., ed. W. Stubbs, Rolls Series, 68 (London, 1876)

The Historical Works of Simeon of Durham, tr. J. Stevenson (London, 1855)

A History of Deeds Done beyond the Sea. Volume 1, ed. Emily Atwater Babcock and A. C. Krey (New York, 1943)

The History of the Tyrants of Sicily by 'Hugo Falcandus', 1154–69, tr. G. A. Loud and Thomas Wiedemann (Manchester, 1998)

Die 'Honorantie Civitatis Papie': Transkription, Edition, Kommentar, tr. Carlrichard Brühl (Cologne, 1983)

Imperial Lives and Letters of the Eleventh Century, tr. Theodore E. Mommsen and Karl F. Morrison (New York, 2000)

International Law Commission's Articles on the Responsibility of States for Internationally Wrongful Acts at https://legal.un.org/ilc/texts/instruments/english/draft_articles/9_6_2001.pdf (accessed 16 July 2021)

International Tribunals (Sierra Leone) Act 2007 at www.legislation.gov.uk/ukpga/2007/7/introduction (accessed 16 July 2021)

Isidori Hispalensis episcopi Etymologiarum sive Originum libri XX, ed. W. M. Lindsay, 2 vols (Oxford, 1911)

The Islamic Law of Nations. Shaybānī's Siyar, tr. Majid Khadduri (Baltimore, 1966)

John of Salisbury, *Policraticus*, tr. John Dickinson (New York, 1927)

King Alfred's West-Saxon Version of Gregory's Pastoral Care, 2 vols., ed. Henry Sweet (London, 1871–2)

The King's Mirror, tr. L. M. Larson (New York, 1917)

Knytlingasaga: The History of the Kings of Denmark, tr. Hermann Pálsson and Paul Edwards (Odense, 1986)

Konungs Skuggsià, ed. L. Holm-Olsen (Oslo, 1983)

Lamperti Monachi Hersfeldensis Opera, ed. O. Holder-Egger, *MGH SRG*, 38 (Hanover, 1894)

The Law of Hywel Dda. Law Texts Translated from Medieval Wales, tr. Dafydd Jenkins (Llandysul, 1986)

Laws of the Salian and Ripuarian Franks, tr. T. J. Rivers (New York, 1986)

Leges Henrici Primi, ed. L. J. Downer (Oxford, 1972)

Letters of Medieval Jewish Traders, tr. S. D. Goitein (Princeton, NJ, 2015)

The Letters and Poems of Fulbert of Chartres, ed. F. Behrends (Oxford, 1976)

Le Liber Censuum de l'eglise romaine, 3 vols., eds. P. Fabre and L. Duchesne (Paris, 1910)

Le Liber Pontificalis: texte, introduction et commentaire, 3 vols., ed. L. Duchesne (Paris, 1886)

Liber Feudorum maior: Cartulario real que se conserva en el Archivo de la Corona de Aragon, 2 vols., ed. Francisco Miquel Rosell (Barcelona, 1945–7)

Liber maiolichinus de gestis pisanorum illustribus, ed. C. Calisse (Rome, 1904)

I libri iurium della repubblica di Genova, 11 vols., eds. Dino Puncuh, Antonella Rovere, et al. (Rome, 1992–2011)

The Lombard Laws, tr. Katherine Fischer Drew (Philadelphia, 1973; repr. 1989)

Magni Presbiteri Chronicon, ed. Wilhelm Wattenbach, *MGH SS*, 17 (Hanover, 1861)

Mas Latrie, M. L. de, *Traités et documents concernant les relations des chrétiens avec les Arabes de l'Afrique septentrionale au moyen âge, part II: documents* (Paris, 1865)

Medieval Italy: Texts in Translation, eds. Katherine L. Jansen et al. (Philadelphia, 2009)

Medieval Trade in the Mediterranean World, tr. Robert S. Lopez and Irving W. Raymond (New York, 1955; repr. 1990)

MGH Capitularia regum Francorum, 2 vols., eds. A. Boretius and V. Krause (Hanover, 1883–97)

MGH Constitutiones et acta publica imperatorum et regum, 2 vols., ed. L. Weiland (Hanover, 1893–6)

De moribus et actis primorum Normannorum Ducum auctore Dudone Sancti Quintini decano, ed. J. Lair (Caen, 1865)

Nazi-Soviet Relations: Documents from the German Foreign Office, eds. Raymond James Sontag and James Stuart Beddie (Washington, DC, 1948)

Nithard: Histoire des fils de Louis le Pieux, ed. and tr. P. Lauer (Paris, 1926)

Olafs saga Tryggvasonar, ed. Olafur Halldorsson (Reykjavik, 2006)

Ottonis et Rahewini Gesta Friderici I Imperatoris, ed. B. de Simson, *MGH SRG*, 46 (Hanover, 1912)

Pactus Legis Salicae, in *MGH LL nat. Germ.* 4:1, ed. K. A. Eckhardt (Hanover, 1962)

Pleas before the King or his Justices 1198–1202. Volume I, ed. D. M. Stenton (London, 1953)

Prisci Panitae Historia Byzantina, in *Fragmenta Historicorum Graecorum, volume 4*, ed. C. Müller (Paris, 1851)

Prosecutor v. Taylor, Case No. SCSL-03–01-A, Appeals Judgment (Spec. Ct. Sierra Leone Sept. 26, 2013) at www.rscsl.org/Documents/Decisions/Taylor/Appeal/1389/SCSL-03-01-A-1389.pdf (accessed 16 July 2021)

Radulphi de Coggeshall Chronicon Anglicanum, ed. Joseph Stevenson, Rolls Series, 66 (London, 1875)

Recueil des actes de Philippe Auguste, 4 vols., ed. H. F. Delaborde (Paris, 1916–79)

Das Register Gregors VII, 2 vols., ed. E. Caspar, *MGH Epp. sel.* 2,1–2 (Berlin, 1920–3)

The Register of Pope Gregory VII, 1073–85: An English Translation, tr. H. E. J. Cowdrey (Oxford, 2002)

Les registres de Philippe Auguste, 1: Texte, ed. John Baldwin (Paris, 1992)

The Reign of Charlemagne: documents on Carolingian Government and Administration, eds. H. R. Loyn and John Percival (London, 1975)

El reino de Castilla el la epoca de Alfonso VIII, vol. II: Documentos 1145 a 1190, ed. Julio Gonzalez (Madrid, 1960)

Richer von Saint-Remi Historiae, ed. Hartmut Hoffmann, *MGH SS*, 38 (Hanover, 2000)

Roger II and the Creation of the Kingdom of Sicily, tr. Graham A. Loud (Manchester, 2012)

Rome Statute of the International Criminal Court, available at www.icc-cpi.int/NR/rdonlyres/ADD16852-AEE9-4757-ABE7-9CDC7CF02886/283503/RomeStatutEng1.pdf (accessed 16 July 2021)

Rufinus of Sorrento's *De Bono Pacis*, tr. Roman Deutinger (Hanover, 1997)

The Ruodlieb, tr. Gordon B. Ford (Leiden, 1965)

The Russian Primary Chronicle. The Laurentian Text, eds. S. H. Cross and O. P. Sherbowitz-Wetzor (Cambridge, MA, 1953)

Saga om baglarar og birkebeinar, in *Noregs kongesoger*, vol. 3, ed., Finn Hødnebø and Hallvard Magerøy (Oslo, 1979)

Sawyer, P. H., *Anglo-Saxon Charters: An Annotated List and Bibliography* (London, 1968), in its revised form available as the 'Electronic Sawyer' (www.esawyer.org.uk)

Saxo Grammaticus, *Gesta Danorum: the History of the Danes*, 2 vols., eds. Peter Fisher and Karsten Friis-Jensen (Oxford, 2015)

'Secret Supplementary Protocols of the Molotov-Ribbentrop Non-Aggression Pact, 1939', *History and Public Policy Program Digital Archive. Nazi-Soviet Relations, 1939–1941: Documents from the Archives of the German Foreign Office*, available at https://digitalarchive.wilsoncenter.org/document/110994 (accessed 16 July 2021)

Select Charters and Other Illustrations of English Constitutional History, ed. William Stubbs, 9th edn, rev. by H. W. C. Davis (Oxford, 1921)

Las Siete Partidas, Volume 4: Family, Commerce, and the Sea: the Worlds of Women and Merchants (Partidas IV and V), ed. Robert I. Burns (Philadelphia, 2000)

Some Letters of Saint Bernard, Abbott of Clairvaux, ed. F. A. Gasquet and tr. Samuel J. Eales (London, 1904)

A Sourcebook for Mediæval History, eds. Oliver J. Thatcher and Edgar Holmes McNeal (New York, 1905)

Sources for the History of Medieval Europe from the Mid-eighth to the Mid-thirteenth Century, ed. B. Pullan (Oxford, 1966)

Sources of Tibetan Tradition, eds. Kurtis R. Schaeffer et al. (New York, 2012)

Storia documentata di Venezia. Tomo 1, ed. S. Romanin (Venice, 1853)

Sveriges traktater med främmande magter. Första delen 822–1335, ed. O. S. Rydberg (Stockholm, 1877)

Symeonis monachis Opera Omnia, 2 vols., ed. T. Arnold (London, 1885)

Thietmari Merseburgensis Episcopi Chronicon, ed. J. M. Lappenberg (Hanover, 1889)

I trattati con Bisanzio, 992–1198, eds. M. Pozza and G. Ravegnani (Venice, 1993)

The Treatise on the Laws and Customs of the Realm of England commonly called Glanvill, ed. and tr. G. D. G. Hall (Oxford, 1993)

The Truce of Safar A.H. 359. December-January 969–970, ed. Wesam Farag (Birmingham, 1977)

Two of the Saxon Chronicles Parallel, 2 vols., ed. C. Plummer (Oxford, 1889–92; repr. 1952)

Die Urkunden der deutschen Könige und Kaiser. Erster Band. Die Urkunden Konrad I, Heinrich I und Otto I, ed. T. Sickel (Hanover, 1879–84)

Die Urkunden der deutschen Könige und Kaiser. Zweiten Bandes erster Theil. Die Urkunden Otto des II (Hanover, 1888)

Die Urkunden Friedrichs I, 4 vols., ed. H. Appelt (Hanover, 1975–90)

Die Urkunden Heinrichs V. und der Königin Mathilde, eds. Matthias Thiel and Alfred Gawlik, available at https://data.mgh.de/databases/ddhv/index.htm (accessed 16 July 2021)

Urkunden Heinrichs des Löwen, part I, ed. K. Jordan (Leipzig, 1941; repr. 1957)

Die Urkunden Lothars III. und der Kaiserin Richenza, eds. E. von Ottenthal and H. Hirsch (Berlin, 1927)

Urkunden zur älteren Handels und Staatsgeschichte der Republik Venedig, eds. G. Tafel and G. Thomas, 3 vols. (Vienna, 1857)

van Houts, E., 'The Anglo-Flemish treaty of 1101', *ANS*, 21 (1998)

The Visigothic Code: (Forum judicum), ed. S. P. Scott (Boston, 1910)

Walter Map, *De Nugis Curialium. Courtiers' Trifels*, tr. M. R. James, revised by C. N. L. Brooke and R. A. B. Mynors (Oxford, 1983)

Die Werke Wipos, ed. H. Bresslau, *MGH SRG*, 61 (Hanover, 1915)

Widukind of Corvey, *Deeds of the Saxons*, tr. Bernard S. Bachrach and David S. Bachrach (Washington, DC, 2014)

Widukindi monachi Corbeiensis Rerum gestarum Saxonicarum libri tres, eds. H. E. Lohmann and Paul Hirsch, *MGH SRG*, 60 (Hanover, 1935)

William of Newburgh, *The History of English Affairs, Book II*, eds. P. G. Walsh and M. J. Kennedy (Oxford, 2007)

Zimmermann, H., *Papsturkunden 896–1046*, 3 vols. (Vienna, 1984–9)

2002/584/JHA: Council Framework Decision of 13 June 2002 on the European arrest warrant and the surrender procedures between Member States, available at http://eur-lex.europa.eu/legal-content/EN/ALL/?uri=CELEX:32002F0584 (accessed 16 July 2021)

Secondary literature

Abbott, Kenneth W., and Snidal, Duncan, 'Hard and Soft Law in International Governance', *International Organization*, 54 (2000)

Abulafia, David, *The Two Italies. Economic Relations between the Norman Kingdom of Sicily and the Northern Communes* (Cambridge, 1977)

Airlie, Stuart, 'Narratives of Triumph and Rituals of Submission: Charlemagne's Mastering of Bavaria', *Transactions of the Royal Historical Society*, 9 (1999)

Allen, Richard, 'The Earliest Known List of Excommunicates from Ducal Normandy', *Journal of Medieval History*, 39 (2013)

Allott, Philip, 'The Concept of International Law', *European Journal of International Law*, 10 (1999)

—— 'State Responsibility and the Unmaking of International Law', *Harvard International Law Journal*, 29 (1988)

Althoff, Gerd, *Amicitiae und Pacta. Bündnis, Einigung, Politik und Gebetsgedenken im beginnenden 10. Jahrhundert* (Hanover, 1992)

—— 'Compositio. Wiederherstellung verletzter Ehre im Rahmen gütlicher Konfliktbeendigung', in *Verletzte Ehre. Ehrkonflikte in Gesellschaften des Mittelalters und der Frühen Neuzeit*, eds. Klaus Schreiner and G. Schwerhoff (Cologne, 1995)

—— *Die Macht der Rituale. Symbolik und Herrschaft im Mittelalter* (Darmstadt, 2003)

—— 'Satisfaction: Peculiarities of the Amicable Settlement of Conflicts in the Middle Ages', in *Ordering Medieval Society. Perspectives on Intellectual and Practical Modes of Shaping Social Relations*, ed. Bernhard Jussen, tr. Pamela Selwyn (Philadelphia, 2001)

—— *Spielregeln der Politik im Mittelalter: Kommunikation in Frieden und Fehde* (Darmstadt, 1997)

—— *Verwandte, Freunde und Getreue. Zum politischen Stellenwert der Gruppenbindungen im frühen Mittelalter* (Darmstadt, 1990)

Altman, Amnon, 'The Role of the "Historical Prologue" in the Hittite Vassal Treaties: An Early Experiment in Securing Treaty Compliance', *Journal of the History of International Law*, 6 (2004)

Amend-Traut, Anja, 'Legal Structure of Early Enterprises – from *Commenda*-like Arrangements to Chartered Joint-stock Companies', in *The Company in Law and Practice: Did Size Matter? (Middle Ages to Nineteenth Century)*, eds. Dave De Ruysscher et al. (Leiden, 2017)

Amerasinghe, C. F., 'The Historical Development of International Law – Universal Aspects', *Archiv des Völkerrechts*, 39 (2001)

Andersen, Per, *Legal Procedure and Practice in Medieval Denmark* (Leiden, 2011)

_____ 'The Use of Mediation and Arbitration in the Legal Revolution of 13th-century Denmark', in *Law and Disputing in the Middle Ages*, eds. Per Andersen et al. (Copenhagen, 2013)

Andersen, Per, et al., eds., *Law and Disputing in the Middle Ages* (Copenhagen, 2013)

Anderson, Stanley, 'Human Rights and the Structure of International Law', *New-York Law School Journal of International and Comparative Law*, 12 (1991)

Anderson, T. M., 'The Viking Policy of Ethelred the Unready', *Scandinavian Studies*, 53 (1987)

Arthur, Paige, 'How "Transitions" Reshaped Human Rights: A Conceptual History of Transitional Justice', *Human Rights Quarterly*, 31 (2009)

Asbridge, Thomas S., *The Creation of the Principality of Antioch 1098–1130* (Woodbridge, 2000)

Astuti, G., *Origini e svolgimento storico della commenda fino al secolo XIII* (Milan, 1933)

Baderin, Mashood A., 'Muhammad Al-Shaybānī (749/50–805)', in *Oxford Handbook of the History of International Law*, eds. Bardo Fassbender and Anne Peters (Oxford, 2012)

Baker, C., and Obradovic-Wochnik, J., 'Mapping the Nexus of Transitional Justice and Peacebuilding', *Journal of Intervention and Statebuilding*, 10 (2016)

Balasco, L. M., 'Reparative Development: Re-conceptualising Reparations in Transitional Justice Processes', *Conflict, Security and Development*, 17 (2017)

Banteka, Nadia, 'Mind the Gap: A Systematic Approach to the International Criminal Court's Arrest Warrants Enforcement Problem', *Cornell International Law Journal*, 49 (2016)

Bartlett, Robert, *The Making of Europe. Conquest, Colonization and Cultural Change 950–1350* (London, 1994)

_____ *Trial by Fire and Water: The Medieval Judicial Ordeal* (Oxford, 1986)

Bass, Gary J., *Stay the Hand of Vengeance: The Politics of War Crimes Tribunals* (Princeton, NJ, 2000)

Bauden, Frédéric, 'Due trattati di pace conclusi nel dodicesimo secolo tra i Banū Ġāniya, signori delle isole Baleari, e il commune di Genova', in *Documentos y manuscritos árabes del occidente musulmán medieval*, ed. Nuria Martínez de Castilla (Madrid, 2010)

Bauduin, Pierre, 'La papauté, les Vikings et les relations Anglo-Normandes: autour du traité de 991', in *Échanges, communications et réseaux dans le haut Moyen Âge*, eds. Alban Gautier and Céline Martin (Turnhout, 2011)

Beck, Jonathan, ' "Pro... salvament" in the Strasbourg Oaths: "Safety" or "Salvation"?', *Romance Philology*, 30 (1976)

Bederman, David J., *International Law in Antiquity* (Cambridge, 2004)

Behrens-Abouseif, Doris, *Practising Diplomacy in the Mamluk Sultanate: Gifts and Material Culture in the Medieval Islamic World* (London, 2016)

Bell, Christine, *On the Law of Peace: Peace Agreements and the Lex Pacificatoria* (Oxford, 2008)

——— 'Peace Agreements: Their Nature and Legal Status', *American Journal of International Law*, 100 (2006)

Bellomo, Elena, *The Templar Order in North-West Italy (1142–c.1330)* (Leiden, 2008)

Bellomo, Manlio, *The Common Legal Past of Europe, 1000–1800* (Washington, DC, 1995)

Benham, Jenny, 'Battle Writing and the Transition from Conflict to Peace', in *Writing Battles: Medieval and Modern Perspectives on Warfare and Memory in Northern Europe*, eds. Máire Ní Mhaonaigh, Rory Naismith, and Elizabeth Ashman Rowe (London, 2020)

——— 'A Changing Perception of War: The Role of Treaties from the Tenth to the Early Thirteenth Centuries', in *Battle and Bloodshed: The Medieval World at War*, eds. Lorna Bleach and Keira Borrill (Newcastle, 2013)

——— 'The Context of Peacemaking', in *The Nordic Civil Wars*, eds. Hans Jacob Orning, Jón Viðar Sigurðsson, and Kim Esmark (forthcoming 2022)

——— 'The Earliest Arbitration Treaty? A Re-assessment of the Anglo-Norman Treaty of 991', *Historical Research*, 93 (2020)

——— 'Law or Treaty? Defining the Edge of Legal Studies in the Early and High Medieval Periods', *Historical Research*, 86 (2013)

——— 'Peace, Security and Deterrence', in *A Cultural History of Peace in the Medieval Age 800–1450*, ed. Walter P. Simons (London, 2020)

——— 'The Peace of Venice (1177)', in *Encyclopedia of Diplomacy*, ed. Gordon Martel (London, 2018)

——— *Peacemaking in the Middle Ages: Principles and Practice* (Manchester, 2011; repr. 2017)

———— 'The Treaty of Verdun, 843' in *Encyclopedia of Diplomacy*, ed. Gordon Martel (London, 2018)

———— 'Writing Peace, Writing War: Roger of Howden and Saxo Grammaticus Compared', in *History and Intellectual Culture in the Long Twelfth Century: The Scandinavian Connection*, eds. Sigbjørn Sønnesyn, Mia Münster-Swendsen, and Thomas Heebøll-Holm (Durham, 2016)

———— 'Wounding in the High Middle Ages: Law and Practice', in *Wounds in the Middle Ages*, eds. Cordelia Warr and Anne Kirkham (Farnham, 2014)

Benham, Jenny, and Smith, Jamie, 'Transitional Justice in the Medieval World', in *Oxford Handbook of Transitional Justice*, eds. Lawrence Douglas, Alex Hinton, and Jens Meierheinrich (Oxford, forthcoming)

Benjamin, R., 'A Forty Years War: Toulouse and the Plantagenets, 1156–96', *Historical Research*, 61 (1988)

Benveniste, Henriette, 'Le système des amendes pénales en France au moyen âge: une première mise en perspective', *Revue historique de droit français et étranger*, 70 (1992)

Berdal, Mats, 'The "New Wars" Thesis Revisited', in *The Changing Character of War*, eds. H. Strachan and S. Scheipers (Oxford, 2011)

Bergeron, J., 'Transnational Organised Crime and International Security: A Primer', *The RUSI Journal*, 158 (2013)

Berglund, Cristofer, 'What is (Not) Asymmetric Conflict? From Conceptual Stretching to Conceptual Structuring', *Dynamics of Asymmetric Conflict*, 13 (2020)

Berman, Paul S., *Global Legal Pluralism. A Jurisprudence of Law Beyond Borders* (Cambridge, 2012)

Bernwieser, Johannes, *Honor civitatis. Kommunikation, Interaktion und Konfliktbeilegung im hochmittelalterlichen Oberitalien* (Munich, 2012)

Berto, Luigi Andrea, *The Political and Social Vocabulary of John the Deacon's 'Istoria Veneticorum'* (Turnhout, 2013)

Bertolini, O., 'Osservazioni sulla Constitutio Romana e sull Sacramentum Cleri et Populi Romani dell'anno 824', in his *Scritti scelti di storia medioevale*, 2 vols., ed. O. Banti (Livorno, 1968), II, 705–38

Binder, Christina, 'Stability and Change in Times of Fragmentation: The Limits of *Pacta Sunt Servanda* Revisited', *Leiden Journal of International Law*, 25 (2012)

Binder, Denis, 'Act of God? Or Act of Man? A Reappraisal of the Act of God Defense in Tort Law', *Review of Litigation*, 15 (1995)

Blaney, D., and Inayatullah, N., 'The Westphalian Deferral', *International Studies Review*, 2 (2000)

Blunt, C. E., 'The Coinage of Offa', in *Anglo-Saxon Coins Studies Presented to F.M. Stenton*, ed. R. H. M. Dolley (London, 1961)

Bohrer, Ziv, 'International Criminal Law's Millennium of Forgotten History', *Law and History Review*, 34 (2016)

Bongert, Y., *Recherches sur les cours laïques du Xe au XIIIe siècle* (Paris, 1949)

Boorman, J., 'The Sheriffs of Henry II and the Significance of 1170', in *Law and Government in Medieval England and Normandy. Essays in Honour of Sir James Holt*, eds. George Garnett and John Hudson (Cambridge, 1994)

Booth, Paul, 'King Alfred versus Beowulf: The Re-Education of the Anglo-Saxon Aristocracy', *Bulletin John Rylands Library*, 79 (1997)

Born, G. B., *International Arbitration: Cases and Materials* (Alphen, 2011)

Boudignon, Christian, ' "How am I to Love the One Who Hates Me?" Love for One's Enemy, Persecution and Human Rights in Maximus the Confessor', in *The Quest for a Common Humanity: Human Dignity and Otherness in the Religious Traditions of the Mediterranean*, ed. Matthias Morgenstern (Leiden, 2011)

Bourdieu, Pierre, 'The Force of Law: Toward a Sociology of the Juridical Field', *Hastings Law Journal*, 38 (1987)

Bowett, Derek, 'Treaties and State Responsibility', in *Le droit international au service de la paix, de la justice et du développement, Mélanges Michel Virally* (Paris, 1991)

Bowlus, Charles, 'The Early Hungarians as Mercenaries 860–955', in *Mercenaries and Paid Men. The Mercenary Identity in the Middle Ages*, ed. John France (Leiden, 2008)

Brady, Lindy, *Writing the Welsh Borderlands in Anglo-Saxon England* (Manchester, 2017)

Brown, K., 'Commemoration as Symbolic Reparation: New Narratives or Spaces of Conflict?', *Human Rights Review*, 14 (2013)

Brunner, Otto, *Land und Herrschaft* (Darmstadt, 1956)

Butler, William E., ed., *On the History of International Law and International Organization. Collected Papers of Sir Paul Vinogradoff* (Clark, NJ, 2009)

Byock, Jesse, *Viking Age Iceland* (London, 2001)

Byrne, E. H., 'Genoese Trade with Syria', *American Historical Review*, 25 (1920)

Calasso, Francesco, 'La città nell'Italia meridionale durante l'età Normanna', *Archivio Storico Pugliese*, 12 (1959)

Calmette, Joseph, *La diplomatie Carolingienne du traité de Verdun à la mort de Charles de Chauve (843–877)* (Paris, 1901)

Canning, Joseph, *History of Medieval Political Thought, 300–1450* (London, 2005)

Caporaso, J., 'Changes in the Westphalian Order: Territory, Public Authority, and Sovereignty', *International Studies Review*, 2 (2000)

Capps, Patrick, *Human Dignity and the Foundations of International Law* (Oxford, 2009)

Carabelli, Anna, and Cedrini, Mario, 'Global Imbalances, Monetary Disorder and Space: Keynes' Legacy for our Troubled World', *European Journal of Economics and Economic Policies: Intervention*, 7 (2010)

Carré, Yannick, *Le baiser sur la bouche au Moyen Âge* (Paris, 1992)

Cartelliere, Alexander, *Philipp II August. König von Frankreich*, 4 vols. (Leipzig, 1899–1906)

Cavaglieri, Arrigo, *I diritti fondamentali degli stati nella Società Internazionale* (Padua, 1906)

Chaplais, Pierre, *English Diplomatic Practice in the Middle Ages* (London, 2003)

—— 'The Letter from Bishop Wealdhere of London to Archbishop Brihtwold of Canterbury; the Earliest Original "Letter Close" Extant in the West', in *Medieval Scribes, Manuscripts and Libraries: Essays Presented to N. R. Ker*, eds. M. B. Parkes and A. G. Watson (London, 1978)

Chavarot, Marie-Claire, 'La pratique des lettres de marque d'après les arrêts du parlement (xiie-début xve siècle)', *Bibliothèque de l'école des chartes*, 149 (1991)

Cheyette, Frederic L., 'Giving Each His Due', in *Debating the Middle Ages*, eds. Lester K. Little and Barbara H. Rosenwein (Oxford, 1998)

—— '*Suum cuique tribuere*', *French Historical Studies*, 6 (1970)

Chick, Derek, 'Towards a Chronology for Offa's Coinage: An Interim Study', *The Yorkshire Numismatist*, 3 (1997), revised and repr. in *The Coinage of Offa and his Contemporaries*, eds. Mark Blackburn and Rory Naismith (London, 2010)

Chinking, C. M., 'Third-Party Intervention before the International Court of Justice', *American Journal of International Law*, 80 (1986)

Church, S. D., *King John, England and the Making of a Tyrant* (London, 2015)

Clapham, Christopher, 'Rwanda: The Perils of Peacemaking', *Journal of Peace Research*, 35 (1998)

Clark, Ian et al., 'Crisis in the Laws of War? Beyond Compliance and Effectiveness', *European Journal of International Relations*, 24 (2017)

Clark, J. N., 'The Three Rs: Retributive Justice, Restorative Justice, and Reconciliation', *Contemporary Justice Review*, 11 (2008)

Clarke, Peter D., *Interdict in the Thirteenth Century: A Question of Collective Guilt* (Oxford, 2007)

Classen, Peter, 'Bayern und die politischen Mächte im Zeitalter Karls des Grossen und Tassilos III', in *Ausgewählte Aufsätze*, ed. J. Fleckenstein (Sigmaringen, 1983)

Close, Josepha, *Amnesty, Serious Crimes and International Law. Global Perspectives in Theory and Practice* (Abingdon, 2019)

Colonna de Cesari-Rocca, R., *Recherches sur la Corse au Moyen âge: Origine de la rivalité des Pisans et des Génois en Corse, 1014–1174* (Genoa, 1901)

Colonomos, Ariel, and Armstrong, Andrea, 'German Reparations to the Jews after World War II: A Turning Point in the History of Reparations', in *The Handbook of Reparations*, ed. P. de Greiff (Oxford, 2006)

Constable, Giles, 'The Second Crusade as Seen by Contemporaries', *Traditio*, 9 (1953)

Corral, F. Luis, 'Alfonso VIII of Castile's Judicial Process at the Court of Henry II of England: An Effective and Valid Arbitration?', *Nottingham Medieval Studies*, 50 (2006)

Coupland, Simon, 'From Poachers to Gamekeepers: Scandinavian Warlords and Carolingian Kings', *Early Medieval Europe*, 7 (1998)

Cowen, Tyler, 'The Marshall Plan: Myths and Realities', in *US Aid to the Developing World*, ed. D. Bandow (Washington, DC, 1985)

Cox, Rory, 'The Ethics of War up to Thomas Aquinas', in *The Oxford Handbook of Ethics of War*, eds. S. Lazar and H. Frowe (Oxford, 2018)

Crawford, James, *The Creation of States in International Law*, 2nd edn. (Oxford, 2006)

—— *State Responsibility. The General Part* (Cambridge, 2013)

—— 'The System of International Responsibility', in *The Law of International Responsibility*, eds. James Crawford, Alain Pellet, and Simon Olleson (Oxford, 2010)

Cushing, Kathleen G., 'Papal Authority and its Limitations', in *Oxford Handbook of Medieval Christianity*, ed. John H. Arnold (Oxford, 2014)

Cutler, Anthony, 'Significant Gifts: Patterns of Exchange in Late Antique, Byzantine, and Early Islamic Diplomacy', *Journal of Medieval and Early Modern Studies*, 38 (2008)

Davies, Margaret, 'Legal Pluralism', *The Oxford Handbook of Empirical Legal Research*, eds. Peter Cane and Herbert M. Kritzer (Oxford, 2010)

Davies, R. H. C., 'Alfred and Guthrum's Frontier', *English Historical Review*, 97 (1982)

Davies, R. R., 'Frontier Arrangements in Fragmented Societies: Ireland and Wales', in *Medieval Frontier Societies*, eds. R. Bartlett and Angus MacKay (Oxford, 1989)

—— 'The Medieval State: The Tyranny of a Concept?', *Journal of Historical Sociology*, 16 (2003)

Davis, Jennifer R., 'A Pattern for Power: Charlemagne's Delegation of Judicial Responsibilities', in *The Long Morning of Medieval Europe*, eds. Jennifer R. Davis and Michael McCormick (Aldershot, 2008)

Davison-Vecchione, D., 'Beyond the Forms of Faith: *Pacta Sunt Servanda* and Loyalty', *German Law Journal*, 16 (2015)

de Jong, Mayke, 'The Two Republics. *Ecclesia* and the Public Domain in the Carolingian World', in *Italy and Early Medieval Europe. Papers for Chris Wickham*, eds. Ross Balzaretti, Julia Barrow, and Patricia Skinner (Oxford, 2018)

Depreux, Philippe, 'Gestures and Comportment at the Carolingian Court: Between Practice and Perception', *Past & Present*, 203 (2009)

—— 'Tassilon III et le roi des Francs: examen d'une vassalité controversée', *Revue Historique*, 293 (1995)

de Robertis, F. M., *La responsabilità contrattuale nel diritto romano dalle origini a tutta l'età postclassica* (Bari, 1996)

Desierto, Diane A., *Necessity and National Emergency Clauses: Sovereignty in Modern Treaty Interpretation* (Leiden, 2012)

Devroey, Jean-Pierre, 'Monastic Economics in the Carolingian Age', in *The Cambridge History of Medieval Monasticism in the Latin West*, eds. Alison I. Beach and Isabelle Cochelin (Cambridge, 2020)

Dickerhof, Harald, 'Wandlungen im Rechtsdenken der Salierzeit am Beispiel der lex naturalis and des ius gentium', in *Die Salier und das Reich*, 3 vols., ed. Stefan Weinfurter (Sigmaringen, 1991)

Dilcher, Gerhard, 'Fehde, Unrechtsausgleich und Strafe im älteren langobardischen Recht: Eine Skizze', in *Hoheitliches Strafen in der Spätantike und im frühen Mittelalter*, ed. Jürgen Weitzel (Cologne, 2002)

Dixon, Martin, *Textbook on International Law*, 7th edn. (Oxford, 2013)

Dolezalek, G., 'I commentari di Odofredo e Baldo alla pace di Constanza', in *La pace di Costanza 1183* (Bologna, 1984)

Downs, George W., and Jones, Michael A., 'Reputation, Compliance and International Law', *The Journal of Legal Studies*, 31 (2002)

Dreillard, Rodolphe, ' "A jure foederis recedente": respect et irrespect des traités dans le monde franc au VIII siècle', in *L'autorité du passé dans les sociétés médiévales*, ed. Jean-Maries Sansterre (Rome, 2004)

Drocourt, Nicholas, 'Les animaux comme cadeaux d'ambassade entre Byzance et ses voisins (VIIe–XIIe siècle)', in *Byzance et ses périphéries: Hommage à Alain Ducellier*, eds. Bernard Doumerc and Christophe Picard (Toulouse, 2004)

—— 'Passing on Political Information between Major Powers: The Key Role of Ambassadors between Byzantium and Some of its Neighbours', *Al-Masaq: Journal of the Medieval Mediterranean*, 24 (2012)

Duchhardt, H., ' "Westphalian System". Zur Problematik einer Denkfigur', *Historische Zeitschrift*, 269 (1999)

Dubber, Markus, and Hörnle, Tatjana, *Criminal Law: A Comparative Approach* (Oxford, 2014)

Dunoff, Jeffrey L., Ratner, Steven R., and Wippman, David, *International Law: Norms, Actors, Process* (Aspen, 2006)

Druzin, Brian, 'Towards a Theory of Spontaneous Legal Standardization', *Journal of International Dispute Settlement*, 8 (2017)

Elster, Jon, *Closing the Books: Transitional Justice in Historical Perspective* (Cambridge, 2004)

Engels, O., 'Friedrich Barbarossa und Dänemark', *Vorträge und Forschungen*, 40 (1992)

Epstein, Steven A., *Genoa and the Genoese 958–1528* (Chapel Hill, NC, 1996)

Esders, Stefan, 'Wergeld und soziale Netzwerke im Frankenreich', in *Verwandtschaft, Name und soziale Ordnung (300–1100)*, eds. Steffen Patzold and Karl Ubl (Berlin, 2014)

Esders, Stefan, and Schuppert, Gunnar Folke, *Mittelalterliches Regieren in der Moderne oder modernes Regieren im Mittelalter?* (Baden-Baden, 2015)

Falkner, Robert, 'Rethinking Europe's External Relations in an Age of Global Turmoil: An Introduction', *International Politics*, 54 (2017)

Fanta, A., 'Die Verträge der Kaiser mit Venedig bis zum Jahre 983', *Mitteilungen des Instituts für Österreichische Geschichtsforschung, Ergänzungsband*, 1 (1885)

Farhang, Cliff, 'The Notion of Consent in Part One of the Draft Articles on State Responsibility', *Leiden Journal of International Law*, 27 (2014)

Farquharson, J., 'Marshall Aid and British Policy on Reparations from Germany, 1947–1949', *Review of International Studies*, 22 (1996)

Fedele, Dante, 'Indemnities in Diplomacy', in *The Encyclopedia of Diplomacy*, ed. Gordon Martel (London, 2018)

Feldbrugge, F., *Law in Medieval Russia* (Leiden, 2009)

Fell, C., 'Unfrið: An Approach to a Definition', *Saga-Book of the Viking Society for Northern Research*, 21 (1982–3)

Fenster, Thelma S., and Smail, Daniel Lord (eds.), *Fama: The Politics of Talk and Reputation in Medieval Europe* (Ithaca, NY, 2003)

Fisch, Jörg, 'Peoples and Nations', in *Oxford Handbook of the History of International Law*, eds. Bardo Fassbender and Anne Peters (Oxford, 2012)

Fletcher, George P., 'Parochial Versus Universal Criminal Law', *Journal of International Criminal Justice*, 3 (2005)

Ford, Lisa, *Settler Sovereignty: Jurisdiction and Indigenous People in America and Australia, 1788–1836* (Cambridge, MA, 2010)

Fordham, Michael, 'Peacekeeping and Order on the Anglo-Welsh Frontier in the Early Tenth Century', *Midland History*, 32 (2007)

Forstein, C., 'Challenging Extradition: The Doctrine of Specialty in Customary International Law', *Columbia Journal of International Law*, 53 (2015)

Fowler, Linda, 'Forms of Arbitration', in *Proceedings of the Fourth International Congress of Medieval Canon Law*, ed. S. Kuttner (Vatican City, 1972)

Fraley, Jill M., 'Re-examining Acts of God', *Pace Environmental Law Review*, 27 (2010)

Frankopan, Peter, 'Byzantine Trade Privileges to Venice in the Eleventh Century: The Chrysobull of 1092', *Journal of Medieval History*, 30 (2004)

Frankot, Edda, *Of Laws of Ship and Shipmen: Medieval Maritime Law and its Practice* (Edinburgh, 2012)

Fraser, Henry S., 'Sketch of the History of International Arbitration', *Cornell Law Review*, 11 (1926)

Fried, Johannes, 'Der karolingische Herrschaftsverband im 9. Jahrhundert zwischen "Kirche" und "Königshaus"', *Historische Zeitschrift*, 235 (1982)

Gaiser, Adam, 'Slaves and Silver across the Strait of Gibraltar: Politics and Trade between Umayyad Iberia and Khārijite North Africa', *Medieval Encounters*, 19 (2013), 41–70.

Galanter, Marc, and Luban, David, 'Poetic Justice: Punitive Damages and Legal Pluralism', *American University Law Review*, 42 (1993)

Ganshof, F. L., 'The Genesis and Significance of the Treaty of Verdun (843)', in *The Carolingians and the Frankish Monarchy*, tr. J. Sondheimer (London, 1971)

——— 'Les traités des rois mérovingiens', *Tijdschrift voor Rechsgeschiedenis*, 32 (1964)

——— *The Middle Ages. A History of International Relations*, 4th edn., tr. Rémy Inglis Hall (London, 1968)

——— 'Note sur le premier traité anglo-flamand de Douvres', *Revue du Nord*, 40 (1958)

——— 'The Treaties of the Carolingians', *Medieval and Renaissance Studies*, 3 (1967)

Gasparri, Stefano, 'The First Dukes and the Origins of Venice', in *Venice and its Neighbors from the 8th to the 11th Century. Through Renovation and Continuity*, eds. Sauro Gelichi and Stefano Gasparri (Leiden, 2017)

——— 'Venezia fra l'Italia bizantina e il regno italico: la civitas e l'assemblea', in *Venezia. Itinerari per la storia della città*, eds. S. Gasparri, G. Levi, and P. Moro (Bologna, 1997)

Gazzini, Tarcisio, Werner, Wouter G., and Dekker, Ige F., 'Necessity across International Law: An Introduction', *Netherlands Yearbook of International Law*, 41 (2010)

Geary, Patrick J., 'Land, Language and Memory in Europe, 700–1100', *Transactions of the Royal Historical Society*, 9 (1999)

———— 'Oathtaking and Conflict Management in the Ninth Century', in *Rechtsverständnis und Handlungsstrategien im mittelalterlichen Konfliktaustrag: Festschrift für Hanna Vollrath*, eds. Stefan Esders and Christine Reinle (Munich, 2007)

Gebhardt, J. H., '*Pacta Sunt Servanda*', *Modern Law Review*, 10 (1947)

Géraud, H., 'Les routiers au douzième siècle', *Bibliothèque de l'école des chartes*, 3 (1842)

Ghignoli, Antonella, and Bougard, François, 'Elementi romani nei documenti longobardi?', in *L'héritage byzantin en Italie (VIIIe-XIIe siècle). I. La fabrique documentaire*, ed. J.-M. Martin, A. Peters-Custot, and V. Prigent (Rome, 2011)

Gialdroni, Stefania, '*Propter Conversationem Diversarum Gentium*: Migrating Words and Merchants in Medieval Pisa', in *Migrating Word, Migrating Merchants, Migrating Law*, eds. Stefania Gialdroni et al. (Leiden, 2020)

Giese, Wolfgang, 'Venedig-Politik und Imperiums-Idee bei den Ottonen', in *Herrschaft, Kirche, Kultur. Beiträge zur Geschichte des Mittelalters. Festschrift für Friedrich Prinz zu seinem 65. Geburtstag*, ed. Georg Jenal (Stuttgart, 1993)

Gillet, Andrew, *Envoys and Political Communication in the Late Antique West, 411–533* (Cambridge, 2003)

Gillingham, John, *Richard I* (New Haven, 1999)

———— 'Surrender in Medieval Europe – an Indirect Approach', in *How Fighting Ends: A History of Surrender*, eds. Holger Afflerbach and Hew Strachan (Oxford, 2012)

Gniazdowski, Mateusz, 'The Problem of War Reparations: The Perspective of the Czech Republic', *The Polish Foreign Affairs Digest*, 4 (2004)

Godfrey, John, 'The Defeated Anglo-Saxons Take Service with the Eastern Emperor', *Anglo-Norman Studies*, 1 (1978)

Goebel, Julius, *Felony and Misdemeanor: A Study in the History of English Criminal Procedure* (New York, 1937; repr., 1976)

Goetz, Hans-Werner, 'Die Wahrnehmung von "Staat" und "Herrschaft" im frühen Mittelalter', in *Staat im frühen Mittelalter* (Vienna, 2006)

———— '*Regnum*. Zum politischen Denken der Karolingerzeit', *Zeitschrift der Savigny-Stiftung für Rechtsgeschichte, Germanische Abteilung*, 104 (1987)

Goffart, Walter, ' "Defensio Patriae" as a Carolingian Military Obligation', *Francia*, 43 (2016)

Goodhand, J., 'Corrupting or Consolidating the Peace? The Drugs Economy and Post-Conflict Peacebuilding in Afghanistan', *International Peacekeeping*, 15 (2008)

Grewe, Wilhelm G., *The Epochs of International Law*, tr. Michel Byers (Berlin, 2000)

—— 'Peace Treaties', in *Encyclopedia of Public International Law: Use of Force. War and Neutrality. Peace Treaties, vol. 4*, ed. Rudolf Bernhardt (Amsterdam, 1982)

Grierson, Philippe, 'The Relations between England and Flanders before the Norman Conquest', *Transactions of the Royal Historical Society*, 4th ser., 23 (1941)

Grygiel, Jakub, 'The Primacy of Premodern History', *Security Studies*, 22 (2013)

Gupta, Sunil Kumar, 'Sanctum for the War Criminal: Extradition Law and the International Criminal Court', *Berkeley Journal of Criminal Law*, 3 (2000)

Güterbock, Ferdinand, 'Alla vigilia della Lega Lombarda', *Archivio storico italiano*, 95 (1937)

Görich, Knut, *Die Ehre Friedrich Barbarossas: Kommunikation, Konflikt und politisches Handeln im 12. Jahrhundert* (Darmstadt, 2001)

Hahn, Adalheid, 'Das *Hludowicianum*. Die Urkunde Ludwig den Fromme für die römische Kirche von 817', *Archiv für Diplomatik*, 21 (1975)

Hallenbeck, Jan T., 'Instances of Peace in Eighth-Century Lombard-Papal Relations', *Archivum Historiae Pontificae*, 18 (1980)

Halphen, Louis, 'La justice en France au XIᵉ siècle', in *A travers l'histoire du moyen âge* (Paris, 1950)

Halsall, Guy, *Warfare and Society in the Barbarian West, 450–900* (London: Routledge, 2003)

Haltern, Ulrich, *Was bedeutet Souveränität?* (Tübingen, 2007)

Harding, Alan, *Medieval Law and the Foundations of the State* (Oxford, 2002)

Hartmann, L. M., *Zur Wirtschaftsgeschichte Italiens im frühen Mittelalter* (Gotha, 1904)

Hathaway, O., 'Do Human Rights Treaties Make a Difference?', *The Yale Law Journal*, 111 (2002)

Hathaway, O., and Shapiro, S. J., 'Outcasting: Enforcement in Domestic and International Law', *The Yale Law Journal*, 121 (2011)

Haug, Henrike, 'The Struggle for Sardinia in the Twelfth Century: Textual and Architectural Evidence from Genoa and Pisa', in *A Companion to Sardinian History 500–1500*, ed. M. Hobart (Leiden, 2017)

Heebøll-Holm, Thomas, *Ports, Piracy and Maritime War: Piracy in the English Channel and the Atlantic, c. 1280-c. 1330* (Leiden, 2013)

Heinemeyer, W., 'Der Friede von *Montebello* (1175)', *Deutsches Archiv für Erforschung des Mittelalters*, 11 (1954)

Helfer, Laurence R., 'The Effectiveness of International Adjudicators', in *The Oxford Handbook of International Adjudication*, eds. Cesare P. R. Romano, Karen J. Alter, and Yuval Shany (Oxford, 2013)

Hershey, A. S., 'The History of International Relations during Antiquity and the Middle Ages', *American Journal of International Law*, 5 (1911)

Hines, John, 'Units of Account in Gold and Silver in Seventh-Century England: *Scillingas, Sceattas* and *Pæningas*', *The Antiquaries Journal*, 90 (2010)

—————— 'Erratum – Units of Account in Gold and Silver in Seventh-Century England: *Scillingas, Sceattas* and *Pæningas*', *The Antiquaries Journal*, 91 (2011)

Hoffman, Geoffrey A., 'Critique, Culture and Commitment: The Dangerous and Counterproductive Paths of International Legal Discourse', *Dalhousie Law Journal*, 27 (2004)

Holdsworth, Christopher, 'Peacemaking in the Twelfth Century', *Anglo-Norman Studies*, 19 (1998)

Holzgrefe, J. L., 'The Origins of Modern International Relations Theory', *RIS*, 15 (1989)

Hough, Carole, 'Cattle-tracking in the Fonthill Letter', *English Historical Review*, 115 (2000)

Houlihan, James W., '*Lex Innocentium* (697 AD): Adomnán of Iona – Father of Western *jus in bello*', *International Review of the Red Cross*, 101 (2019)

Hudson, J. G. H., *The Oxford History of the Laws of England. Volume II, 871–1216* (Oxford, 2012)

—————— 'Feud, Vengeance and Violence in England from the Tenth to the Twelfth Centuries', in *Feud, Violence and Practice: Essays in Medieval Studies in Honor of Stephen D. White*, eds. Belle S. Tuten and Tracy L. Billado (Farnham, 2010)

—————— 'Court Cases and Legal Arguments in England, c. 1066–1166', *Transactions of the Royal Historical Society*, 10 (2000)

Humfress, Caroline, 'Thinking through the Lens of Legal Pluralism: "Forum Shopping" in the Later Roman Empire', in *Law and Empire: Ideas, Practices, Actors*, eds. J. Duindam, Jill Harries, Caroline Humfress, and N. Hurvitz (Leiden, 2013)

Hyams, Paul R., 'Henry II and Ganelon', *Syracuse Scholar*, iv (1983)

—————— *Rancor and Reconciliation in Medieval England* (Ithaca, NY, 2003)

Iverson, J., 'Transitional Justice, Jus Post Bellum and International Criminal Law: Differentiating the Usages, History and Dynamics', *The International Journal of Transitional Justice*, 7 (2013)

Jamieson, Neil, '"Sons of Iniquity": The Problem of Unlawfulness and Criminality amongst Professional Soldiers in the Middle-Ages', in *Outlaws in Medieval and Early Modern England*, eds. John C. Appleby and Paul Dalton (Burlington, VT, 2009)

Jaspert, Nikolas, ' "Capta est Dertosa clavis Cristianorum": Tortosa and the Crusades', in *The Second Crusade: Scope and Consequences*, eds Jonathan Phillips and Martin Hoch (Manchester, 2001)

Jenks, Stuart, 'Friedensvorstellungen der Hanse (1356–1474)', *Vorträge und Forschungen: Träger und Instrumentarien des Friedens im hohen und späten Mittelalter*, 43 (1996)

John, Eric 'War and Society in the Tenth Century: The Maldon Campaign', *Transactions of the Royal Historical Society*, 5th ser., 27 (1977)

Johnson, Ewan, 'The Process of Norman Exile into Southern Italy', in *Exile in the Middle Ages*, eds. Laura Napran and Elisabeth van Houts (Turnhout, 2004)

Johnson, Tom, 'Medieval Law and Materiality: Shipwrecks, Finders, and Property on the Suffolk Coast, ca. 1380–1410', *American Historical Review*, 120 (2015)

Jordan, William Chester, *From England to France: Felony and Exile in the High Middle Ages* (Princeton, NJ, 2015)

Judde de Larivière, Claire, 'Du sceau au passeport: genèse des pratiques médiévales de l'identification', in *L'identification. Genèse d'un travail d'État*, ed. Gérard Noiriel (Paris, 2007)

Kaeding, Susanne, Seidel, Kerstin, and Kümmerlen, Britta, 'Heinrich I. – ein Freundschaftskönig?', *Concilium medii aevi*, 3 (2000)

Kaldor, Mary, 'In Defence of New Wars', *Stability*, 2 (2013)

_____ 'How Peace Agreements Undermine the Rule of Law in New War Settings', *Global Policy*, 7 (2016)

Kamp, Hermann, *Friedensstifter und Vermittler im Mittelalter* (Darmstadt, 2001)

_____ 'Soziologie der Mediation aus historischer Perspektive', *Zeitschrift für Rechtssoziologie*, 36 (2016)

_____ 'Vermittlung in der internationalen Politik des spaten Mittelalters', in *Frieden stiften. Vermittlung und Konfliktlösung vom Mittelalter bis heute*, ed. Gerd Althoff (Darmstadt, 2011)

Karn, Nicholas, *Kings, Lords and Courts in Anglo-Norman England* (Woodbridge, 2020)

Kedar, Benjamin Z., 'Again, Genoa's Golden Inscription and King Baldwin I's Privilege of 1104', in *Chemins d'outre-mer. Etudes d'histoire sur la Méditerranée médiévale offertes à Michel Balard*, eds. Damien Coulon et al. (Paris, 2004)

Keen, Maurice, *Laws of War in the Late Middle Ages* (London, 1965)

_____ *The Outlaws of Medieval Legend* (London, 2000; repr. 2007)

Kennedy, Hugh, *Muslim Spain and Portugal. A Political History of al-Andalus* (London, 1996)

Kern, Fritz, *Kingship and Law in the Middle Ages* (New York, 1970)

Kershaw J., and Naismith, R., 'A New Late Anglo-Saxon Seal Matrix', *Anglo-Saxon England*, 42 (2013)

Kershaw, Paul J. E., 'The Alfred-Guthrum Treaty: Scripting Accommodation and Interaction in Viking Age England', in *Cultures in Contact: Scandinavian Settlement in England in the Ninth and Tenth Centuries*, eds. Dawn Hadley and Julian D. Richards (Turnhout, 2000)

—— *Peaceful Kings. Peace, Power and the Early Medieval Political Imagination* (Oxford, 2011)

Keynes, Simon, 'Historical Context', in *The Battle of Maldon AD 991*, ed. Donald Scragg (Oxford, 1991)

Khalilieh, Hassan S., *Admiralty and Maritime Laws in the Mediterranean Sea (ca. 800–1050): The Kitāb Akriyat Al-Sufun Vis-a-vis the Nomos Rhodion Nautikos* (Leiden, 2006)

Kilger, Christoph, 'Silver, Land, Towns, and the Elites. Social and Legal Aspects of Silver in Scandinavia c. 850–1150', in *Nordic Elites in Transformation c. 1050–1250. Volume I: Material Resources*, eds. Bjørn Poulsen, Helle Vogt, and Jón Viðar Sigurðsson (London, 2019)

King, Henry T. Jr., and Le Forestier, Marc A., 'Papal Arbitration: How the Early Roman Catholic Church Influenced Modern Dispute Resolution', *Dispute Resolution Journal*, 52 (1997)

Kinsella, Helen M., and Mantilla, Giovanni, 'Contestation before Compliance: History, Politics, and Power in International Humanitarian Law', *International Studies Quarterly*, 64 (2020)

Kintzinger, Martin, 'From the Late Middle Ages to the Peace of Westphalia', in *Oxford Handbook of the History of International Law*, eds. Bardo Fassbender and Anne Peters (Oxford, 2012)

Koh, Harold Hongju, 'Why Do Nations Obey International Law?', *Yale Law Journal*, 106 (1997)

Kolb, Werner, *Herrscherbegegnungen im Mittelalter* (Frankfurt, 1988)

Koskenniemi, Martti, 'Histories of International Law: Dealing with Eurocentrism', *Rechtsgeschichte*, 19 (2011)

Kosto, Adam J., *Hostages in the Middle Ages* (Oxford, 2012)

—— *Making Agreements in Medieval Catalonia. Power, Order and the Written Word,1000–1200* (Cambridge, 2001)

Koziol, Geoffrey, *Begging Pardon and Favor: Ritual and Political Order in Early Medieval France* (Ithaca, NY, 1992)

—— *The Peace of God* (Leeds, 2018)

—— *The Politics of Memory and Identity in Carolingian Royal Diplomas. The West Frankish Kingdom (840–987)* (Turnhout, 2012)

Kreutz, Barbara M., *Before the Normans* (Philadelphia, 1996)

Kuklick, B., *American Policy and the Division of Germany: The Clash with Russia over Reparations* (Ithaca, NY, 1972)

Lacarra, J. M., 'Dos Tratados de paz y alianza entre Sancho el de Peñalén y Moctádir de Zaragoza (1069 y 1073)', in *Homenaje a Johannes Vincke*, 2 vols. (Madrid, 1962–3)

Lambert, Tom, *Law and Order in Anglo-Saxon England* (Oxford, 2016)

Lambton, A. K. S., 'Justice in the Medieval Persian Theory of Kingship', *Studia Islamica*, 17 (1962)

Landauer, Carl, 'The Ever-Ending Geography of International Law: The Changing Nature of the International System and the Challenge to International Law: A Reply to Daniel Bethlehem', *European Journal of International Law*, 25 (2014)

Landon, L., *The Itinerary of King Richard I* (London, 1935)

Lanoszka, Alexander, 'Russian Hybrid Warfare and Extended Deterrence in Eastern Europe', *International Affairs*, 92 (2016)

Laudage, Johannes, *Alexander III. und Friedrich Barbarossa* (Cologne, 1997)

Le Goff, Jacques, 'The Symbolic Ritual of Vassalage', in *Time, Work and Culture in the Middle Ages*, tr. Arthur Goldhammer (Chicago, 1980)

Le Jan, Régine, 'Les relations diplomatique pendant le premier Moyer Age (VIᵉ–XIᵉ siècle)', in *Les relations diplomatiques au Moyen Age. Formes et Enjeux*, ed. Société des historiens médiévistes de l'Enseignement supérieur public (Paris, 2011)

Lesaffer, Randall, 'International Law and its History: The Story of an Unrequited Love', in *Time, History and International Law*, eds. M Craven et al. (Leiden, 2006)

―――― 'Peace Treaties and the Formation of International Law', in *The Oxford Handbook of the History of International Law*, eds. Bardo Fassbender and Anne Peters (Oxford, 2012)

―――― 'Wiping the Slate Clean… for Now: Amnesty Clauses in Early-Modern Peace Treaties', available at https://opil.ouplaw.com/page/amnesty-peace-treaties (accessed 16 July 2021)

Lewis, Kevin James, *The Counts of Tripoli and Lebanon in the Twelfth Century: Sons of Saint-Gilles* (Abingdon, 2017)

Leyser, Karl, 'Henry I and the Beginnings of the Saxon Empire', *English Historical Review*, 83 (1968)

Li, Fang-Kuei, 'The Inscription of the Sino-Tibetan Treaty of 821–2', *T'oung Pao*, 44 (1956)

Loud, Graham A., *The Age of Robert Guiscard: Southern Italy and the Norman Conquest* (Harlow, 2000)

Lowe, Vaughan, 'Precluding Wrongfulness or Responsibility: A Plea for Excuses', *European Journal of International Law*, 10 (1999)

Lund, Niels, 'Peace and Non-Peace in the Viking Age: Ottar in Biarmaland, the Rus in Byzantium and Danes and Norwegians in

England', in *Proceedings of the Tenth Viking Congress*, ed. J. E. Knirk (Oslo, 1987)

Lung, Ecaterina, 'Barbarian Envoys at Byzantium in the 6th Century', *Hiperboreea Journal*, 2 (2015)

Lupoi, Maurizio, *The Origins of the European Legal Order* (Cambridge, 2000)

Lyons, S. W., 'Ineffective Amnesty: The Legal Impact on Negotiating the End to Conflict', *Wake Forest Law Review*, 47 (2013)

Madden, Thomas F., 'The Chrysobull of Alexius I Comnenus to the Venetians: the Date and the Debate', *Journal of Medieval History*, 28 (2002)

Madden Dempsey, Michelle, 'Victimless Conduct and the Volenti Maxim: How Consent Works', *Criminal Law and Philosophy*, 7 (2013)

Magnou-Nortier, Elisabeth, 'The Enemies of the Peace: Reflections on a Vocabulary, 500–1100', in *The Peace of God: Social Violence and Religious Response in France around the Year 1000*, eds. Thomas Head and Richard Landes (Ithaca, NY, 1992)

Maleczek, Werner, 'Das Frieden stiftende Papsttum im 12. und 13. Jahrhundert', *Vorträge und Forschungen: Träger und Instrumentarien des Friedens im hohen und späten Mittelalter*, 43 (1996)

Malegam, Jehangir Y., 'Suspicions of Peace in Medieval Christian Discourse', *Common Knowledge*, 21 (2015)

Mallard, Grégoire, ' "The Gift" Revisited: Marcel Mauss on War, Debt, and the Politics of Reparations', *Sociological Theory*, 29 (2011)

Marmor, Andrei, 'The Nature of Law', *Stanford Encyclopedia of Philosophy*, ed. Edward N. Zalta (2011), available at http://plato.stanford.edu/archives/win2011/entries/lawphil-nature/ (accessed 16 July 2021)

Martin, Jean-Marie, *Guerre, accords et frontières en Italie méridionale pendant le haut Moyen Âge* (Rome, 2005)

Martinez, Jenny S., *The Slave Trade and the Origins of International Human Rights Law* (Oxford, 2012)

Mas Latrie, René de, *Du droit de marque ou droit de représailles au moyen-âge* (Paris, 1875)

Matthew, D., *The Norman Kingdom of Sicily* (Cambridge, 1992)

Mavroidis, Petros C., 'Licence to Adjudicate: A Critical Evaluation of Appellate Body So Far', in *Trade Disputes and the Dispute Settlement of the WTO: An Interdisciplinary Assessment*, ed. James C. Hartigan (Bingley, 2009)

McEvoy, Kieran, and Mallinder, Louise, 'Amnesties in Transition: Punishment, Restoration, and the Governance of Mercy', *Journal of Law and Society*, 39 (2012)

McHaffie, Matthew, 'Law and Violence in Eleventh-century France', *Past & Present*, 238 (2018)

—— 'Mercy and the Violence of Law', *The Mediaeval Journal* (forthcoming).

McKitterick, Rosamond, 'Latin and Romance: An Historian's Perspective', in *The Frankish Kings and Culture in the Early Middle Ages*, ed. Rosamond McKitterick (Aldershot, 1995)

Meens, Rob, 'Penitential Questions: Sin, Satisfaction and Reconciliation in the Tenth and Eleventh Centuries', *Early Medieval Europe*, 14 (2006)

Mercer, Jonathan, *Reputation and International Politics* (Ithaca, NY, 2018)

Merrell, James H., '"I Desire All That I Have Said ... May Be Taken down Aright": Revisiting Teedyuscung's 1756 Treaty Council Speeches', *The William and Mary Quarterly*, 63 (2006)

Middleton, Neil, 'Early Medieval Port Customs, Tolls and Controls on Foreign Trade', *Early Medieval Europe*, 13 (2005)

Milani, Giuliano, *L'esclusione dal comune: conflitti e bandi politici a Bologna e in altre città italiane tra XII e XIV secolo* (Rome, 2003)

Miller, William I., 'Avoiding Legal Judgment. The Submission of Disputes to Arbitration in Medieval Iceland', *American Journal of Legal History*, 28 (1984)

Millward, A. S., *The Reconstruction of Western Europe, 1945–1951* (Berkeley, 1984)

Moeglin, Jean-Marie, 'Harmiscara – harmschar – hachée. Le dossier des rituels d'humiliation et de soumission au Moyen Age', *Archivum Latinitatis Medii Aevi*, 54 (1996)

—— 'Pénitence publique et amende honorable au Moyen Âge', *Revue Historique*, 298 (1997)

—— '"Performative turn", "communication politique" et rituels au Moyen Age. À propos de deux ouvrages récents', *Le Moyen Age*, 113 (2007)

Moeglin, Jean-Marie, and Péquignot, Stéphane, *Diplomatie et 'relations internationales' au Moyen-Âge (IXe – XVe siècle)* (Paris, 2017)

Molyneaux, George, 'The *Ordinance Concerning the Dunsæte* and the Anglo-Welsh Frontier in the Late Tenth and Eleventh Centuries', *Anglo-Saxon England*, 40 (2012)

Montanari, Massimo, 'Il capitolare di Liutprando: note di storia dell'economia e dell'alimentazione', in *La Civiltà Comacchiese e Pomposiana dalle origini preistoriche al tardo medioevo* (Bologna, 1986)

Moore, Michael E., 'Wolves, Outlaws and Enemy Combatants', in *Cultural Studies of the Modern Middle Ages*, eds. E. Joy et al. (New York, 2007)

Morgan, Patrick M., 'The State of Deterrence in International Politics Today', *Contemporary Security Policy*, 33 (2012)

Murphy, Anthony, and Stancescu, Vlad, 'State Formation and Recognition in International Law', *Juridical Tribune*, 7 (2017)

Murray, Williamson, and Mansoor, Peter R., *Hybrid Warfare: Fighting Complex Opponents from the Ancient World to the Present* (Cambridge, 2012)

Muthesius, Anna Maria, 'Silk, Power and Diplomacy in Byzantium', in *Textiles in Daily Life. Proceedings of the Third Biennial Symposium of the Textile Society of America, September 24–26, 1992, Seattle* (Textile Society of America, 1993)

Napran, Laura, and Houts, Elisabeth van (eds.), *Exile in the Middle Ages* (Turnhout, 2004)

Neff, Stephen C., *Justice among Nations: A History of International Law* (Cambridge, MA, 2014)

––––––– *War and the Law of Nations* (Cambridge, 2005)

Nelson, Janet L., 'Alfred of Wessex at a Cross-roads in the History of Education', *History of Education*, 6 (2013)

––––––– 'Dispute Settlement in Carolingian West Frankia', in *The Settlement of Disputes in Early Medieval Europe*, eds. Wendy Davis and Paul Fouracre (Cambridge, 1986)

––––––– ' "A King Across the Sea": Alfred in Continental Perspective', *Transactions of the Royal Historical Society*, 36 (1986)

––––––– 'Kingdom and Empire in the Carolingian World', in *Carolingian Culture: Emulation and Innovation*, ed. Rosamond McKitterick (Cambridge, 1993)

––––––– 'Public Histories and Private History in the Work of Nithard', *Speculum*, 60 (1985)

––––––– 'The Role of the Gift in Early Medieval Diplomatic Relations', in *Le relazioni internazionali nell'alto medioevo: Spoleto, 8–12 aprile 2010, Settimane di studio della Fondazione Centro italiano di studi sull'alto Medioevo*, 58 (Spoleto, 2011)

Newman, Edward, 'The "New Wars" Debate: A Historical Perspective is Needed', *Security Dialogue*, 35 (2004)

Nicovich, John Mark, 'The Poverty of the Patriarchate of Grado and the Byzantine-Venetian Treaty of 1082', *Mediterranean Historical Review*, 24 (2009)

Nijdam, Han, *Lichaam, eer en recht in middeleeuws Friesland: Een studie naar de Oudfriese boeteregisters*, 2 vols. (Hilversum, 2008)

Niles, John D., 'The Myth of the Feud in Anglo-Saxon England', *Journal of English and Germanic Philology*, 114 (2015)

Nip, Renée, 'The Political Relations between England and Flanders (1066–1128)', *Anglo-Norman Studies*, 21 (1998)

Nobile Mattei, Gustavo Adolfo, 'Il problema della qualificazione giuridica della "Divisio Ducatus" ', *Historia et Ius*, 4 (2013)

Nys, Ernest, *Les origines du droit international* (Paris, 1894)

Obregón, Liliana, 'The Civilized and the Uncivilized', in *The Oxford Handbook of The History of International Law*, eds. Bardo Fassbender and Anne Peters (Oxford, 2012)

O'Connell, Mary Ellen, and VanderZee, Lenore, 'The History of International Adjudication', in *The Oxford Handbook of International Adjudication*, eds. Cesare P. R. Romano, Karen J. Alter, and Yuval Shany (Oxford, 2013)

Oksanen, Eljas, 'The Anglo-Flemish Treaties and Flemish Soldiers in England 1101–1163', in *Mercenaries and Paid Men: the Mercenary Identity in the Middle Ages*, ed. John France (Leiden, 2008)

—— *Flanders and the Anglo-Norman World, 1066–1216* (Cambridge, 2012)

Oldfield, Paul, 'Urban Government in Southern Italy, c.1085–c.1127', *English Historical Review*, 122 (2007)

Oliver, Lisi, *The Body Legal in the Barbarian Laws* (Toronto, 2011)

Onuma, Yasuaki, *A Transcivilizational Perspective of International Law* (Leiden, 2010)

—— 'When was the Law of International Society born? An Inquiry of the History of International Law from an Intercivilizational Perspective', *Journal of the History of International Law*, 2 (2000)

Oppl, F., 'La politica cittadina di Federico I Barbarossa nel "Regnum Italicum"', *Bullettino dell'Istituto Storico Italiano per il Medio Evo*, 96 (1990)

Orvietani Busch, Silvia, *Medieval Mediterranean Ports. The Catalan and Tuscan Coasts, 1100 to 1235* (Leiden, 2001)

Ostdiek, Bennett, and Witt, John Fabian, 'The Czar and the Slaves: Two Puzzles in the History of International Arbitration', *American Journal of International Law*, 113 (2019)

Ottewill-Soulsby, Samuel, 'The Camels of Charles the Bald', *Medieval Encounters*, 25 (2019)

Ouerfelli, Mohamed, 'Diplomatic Exchanges between the City of Pisa and the States of the Maghrib (from the 12th to the 14th Century)', *Mediterranean World*, 22 (2015)

Paddeu, Federica, 'A Genealogy of Force Majeure in International Law', *The British Yearbook of International Law*, 82 (2012)

—— *Justification and Excuse in International Law. Concept and Theory of General Defences* (Cambridge, 2018)

Padoa-Schioppa, Antonio, 'Profili del diritto internazionale nell'alto medioevo', in *Le relazioni internazionali nell'alto medioevo: Spoleto, 8–12 aprile 2010, Settimane di studio della Fondazione Centro italiano di studi sull'alto Medioevo*, 58 (Spoleto, 2011)

Paik, Jin-Hyun, 'Globalisation and International Adjudication', in *Asian Approaches to International Law and the Legacy of Colonialism: The Law of the Sea, Territorial Disputes and International Dispute Settlement*, eds. Jin-Hyun Paik, Seok-Woo Lee, and Kevin Y. L. Tan (London, 2012)

Panaite, Viorel, *Ottoman Law of War and Peace* (Leiden, 2019)

Paradisi, Bruno, *Storia del diritto internazionale nel medio evo: L'età de transizione* (Naples, 1956)

—— *Civitas Maxima*, 2 vols. (Florence, 1974)

Pascua, Esther, 'Peace among Equals: War and Treaties in Twelfth-century Europe', in *War and Peace in Ancient and Medieval History*, eds. Philip de Souza and John France (Cambridge, 2008)

—— 'South of the Pyrenees: Kings, Magnates and Political Bargaining in Twelfth-century Spain', *Journal of Medieval History*, 27 (2001)

Patout Burns, J., 'The Concept of Satisfaction in Medieval Redemption Theory', *Theological Studies*, 36 (1975)

Patzold, Steffen, 'Human security, fragile Staatlichkeit und Governance im Frühmittelalter. Zur Fragwürdigkeit der Scheidung von Vormoderne und Moderne', *Geschichte und Gesellschaft*, 38 (2012)

Pavlac, Brian A., 'Excommunication and Territorial Politics in High Medieval Trier', *Church History*, 60 (1991)

Pelteret, David, 'Not All Roads Lead to Rome', in *England and Rome in the Early Middle Ages: Pilgrimage, Art and Politics*, ed. Francesca Tinti (Turnhout, 2014)

Pennington, K., 'Feudal Oath of Fidelity and Homage', in *Law as Profession and Practice in Medieval Europe: Essays in Honor of James A. Brundage*, eds. K. Pennington and M. Harris Eichbauer (Farnham, 2011)

—— 'The Formation of the Jurisprudence of the Feudal Oath of Fealty', *Rivista internazionale di diritto comune*, xv (2004)

—— 'The Jurisprudence of Procedure', in *The History of Courts and Procedure in Medieval Canon Law*, eds. Wilfried Hartmann and Kenneth Pennington (Washington, DC, 2016)

Péquignot, Stéphane, 'Fragiles traités? L'exemple des relations diplomatiques des rois d'Aragon avec les rois de France et de Castille (XIIe siècle-début du XVe siècle)', in *Der Bruch des Vertrages. Die Verbindlichkeit spätmittelalterlicher Diplomatie und ihre Grenzen*, ed. G. Jostkleigrewe, *Zeitschrift für Historische Forschung*, 55 (Berlin, 2018).

Perez, Oren, 'Fuzzy Law: A Theory of Quasi-Legal Systems', *Canadian Journal of Law and Jurisprudence*, 28 (2015)

Petkov, Kiril, *The Kiss of Peace: Ritual, Self, and Society in the High and Late Medieval West* (Leiden, 2003)

Pitts, Jennifer, 'Empire and Legal Universalisms in the Eighteenth Century', *American Historical Review*, 117 (2012)

Plechl, Helmut, 'Studien zur Tegernseer Briefsammlung des 12. Jahrhunderts II: Briefe zur Reichspolitik aus der Zeit der Verhandlungen in Anagni und der Vorbereitungen des Venetianer Friedenskongresses (Oktober 1176–Januar 1177)', *Deutsches Archiv für Erforschung des Mittelalters*, 12 (1956)

Pohl, Walter, 'The Empire and the Lombards: Treaties and Negotiations in the Sixth Century', in *Kingdoms of the Empire. The Integration of Barbarians in Late Antiquity*, ed. Walter Pohl (Leiden, 1997)

—— 'Frontiers in Lombard Italy: the Laws of Ratchis and Aistulf', in *The Transformation of Frontiers. From Late Antiquity to the Carolingians*, eds. Walter Pohl, Ian Wood, and Helmut Reimitz (Leiden, 2001)

—— 'Memory, Identity and Power in Lombard Italy', in *The Uses of the Past in the Early Middle Ages*, eds. Yitzhak Hen and Matthew Innes (Cambridge, 2000)

Pohl-Resl, Brigitte, 'Legal Practice and Ethnic Identity in Lombard Italy', in *Strategies of Distinction: The Construction of Ethnic Communities 300–800*, eds. Walter Pohl and Helmut Reimitz (Leiden, 1998)

Portilla, J. C., 'Amnesty: Evolving 21st Century Constraints Under International Law', *The Fletcher Forum of World Affairs*, 38 (2014)

Posner, Eric A., 'Do States Have a Moral Obligation to Obey International Law?', *Stanford Law Review*, 55 (2003)

Power, D. J., *The Norman Frontier in the Twelfth and Early Thirteenth Centuries* (Cambridge, 2004)

—— 'L'aristocratie Plantagenêt face aux conflits capétiens-angevins: l'example du traité de Louviers', in *Noblesses de l'espace Plantagenêt (1154–1224)*, ed. Martin Aurell (Poitiers, 2001)

Powicke, F. M., 'Presidential Address: Reflections on the Medieval State', *Transactions of the Royal Historical Society*, 19 (1936)

Pratt, David, *The Political Thought of King Alfred the Great* (Cambridge, 2007)

Procter, Evelyn S., *Curia and Cortes in Leon and Castile 1072–1295* (Cambridge, 1980)

Pryor, John H., 'Mediterranean Commerce in the Middle Ages. A Voyage under the Contract of Commenda', *Viator*, 14 (1983)

Quinton-Brown, Patrick, 'The South, the West, and the Meanings of Humanitarian Intervention in History', *Review of International Studies*, 46 (2020)

Raccagni, Gianluca, *The Lombard League, 1167–1225* (Oxford, 2010)

—— 'When the Emperor Submitted to his Rebellious Subjects: A Neglected and Innovative Legal Account of the Peace of Constance, 1183', *English Historical Review*, 131 (2016)

Ramel, Frédéric, 'Marcel Mauss et l'étude des relations internationales: un héritage oublié', *Sociologie et sociétés*, 36 (2004)

Rasilla Del Moral, Ignacio De La, 'Medieval International Law', in *Oxford Bibliographies. International Law* (Oxford, 2014)

Reuter, Timothy, 'Gedenküberlieferung und -praxis im Briefbuch Wibalds von Stablo', in *Der Liber Vitae von Corvey*, eds. Karl Schmid and Joachim Wollasch, 2 vols (Wiesbaden, 1989)

—— 'Mandate, Privilege, Court Judgment: Techniques of Rulership in the Age of Frederick Barbarossa', in *Medieval Polities and Modern Mentalities*, ed. Janet L. Nelson (Cambridge, 2006)

—— 'Plunder and Tribute in the Carolingian Empire', *Transactions of the Royal Historical Society*, 5th ser., 35 (1985)

—— 'Rechtliche Argumentation in den Briefen Wibalds von Stablo', in *Papsttum, Kirche und Recht im Mittelalter: Festschrift für Horst Fuhrmann zum 65. Geburtstag*, ed. Hubert Mordek (Tübingen, 1991)

Reynolds, Susan, *Before Eminent Domain. Toward a History of Expropriation of Land for the Common Good* (Chapel Hill, NC, 2010)

—— 'There Were States in Medieval Europe. A Response to Rees Davies', *Journal of Historical Sociology*, 16 (2003)

—— *Kingdoms and Communities in Western Europe 900–1300*, 2nd edn. (Oxford, 1997)

Richardson, H. E., 'The Sino-Tibetan Treaty Inscription of A.D. 821/823 at Lhasa', *The Journal of the Royal Asiatic Society of Great Britain and Ireland*, 2 (1978)

Riedmann, Josef, *Die Beurkundung der Verträge Friedrich Barbarossas mit italienischen Städten: Studien zur diplomatischen Form von Vertragsurkunden im 12. Jahrhundert* (Vienna, 1973)

Rio, Alice, 'Formulae, Legal Practice and the Settlement of Disputes', in *Law before Gratian. Law in Western Europe c. 500–1100*, eds. Per Andersen, Mia Münster-Swendsen, and Helle Vogt (Copenhagen, 2007)

Rivkin, David W., 'The Impact of International Arbitration on the Rule of Law', *Arbitration International*, 29 (2013)

Roach, Levi, *Æthelred the Unready* (London, 2016)

Robinson, I. S., *The Papacy, 1073–1198: Continuity and Innovation* (Cambridge, 1990)

Roche, Jason T., 'The Second Crusade, 1145–49: Damascus, Lisbon and the Wendish Campaigns', *History Compass*, 13 (2015)

Roht-Arriaza, Naomi, *Impunity and Human Rights in International Law and Practice* (Oxford, 1995)

Rösch, G., *Venedig und das Reich. Handels- und verkehrspolitische Beziehungen in der deutschen Kaiserzeit* (Tübingen, 1982)

———— *Venezia e l'Impero, 962–1250. I rapporti politici, commerciali e di traffico nel periodo imperiale germanico* (Rome, 1985)

Rosenstock, Robert, 'The ILC and State Responsibility', *American Journal of International Law*, 96 (2002)

Rosenwein, Barbara H., ed., *Reading the Middle Ages: Sources from Europe, Byzantium, and the Islamic World*, 3rd edn. (Toronto, 2018)

Roumy, Franck, 'L'origine et la diffusion de l'adage canonique *Necessitas non habet legem* (VIIIe–XIIIe s.)', in *Medieval Church Law and the Origins of the Western Legal Tradition. A Tribute to Kenneth Pennington*, eds. Wolfgang P. Müller and Mary E. Sommar (Washington, DC, 2006)

Ruda, José María, 'Recognition of States and Governments', in *International Law: Achievements and Prospects*, ed. M. Bedjaoui (Dordrecht, 1991)

Ruggie, John G., 'Continuity and Transformation in the World Polity: Toward a Neorealist Synthesis', *World Politics*, 35 (1983)

Rundall, M. T., 'Act of God as a Defense in Negligence Cases', *Drake Law Review*, 25 (1975–6)

Russell, F. H., *The Just War in the Middle Ages* (Cambridge, 1975; repr. 1979)

Ryan, M., 'The Oath of Fealty and the Lawyers', in *Political Thought and the Realities of Power in the Middle Ages*, eds. J. P. Canning and O. G. Oexle (Göttingen, 1998)

Sadat, Leila, 'Exile, Amnesty and International Law', *Notre Dame Law Review*, 81 (2006)

Sahgal, Smita, 'Situating Kingship within an Embryonic Frame of Masculinity in Early India', *Social Scientist*, 43 (2015)

Scalia, Giuseppe, 'Contributi pisani alla lotta anti-islamica nel Mediterraneo centro-occidentale durante il secolo XI e nei prime deceni del XII', *Anuario de estudios medievales*, 10 (1980)

Scharf, Michael P., 'From the eXile Files: An Essay on Trading Justice for Peace', *Washington and Lee Law Review*, 63 (2006)

Schillings, Sonja, *Enemies of All Humankind. Fictions of Legitimate Violence* (Hanover, NH, 2017)

Schmitt, Joseph, *Die Selbsthilfe im römischen Privatrecht* (Erlangen, 1868)

Schneider, Reinhard, *Brüdergemeine und Schwurfreundschaft der Auflösungsprozess des Karlingerreiches im Spiegel der Caritas-Terminologie in den Verträgen der karlingischen Teilkönige des 9. Jahrhunderts* (Lübeck, 1964)

Schneidmüller, Bernd, 'Die Begegnung der Könige und die erste Nationalisierung Europas (9.-11. Jahrhundert)', in *Le relazioni internazionali nell'alto medioevo* (Spoleto, 2011)

Schuit, Anne, 'Recognition of Governments in International Law and the Recent Conflict in Libya', *International Community Law Review*, 14 (2012)

Semmler, Josef, 'Eine Herrschaftsmaxime im Wandel: Pax und Concordia im karolingischen Frankenreich', in *Frieden in Geschichte und Gegenwart*, ed. Historisches Seminar der Universität Düsseldorf (Düsseldorf, 1985)

Sen, Tansen, 'In Search of Longevity and Good Karma: Chinese Diplomatic Missions to Middle India in the Seventh Century', *Journal of World History*, 12 (2001)

Shadis, Miriam, *Berenguela of Castile (1180–1246) and Political Women in the High Middle Ages* (New York, 2009)

Sharlet, Jocelyn, 'Tokens of Resentment: Medieval Arabic Narratives about Gift Exchange and Social Conflict', *Journal of Arabic and Islamic Studies*, 11 (2011)

Sharma, Surya P., *Territorial Acquisition, Disputes and International Law* (The Hague, 1997)

Shaw, Malcolm N., *International Law*, 6th edn. (Cambridge, 2008)

Shoemaker, Karl, *Sanctuary and Crime in the Middle Ages* (New York, 2011)

Sicilianos, L.-A., 'The Relationship between Reprisals and Denunciation or Suspension of a Treaty', *European Journal of International Law*, 4 (1993)

Sickel, T. H., *Das Privilegium Otto I. für die römische Kirche vom Jahre 962* (Innsbruck, 1883)

Siems, Harald, *Handel und Wucher im Spiegel frühmittelalterlicher Rechtsquellen* (Hanover, 1992)

Sigurðsson, Jón Viðar, 'The Role of Arbitration in the Settlement of Disputes in Iceland c. 1000–1300', in *Law and Disputing in the Middle Ages*, eds. Per Andersen et al. (Copenhagen, 2013)

Skinner, Patricia, *Family Power in Southern Italy. The Duchy of Gaeta and its Neighbours, 850–1139* (Cambridge, 1995)

Sluiter, Göran, 'The Surrender of War Criminals to the International Criminal Court', *Loyola of Los Angeles International and Comparative Law Review*, 25 (2003)

Smail, Daniel Lord, *Legal Plunder. Households and Debt Collection in Late Medieval Europe* (Cambridge, MA, 2016)

Stantchev, Stefan, 'The Medieval Origins of Embargo as a Policy Tool', *History of Political Thought*, 33 (2012)

—— *Spiritual Rationality: Papal Embargo as Cultural Practice* (Oxford, 2014)

Stanton, Charles D., *Medieval Maritime Warfare* (Barnsley, 2015)

Steenkamp, Christina, 'The Crime-Conflict Nexus and the Civil War in Syria', *Stability: International Journal of Security and Development*, 6 (2017)

Steiger, Heinhard, 'From the International Law of Christianity to the International Law of the World Citizen. Reflections on the Formation of the Epochs of the History of International Law', *Journal of the History of International Law*, 3 (2001)

—— *Die Ordnung der Welt. Eine Völkerrechtsgeschichte des karolingischen Zeitalters (741–840)* (Cologne, 2010)

—— 'Peace Treaties from Paris to Versailles', in *International Law in European History. From the Late Middle Ages to World War One*, ed. Randall Lesaffer (Cambridge, 2004)

Steinbach, Armin, 'The Trend towards Non-Consensualism in Public International Law: A (Behavioural) Law and Economics Perspective', *European Journal of International Law*, 27 (2016)

Stenton, F. M., 'St Benet of Holme and the Norman Conquest', *English Historical Review*, 37 (1922)

Stewart, James G., and Kiyani, Asad, 'The Ahistoricism of Legal Pluralism in International Criminal Law', *American Journal of Comparative Law*, 65 (2017)

Storti, Claudia, 'Ascertainment of Customs and Personal Laws in Medieval Italy from the Lombard Kingdom to the Communes', *Rechtsgeschichte-Legal History*, 24 (2016)

Story, Joanna, *Carolingian Connections: Anglo-Saxon England and Carolingian Francia c. 750–870* (Aldershot, 2003)

Struve, Tilman, 'Lampert von Hersfeld. Persönlichkeit und Weltbild eines Geschichtsschreibers am Beginn des Investiturstreits', *Hessisches Jahrbuch für Landesgeschichte*, 20 (1970)

Suchodolski, S., 'La date de la grande réforme monétaire de Charlemagne', *Quaderni Ticinesi di Numismaticae Antichità Classiche*, 10 (1981)

Tan, Kevin Y. L., 'The Role of History in International Territorial Dispute Settlement: The Pedra Branca Case (Singapore v Malaysia)', in *Asian Approaches to International Law and the Legacy of Colonialism: The Law of the Sea, Territorial Disputes and International Dispute Settlement*, eds. Jin-Hyun Paik, Seok-Woo Lee, and Kevin Y. L. Tan (London, 2012)

Tanaka, Yoshifumi, *The Peaceful Settlement of International Disputes* (Cambridge, 2017)

Tangheroni, Marco, 'Sardinia and Corsica from the Mid-Twelfth to the Early Fourteenth Century', in *The New Cambridge Medieval History, volume V, c. 1198–c.1300*, ed. D. Abulafia (Cambridge, 1999)

Tangl, Georgine, 'Die Paßvorschrift des Königs Ratchis und ihre Beziehung zu dem Verhaltnis zwischen Franken und Langobarden vom 6.–8. Jahrhundert', *Quellen und Forschungen aus italienischen Archiven und Bibliotheken*, 38 (1958)

Taylor, Alice, 'Homage in the Latin Chronicles of Eleventh- and Twelfth-century Normandy', in *People, Texts and Artefacts. Cultural Transmission in the Medieval Norman Worlds*, eds. David Bates, Edoardo D'Angelo, and Elisabeth van Houts (London, 2017)

Teitel, Ruti G., 'Transitional Justice Genealogy', *Harvard Human Rights Journal*, 16 (2003)

Tierney, B., *The Crisis of Church and State: 1050–1300* (Toronto, 1988)

Teubner, Gunther, 'The King's Many Bodies: The Self-Deconstruction of Law's Hierarchy', *Law & Society Review*, 31 (1997)

Tolan, J., '*Lex alterius*: Using Law to Construct Confessional Boundaries', *History and Anthropology*, 26 (2015)

Torpey, John, *Making Whole What Has Been Smashed: On Reparations Politics* (Cambridge, MA, 2006)

—— (ed.) *Politics and the Past: On Repairing Historical Injustices* (New York, 2003)

Treviño, A. Javier, *The Sociology of Law. Classical and Contemporary Perspectives* (New Brunswick, NJ, 2001)

Tucci, Pier Luigi, *The Temple of Peace in Rome* (Cambridge, 2017)

Twining, William, 'Normative and Legal Pluralism: A Global Perspective', *Duke Journal of Comparative and International Law*, 20 (2010)

Ullmann, Walter, 'The Medieval Papal Court as an International Tribunal', repr. In *The Papacy and Political Ideas in the Middle Ages* (London, 1976)

—— 'The Origins of the *Ottonianum*', *The Cambridge Historical Journal*, 11 (1953)

van Eickels, Klaus, 'Homagium and Amicitia: Rituals of Peace and their Significance in the Anglo-French Negotiations of the Twelfth Century', *Francia*, 24 (1997)

—— 'Um 1101: Wo man im Mittelalter zwei Herren dienen konnte – und welche Folgen dies hatte', in *Die Macht des Königs: Herrschaft in Europa vom Frühmittelalter bis in die Neuzeit*, ed. Bernhard Jussen (Munich, 2005)

van Houts, Elisabeth, 'The Vocabulary of Exile and Outlawry in the North Sea Area around the First Millenium', in *Exile in the Middle Ages*, eds. Laura Napran and Elisabeth van Houts (Turnhout, 2004)

—— 'L'exil dans l'espace Anglo-Normand', in *La Normandie et l'Angleterre au Moyen Âge*, eds. Pierre Bouet and Véronique Gazeau (Caen, 2003)

Vogt, Helle, *The Function of Kinship in Medieval Nordic Legislation* (Leiden, 2010)

Voss, Ingrid, *Herrschertreffen im frühen und hohen Mittelalter* (Cologne, 1987)

Walters, William, 'Deportation, Expulsion, and the International Police of Aliens', *Citizenship Studies*, 6 (2002)

Wanner, Peter, 'Der staufisch-kastilische Ehepakt des Jahres 1188. Erkenntnisse aus Anlass einiger "Kleiner" Stadtteilsund Gemeindejubiläen 2013', *Quellen und Forschungen zur Geschichte der Stadt Heilbronn*, 22 (2016)

Watkins, John, 'Toward a New Diplomatic History of Medieval and Early Modern Europe', *Journal of Medieval and Early Modern Studies*, 38 (2008)

Wehberg, Hans, '*Pacta Sunt Servanda*', *American Journal of International Law*, 53 (1959)

Weiler, Björn, 'Describing Rituals of Succession and the Legitimation of Kingship in the West, ca.1000–ca.1150', in *Court Ceremonies and Rituals of Power in Byzantium and the Medieval Mediterranean: Comparative Perspectives*, eds. Alexander D. Beihammer, Stavroula Constantinou, and Maria G. Parani (Leiden, 2013)

West, G. V. B., 'Communities and *Pacta* in Early Medieval Italy: Jurisdiction, Regulatory Authority and Dispute Avoidance', *Early Medieval Europe*, 18 (2010)

White, Stephen D., 'A Crisis of Fidelity in c.1000', in *Building Legitimacy: Political Discourses and Forms of Legitimacy in Medieval Societies*, eds. I. Alfonso, H. Kennedy, and J. Escalona (Leiden, 2004)

—— '"Pactum... Legem Vincit et Amor Judicium": The Settlement of Disputes by Compromise in Eleventh-Century Western France', *American Journal of Legal History*, 22 (1978)

Wickham, Chris, *Early Medieval Italy. Central Power and Local Society 400–1000* (London, 1981)

—— 'Gossip and Resistance among the Medieval Peasantry', *Past & Present*, 160 (1998)

—— 'Problems in Doing Comparative History', in *Challenging the Boundaries of Medieval History. The Legacy of Timothy Reuter*, ed. Patricia Skinner (Turnhout, 2009)

Wubs-Mrozewicz, Justyna, 'The Late Medieval and Early Modern Hanse as an Institution of Conflict Management', *Continuity and Change*, 32 (2017)

Yerkes, David, 'The Full Text of the Metrical Preface to Wærferth's Translation of Gregory', *Speculum*, 55 (1980)

Zahid, M. A., and Shapiee, R., '*Pacta Sunt Servanda*: Islamic Perception', *Journal of East Asia and International Law*, 3 (2010)

Ziegler, K.-H., 'Arbiter, Arbitrator und Amicabilis Compositor', *Zeitschrift der Savigny-Stiftung für Rechtsgeschichte*, 84 (1967)

—— 'Conclusion and Publication of International Treaties in Antiquity', *Israel Law Review*, 29 (1995)

—— 'From *foedera pacis* to *foedera paces*', in *Peace Treaties and International Law in European History*, ed. R. Lesaffer (Cambridge, 2004)

——— 'The Influence of Medieval Roman Law on Peace Treaties', in *Peace Treaties and International Law in European History*, ed. R. Lesaffer (Cambridge, 2004)

——— *Völkerrechtsgeschichte* (Munich, 1994)

Zielonka, Jan, 'The International System in Europe: Westphalian Anarchy or Medieval Chaos?', *Journal of European Integration*, 35 (2013)

Zwass, Adam, *The Council for Mutual Economic Assistance: The Thorny Path from Political to Economic Integration* (London, 1989)

Unpublished

Benham, Jenny, 'Law, Violence and the Practice of Political Power in England and Denmark in the Late Twelfth and Early Thirteenth Centuries', available at www.academia.edu/2506393/Law_violence_ and_the_practice_of_political_power (accessed 16 July 2021)

Colafranceso, Sonia, 'Interferenze e commistioni tra diritto longobardo e diritto romano-bizantino nei documenti del *Codex diplomaticus Cavenis*', unpublished PhD thesis (University of Chieti-Pescara, 2016)

Penna, Daphne, 'The Byzantine imperial acts to Venice, Pisa and Genoa, 10th–12th Centuries: A Comparative Legal Study', unpublished PhD thesis (Groningen, 2012)

Tindal-Robertson, C., 'Peacemaking in Medieval Léon and Castile, c.1100–1230', unpublished PhD thesis (Exeter, 2014)

Wielers, M., 'Zwischenstaatliche Beziehungsformen im frühen Mittelalter (*Pax, Foedus, Amicitias, Fraternitas*)', unpublished PhD thesis (Münster, 1959)

Index